Expanding the Rainbow

Teaching Gender

Scope

Teaching Gender publishes monographs, anthologies and reference books that deal centrally with gender and/or sexuality. The books are intended to be used in undergraduate and graduate classes across the disciplines. The series aims to promote social justice with an emphasis on feminist, multicultural and critical perspectives.

Please consult www.patricialeavy.com for submission requirements (click the book series tab).

VOLUME 12

The titles published in this series are listed at *brill.com/gend*

Expanding the Rainbow

*Exploring the Relationships of Bi+, Polyamorous,
Kinky, Ace, Intersex, and Trans People*

Edited by

Brandy L. Simula, J. E. Sumerau and Andrea Miller

BRILL

SENSE

LEIDEN | BOSTON

All chapters in this book have undergone peer review.

The Library of Congress Cataloging-in-Publication Data is available online at
http://catalog.loc.gov

ISSN 2542-9205
ISBN 978-90-04-41408-2 (paperback)
ISBN 978-90-04-41409-9 (hardback)
ISBN 978-90-04-41410-5 (e-book)

ADVANCE PRAISE FOR
EXPANDING THE RAINBOW

"If you want to understand the identities, relationships, and family forms in the contemporary US, you need this book. Too much in the sociology (often unconsciously) treats the terms that define what's largely considered 'normal' as essential to humanity and society: that sex and gender are binaries; that true love occurs only in sexual pairings; that intimate relationships, while usually full of power relations, only work when that power remains invisible; that there's something wrong with the people who reveal how wrong these assumptions can be. *Expanding the Rainbow* shows us how the world works from the perspectives of people who are bi/pan+, asexual, polyamorous, intersex, trans, and into BDSM—the very people whose experiences, because they have been marginalized, stand to teach us the most about what it means to relate intimately to others, to form families and communities, to be human."
Dawne Moon, Associate Professor of Sociology and Gender/Sexuality Studies, Marquette University

"This book is the urgently needed next step in examining relationships and families, as well as the lives of LGBTIQ+ people. Through theoretical, empirical, and personal pieces, the authors in *Expanding the Rainbow* push sociological work on 'the family' to take seriously types of families that are systematically ignored by researchers. They push us past the mainstream (even normative) profile of 'same-sex families': two middle-class white cisgender gay men (sometimes lesbian women) who are married and have 2.5 kids. The text introduces readers to relationships and families that are hardly ever visible in the mainstream, even in this time of 'marriage equality.' It also does the important work of pushing us to stop viewing trans and intersex individuals as just 'individuals,' as though these members of the LGBTIQ+ community are perpetually single, sexless, and lonely. As a Black queer non-binary person, I'm so happy to finally encounter a book that reflects me, my identities, and my family."
Eric Anthony Grollman, Associate Professor of Sociology, University of Richmond

"*Expanding the Rainbow* is a breath of fresh air in the field of sexualities and gender. The current lack of scholarship on bi+, poly, kink, asexual, intersex, and/or trans presents a challenge in the classroom when discussing the intricacies of these relationships and identities. Now, *Expanding the Rainbow* offers a comprehensive review of the LGBTQQIAP spectrum that's accessible to academic and non-academic audiences alike. The insightful and deeply personal narratives of members from these diverse communities, including activists and scholars, help readers to better relate to experiences outside their own purview. This timely volume would make a great addition to undergraduate courses addressing sexualities, gender identities, relationships and the intersectionality of race, ethnicity, socioeconomic status, religious affiliation, and nationality."
Mandi Barringer, Assistant Professor of Sociology, University of North Florida

"*Expanding the Rainbow* illuminates complexities of sex, gender, and sexuality that remain largely overlooked and underemphasized within sociology. Editors Brandy L. Simula, J. E. Sumerau, and Andrea Miller begin this volume with great care, introducing readers to the marginalized identities and corresponding terminology that the content showcases: bisexuality, polyamory, kink, asexuality, intersex, and transgender. The ensuing content is carefully curated, featuring the research and personal experiences of established scholars alongside the innovative perspectives of emerging scholars. The diverse standpoints, methods, and theoretical insights of these writers highlight complex hues of the rainbow that many people struggle to see."
Helana Darwin, Doctoral Candidate, Stony Brook University

CONTENTS

R. F. PLANTE

FOREWORD

In a previous life, far removed from the one I now live, I was hired to teach courses in "the sociology of the family." Sexualities-specific gigs were few and far between, and it seemed that courses on "the family" would at least offer an opportunity to teach and think about relationships, intimacies, and connections. Unfortunately, 20+ years ago, these courses seemed to traffic in unexamined assumptions, not least of which was evident in the definite article "the." Textbooks and related materials were organized around the argument that there was a hegemonic "family," and by inference, one primary set of relationships, roles, connections, and paths into and out of these relationships. Anyone wishing to learn about multiplicities of intimacies, families in the plural, relationships, and selves had to search hard for even a little information.

This book – an extensive exploration of multiple aspects and forms of relationships, intersections, identities, paths, experiences, and sociocultural contexts – is delightfully removed from the sociology of intimacies of the past. It is a timely, fundamentally necessary volume. How do we live, love, desire, and choose within our contexts? How do we narrate ourselves and our relationships? How do we make sense of who we are, how we share our lives, and how we create connections with others? How do we understand and navigate barriers, challenges, and structural inequalities?

Several things would seem to be useful in a nuanced, sensitive exploration of these issues. First, application and development of empirical and theoretical frames so that thinker/activists within and beyond the 'full range of the rainbow' can find one another. Second, clarity about the ways in which intimate and sexual citizenship is both a micro- and macro- sociological project, ever changing but always grounded in entangled social contexts. And finally, an acknowledgment of the pleasures and pains involved in (re)developing the language, systems, and structures that underlie relationships and identities.

Let's address theoretical and empirical frames first. As the contributions to this volume make clear, community seems to be a basic building block for enabling us to find one another and find ourselves. As a scholar-activist, and to the extent that I desire any public, social change regarding expanded understandings of relationships, it is vital to connect with others. Sociologists know all too well the pitfalls of overgeneralization ("an *n* of one does not a sample make" was drilled into us in methods classes). Multiple sources and forms of data, from autoethnographic to focus group to quantitative to interview, add textured layers of knowledge to the still exploratory data on most aspects of relationships across and within the rainbow. A community of scholar-activists, adding to the fund of knowledge and action, will help advance our collective goals and understanding.

To this end, acknowledgment of the complexities of intimate, sexual citizenship is warranted. In imagining sexual and intimate citizenship as a privilege, or a right, perhaps, we can envision the best-case scenarios of individuals and groups, freed to live authentically. Still, we cannot help but see complexities still to be disentangled. In what ways is the privilege of intimate/sexual citizenship still mired within an unequal world and unequal nations? What disrupts individuals from finding space, time, and resources to create and live in the relational spaces that nurture them? How do things like race, ethnicity, class, health, age, place, and spirituality matter? In what ways do complex bureaucracies, stagnant social institutions, and antiquated customs block us from finding each other, our selves, and our relational, romantic, familial, sexual and communal bonds?

There is pleasure and pain in these journeys, and in those described so critically in this book. The authors and editors utilize a range of tools to illuminate communities, stories, and struggles. We carve out spaces for connection, for seeing ourselves reflected online and 'in real life,' for using our voices to narrate our experiences. We see the limitations of those spaces and of our selves. We name the pain, or try to – stigma, shame, isolation, depression, loneliness, aloneness, fear, sadness. We chase the pleasures – a sense of unity, connection, belonging; self-awareness; choices, friendships, meanings, intensities; love, acceptance, feelings. In the pages that follow, we are called to speak, listen, hear, see, think, reflect, and feel. In acknowledging the beauty of the full range of the rainbow, we acknowledge our connections with each other as much as we recognize the varied scholarship, activism, and arguments herein.

PREFACE

This coedited volume was designed as a resource for a wide range of courses in gender and sexuality studies. We bring together in this volume contributions from individuals representing a diversity of academic and personal engagements. We conceptualized the volume as being highly accessible and readable without forgoing the complexities of the identities, communities, and experiences it explores. Rather than extracting or reprinting previous work, we have included only new contributions that were written expressly for an undergraduate audience.

Throughout the text, the readings vary in terms of their approaches. The volume includes a range of contributions that span empirical reports on recent findings, theoretical approaches to the most pressing issues in the communities represented in this volume, and personal reflections from members of these communities.

We bring a strong background in gender and sexuality studies to the project, spanning more than 50 combined years of work in the field. Each of us have engaged in empirical research in sexuality studies from a sociological approach, each have published in one or more of the specific areas of genders and sexualities represented in the volume and we each have extensive experience centering the identities and communities that are the focus of this volume across a range of courses in our research and teaching.

ACKNOWLEDGEMENTS

Thank you to Patricia Leavy, John Bennett, Jolanda Karada, Paul Chambers, Robert van Gameren, and everyone else at Brill | Sense for your faith in us, your willingness to support creativity, and your invaluable guidance. We would also like to especially thank Shalen Lowell for your considerable assistance and support.

Brandy Simula: I owe the warmest of thanks to my co-editors, J. E. Sumerau and Andrea Miller, who shared my excitement over the earliest, inchoate idea for the volume. Their collegiality and dedication to the project made the process of bringing this volume from inception to print a thoroughly enjoyable one. I am enormously grateful to my partner, M, who has supported all of my interests and projects over the past two decades, including this one, and whose partnership continues to help me flourish both personally and professionally. Molly & Lucy have been my constant and steadfast companions throughout the process of developing and bringing the book to fruition, and I could not have had better. The love and support of my family of choice and their willingness to think and live together toward expanding the light of our own rainbows has sustained me in more ways than they can know.

J. E. Sumerau: As always, I cannot overstate how much gratitude I owe to Xan Nowakowski and Lain Mathers for this and all my other books. I also owe deep gratitude to my co-editors in this project who came up with the idea in the first place and walked with me every step of the way. I also am always thankful for my own chosen family and the ways they each bring something fantastic to my life even when they don't quite realize they are doing so. Thanks especially to Eve, Nik, M, Eric, Brittany, Kate, Bran, and Shay for all you do that helps me think, create, and exist in this world. I also wish to thank all the contributors to this volume, and to my own development as a scholar, novelist, and teacher over the past decade. Special thanks in these regards to Irene Padavic, Doug Schrock, Koji Ueno, Dawne Moon, Katie Acosta, Kristen Schilt, Rebecca Plante, Allen Scarboro, John Reynolds, Orit Avishai, Patricia Leavy, and Kim Davies for better mentorship than I could have ever hoped to find as I made my want into the academy. Finally, as always, thank you especially to all the other LGBTQIA people who have allowed me to learn about their lives, tell their stories in scholarship and novels, and grow from their life lessons.

Andrea Miller: This work was inspired during the last day of the 2017 American Sociological Association when I turned to one of the co-editors of this volume, Brandy Simula and asked her "where were the books by scholars doing work on alt sexualities?" Mere days after that conversation Brandy told me I had to meet her friend J Sumerau who was doing vital work on Bi+ identities and alt family relationships. In quick succession this book came to fruition.

Based on this conversation I have had the pleasure of working with my co-editors and the authors in this volume.

As a life-long bisexualities scholar this is the kind of book I have wanted to have to teach to the newer generation of undergraduate sociology students. Thank you to my long time mentor Betsy Lucal, and my partners in crime, Charlie, Theo and Levi. These folks, along with my students have continued to encourage me to reach outside the rainbow.

BRANDY L. SIMULA, ANDREA MILLER AND J. E. SUMERAU

INTRODUCTION

Gender identity, performance, and expression and sexual identities, interests, and activities are conceptually distinct categories. The frequent collapsing of gender identity and sexual identity as they are currently constructed in the contemporary U.S., however, has led to the construction of an umbrella group, LGBTQQIAP. That umbrella group includes individuals across a variety of sexual identities, as well as gender identifications. While work on lesbian and gay relationships has exploded over the last several decades, this volume represents the first collection of original research in the sociology of gender and sexualities that explicitly and intentionally gives voice to the margins of the LGBTQQIAP rainbow and beyond. Representing a range of voices and issues in bi+, consensually non-monogamous, BDSM, ace, intersex, and trans identities and relationships, the chapters in this book highlight the variety of experiences of individuals in the less commonly studied and written about hues of the rainbow. We intend this volume not as a definitive representation of these relationships and identities, but as an urgent call to include and center these relationships, identities, and practices in sexualities and gender work and beyond.

We note at the outset that the limited extant scholarship in many of these areas means that our knowledge of many of these identities, experiences, and communities, suffers from the serious lacuna that has long plagued U.S.-based sexuality scholarship: the experiences of people of color, people from poor and working class backgrounds, and people with disabilities are severely underrepresented in most existing scholarship in these areas (see Loeser, Pini, & Crowley, 2018; Martino, 2017), with the possible exceptions of the bi+ and trans literatures, which are the largest and most academically visible among the communities and identities represented in this book. Second, the small handful of scholars currently publishing in these areas are overwhelmingly white. We intend this volume specifically to help legitimize the academic study of these identities, relationships, and communities and to open up space for a wider community of scholars in these areas. We have intentionally solicited contributions from a diverse range of scholars

© KONINKLIJKE BRILL NV, LEIDEN, 2019 | DOI:10.1163/9789004414105_001

and community members representing different personal and academic relationships to the identities and/or relationships on which they write in this volume, and have sought to include both senior scholars widely recognized as experts in their respective areas of specialization as well as to highlight the work of emerging scholars in these areas.

As with all sexualities projects, both the editors and individual chapter authors have wrestled seriously with questions of language and labels. Rather than imposing a standard lexicon across the volume, we have invited contributors to the volume to discuss their own use of terminology and labels in the context of their chapters. We encourage readers to follow closely the ways in which language and terminology are deployed—both in this volume and in the broader culture—and to be attentive to the effects of particular kinds of linguistic representations. We frequently identify and use umbrella terms such as bi+, trans, polyamorous, and kinky as a general starting point, while recognizing that very move as in itself problematic. Many identities are subsumed under each of those broad umbrellas, and some individuals whose identities we might broadly categorize under one of those umbrella terms explicitly *dis*identify with such umbrella terms for important reasons. For instance, some pansexuals identify not with but *against* the term bi+ (see for instance, Green, this volume), some genderqueer and nonbinary individuals identify in those ways rather than as trans as a way to represent their specific experience, and some individuals who engage in consensual power exchange or pain play strongly reject the "kink" identity, pushing back against the notion implied in the term "kink" that what they do is (just) about sex or that there is a "normal" straight as opposed to an "abnormal" kink. Throughout the volume, we and the individual contributors have tried to draw the readers' attention to moments where our own uses of language are particularly fraught.

For ease of structural organization of the text we have organized the sections by specific relationships, identities and communities, but there are multiple and frequent points of intersection among them (e.g. Bauer, 2014). The chapters in this volume focus on both specific identities and relationships, and the ways in which those identities and relationships intersect with one another, as well as with other social identities and categories, including race, ethnicity, socioeconomic status, ability, religion, nationality, and others. Research exploring some of these intersections, for example, already finds that bi+ and trans people are often evaluated more negatively by both gay/lesbian and straight populations in the U.S. (Cragun & Sumerau, 2015, 2017), and that scholarship has largely remained within the lesbian and gay hues of the rainbow overall in the social sciences to date (see Monro et al., 2017; Schilt & Lagos, 2017 for reviews). Further, researchers have shown how experiences throughout these groups often rely heavily upon contextual factors related to locations in race, class, sex, gender, sexual, religious, relationship, and ability hierarchies embedded within the broader society (see, e.g., Moore, 2011; Schrock et al., 2014; Worthen, 2013 for reviews). Here we seek to engage and explore many of these variations while providing introductions to varied relationship forms in society that often receive less academic or public attention at present.

Although each of the identities and relationship structures across bi+, consensually non-monogamous, kink, ace, intersex, and trans experiences have unique histories and experiences, common themes also emerge across these groups. Marginalization, stigma, and discrimination are frequent experiences for individuals who identify with one or more of these identities. Processes of discovering, recognizing and claiming—or contesting—identities and labels that reflect an individual's life experience are also frequent across many of these identities. Similarly, the role of community in creating visibility and support is shared by many individuals in these groups. At both the individual and broader sociocultural levels, the experiences reflected in these categories challenge many of the most persistent, embedded notions in Western culture about relationships, bodies, sexualities, gender, and identities. Here, we provide a brief introduction to each of the identities and relationship structures highlighted in this book.

BI+ INDIVIDUALS AND RELATIONSHIPS

Although sexuality has long been understood as a binary in western cultures, a range of plurisexual identities (identities that involve attraction to people of more than one gender identification, such as bisexual, queer, pansexual, heteroflexible, homoflexible, bicurious and others) exist in addition to monosexual identities (identities that involve attraction to people of one gender identification, e.g. lesbian, gay, heterosexual) (Galupo, Ramirez, & Pulice-Farrow, 2017). "Polysexual," "pomosexual," "multisexual," and "non-monosexual" are other identity terms with similar meanings to "plurisexual" (Flanders, 2017). Non-binary sexual identities, such as bisexual, queer, pansexual, heteroflexible, homoflexible, bicurious, and others are collectively referred to here with the umbrella term bi+ to indicate bisexual as well as a range of other plurisexual identities. While the term bi+ is used here for the sake of brevity, it is important to note that identities such as "queer," "bisexual," and "pansexual" have distinct meanings, and that the meanings of these identities are often a source of debate among members of the bi+ community. It is also important to note that not everyone who identifies as pansexual, queer, etc. themselves identify as being under the bi+ umbrella.

People of all genders identify under the bi+ umbrella, though ciswomen as well as members of the transgender community are more likely than cismen to do so (Compton, Farris, & Chang, 2015). Bi+ identified people may be attracted to men and women, to people of a range of genders, to people based on categories other than gender, and/or may have attractions that change over time (Robinson, 2017). Younger people are more likely to identify as pansexual, while older people are more likely to identify as bisexual. Transgender people are more likely to identify with queer and pansexual identities than with bisexual identities (Morandini, Blaszcynski, & Dar-Nimrod, 2017). While some bi+ individuals have consensually non-monogamous relationships, others identify with and practice relational monogamy (Benson, 2017).

Bi+ individuals face a range of challenges, including disbelief in the bi+ identity and experience itself from individuals who see bi+ identities as transitional or confused (Barringer, Sumerau, & Gay, 2017). Bi+ individuals face stigma and discrimination in both heterosexual and lesbian/gay communities, where they are less likely to be accepted and more likely to face exclusion than their heterosexual, lesbian, or gay counterparts (Callis, 2013). Bi+ individuals experience higher rates of negative mental and physical health outcomes than do individuals who identify as lesbian, gay, or heterosexual (Baldwin et al., 2017). Monosexism (the belief that monosexual identities— heterosexual, gay, lesbian—are valid and legitimate while plurisexual sexualities are not) and biphobia (devaluing bi+ individuals based on their sexual identity) create significant social stress for bi+ individuals (Flanders, Dobinson, & Logie, 2015).

Bi+ individuals challenge the deeply-seated Western cultural understanding of sexual identity as a binary (Mathers, Sumerau, & Cragun, 2018). While for some bi+ individuals, gender is important in choosing a partner or partners, many bi+ individuals reject gender as an important category when selecting partners, further challenging the notion that gender does or should influence romantic, sexual, and intimate relationships (Toft & Kam-Tuck Yip, 2018). Additionally, the fluidity in attraction over time experienced by some bi+ individuals undermines the assumption that sexual identity and attraction are fixed rather than variable (Flanders et al., 2017).

In this volume, Ashley Green explores the tensions between the identities bisexual and pansexual, exploring the processes through which individuals claim identities and create meanings around those identities. In an auto-ethnographic account of their experiences navigating their identity as a bi+ person in the context of family settings, Nik Lampe presents an analysis of the ways bi+ individuals experience coming out. Lain Mathers explores how sibling relationships factor into and are affected by bi+ individuals' decisions about whether to come out to their siblings, focusing on the important role siblings often play as "gatekeepers" in the family context. Brittany Harder presents an autoethnographic account of the ways bi+ individuals and relationships are depicted in popular media, showing how these accounts shape perceptions of bi+ people and their relationships.

CONSENSUALLY NON-MONOGAMOUS IDENTITIES AND RELATIONSHIPS

Consensual nonmonogamy refers to intimate relationships negotiated between more than two people, and can be nonexclusive in terms of sexuality, emotional connection, and a variety of other relationship experiences (Grunt-Mejer & Campbell, 2016). There are multiple types of relationship agreements and individual identities that fall under the broad umbrella of consensual nonmonogamies (CNM), including polyamory, open relationships, swinging, and others (Rubel & Bogeart, 2014). While there is significant debate over what each of these relationship styles mean and how they are most accurately defined (see Barker, 2005), we provide here very broad brush definitions, recognizing that there are myriad individuals who would define these terms differently.

Swinging usually involves a couple having sex with others, usually with both members of the couple present. Open relationships usually involve a relationship in which all/both partners can have sex with others without the other partner present. Polyamory usually permits all partners in a relationship to have both sexual and emotional connection with other partners (Phillips, 2010). Among the range of varieties of polyamorous relationship structures, common arrangements include primary/secondary (where one individual is regarded as the main partner and others as secondary), triads and quads (three or four partners make up one main relationship unit), Vs (one person is equally involved with two other individuals, who are not themselves involved with one another), and broader polyamorous webs and families (Balzarini et al., 2017).

People who engage in CNM relationships discuss the terms of the relationships with their partner(s), and set those terms based on what each individual involved needs (Franke & DeLamater, 2010). People in CNM relationships report a high degree of satisfaction with their relationships (Balzarini et al., 2017) and report having greater emotional and sexual need fulfillment than if they had only one partner (Mitchell, Bartholomew, & Cobb, 2014). While for some BDSM is a sexual experience that violate the boundaries of a relationship agreement—can and does happen in CNM relationships, just as it does in the context of monogamous relationships, in the context of CNM relationships, interactions with others do not necessarily violate the relationship agreement (Schippers, 2016). CNM relationship agreements are usually created to protect members from unpleasant feelings of jealousy and insecurity and to foster compersion (experiencing happiness at a partner's happiness with another partner) (Wosick-Correa, 2010).

People whose relationships and/or identities fall under the CNM umbrella are often subject to stigma, misunderstanding, and discrimination (Moors, 2017). Because contemporary Western cultures valorize and normalize monogamy over other relationship forms—known as mononormativity—(Anderson, 2010), CNM is rarely recognized as a legitimate relationship structure (Klesse, 2014), and is not subject to the same legal protections and benefits as those extended to monogamous relationships (Sheff, 2011). For example, marriage to multiple partners is not legally available in the United States, most spousal and domestic partner privileges are limited to one partner. Because polyamory is not widely recognized or visible as a legitimate relationship structure, polyamorous individuals create their own language to describe their relationship structures and experiences (Ritchie & Barker, 2006). For example, polyamorists commonly refer to their partner's partner as their "metamour." Individuals with greater socioeconomic resources and class and racial privilege may face fewer risks related to their CNM relationships and have more resources available to manage those that they do encounter in comparison with individuals of color and/or with fewer socioeconomic resources (Sheff & Hammers, 2011).

CNM relationships and identities challenge the notion that only one individual should be responsible for fulfilling all of one's sexual and emotional needs (Wolkomir, 2015). These relationships also challenge the dominant cultural assumption that sexuality, romance, and emotional intimacy can and should be linked tightly together, and should be experienced in tandem, with one and only one individual. CNM relationship structures also push us to think more critically about *why* sexuality, romance, and intimacy are so commonly culturally linked, and what interests those linkages serve—or not.

In this volume, Mimi Schippers explores notions of happiness and the good life, examining how queer polyamorous individuals develop what Schippers terms a "poly identity to the world," disentangling conventional understandings of happiness and a good life from mononormative expectations. Krista Benson examines moments of failure in attempts at stable polyamorous identities, focusing on the experiences of queer polyamorous women. Emily Pain explores the ways disparities in race, class, and gender influence how individuals negotiate and experience polyamorous relationships. And J. E. Sumerau and Alexandra "Xan" C. H. Nowakowski write about how they have developed and negotiated their polyamorous relationship.

KINKY/BDSM IDENTITIES AND RELATIONSHIPS

BDSM (or kink) is an umbrella term that encompasses a variety of terms used interchangeably both in the literature and by participants to refer to a range of consensual practices/activities, desires, communities/sub-cultures, identities/roles, and meanings related to bondage and discipline, dominance and submission, and/or sadomasochism (Simula, 2017). Consensual activities that fall under the BDSM umbrella include impact play (e.g. spanking, whipping), bondage (e.g. handcuffs, rope), humiliation (e.g. begging, crawling), deprivation (e.g. orgasm control, sensory deprivation), service (e.g. preparing a meal for or doing laundry for a partner), body modification (e.g. piercing, tattooing), power exchange (allowing someone to control negotiated aspects of one's behavior and/or experiences), and many others. While for some BDSM is a sexual experience (Faccio, Casini, & Cipolletta, 2014), for others, it does not have a sexual meaning, or has a sexual meaning that is secondary to other meanings (Newmahr, 2011). Some BDSM participants describe BDSM experiences as being therapeutic or healing (Lindemann, 2012), while for others, BDSM is often a spiritual experience (Schneider, 2009). The terms "scene" and "play" are commonly used to refer to a specific interaction participants engage in agreed-upon activities and/or roles.

Regardless of the specific activities or relationship dynamics involved, the common theme that underlies BDSM activities is that they are consented to by all individuals involved (Weinberg, 2006). Participants commonly share their "limits" (things that they are unwilling to participate in) with play partners, negotiate what they do and do not want to happen in the context of a BDSM scene, and use "safewords" (terms agreed upon in advance to mean stop) to create consensual scenes. For example, the stoplight system—green means everything is good and keep going, yellow means slow down and check in, red means complete stop—is commonly used by BDSM participants to ensure clear communication of consent.

While BDSM and kink appear more commonly than ever before in mainstream media—prior to and continuing beyond the *Fifty Shades* phenomenon through references on TV shows such as *Law and Order, Will and Grace, Sex and the City, CSI, Weeds, the Surreal Life, House, Desperate Housewives, Family Guy, Nip/Tuck* and many others, and in music videos by well-known artists such as Christina Aguilera, Madonna, Rihanna, Lady Gaga, and others— these representations are often highly problematic, deeply misrepresenting fundamental aspects of BDSM such as consent, portraying BDSM participants as suffering from mental illnesses and/or BDSM itself as a sign of mental illness (Beckmann 2005). Further, while recent changes to the American Psychiatric Association's Diagnostic and Statistical Manual (DSM-5; 2013) remove interest in BDSM from being labeled a disorder, BDSM continues to be highly stigmatized and pathologization of BDSM persists in both academic and mental health settings (Tellier, 2017). However, BDSM participants do not report higher psychopathology or psychological distress than non-BDSM-involved individuals (Richters et al., 2008). In sum, BDSM remains a frequently marginalized and misunderstood practice.

As with other marginalized identities, community is an integral part of the experience of BDSM for many kink-identified individuals (Graham et al., 2016). BDSM communities provide education, opportunities to meet relationship and/or BDSM play partners, and serve to validate BDSM-specific identities, such as submissive, leatherboy, or puppy (Hale, 2003). However, some research suggests that at least some BDSM participants import normative cultural beliefs about gender that link men and masculinity with dominance and power and women and femininity with powerlessness and submissiveness and that men may be more likely to identify as dominant and women more likely to identify as submissive (Simula & Sumerau, 2017). Many BDSM participants nonetheless report that BDSM communities and settings can provide spaces for exploring alternative gendered selves, and that gender is sometimes less relevant in BDSM spaces than other social settings (Simula, 2013). However, access to BDSM spaces often requires a significant investment of economic resources—a fee for a membership to a dungeon (BDSM social club, educational venue, and play setting), entrance fee for each event one attends, appropriate clothing (leather, latex and other fetish gear), BDSM implements, and a host of related expenses—making access to BDSM community spaces available only to those with relatively high socioeconomic status (Sheff & Hammers, 2011).

BDSM participants challenge the normative meanings of bodily sensations, assumptions about the operation of power dynamics in interpersonal dynamics, and the relationships among sex, eroticism, and physical pleasure (Simula, 2017). BDSM participants also provide models for explicitly negotiating relationship structures as well as sexual and other experiences, undermining the common notion that explicit discussion and consent are challenging or spontaneity-reducing. The experiences of BDSM participants push us to think more critically about the relationships among physical sensations, power exchange, sexuality, erotic experience, and intimate relationships.

In this volume, Robin Bauer explores the diverse ways that BDSM participants construct relationships, drawing attention to the ways that power and consent influence those processes and outcomes. Angela Jones explores how the camming industry provides space for the exploration of kinky sexual desires, examining the ways that practices often marginalized even within the kink community are explored through the context of the camming industry. Katherine Martinez examines when and how BDSM participants disclose their kink identities to others and discusses how participants perceive others to respond to those disclosures. Mar Middlebrooks provides a personal reflection on experiences of healing from trauma through the context of kink.

ASEXUAL IDENTITIES AND RELATIONSHIPS

The term "asexual," or "ace," refers to a broad range of individuals who do not experience sexual attraction to others (Cuthbert, 2017).[1] Some aces are not interested in physical contact with others, while some desire and engage in physical closeness such as kissing, cuddling, and holding hands. Some aces engage in self-sex acts, such as fantasizing and masturbating, and some aces are willing to have sex if it is important to a partner, while others choose not to have sex (Scherrer, 2008). Within the asexual umbrella, some individuals identify as romantic, while others identify as aromantic—not interested in romantic relationships or experiences (Dawson, McDonnell, & Scott, 2016). Asexuals who are interested in romantic relationships describe their relationship interests as seeking closeness and intimate bonds, often in terms of a "close friendship" (Vares, 2018). For some aces, the gender of a potential partner matters, while for others, gender is irrelevant (Carrigan, 2011). Asexuals identify across the entire spectrum of gender-based relational identities (e.g. heteroromantic, homoromantic, panromantic) and identify across a spectrum of monogamous and non-monogamous relationship preferences. Additionally, there is a significant range of experiences and identifications that fall under the "ace umbrella" or on the "Grey-A" spectrum, both of which describe the continuum that exists between sexual and asexual identification (Brotto & Yule, 2017). Demisexuals, for example, experience sexual attraction and desire only after a strong emotional or romantic connection.

Historically conceptualized within medical discourse as a disability or disorder (Scott & Dawson, 2015), since the early 2000s—spurred by the creation of the online community site Asexuality Visibility and Education Network (AVEN) in 2001—asexuality emerged as an identity category, with some suggesting that asexuality can be understood as a sexual identity (Van Houdenhouve, Enzlin, & Gijs, 2017). Despite the increasing recognition of asexuality as an identity, asexuality continues to be widely misunderstood and stigmatized within both academic literature and the popular media, with disbelief concerning its very existence, claims that asexuality is manifestation of trauma or a personality or other disorder remain prevalent (Chasin, 2014). Stigma against and delegitimation of asexual identities lead to challenges for asexually-identified individuals, including fear of or actual exclusion from family and friend groups, feelings of being not good enough, pressure to engage in sexual activities to fit in, social isolation and feelings of confusion about one's self and identity (Scott & Dawson, 2015).

Due in part to the assumption of sexual interest and the relative invisibility of aces and the asexual community, finding the asexual community is often a pivotal life experience for aces. Like LGBTQ and BDSM identities, asexuality is a shared, community-based identity (Scherrer & Pfeffer, 2017). Common experiences in developing an asexual identity include a sense of differences from one's peers or friends, wondering whether there is something wrong with oneself, and finally developing a communal identity, often through discovering AVEN or other asexual community organizations (Cuthbert, 2017). A key part of the process of developing an asexual identity, similarly to developing other alternative sexual identities, is the process of coming out to others (Robbins, Graff Low, & Query, 2016). Many aces describe feeling that they are "naturally" asexual or have always been asexual, even before learning there was a name for how they feel (Scherrer, 2008).

Aces challenge the idea that sex is the best, easiest, or only route to achieving intimacy or connections with others. As Kim (2010) explains, being asexual does not mean being uninterested in pleasure, but rather focusing on non-sexual pleasures and ways of connecting to others and forming intimate interpersonal bonds. The experiences of aces call into question normative assumptions about the relationships among sex, physical closeness, romantic experience, and interpersonal intimacy, demonstrating that there are a variety of ways of creating meaningful intimate bonds with others that do not focus on sex or even necessarily on romantic connections.

In this volume, Tina Vares examines how asexually-identified individuals construct and navigate intimate relationships, focusing on the ways that the relationships of asexuals challenge conventional boundaries around intimacy. Daniel Copulsky explores the intersection of polyamory and asexuality, showing how asexuals may be more likely to consider polyamory as a relationship arrangement because both identities challenge common relationship assumptions. CJ Chasin investigates the (potential) relationship between asexuality and the traditional concept of sexual identity, examining the ways in which different models of sexual identity may fit—or not—the experiences of asexual individuals. Katie Linder provides a personal reflection on navigating family relationships as an asexual person, arguing that asexual familial relationships may queer the traditional concept of the nuclear family.

INTERSEX IDENTITIES AND RELATIONSHIPS

People with intersex traits are born with ambiguous chromosomes, sexual and reproductive organs, and/or genitalia, neither clearly male nor clearly female (Davis & Preves, 2017). Despite the long historical existence of intersex traits—formerly known as hermaphroditism (Topp, 2012)— intersex as an identity category did not develop until the 1990s, when intersex individuals began to work together to push back against the medicalization of intersex traits (Turner, 1999). Historically, the medical profession "treated" intersex individuals by surgically modifying perceived "abnormalities," despite the lack of medical necessity for such surgeries (Preves, 2003). Critiques of medical interventions by scholars and intersex activists, such as the Intersex Society of North America (ISNA), have made clear that intersexuality is a social, not medical issue (Fausto-Sterling, 2000).

Medical professionals historically made decisions about which sex category (male or female) to assign an infant with intersex traits, often concealing information from parents, and performing surgeries without fully informing parents and for cosmetic and social, rather than medical reasons (Costello, 2016). Surgical and other medical interventions performed on the bodies of intersex individuals are rarely necessary for health purposes, yet are routinely performed (Kessler, 1998). Medical professionals routinely work from the assumption that an individual with sex traits that vary from what is considered "normal" will be ostracized in society, despite lack of evidence for that view, and reports from intersex individuals themselves that contradict that belief (Davis, Dewey, & Murphy, 2015). Intersex activists challenge both the standard of medically unnecessary surgical and other medical interventions and the carrying out of those procedures on the bodies of intersex individuals without regard for individuals' own experiences and preferences (Jenkins & Short, 2017).

Intersex activist and support organizations, such as ISNA, the Ambiguous Genitalia Support Network, the Hermaphrodite Education and Listening Post, Bodies Like Ours, the Coalition for Intersex Support, Activism, and Education, and others have provided support, resources, and community for intersex individuals (Dreger & Herndon, 2009). Drawing on the success of LGBT rights movements in the late 20th century, intersex activists have worked to destigmatize intersexuality and to reduce the medicalization and pathologization of intersex individuals and bodies (Davis, 2015).

Intersex individuals challenge the binary understanding of sex and gender (i.e., one is *either* male or female, man or woman) (Butler, 1999[1990]). Intersex individuals also push back on the notion that one must have a sex or gender to exist as an intelligible human being, and that there is a *true* or essential sex or gender category for any individual, demonstrating that the reliance on sex and gender is itself a social rather than medical or biological imperative (Turner, 1999). Intersex activist movements further destabilize the cultural desire to "know" an individual's sex and/or gender (Chase, 2003), raising important questions about what, precisely, we think we "know" about an individual when we know their sex and/or gender.

In this volume, Cary Gabriel Costello explores the challenges and rewards of romantic and sexual relationships for intersex people, showing how contemporary models of bodies and relationships shape intersex individuals' relationship experiences. Georgiann Davis and Jonathan Jimenez investigate the experiences of intersex youth, focusing specifically on whether and how young intersex individuals develop expectations and desires for marriage. Sarah Topp explores the history of relationships between intersex individuals and medical professionals, tracing changes within shifting healthcare paradigms since the late nineteenth century.

TRANS IDENTITIES AND RELATIONSHIPS

The term "gender binary" refers to the social system that categorizes sex and gender into two categories, male/man and female/woman (Sumerau, Cragun, & Mathers, 2016). "Transgender" is an umbrella term that refers to a range of individuals whose gender identification does not align with the sex category to which they were assigned at birth[2]; the term "cisgender" refers to individuals who feel that their gender identification is in line with the sex category they were assigned at birth. (Serano, 2013). "Trans" and "cis" are common abbreviations. Gender nonconforming, gender queer, gender fluid, and nonbinary are identities that fall under the trans umbrella, but have distinct meanings (Grant et al., 2011). For the sake of brevity here, we use the term trans to refer to all individuals under the trans umbrella, while recognizing that not all individuals who fall under the umbrella identify with trans terminology.

Some trans individuals choose to pursue medical transition for their bodies, including using hormones and/or pursuing gender confirmation surgery (Schilt & Windsor, 2014). Changes in embodiment are often accompanied by complex social processes, requiring trans individuals to navigate the opinions of relationship partners (Pfeffer, 2008), friends and family (Whitley, 2016), health care professionals (Nordmarken & Kelly, 2014), and others (Schilt, 2010). Although not all friends and family support gender transition and/ or disclosures of gender identifications under the trans umbrella, a growing number of parents support gender transitions and gender fluidity (Meadow, 2011). Disclosing trans identity, like disclosing other marginalized identities, is a complex process, rather than a one-time decision or action (Cavalcante, 2016). Finding the trans community provides recognition and support for many trans individuals, and can function as an important step in the process of claiming a trans identity (Testa, Jimenez, & Rankin, 2014).

Historically treated as subjects of medical and psychological study in need of diagnosis and treatment (Stryker, 2008), the lives of transgender individuals often continue to be approached through a pathologizing framework. "Cisnormativity," the assumption that people are or should be cisgender, is deeply embedded in western cultures in ways that privilege the lives of cisgender individuals while devaluing those of transgender individuals (Sumerau, Cragun, & Mathers, 2016), including in the context of the broader LGBT community (Stone, 2013). Trans individuals face a range of forms of discrimination and violence beyond the medical establishment, including being subject to various forms of harassment, physical violence, mistreatment and lack of access to healthcare, higher rates of unemployment, and educational and workplace policies that deny gender identities (shuster, 2017). Trans individuals also navigate a host of "administrative recognitions," such as being denied the alignment of government documents such as driver's licenses and passports with their gender identities (Meadow, 2010). Transwomen, particularly women of color, experience the highest rates of discrimination and violence (Vidal-Ortiz, 2009).

The experiences of people who identify under the trans umbrella challenge deep-rooted sex and gender binaries such as male/female, masculine/feminine, and man/woman, along with the assumptions that such binaries are natural rather than socially shaped (Westbrook & Schilt, 2014). The experiences of trans people also undermine the dominant Western cultural conception that biological sex can or should align with gender identification and experience (Schilt & Westbrook, 2009). Additionally, some trans people, like some ace and BDSM identified individuals, decenter normative markers of sexual experience in favor of other bodily as well as emotional and interpersonal experiences in constructing the meaning of sex and intimacy (Latham, 2016).

In this volume, Carey Jean Sojka explores what they call the "trans partnership narrative" and its limiting and often negative effects on the ways that trans people and their partners develop relationships. stef shuster examines tensions between binary and non-binary trans people, examining the ways that inequalities are reproduced within trans communities. alithia zamantakis investigates how trans and nonbinary individuals negotiate race and gender in the context of intimate relationships, identifying the types of preemptive labor trans and nonbinary individuals engage in with potential relationship partners. Griffin Lacy provides a critical assessment of the current state of the literature on gender identity and youth, articulating an urgent call for more intersectional research, particularly in relation to studies of trans and gender nonconforming youth. Shalen Lowell provides a personal reflection on sex and relationships among trans people, detailing the symbiotic aspects of their own relationship experiences.

CONCLUSION

The chapters in this volume raise important questions about a range of gendered and sexual identities, identifications, relational styles, and communities. How do media representations (or lack thereof) contribute to awareness of these communities and experiences? How does access to information and community shape individuals' experiences of coming to one's own identity? How do stigma, bias, and inequality shape the experiences of living as an ace, trans, intersex, bi+, kinky, and/or poly individual? How do particular intersections across these communities, identities, and relational styles shape the experience of each? How do other identities along axes of race, ethnicity, socio-economic status, ability, religion, nationality, citizenship status, and others shape participation in and identification with these communities? To what extent do individual identification and community access and participation overlap? How and when do the experiences of romance, interpersonal attraction, sex, relationship development and maintenance intersect?

The chapters that follow engage with these and many other questions, covering a range of topics and issues related to the relationships, identities, and experiences of bi+, consensually non-monogamous, BDSM, ace, intersex, and trans individuals. Across each of the sections, the chapters include a range of empirical, pedagogical, theoretical, and/or personal experience and expertise. The concluding section of the book, intended specifically for teachers, includes reflections on and resources for pedagogical approaches to these relationships and identities.

NOTES

[1] Yet some asexually-identified individuals experience sexual attraction in specific circumstances, or in relation to specific individual (Brotto & Yule, 2017).

[2] As with the bisexual umbrella, not all individuals we describe here would themselves identify under the trans umbrella. We choose that term, like the term bi+, because it is among the most inclusive and recognizable, while noting here, too, that not everyone we describe in this section would identify with the trans umbrella. For instance, some individuals who identify as genderqueer or nonbinary actively disidentify from the term "trans."

REFERENCES

Anderson, E. (2010). 'At least with cheating there is an attempt at monogamy': Cheating and monogamism among undergraduate heterosexual men. *Journal of Social and Personal Relationships, 27*, 851–872.

Baldwin, A., Dodge, B., Schick, V., Herbenick, D., Sanders, S., Dhoot, R., & Fortenberry, J. D. (2017). Health and identity-related interactions between lesbian, bisexual, queer, and pansexual women and their healthcare providers. *Culture, Health, and Sexuality, 19*(11), 1181–1196.

Balzarini, R., Campbell, L., Kohut, T., Holmes, B., Lehmiller, J., Harman, J., & Atkins, N. (2017). Perceptions of primary and secondary relationships in polyamory. *PLOS, One, 12*, 1–20.

Barker, M. (2005). 'This is my partner, and this is my…partner's partner': Constructing a polyamorous identity in a monogamous world. *Journal of Constructivist Psychology, 18*, 75–88.

Barringer, M. N., Sumerau, J. E., & Gay, D. A. (2017). Examining differences in identity disclosure between monosexuals and bisexuals. *Sociological Spectrum, 37*(5), 319–333.

Bauer, R. (2014). *Queer BDSM intimacies: Critical consent and pushing boundaries.* New York, NY: Palgrave Macmillan.

Beckmann, A. (2005). Representing 'healthy' and 'sexual' bodies: The media, 'disability' and consensual 'SM'. In M. King and K. Watson (Eds.), *Representing health: Discourses of health and illness in the media* (pp. 206–225). Basingstoke: Palgrave MacMillan.

Benson, K. (2017). Tensions of subjectivity: The instability of queer polyamorous identity and community. *Sexualities, 20*(1–2), 24–40.

Brotto, L., & Yule, M. (2017). Asexuality: Sexual identity, paraphilia, sexual dysfunction, or none of the above? *Archives of Sexual Behavior, 46*, 619–627.

Butler, J. (1999[1990]). *Gender trouble: Feminism and the subversion of identity.* New York, NY: Routledge.

Callis, A. S. (2013). "The black sheep of the pink flock: Labels, stigma, and bisexuality identity. *Journal of Bisexuality, 13*(1), 82–105.

Carrigan, M. (2011). 'There's more to life than sex?' Difference and commonality within the asexual community. *Sexualities, 14*(4), 462–478.

Cavalcante, A. (2016). 'I did it all online': Transgender identity and the management of everyday life. *Critical Studies in Media Communication, 33*(1), 109–122.

Chase, C. (2003). What is the agenda of the intersex patient advocacy movement? *Endocrinologist, 13*(3), 240–242.

Chasin, C. J. D. (2014). Making sense in and of the asexual community: Navigating relationships and identities in a context of resistance. *Journal of Community and Applied Social Psychology, 25*, 167–180.

Compton, D., Farris, N., & Chang, Y.-T. (2015). Patterns of bisexuality in America. *Journal of Bisexuality, 15*(4), 481–497.

Costello, C. G. (2016). Intersex and trans* communities: Commonalities and tensions. In S. Horlacher (Ed.), *Transgender and intersex: Theoretical, practical, and artistic perspectives* (pp. 83–113). New York, NY: Palgrave Macmillan.

Cuthbert, K. (2017). You have to be normal to be abnormal: An empirically grounded exploration of the intersection of asexuality and disability. *Sociology, 51*(2), 241–257.

Davis, G. (2015). *Contesting intersex: The dubious diagnosis.* New York, NY: NYU Press.

Davis, G., Dewey, J., & Murphy, E. (2015). Giving sex: Deconstructing intersex and trans medicalization practices. *Gender & Society, 30*(3), 490–514.

Davis, G., & Preves, S. (2017). Intersex and the social construction of sex. *Contexts, 16*(1), 80.

Dawson, M., McDonnell, L., & Scott, S. (2016). Negotiating the boundaries of intimacy: The personal lives of asexual people. *The Sociological Review, 64*, 349–365.

Dreger, A., & Herndon, A. (2009). Progress and politics in the intersex rights movement: Feminist theory in action. *GLQ, 15*(2), 199–224.

Faccio, E., Casini, C., & Cipolletta, S. (2014). Forbidden games: The construction of sexuality and sexual pleasure by BDSM 'players'. *Culture, Health, and Sexuality, 16*(7), 752–764.

Fausto-Sterling, A. (2000). *Sexing the body: Gender politics and the construction of sexuality.* New York, NY: Basic Books.

Flanders, C. (2017). Under the bisexual umbrella: Diversity of identity and experience. *Journal of Bisexuality, 17*(1), 1–6.

Flanders, C., Dobinson, C., & Logie, C. (2015). 'I'm never really my full self': Young bisexual women's perceptions of their mental health. *Journal of Bisexuality, 15*(4), 454–480.

Flanders, C., LeBreton, M., Robinson, M., Bian, J., & Alonso Caravaca-Morera, J. (2017). Defining bisexuality: Young bisexual and pansexual people's voices. *Journal of Bisexuality, 17*(1), 39–57.

Franke, K., & DeLamater, J. (2010). Deconstructing monogamy: Boundaries, identities, and fluidities across relationships. In M. Barker & D. Langdridge (Eds.), *Understanding non-monogamies* (pp. 9–20). New York, NY: Routledge.

Galupo, M. P., Ramirez, J., & Pulice-Farrow, L. (2017). 'Regardless of their gender': Descriptions of sexual identity among bisexual, pansexual, and queer identified individuals. *Journal of Bisexuality, 17*(1), 108–124.

Graham, B., Butler, S., McGraw, R., Cannes, S. M., & Smith, J. (2016). Member perspectives on the role of BDSM communities. *The Journal of Sex Research, 53*(8), 895–909.

Grant, J. M., Mottet, L. A., Tanis, J., Harrison, J., Herman, J. L., & Keisling, M. (2011). *Injustice at every turn: A report of the national transgender discrimination survey.* Washington, DC: US Department of Health and Human Services.

Grunt-Mejer, K., & Campbell, C. (2016). Around consensual nonmonogamies: Assessing attitudes toward nonexlcusive relationships. *Journal of Sex Research, 53*(1), 45–53.

Hale, C. J. (2003). Leatherdyke boys and their daddies: How to have sex without women or men. In R. Corber & S. Valocchi (Eds.), *Queer studies: An interdisciplinary reader* (pp. 61–70). Malden: Blackwell.

Jenkins, T., & Short, S. (2017). Negotiating intersex: A case for revising the theory of social diagnosis. *Social Science and Medicine, 175*, 91–98.

Kessler, S. (1998). *Lessons from the intersexed.* New Brunswick, NJ: Rutgers University Press.

Kim, E. (2010). How much sex is healthy? The pleasures of asexuality. In J. Metzl & A. Kirkland (Eds.), *Against health: How health became the new morality.* New York, NY: New York University Press.

Klesse, C. (2014). Polyamory: Intimate practice, identity, or sexual identity? *Sexualities, 17*(1–2), 81–99.

Latham, J. R. (2016). Trans men's sexual narrative-practices: Introducing STS to trans and sexuality studies. *Sexualities, 19*(3), 347–368.

Lindemann, D. (2012). *Dominatrix: Gender, eroticism, and control in the dungeon.* Chicago, IL: University of Chicago Press.

Loeser, C., Pini, B., & Crowley, V. (2018). Disability and sexuality: Desires and pleasures. *Sexualities, 21*(3), 255–270.

Martino, A. S. (2017). Cripping sexualities: An analytic review of theoretical and empirical writing on the intersection of disabilities and sexualities. *Sociology Compass, 11*, e12471.

Mathers, L. A. B., Sumerau, J. E., & Cragun, R. (2018). The limits of homonormativity: Constructions of bisexual and transgender people in the post-gay era. *Sociological Perspectives*, 1–19.

Meadow, T. (2011). Deep down where the music plays: How parents account for gender variance. *Sexualities, 14*, 725–747.

Mitchell, M. E., Bartholomew, K., & Cobb, R. J. (2014). Need fulfillment in polyamorous relationships. *Journal of Sex Research, 51*, 329–339.

Moors, A. (2017). Has the American public's interest in information related to relationships beyond "the couple" increased over time? *The Journal of Sex Research. 54*(6), 677–684.

Morandini, J., Blaszcynski, A., & Dar-Nimrod, I. (2017). Who adopts queer and pansexual sexual identities? *The Journal of Sex Research, 54*(7), 911–922.

Newmahr, S. (2011). *Playing on the edge: Sadomasochism, risk, and intimacy.* Bloomington, IN: Indiana University Press.

Nordmarken, S., & Kelly, R. (2014). Limiting transgender health: Administrative violence and microaggressions in health care systems. In V. L. Harvey & T. Heinz (Eds.), *Health care disparities and the LGBT population.* New York, NY: Lexington.

Pfeffer, C. (2008). Bodies in relation – Bodies in transition: Lesbian partners of trans men and body image. *Journal of Lesbian Studies, 12*(4), 325–345.

Phillips, S. (2010). There were three in the bed: Discursive desire and the sex lives of swingers. In M. Barker and D. Langdridge (Eds.), *Understanding non-monogamies* (pp. 82–86). New York, NY: Routledge.

Preves, S. (2003). *Intersex and identity: The contested self.* New Brunswick, NJ: Rutgers University Press.

Richters, J., de Visser, R., Riseel, C., Grulich, A., & Smith, A. (2008). Demographic and psychosocial features of participants in Bondage and Discipline, "Sadomasochism" or Dominance and Submission (BDSM): Data from a national survey. *Journal of Sexual Medicine, 5,* 1660–1668.

Ritchie, A., & Barker, M. (2006). 'There aren't words for what we do or how we feel so we have to make them up': Constructing polyamorous languages in a culture of compulsory monogamy. *Sexualities, 9*(5), 584–601.

Robbins, N., Graff Low, K., & Query, A. (2016). A qualitative exploration of the "coming out" process for asexual individuals. *Archives of Sexual Behavior, 45,* 751–760.

Robinson, M. (2017). Two-spirit and bisexual people: Different umbrella, same rain. *Journal of Bisexuality, 17*(1), 7–29.

Rubel, A. N., & Bogeart, A. F. (2014). Consensual nonmonogamy: Psychological well-being and relationship quality correlates. *Journal of Sex Research, 4,* 1–22.

Scherrer, K. (2008). Coming to an asexual identity: Negotiating identity, negotiating desire. *Sexualities, 11*(5), 621–641.

Scherrer, K., & Pfeffer, C. (2017). None of the above: Toward identity and community-based understandings of (A)Sexualities. *Archives of Sexual Behavior, 46,* 643–46.

Schilt, K. (2010). *Just one of the guys? Transgender men and the persistence of gender inequality.* Chicago, IL: University of Chicago Press.

Schilt, K., & Lagos, D. (2017). The development of transgender studies in sociology. *Annual Review of Sociology, 43,* 425–443.

Schilt, K., & Westbrook, L. (2009). Doing gender, doing heteronormativity: 'Gender normals', transgender people, and the social maintenance of heterosexuality. *Gender & Society, 23*(4), 440–464.

Schilt, K., & Windsor, E. (2014). The sexual habitus of transgender men: Negotiating sexuality through gender. *Journal of Homosexuality, 61*(5), 732–748.

Schippers, M. (2016). *Beyond monogamy: Polyamory and the future of polyqueer sexualities.* New York, NY: New York University Press.

Schneider, A. (2009). The rhythm of the whip. *Social Psychology Quarterly, 72*(4), 285–289.

Scott, S., & Dawson, M. (2015). Rethinking asexuality: A symbolic interactionist account. *Sexualities, 18*(1–2), 3–19.

Serano, J. (2013). *Excluded: Making feminist and queer movements more inclusive.* Seattle, WA: Seal Press.

Sheff, E. (2005). Polyamorous women, sexual subjectivity, and power. *Journal of Contemporary Ethnography, 34*(3), 251–283.

Sheff, E., & Hammers, C. (2011). The privilege of perversities: Race, class, and education among polyamorists and kinksters. *Sexuality and Psychology, 2*(3), 198–223.

shuster, s. (2017). Punctuating accountaibility: How discursive aggression regulates transgender people. *Gender & Society, 31*(4), 481–502.

Simula, B. (2013). Queer utopias in painful spaces: BDSM participants resisting heteronormativity and gender regulation. In A. Jones (Ed.), *A critical inquiry into queer utopias* (pp. 71–100). New York, NY: Palgrave Macmillan.

Simula, B. (2017). A 'different economy of bodies and pleasures'?: Differentiating and evaluating sex and sexual BDSM experiences. *Journal of Homosexuality*.

Simula, B., & Sumerau, J. E. (2017). The use of gender in the interpretation of BDSM. *Sexualities*.

Stone, A. (2013). Flexible queers, serious bodies: Transgender inclusion in queer spaces. *Journal of Homosexuality, 60*(12), 1647–1665.

Stryker, S. (2008). *Transgender history*. Seattle, WA: Seal Press.

Sumerau, J. E., Cragun, R., & Mathers, L. A. B. (2016). Contemporary religion and the cisgendering of reality. *Social Currents, 3*, 239–311.

Tellier, S. (2017). Advancing the discourse: Disability and BDSM. *Sexuality and Disability, 35*, 485–493.

Testa, R., Jimenez, C., & Rankin, S. (2014). Risk and resilience during transgender identity development: The effects of awareness and engagement with other transgender people on affect. *Journal of Gay and Lesbian Mental Health, 18*(1), 31–46.

Toft, A., & Kam-Tuck Yip, A. (2018). Intimacy negotiated: The management of relationships and the construction of personal communities in the lives of bisexual women and men. *Sexualities, 21*(1–2), 233–250.

Topp, S. (2012). Againt the revolution: The rhetorical construction of intersex individuals as disordered. *Sexualities, 16*(1–2), 180–194.

Turner, S. (1999). Intersex identities: Locating new intersections of sex and gender. *Gender & Society, 13*(4), 457–479.

Van Houdenhouve, E., Enzlin, P., & Gijs, L. (2017). A positive approach toward asexuality: Some first steps, but still a long way to go. *Archives of Sexual Behavior, 46*, 647–651.

Vares, T. (2018). 'My [asexuality] is playing hell with my dating life': Romantic identified asexuals negotiate the dating game. *Sexualities, 21*(4), 520–536.

Vidal-Ortiz, S. (2009). The figure of the transwoman of color through the lens of 'doing gender'. *Gender & Society, 23*, 99–105.

Weinberg, T. (2006). Sadomasochism and the social sciences: A review of the sociological and social psychological literature. *Journal of Homosexuality, 50*(2–3), 17–40.

Westbrook, L., & Schilt, K. (2014). Doing gender, determining gender: Transgender people, gender panics, and the maintenance of the sex/gender/sexuality system. *Gender & Society, 28*(1), 32–57.

Whitley, C. (2016). Trans-kin undoing and redoing gender: Negotiating relational identity among friends and family of transgender persons. *Sociological Perspectives, 56*, 597–621.

Wolkomir, M. (2015). One but not the only one: Reconfiguring intimacy in multiple partner relationships. *Qualitative Sociology, 38*, 417–438.

Wosick-Correa, K. (2010). Agreements, rules, and agentic fidelity in polyamorous relationships. *Psychology and Sexuality, 1*, 44–61.

PART 1

BI+ AND PLURISEXUAL RELATIONSHIPS

ASHLEY GREEN

1. "BY DEFINITION THEY'RE NOT THE SAME THING"

Analyzing Methods of Meaning Making for Pansexual Individuals

INTRODUCTION

As transgender and gender non-conforming identities gain visibility in the media, an increasing number of individuals are beginning to understand gender as more fluid than the traditional notion of binary "man" and "woman" identities would suggest. As a result, an increasing number of individuals are adopting sexual identities that account for this fluidity. One such identity, pansexual, has been defined by those who use it as having the potential to be attracted to individuals of all genders (Callis, 2014; Guittar, 2014; Elizabeth, 2013; Rupp & Taylor, 2013). However, despite the increasing adoption of this sexual identity, very little research has explored the use of this label or what makes it meaningful to individuals who identify as pansexual. The purpose of this chapter is to explore some of the themes that emerge in the stories that individuals tell about their pansexual identities and to examine how pansexual individuals construct this identity when crafting these narratives. I do so by drawing on interviews with 10 individuals who use the label pansexual that I collected as part of an exploratory project. This project sought to better understand why some people chose to use this particular identity label and what meaning it held for them. The participants in this study claimed that they were drawn to the identity label because it was more inclusive of a variety of gender identities. However, as they spoke about their experiences they often relied on discovery narratives, which tell the tell the story of "discovering a truth" about one's identity (Plummer, 1995, p. 83). Moreover, they often sought to authenticate their own identity by juxtaposing it with the identity of bisexual, at times in ways that seemed to contradict their alleged goal of inclusivity.

My analysis of this data is grounded in ethnomethodology, which "appreciated the necessity of studying how reality is accomplished" (Gubrium & Holstein, 1997, p. 120). Reflecting on ethnomethodology as an analytic tool, it seems a

© KONINKLIJKE BRILL NV, LEIDEN, 2019 | DOI:10.1163/9789004414105_002

useful lens through which to derive a better understanding of how individuals use language to make meaning of their sexual identity in everyday interactions. Indeed, a significant body of literature on gender as socially constructed is grounded in phenomenology and ethnomethodology (Brickell, 2006; Crawley & Broad, 2004; Crawley, Foley, & Shehan, 2008; West & Zimmerman, 1987). Sexual identity labels used by individuals who understand their identity as existing outside the binary of heterosexual and gay/or lesbian present something of a paradox when put in conversation with existing literature. The use of labels like pansexual and queer represents an increasing attempt to deconstruct the widely held notion of gender as being biologically determined and existing solely within a binary. However, if, as Butler (1997) claims, "identity categories tend to be instruments of regulatory regimes," then the proliferation of these labels is counterintuitive to deconstructive calls of queer theory that some individuals claim to be answering (p. 301). Rather than eliminating identity categories, the number of categories with which one can identify are increasing, at times causing conflict within the larger LGBTQ+ community. Such animosity is far from new, but rather contributes to a history of biphobia that has long been perpetuated by gay and lesbian individuals (Firestein, 1996; Rust, 1992, 1993; Udis-Kessler, 1996; Ochs, 1996; Coleman, 1998).

By analyzing the methods some individuals use when crafting their pansexual identities, we might gain more insight into this seemingly contradictory phenomenon. Thus, I focus particularly on the methods individuals used to describe their experiences discovering the label pansexual and adopting it as their own identity. Recognizing that "the whats and hows of meaningful interaction are equally important to understanding whatever has interactionally transpired" (Gubrium & Holstein, 1997, p. 120; emphasis in original), my goal is to look at patterns of both what individuals are saying as well as how they engage in conversation about identity.

METHODOLOGY

In-person interviews were conducted with 10 participants in spring of 2015, none of which last more than an hour. Advertisements for participants were placed both on campus at a mid-size university in southern California, as well as in coffee shops and local businesses in LGBTQ+ friendly neighborhoods. Convenience and snowball sampling were used due to time constraints on the original project, and the first ten participants to respond were accepted, likely impacting the potential diversity of the sample. Table 1 presents all demographic information at the time interviews were conducted.

Table 1. Participant demographics

Name[a]	Age	Race/Ethnicity[b]	Gender identity
Zander	18	White	Trans man
Shayla	18	White	Cis woman
Emilia	18	White	Genderqueer, Nonbinary, Trans
Kaylee	25	European American & Native American	Cis woman
Shane	25	White	Cis man
Victor	26	Mexican, Spanish, Irish, & French	Trans man
Vanessa	27	White	Cis woman
Bryant	27	African American	Cis man
Kenichi	32	Japanese and White	Genderqueer, Agender
Mike	54	White	Cis man

[a] All names listed are pseudonyms. Nonbinary participants chose their own pseudonyms.

[b] Participants were asked how they identified their race and ethnicity, so all identifiers are in their own words.

DISCUSSION

Attempting Inclusivity

Before analyzing how participants constructed the reality of their identities, I want to explore commonalities between what participants discussed as having been important to their use of pansexual as an identity label. One of the most prevalent themes to emerge from the interviews was a connection between labelling one's sexuality as pansexual and either identifying as transgender or nonbinary,[1] or engaging in a relationship with someone who identified as such. All but one individual either identified with a gender that did not match the sex they were assigned at birth or had engaged in romantic or sexual relationships with individuals who identified as transgender. Moreover, the participants stated that their own gender identities or relationships with transgender individuals impacted their understanding of pansexual as a label that allowed them to account for the experiences. For example, transgender and nonbinary participants stated:

Emilia, genderqueer: It's one of the few all-encompassing, inclusive identities and part of my identity is being genderqueer. I'm on the trans spectrum. I self-identify as trans or genderqueer, and pansexual is important to me personally because it includes me, so that's really nice.

Victor, Transman: I had for example, gay guys attracted to me but then that becomes problematic because they expect me to have a penis. And then when I have women that are attracted to me they sometimes expect me to have breasts and so that's problematic in itself. So really, pansexuality kind of gave me like this, breathing room that I didn't have to, because sexual orientation is so based on um, your gender identity.

Zander, Transman: I started as androgynous, and then I went to genderqueer, and then I finally decided on trans male. And so through that and my own self-discovery I went through my own mental crisis of, because I identify this way no one could ever like me or love me. And so that was probably one of the major factors in me deciding like, but then I realized that other people can love me for who I am, and I can like other people for who they are, that their gender doesn't really matter, doesn't define who they are.

The assumptions made by people with whom he interacted were particularly problematic for Victor. In *Gendering Bodies*, Crawley, Foley, and Shehan (2008) state that "if we believe we know the sex of the person, we also believe we know the gender and sexual orientation of the person," a phenomenon highlighted by use of the "gender box structure" (p. 16). Victor's comment shows that he recognizes that people with whom he interacts with sexually will likely assign him a sex category, and, regardless of which sex category he is assigned, the physical reality of his body is not going to match up. By using the label pansexual when interacting with potential partners, he hopes that individuals who identify similarly will be accepting of his body.

Additionally, four of the cisgender participants cited the gender identity of past or current partners as playing a role in their use of pansexual as a sexual identity label. Participants stated things such as:

Shayla, Ciswoman: I started dating my girlfriend, who's transgender, MTF [male to female], and I started getting more and more comfortable with the fact that, yea, I'm pansexual. Like, that's definitely it.

Bryant, Cisman: One of the like, the turning points in my sexual history that really helped me like, identify as pansexual was uh, I met someone on craigstlist, it was a transsexual [sic] uh, male to female…She was just so chill and normal and everyday and like, it was just a whole new world that I didn't even know existed cuz you're not generally exposed to it.

Shane, Cisman: I was in a relationship about two and a half years ago with a transgender [sic] and that then I was like—I wasn't bisexual but I mean, I wasn't straight. I wasn't anything. So when I heard pansexuality I was like, yea.

For these individuals, engaging in romantic or sexual relationships with someone whose gender identity did not match their sex assigned at birth led them to question the sexual identity labels they previously employed. They believed these labels were not inclusive of transgender individuals, and felt that the label pansexual allowed them to better express their new understanding of their own sexual identities.

Another commonality between the interviewees was that many spoke of the need to be able to communicate their identity to other people. This was particularly important for those who cited gender identity as one of the main reasons they felt that the label pansexual best represented their understanding of their sexual identity. Some examples include:

Vanessa, Ciswoman: Maybe just the ease in conversation. Umm, it requires less of the explaining why I'm not this, more so the easier of why I'm this. So instead of saying 'Well I'm not a lesbian. I'm not bisexual. I like all these other people.' If you can just say 'Well I'm [pansexual] because...'

Kenichi, Genderqueer: It's important to me to communicate to other people. Um, so like talking to my mom...for me to use pansexual to explain to her what that means. I guess it's also easy to say, like 'I'm into anybody.' But if someone doesn't understand that there are more identities than just male or female that's not enough. Because then if I say I'm into anyone they're going to think that I'm referring to men and women only when I want to be very intentional of bringing, um, like visibility or bringing trans people into the conversation.

Here Kenichi and Vanessa speak to the way pansexual creates meaning for them by allowing them to communicate to others that their identity is inclusive of individuals who do not identify within the gender binary, and moreover that they do not believe everyone needs to conform to the notion of a gender binary. This is particularly noteworthy given the importance that phenomenology and ethnomethodology place on language. Citing Schutz, Holstein, and Gubrium (1994) state that "language is the central medium for transmitting typifications and thereby meaning" (p. 263). The importance of language stressed by these theorists is reflected in both Vanessa's and Kenichi's claims that using the label pansexual allows them to place themselves into a category when interacting with others. While Butler (1997) argues against such categorization, these individuals found it useful in helping ease communication. At another point during the interview, Vanessa states that she "didn't really want any label," but ultimately began using pansexual because she would "rather have something that's inclusive than either none or one." Even though she did not believe her sexuality could be defined in such a way, she felt it was easier to communicate her identity to others when using a label.

Finally, many individuals told a version of the "coming out" story as outlined by Kenneth Plummer (1995). However, unlike in these traditional narratives, the stories shared by the participants more closely resemble the ways in which Plummer states that stories are shifting, most notably that "the stories are full of indeterminacies" and that "identities blur and change" (pp. 139–140). This often occurred when participants were discussing labels they used prior to identifying as pansexual:

Mike, Cisman: So, I went through college gay, gay, gay, gay, gay. In my mid-20's I met a girl who was a lesbian, but we had this great relationship at the time, emotionally and physically. And I decided that I'm closer to bisexual than I am to homosexual. So from that time forward I considered myself bisexual and I kept trying to figure out where on the sliding scale I fell: seventy-thirty, forty-sixty, today I'm this, on Tuesday I'm that, full moon it's right in the middle. Um, and that helped me become a little more comfortable with this flexible sexuality.

Zander, Transman: For me up until my freshman year of high school I didn't think I could identify as anything besides straight and so that affected my dating, but there I was opened up to "Oh here, you can date people of the same sex," and I was like, okay that's something I can try too. And then, and then I just like, I ended up dating someone who was transmale [sic] and that for me was way out there. It was super different. Um, and to them, they kind of helped me discover that I was trans and that this was cool and I thought it was very interesting.

According to Plummer (1995), the most basic version of these stories follow a linear progression, beginning with a "strong sense of difference" in childhood, on to adolescence and a "crucial moment…that lead to a concern—or discovery—over being 'gay'," and finally to a resolution "through meeting other lesbians or gays in a community" and achieving a "sense of identity or self" (p. 83). However, the stories shared by Mike and Zander are less linear, with their understandings of their own identity shifting over time.

Additionally, Vanessa told a story of having a constantly shifting understanding of her sexual identity. She states that she went from being "very not focused on sexuality" in high school, to adopting a lesbian identity after fighting for the rights of a lesbian couple in the student senate, to "talking about sexual ambiguity" and not labelling before finally settling on pansexual because she would "rather have something that's inclusive than either none or one." These narratives epitomize what Plummer describes, highlighting the ways in which individuals understanding of their identities blurred as they gained access to new language and began deconstructing notions of a gender binary.

Asserting Authenticity

Despite their rejection of a binary understanding of gender, many of the stories told by participants relied on existing narratives of identity as a method for discussing their adoption of the label pansexual. Thus, I would like to shift into focusing on the "hows" of accomplishing identity that were employed by the participants. In his discussion of shifting sexual stories, Plummer (1995) states that "stories to be told are borrowings, reassembled into pastiche, never-endingly being reassembled to tell the same old new stories in ironic ways" (p. 139). This was most prevalent through the use of a "discovery narrative," in which identity is not "something one chooses or develops but as something that is natural, essential, and free from agency" (Johnson, 2016, p. 485). Participants made statements that implied their identity was something inherent. For example, Zander claimed that the GSA he attended "kind of helped me discover that I was trans." Additionally, Mike stated that "when I say I'm pansexual to someone…that's when I'm closest to being, to describing my most authentic self." By using words such as "authentic" and "discover," these participants are drawing on the assumption that identity is something innate that needs to be described.

Furthermore, when discussing her understanding of the origins of the term pansexual Shayla states "the term kind of came into being when it was really only believed that there was two genders. So pansexuality kind of grew off of that as it became more apparent that there was more than one—I mean there's more than two." Although she is rejecting the existence of a gender binary, Shayla does not use language that shows an understanding of gender as socially constructed. Instead she relies on existing narratives of identity that offer up a "born this way" understanding of gender that simply allows for more options regarding gender identity. The word "apparent" in particular works to craft non-binary genders as something that are real and have been discovered. This is significant because the master narrative that asserts LGBT identities as naturally occurring and innate to the individual has often been used to gain validation in activist circles. Whether or not Shayla's use of this language was intentional, it shows how she constructs identity as something that is valid and thus deserving of respect.

Additionally, some participants sought to authenticate their identity as pansexual by juxtaposing it with bisexuality. These participants often spoke of bisexuality as being inferior to pansexuality, most notably because they felt it excluded individuals who did not identify within the gender binary. For example, participants stated that:

> Zander, Transman: I think that bisexual is important because, for some people, yea it is only two. Like they like male and female and maybe they don't like trans. It's definitely different and its own identity from pansexuality.

> Mike, Cisman: I tried getting into the bisexual community and there was this ferocious almost pressure to be—if you're gonna be bi then you're either having sex with bio men and bio women, but the trans community didn't fit into that, which was kind of bizarre to me.

> Shayla, Ciswoman: Sometimes bisexuality and pansexuality are used interchangeably. By definition they're not the same thing. Bisexual is two, pansexual is all.

These individuals use language that constructs pansexual as different from bisexual, a method used in order to establish it to listeners as its own distinct identity. One participant, Kaylee a ciswoman, took this differentiation a step further, expressing very negative feelings toward bisexual individuals. When the topic of bisexuality came up, she exclaimed "Fuck that! Fuck those bitches," and asked, "Do I get to hate?" before going on to explain her understanding of people who use the label bisexual:

> There are two kinds of bi people, alright?…they either were like me in high school and they don't know there's other things out there, but bi people that I fucking, that I meet, it's usually chicks who want to have like, intimate, not sexual, intimate personal relationships with men,

they see themselves marrying men…they're going to take home to their family a man. But [her emphasis], they're sexually attracted to women and they're gonna go fuck 'em and do that shit. I dunno maybe they'll go to dinner first, maybe not. But, they don't plan to, they don't plan to pursue it any further than that.

Kaylee prefaced this description by stating that although she identified as bisexual in high school, it was only because she was not aware there were other options. Additionally, she claimed that if bisexual individuals were unaware of pansexuality, when they heard the term "they'd be like oh okay, that's better…unless they're cissexist or transphobic." This assertion not only positions pansexuality as being the superior identity as a result of its inclusivity, but also goes on to demonize bisexual individuals as being transphobic if they do not identify as pansexual once they are informed that there is a "better" identity. In doing so she crafts an identity that she feels is not only distinct and legitimate, but superior to bisexuality as a result of its inclusivity. However, in doing so both Kaylee and the other participants who posit pansexuality as superior to bisexuality are contributing to a long history of biphobia that has existed within gay and lesbian communities. Moreover, Kaylee's claim that anyone who actively chooses to identify as bisexual rather than pansexual is inherently cissexist or transphobic does not account for the large percentage of transgender and nonbinary individuals who also identify as bisexual.

While some participants sought to make distinctions between the identities bisexual and pansexual, others spoke favorably of bisexuality, even going so far as to address the tensions between individuals who used the labels. Their responses included statements such as:

Victor, Transman: I mean just like pansexuality, if I wanted my sexual orientation to be recognized I also advocate for bisexuality to be recognized as well. Because just because someone is attracted to women and men and not people that are outside of women and men, um, it doesn't mean that its incorrect or it's wrong or it's not a sexual orientation at all.

Emilia, Genderqueer: I know the people think that pans and bis don't like each other and I'm like, that's dumb. Why would we just argue over petty stuff? It's like personal. If someone wants to identify the way they do that's their choice.

Shane, Cisman: I don't think nothing bad of bisexual as an identity or anything like that. I don't look down upon it cuz everybody has their own identity for themselves. And then identity, the only reason why identity is important in today's society is because we in society survive with being able to apply labels on people or on things.

Rather than position the two identities as in opposition, these participants spoke of the importance of respecting all identities. As with those who highlighted distinctions between the two, these individuals still crafted their identities as meaningful and deserving of respect. Victor in particular was explicit in his use of this method, stating the importance of recognizing the legitimacy of bisexuality if he wants his own identity to be recognized.

CONCLUSION

When describing their use of the sexual identity label pansexual, participants in this study told coming out stories that frequently relied on discovery narratives. This method of storytelling reflects what Plummer (1995) identifies as shifting sexual stories, which "are borrowings, reassembled" (p. 139). In borrowing narratives that they are familiar with, the pansexual individuals interviewed in this study reinforced an essentialist understanding of identity despite their attempts to deconstruct gender binaries. Additionally, participants sought to authenticate the identity pansexual by distinguishing it from the identity bisexual. Some did so by engaging in biphobic rhetoric, while others believed it was important to respect all identities—a strategy that ultimately reflected a desire for respect and acceptance of their own identity.

However, the stories shared here represent only a small snapshot of the experiences of individuals who use adopt the label pansexual. Additional in-depth interviews with individuals who identify as pansexual can expand understanding of why people choose this identity label over others. Moreover, including individuals who identify with labels beyond pansexual, such as bisexual, queer, and fluid, could provide a better picture of how individuals use different labels to communicate attraction to a variety of different gender identities, while also potentially shedding light on the ways in which biphobia continues to be perpetuated by and experienced within the larger LGBTQ+ community.

NOTE

[1] Here nonbinary is being used as an umbrella term for all participants who did not identify as a transgender or cisgender man or woman.

REFERENCES

Brickell, C. (2016). The sociological construction of gender and sexuality. *The Sociological Review, 54*(1), 87–113.

Butler, J. (1997). Imitation and gender insubordination. In L. Nicholson (Ed.), *The second wave: A reader in feminist theory* (pp. 300–315). New York, NY: Routledge.

Callis, A. (2014). Bisexual, pansexual, queer: Non-binary identities and the sexual borderlands. *Sexualities, 17*(1–2), 63–80.

Coleman, E. (1996). Paradigmatic changes in the understanding of bisexuality. In B. Firestein (Ed.), *Bisexualities: The ideology and practice of sexual contact with both men and women* (pp. 217–239). Thousand Oaks, CA: Sage Publications.

Crawley, S., & Broad, K. (2004). "Be your(real lesbian)self": Mobilizing sexual formula stories through personal (and political) storytelling. *Journal of Contemporary Ethnography, 233*(1), 39–71.

Crawley, S., Foley, L., & Shehan, C. (2008). *Gendering bodies*. Lanham, MD: Rowman and Littlefield Publishers.

Elizabeth, A. (2013). Challenging the binary: Sexual identity that is not duality. *The Journal of Bisexuality, 3*(3), 329–337.

Firestein, B. (1996). Bisexuality as paradigm shift: Transforming our disciplines. In B. Firestein (Ed.), *Bisexuality: The psychology and politics of an invisible minority* (pp. 263–291). Thousand Oaks, CA: Sage Publications.

Gubrium, J., & Holstein, J. (1997). *The new language of qualitative method*. New York, NY: Oxford University Press.

Guittar, N. (2014). *Coming out: The new dynamics*. Boulder, CO: Lynne Rienner Publishers.

Holstein, J., & Gubrium, J. (1994). Phenomenology, ethnomethodology, and interpretive practice. In N. K. Denzin & Y. S. Lincoln (Eds.), *Handbook of qualitative research* (pp. 262–272). Thousand Oaks, CA: Sage Publications.

Johnson, A. H. (2016). Transnormativity: A new concept and its validation through documentary film about transgender men. *Sociological Inquiry, 86*(4), 465–491.

Ochs, R. (1996). Biphobia: It goes more than two ways. In B. Firestein (Ed.), *Bisexuality: The psychology and politics of an invisible minority* (pp. 217–239). Thousand Oaks, CA: Sage Publications.

Plummer, K. (1995). *Telling sexual stories: Power, change, and social worlds*. New York, NY: Routledge.

Rupp, L., & Taylor, V. (2013). Queer girls on campus. In A. Frank, P. Clough, & S. Seidman (Eds.), *Intimacies: A new world of relational life* (pp. 82–97). New York, NY: Routledge.

Rust, P. (1992). Who are we and where do we go from here? Conceptualizing bisexuality. In E. Weise (Ed.), *Closer to home: Bisexuality and feminism* (pp. 281–310). Seattle, WA: Seal Press.

Rust, P. (1993). 'Coming out' in the age of social constructionism: Sexual identity formation among lesbian and bisexual women. *Gender and Society, 7*(1), 50–77.

Udis-Kessler, A. (1996). Identity/Politics: Historical sources of the bisexual movement. In B. Beemyn & M. Eliason (Eds.), *Queer studies: A lesbian, gay, bisexual, and transgender anthology* (pp. 52–63). New York, NY: New York University Press.

West, C., & Zimmerman, D. (1987). Doing gender. *Gender and Society, 1*(2), 125–151.

NIK LAMPE

2. YOU CARED BEFORE YOU KNEW

Navigating Bi+ Familial Relationships

INTRODUCTION

It was a stormy June evening in rural Indiana when I first came out to my parents as bi. I remember distinctively hearing the roaring cracks of thunder and witnessing the power of lightning from a safe distance in the house I once grew up in. I flew up from Tampa the day before as part of my semi-annual family visit, during which I make my usual rounds of visiting family members and old friends from high school. I try to see whoever I can, and in so doing, catch up on what has happened to us in between these visits. On that June evening in the midst of my visit, I had a nice dinner with my family as I often do. After dinner, while my mom was washing dishes, my dad and I were sitting in the dining room discussing my big move to Orlando for graduate school after completing college in Tampa earlier in the year. Much like other LGBT folks who grew up in rural areas, I moved away from my small, Midwestern town at the age of 18 to a more urban, LGBT-friendly area of the country—the Tampa Bay area in Florida—and had no intention of ever coming "home" except for the occasional visit. On that night, the remnants of dinner still present, our casual conversation noticeably shifted towards prior romantic relationships, old flames, and exes. My father then asked if there were any men in my life, or more simply, if I was seeing anyone exclusively.

Instead of brushing off the question or laughing it off like I typically would, I briefly reflected on my experiences in Florida, and thought this was my chance to have a much-needed dialogue about sexuality, sex, and sexual fluidity. The majority of families in the United States report challenges in producing and maintaining open conversations about sex, sexuality, and relationships (Elliott, 2012). Evidence-based sex education is almost nonexistent in a significant number of U.S. households, even more so in poor and working class communities like where I originally grew up at (see Fields, 2008). Hell, I never had sex-positive education without the mention of abstinence, virginity, and Jesus until my sophomore year of undergrad, and

© KONINKLIJKE BRILL NV, LEIDEN, 2019 | DOI:10.1163/9789004414105_003

even in this regard, I'm likely luckier than many Americans who grow up in rural areas. While growing up in a predominantly religious and politically conservative state in the Midwest, I was surrounded by people ill-equipped to engage in healthy and open dialogues about sexual and intimate relationships, practices, desires, or options. Moved by the uncomplicated transition into the "coming out" talk I so desperately desired as a bi+ young adult from my parents, I nervously expressed my sexual and romantic interests while fidgeting with fake, plastic grapes that my mother sets out as kitchen décor.

In the above vignette, which I return to later, I am recounting experiences that are beginning to make their way into scholarship on sexualities and relationships with others. Often drawing on respondents' experiences in settings like the one above via the collection of retrospective interviews, researchers have recently started exploring the experiences of bi+ people with others in various contexts (Barringer et al., 2017; Moss, 2012; Sumerau et al., 2017; Sumerau & Nowakowski, Chapter 9 in this volume). For example, Scherrer et al. (2015) examined how bisexual people's disclosure processes are verbally fashioned in desirable ways as they come out to family members, while navigating monosexist and heterosexist expectations in their familial relationships. Similarly, McLean (2007) explored coming out experiences among bi+ people and noted how several social and cultural factors enhance the difficulty to come out to others, which overall challenges assumptions for the need of disclosure or coming out in the first place. In fact, research on bi+ experiences suggest their interactions with family and friends often become fraught as a result of assumptions about hetero and mono sexualities (Monro et al., 2017).

At the same time, these tensions are not surprising considering research noting the pervasive influence of mononormativity (Schippers, 2016; Schippers, Chapter 5 in this volume) and monosexism (Sumerau et al., 2018) in society. Monosexism refers to the privileged position of people who are or identify as romantically and/or sexually attracted to only one sex and/or gender (Roberts et al., 2015). At the same time, mononormativity refers to the elevation of monogamous people and monosexuality over other or multiple romantic and sexual options over the life course (Schippers, 2016; Barringer et al., 2017). Put simply, American society privileges monosexual and monogamous relationships throughout media, government, religion, and other social institutions in ways that negatively influence bi+ and/or poly desires, relationships, and identities (see also Heath, 2012). As such, bi+ people, like myself, face both of these social systems in the assumptions of others when they become visible in interactions, by coming out, or otherwise.

In this chapter, I reflect on my experiences as a bi+ person navigating familial relationships as a window into the day-to-day experiences that occur in concrete situations (Adams, 2011). As with autoethnography (see, e.g., Adams, 2011; Nowakowski, 2016; Sumerau, 2019), I utilize my personal experiences to direct attention to the ways bi+ people may experience coming out to families of origin and negotiating families of choice. In so doing, this chapter compliments empirical and theoretical discussions of the experience of bi+ people, coming out, and family dynamics within this volume and other sources (see also Moss, 2012). Put simply, I utilize my own experiences and a "bisexual lens" (Moss, 2012) to discuss differential expectations when engaging in fluid relationships with families of origin and families of choice. In so doing, this chapter offers a view of variation throughout the landscape of familial relationships bi+ people may experience in a given lifetime.

FAMILIAL RELATIONSHIPS

Families of Origin

As I noted in the beginning of this chapter, I came out to my parents. My coming out experience wasn't the fairytale I longed for, but it didn't compare to the nightmares I have heard from some of my queer and trans siblings. For example, some LGBT people experience homelessness, conversion therapy, and familial abuse due to familial rejection of their sexuality and gender (Adams, 2011). I did not experience these nuisances, but I did encounter a comparable form of familial rejection.

I remember sitting at the kitchen bar as my father was discussing my prior relationships with various (cis)men while my mother was washing dishes nearby. I disclosed to him that I recently had a relationship with someone who is a (cis)woman. As I said the word "woman," my father broke eye contact with me and looked down at the counter. My mother quickly left the room and avoided the rest of the conversation. Stunned, my father gripped his hands into loose fists, while his face turned slightly red as if he stopped breathing.

As someone who considers themselves to be transgender, non-binary, genderqueer, and gender-fluid, my coming-out narrative quickly became messy due to the intersections of my gender fluidity and bi+ identity. I am romantically and sexually attracted to various people with different body types, sex traits, gender identities, and gender expression. This includes cis and trans folks across the gender spectrum. When I came out as bi to my parents, I subconsciously acknowledged that the multifaceted gendered dimensions of my bi+ identity would be too complicated for my cis het parents to comprehend. I intentionally utilized cisnormative language (i.e. saying "woman" while referring to cis women) to frame my coming out narrative in a way that was simpler for my parents to emotionally and intellectually grasp.

After I came out to my parents, I paused for a couple of seconds to see if my dad would say something. He just stared at the counter. Finally ripping off the band-aid of heteronormativity and mononormativity (Barringer et al., 2017), I further clarified my intimate, romantic, and sexual desires for different types of bodies, sex organs, and people. I described how my relationships with partners grow with intimacy, similar political ideology, and mutual love for knowledge. Simply put, I was blurting out the T-M-I conversation many young adults wish to avoid with their parents while my parents sought to avoid or reject this aspect of my selfhood and sexual identity.

In that moment, I felt exposed and completely vulnerable. I felt like my mouth was burning with the truths of my bi+ experiences and this unique sensation was pouring out into their ears, even though anything I said after that moment could of been held against me later on down the road. I felt frightened while knowing the uncertainty of their verbal and non-verbal reactions which could turn into horrible consequences, such as cutting me off financially or forbidding me from visiting my brother, whom I love and cherish dearly. My parents have never physically abused me throughout my childhood—even spanking was off limits in our household—but what was also running through my head was all the violence and trauma I have experienced throughout my life course from other sources beyond the family. I never desire to depict my parents in a negative fashion, but I had mentally prepared myself for all of the worst case scenarios in order to protect myself and brace for any negative consequences.

Much like my queer and trans siblings, I have practiced my coming out conversations repeatedly (Adams, 2011). I individually frame and tailor each of these dialogues in attempt to receive the best possible outcome in my coming out experience (see Scherrer et al., 2015). In this particular conversation, I warmed up my parents by discussing my upcoming plans to earn a career in the academy and any updates I had with my romantic or intimate relationships with various people. I set up the stage to perform my best self or what social theorist Erving Goffman (1959) described as the "presentation of the self." Simply, I am the "performer" and my parents are the "audience." I manipulate my "front stage" to accomplish my goal of getting positive responses from both of my parents while disclosing my bisexuality. In so doing, I was seeking to provide information in a way that maintained the best chance for positive reactions and interpretations of my selfhood from my parents in the moment and going forward. As such, I was watching my parents' reactions just as much as they were watching my performance, a contained drama within the interactional context of a familial experience (Goffman, 1959).

It felt safer to come out in that moment with my parents compared to other interactions with them because I felt like I had some control over the conversation. I also had less concern about showing proper demeanor than at other times due to an inner need I felt about being seen as I am (see also Adams, 2011, for similar experiences among lesbian and gay people in relation to families of origin). In fact, coming out as bi+ for me specifically was much needed at the moment. It felt like a necessity. It was a matter of my quality of life and well-being. I never wanted to hide my sexuality as a bi+ person with the capability to be romantically and sexually attracted to a penumbra of genders and body types. At the same time, however, I was afraid to let others know about my sexuality growing up because of my geographic location and religious upbringing in a Roman Catholic household. Being a sexual minority and Catholic in rural Indiana was practically a death sentence. The only few queer folks that I knew growing up in my hometown all experienced physical violence and emotional abuse tied to their sexuality or gender identity. The only options for surviving as a LGBTQ person were to hide a significant part of your selfhood or get out. Since I had gotten out mostly at this point, I felt more comfortable—and more in need of—coming out than at prior times.

I carefully studied my parent's body language as I come out as bisexual. I watched as my mother practiced avoidance by leaving the room. I watched my father catch his breath and glance down at his drink. When I came out to my father, he became serious and kept repeating "I don't care if you are gay and straight." He then specified how him and my mother "don't care" what I do (sexually), as long as I don't "rub it in their face" like "flamers" he has met over the years. When I said that I am neither gay nor straight and that I am bisexual, the response went over my father's head and kept talking in circles. While he could have asked me any number of questions to make sense of this "new information" (Goffman, 1959), he instead sought to move away from the subject by continuously repeating similar lines and avoiding any engagement with a topic he knew little to nothing about from his prior experiences. As Adams (2011) notes, this type of reaction is a form of rejection that involves seeking to ignore an unexpected aspect of a person in order to maintain previous expectations and assumptions about the person in question.

I should have been proud of myself for at least trying and taking a leap of faith, but I felt defeated. I wasn't sure what was worse—my dad's biphobic responses or my mother leaving the room during a critical moment in my life and our relationship. The next day, I developed a smarter tactic. I brought up the conversation again with my mother while she was driving me into town. Her response was that she "didn't care" about what I do or who I "do it with." The problem with these "I don't care" responses that both of my parents kept repeating was the fact that it didn't come from a good place. It was said as a method to shut me up and to shut down the conversation. It was tactic to silence and erase my experiences as a bi+ person. For example, my parents asking about significant others over the years had already revealed they do care about what I do and who I do it with, but now that they were aware that the what and who might not be heterosexual, they no longer had any interest in the subject. I thought about these things in each of the examples noted here. Throughout these interactions, I kept my physical appearance calm and collected, my poker face as I like to call it, but I felt like my heart shattered. It was too obvious to my eyes—when they could assume I was heterosexual, they wanted information, but the moment they lost that assumption, they wanted to know nothing about my sexual and romantic selfhood.

As suggested above, nothing affirming happened when I came out to my parents. They didn't want to get to know the real me. My parents saw only the version of me and parts of me as heterosexual before I came out. It felt like they didn't want to know or love my queer self. My mother and father avoided having the tough conversations about sexuality and sexual relationships which could have saved me from potential trauma within this and other intimate relationships. Put simply, they could have demonstrated acceptance instead of leaving me feeling isolated, alone, and unworthy of affection and affirmation in ways that could leave me more vulnerable to unhealthy ways of seeking affection and care (see also Adams, 2011). Put simply, I didn't feel like I could tell them about anything about my sexuality or relationships after that weekend in June. This also made me less likely to mention anything about my transgender identity and experience to them as I would assume a similar reaction. There was a metaphorical wall that created after coming out between my parents and me. I needed to build this wall to protect myself in the face of their rejection. Because of these experiences, I haven't been close to my parents since and I don't know if I ever can be. This type of rejection, while subtle impacted, my self-conception.

Looking back at that moment, the critical goal of this conversation was not to come out to my parents and celebrate my sexual potential and fluidity. The objective to this discussion was to be noticed as bi+ person by the most intimate relationships I had at the time—my parents. At the same time, however, my parents had a different goal that emerged the moment I shared my own. Specifically, they avoided the issue and my father drew on his little knowledge of gay and lesbian identities to display disinterest in knowing the full parameters of my bi+ experiences and sexual fluidity. In so doing, both of my parents avoided any questions that could have helped them understand me as a bi+ person. They never gave me the opportunity to openly discuss my feelings about growing up in a rural, conservative area of the Midwest as bi+ and never gave me any reason to open up to them further about anything personal, romantic, or important in my life. My parents were fixed on seeing me as images or reflections of them (see also Elliott, 2012)—heterosexual, cisgender Christians from rural Indiana. However, my parents didn't want to believe I was bi+ and their coping mechanism was to say they don't care about this topic in ways that ultimately told me they simply did not care about me enough to see who I actually am beyond their expectations, dreams, or assumptions.

Since then, I have struggled opening up to my parents about an array of intimate matters that went on in my life. As an emerging scholar in LGBTQIAP studies, I even refrain from sharing the majority of my academic career and brush over the details relating to sex, gender, and sexualities. We dance around the elephant in the room with our phone conversations, talking about the weather, town updates, and the family dog. Whether my parents realized it at the time, I felt like they tried to erase my bi+ experiences and mute my voice as a member of the queer community by practicing avoidance and not being interested in what I have to say. For my own quality of life, I have thus gone alone in muting most of what matters in my life when interacting with them since, and in so doing, we have become more and more distant from each other.

My parents' avoidance of parts of me took a more concrete form at the beginning of my first semester of graduate school. Before Hurricane Irma hit Florida, I unexpectedly flew back to Indiana and stayed with my family for a week. During that week, my mother's extended family had their annual family reunion at a community park nearby. I went with my parents and brother to support my mother, while anticipating I would catch up with relatives. While I was there, I scooped up some food at the pot luck table and sat down with some relatives. My parents joined me soon after. After I finished eating, my great-aunt asked about my upcoming move to Orlando.

The subject shifted to the Pulse Massacre on June 12, 2016 and how 49 people from the LGBTQIAP, Central Florida, and Latinx communities died from a lone gunman. Whether my great-aunt realized it or not, this healthy dialogue quickly became therapeutic for me. She gave me the opportunity to grieve and process this collective trauma openly, something my parents never bothered to do or educate themselves on. Because Pulse was a popular nightclub and safe haven for LGBTQIA people in Orlando and others like me in nearby cities like Tampa, the Pulse mass murder was both a violent assault upon the LGBTQIA community and an assault that feels deeply personal to many of us in Central Florida especially. In fact, many queer and trans folks previously thought violent attacks against LGBTQIA safe havens were a thing of the past, like the attacks at Stonewall Inn and the Black Cat in the late 1960s (Lampe et al., 2018). This was a reminder that the fights for our existence continue every day.

After I explained to my great-aunt how everyone I knew spent that day grieving, an aunt who heard the conversation nearby softly snarled in disgust. Having the burning desire to call my aunt out on her prejudice, I asked why she made that unexpected sound. My aunt rolled her eyes and implied that what happened at Pulse wasn't a big deal, but at the time Pulse was the deadliest mass shooting in U.S. modern history (Lampe et al., 2018). Then my aunt suggested that the patrons at Pulse nightclub "had it coming" since they were "acting on risky [nonheterosexual] behaviors." Meanwhile my mother was sitting down at the other end of the picnic table within, earshot of this conversation. She never spoke up to protect me from my aunt's hurtful, potentially triggering words. She said nothing. My mother failed to redeem herself in that moment, so I took the initiative to come out as bi+ to my aunt in front of all my relatives and to explain the daily horrors queer and trans people experience in a binary world. I saved myself from my aunt's comments in the moment, but I felt abandoned by the person who gave birth to me and even once helped me move 1,200 miles away to pursue higher education. When certain aspects of my selfhood came into play, my mother was no longer a protector or supporter.

I still know my family of origin. I have seen my parents and brother during their best and worst moments, they would echo the same about me. But at the same time, they are only willing to know part of me. The part of me that doesn't involve being queer and sexually fluid. Instead, my parents repeatedly attempt to box me in and put me back into the closet. These experiences demonstrate a case where suggestions from existing research become personal and real in concrete daily life. Stated simply, bi+ people have been boxed in the hetero and mononormative lenses society created and maintained through various social institutions like families, media, and religion (Barringer et al., 2017). As such, our stories and voices are repetitively erased from history, but in this chapter, I join others beginning to bring these stories back into the light.

Families of Choice

Like many people do, I have responded to the relative absence of my family of origin by creating a family of choice (Broad, 2011). Families of choice are familial relationships that we create intimately or socially when we choose to treat specific people in our lives as family. Genetics and reproduction are irrelevant. Families of choice take many forms, such as familial bonds between friends or role models we look up to, or lifelong commitment within and between friendship groups. Families of choice can provide joy and fuller satisfaction for individuals when families or origin fail to do so or are absent through one's life course (Adams, 2011). These families are even more important to people who face rejection from their families of origin.

In my case, I sought out others who would see me in full. The relationships I created in Tampa and Orlando provided me the security and comfort I needed to feel fulfilled in my familial relationships. For example, when I came out as bi+ to my friend and roommate at the time, let's call her Kelly, I was expecting familial rejection or avoidance like my parents practiced when I came out to them. Kelly was upset at me not because I was bi+, but because I never told her until that moment. She asked several questions about my experiences as a bi+ person and what that meant for our friendship. Specifically, Kelly wanted to fulfill her role as an ally and asked what I wanted her familial support to look like. When I told Kelly I wanted her to help be more active in the LGBTQIA community, she took me to multiple queer and trans friendly venues in Tampa while introducing me to all of her queer friends and colleagues. Kelly reshaped my coming out experience and gave me all the reason to continue coming out as bi+ and even share my gender identity and experience with her in time as well.

Families of choice can originate in unusual or unexpected contexts. For instance, I had a mentor in undergrad who gave me the tools I needed to survive on my own while I was living in low-income housing. I have received gently worn clothes, books, and gas money from them when I would visit them. I have slept on their couch before when I was terrified of going home to an empty apartment. I had a classmate in undergrad, they wound up becoming one of my best friends, who would meet me frequently to discuss my future plans of graduate school and having a better life. Much to my surprise, she was the first person I came out to as bi+ and connected me to an expert in bi+ populations. In cases like this, I found affirmation and support that people typically associate with family, but I had to build—or choose—such families because my original familial bonds were not available to me as a bi+ person.

This amazing human, let's call zir[1] Neko, who my classmate put me in touch with is someone I now consider to be my closest mentor and frankly one of my best friends. Even though we live in different geographic areas and only can spend time together in person periodically, Neko took care of me emotionally and professionally as I was starting grad school. Ze encouraged me to open up about my feelings and saved me from spiraling more times than I can count. Neko always has my back and they saved me from slipping out of trauma recovery. I don't have to save myself anymore. Instead, I have Neko and networks of others who provide a safety net of sorts as I continue to grow and pursue my goals. I guess that is what families of choice are for since that is often what people privileged enough to find affirmation of families of origin talk about when they speak of the meaning of family (see also Broad, 2011).

I sought these various, intimate relationships because I wanted connections that centered all of me. My families of choice heal and support what my families of origin were ill-equipped to do as well as the damage from their rejection and avoidance. By opening myself up completely and forming emotional intimacy with people who matter, I became fully myself again while having a loud and proud bi+ voice as my transgender voice continues to develop. I am slowly starting to trust those who give me reason to in my familial relationships. I also sought to become active in groups seeking better options for bi and trans people. In my applied work on queer and trans experiences in health care, I have been working towards making bi+ voices heard and bi+ experiences empirically represented in the social sciences. In fact, I even specifically tried to arrange my life around supportive others. For example, I chose my current roommates when I moved into off-campus student housing for graduate school based on whether they were LGBTQIA. I was too exhausted to deal with roommates who wouldn't be able to understand my queer self fully. Thankfully, I somehow managed to convince the leasing agent at the time, who I later found out is also bi+, to match me with the only queer people they knew who lived in the apartment complex. I can now be validated and seen as a bi+, trans person in my own home and feel safe doing so. In these ways, I centered my bi ness with others via forming my own familial relationships.

CONCLUSION

In closing, I would have to say that my current family of choice reminds me of learning to ride a bike as a child. When I was a child, I got a bicycle from my parents. The other day I watched a parent teaching their child to ride a bike, and I remembered that my parents didn't teach me how to do it. I learned to ride a bike through my own trial and error. I kept getting cuts and bruises from falling while riding my bike. I kept trying, but it was a struggle because I had no guidance about how to handle the bike, maintain balance, and take care of myself when the inevitable falls occurred. I was on my own, forging my own self as one who could operate and enjoy bike riding. I was thinking about this as I wrote about coming out to my families of origin and creating my families of choice because it was a similar type of learning experience. Once again, I had no guidance from my family and the process of building a self as an openly bi+ and trans person was filled with bumps, bruises, and falls that I had to figure out how to navigate, at least at first, on my own. The two experiences are reminiscent of each other in many ways. For example, riding a bike is something you feel like you should do, but you don't have a road map unless someone teaches you. Telling others about your sexual fluidity, or other aspects of your selfhood, is similar in that you don't know what to do unless someone teaches you. There is no automatic script.

The two are also similar because both are frightening. You are scared to ride the bike because you can fall and falling hurts. You have to push through the fear to do it, but the fear is real. This is the same thing you experience disclosing your bisexuality. You are scared to tell people because you don't know how they will react, and they may react in ways that hurt. You have to push through the fear to do it, but the fear, again, is real. And like riding a bike, sometimes it will lead to pain and other times it will lead to pleasure, but you don't know which way it goes before you push through the fear in the first place.

NOTE

[1] There are several varieties of gender pronouns that people can identify themselves with. Since Neko's pronouns are ze/zir/zirs, I am using these pronouns when referring to Neko out of respect for zir and zir's gender identity.

REFERENCES

Adams, T. E. (2011). *Narrating the closet: An autoethnography of same sex attraction.* Walnut Creek, CA: Left Coast Press, Inc.

Barringer, M. N., Sumerau, J. E., & Gay, D. A. (2017). Examining differences in identity disclosure between monosexuals and bisexuals. *Sociological Spectrum, 37*(5), 319–333.

Broad, K. L. (2011). Coming out for parents, families and friends of lesbians and gays: From support group grieving to love advocacy. *Sexualities, 14*(4), 399–415.

Elliott, S. (2012). *Not my kid: What parents believe about the sex lives of their teenagers.* New York, NY: New York University Press.

Fields, J. (2008). *Risky lessons: Sex education and social inequality.* New Brunswick, NJ: Rutgers University Press.

Goffman, E. (1959). *The presentation of self in everyday life.* Garden City, NY: Doubleday.

Heath, M. (2012). *One marriage under god: The campaign to promote marriage in America.* New York, NY: New York University Press.

Lampe, N., Huff-Corzine, L., & Corzine, J. (2018). The pulse scrolls. In W. Regoeczi & J. Jarvis (Eds.), *Homicide on the rise: The resurgence of homicide in Urban America?* (pp. 156–160). Proceedings of the 2018 Meeting of the Homicide Research Working Group Clearwater Beach, FL: Cleveland State University and Washington, DC: FBI.

McLean, K. (2007). Hiding in the closet?: Bisexuals, coming out and the disclosure imperative. *Journal of Sociology, 43*(2), 151–166.

Monro, S., Hines, S., & Osborne, A. (2017). Is bisexuality invisible? A review of sexualities scholarship 1970–2015. *Sociological Review, 65*(4), 663–681.

Moss, A. R. (2012). Alternative families, alternative lives: Married women doing bisexuality. *Journal of GLBT Family Studies, 8*(5), 405–427.

Nowakowski, A. C. H. (2016). Hope is a four-letter word: Riding the emotional rollercoaster of illness management. *Sociology of Health & Illness, 38*(6), 899–915.

Roberts, T. S., Horne, S. H., & Hoyt, W. H. (2015). Between a gay and a straight place: Bisexual individuals' experiences with monosexism. *Journal of Bisexuality, 15*(4), 554–569.

Scherrer, K. S., Kazyak, E., & Schmitz, R. M. (2015). Getting "Bi" in the family: Bisexual people's disclosure experiences. *Journal of Marriage and Family, 77*(3), 680–696.

Schippers, M. (2016). *Beyond monogamy: Polyamory and the future of polyqueer sexualities.* New York, NY: New York University Press.

Sumerau, J. E. (2019). Embodying nonexistence: Experiencing Cis and Mono normativities in everyday life. In S. Kwan & C. Bobel (Eds.), *Body battlegrounds: Transgressions, tensions and transformations.* Nashville, TN: Vanderbilt University Press.

Sumerau, J. E., Mathers, L. A. B., & Cragun, R. T. (2018). Incorporating transgender experience toward a more inclusive gender lens in the sociology of religion. *Sociology of Religion, 79*(4), 425–448. https://doi.org/10.1093/socrel/sry001

Sumerau, J. E., Mathers, L. A. B., Nowakowski, A. C. H., & Cragun, R. T. (2017). Helping quantitative sociology come out of the closet. *Sexualities, 20*(5–6), 644–656.

LAIN A. B. MATHERS

3. SIBLING RELATIONSHIPS AND THE BI+
COMING OUT PROCESS

Disclosing information to loved ones about one's sexual identity and attraction is an important process in the lives of BTQLG[1] individuals (Garcia, 2012; Scherrer, Kazyak, & Schmitz, 2015; Watson, 2014). Although this practice of disclosure, or "coming out," is often an ongoing process (Adams, 2011), some scholars have noted that both the initial disclosure of one's sexual identity, as well as the first time coming out to family of origin, marks a pivotal moment for BTQLG people (Watson, 2014). Furthermore, scholars have pointed to the fact that receiving support and acceptance from family members upon coming out can lessen a negative sense of self and bolster positive mental health outcomes (Shilo & Savaya, 2011). While the body of coming out literature highlights important dynamics of the process of disclosure, much of this literature focuses predominantly on lesbian and gay populations (Biblarz & Savci, 2010). In this chapter, I will build on these findings about coming out in families to include a greater focus on both bi+ experience and sibling relationships, two often-ignored elements of the BTQLG coming out experience.

Researchers have pointed to the fact that support from family and friends is connected to feeling more positive about one's sexuality and, thus, an increased likelihood of lesbian and gay individuals to disclose their identity to others (Shilo & Savaya, 2011). If lesbian and gay people feel shame or negativity about their sexuality, however, they may be less likely to disclose their identity to others (Adams, 2011). Some research that combines lesbian, gay and bisexual populations suggests that the overall structure of one's family and the religious and political ideologies normalized within one's family may impact experiences of coming out (D'Augelli, Grossman, & Starks, 2008). These studies show that the relationships and norms within one's family and the response of family members when another family member comes out significantly influence the lives of BTQLG people. Although these studies lead to a clearer understanding of the coming out process, researchers suggest that much more attention is needed on the specific dynamics of bi+[2] people's

© KONINKLIJKE BRILL NV, LEIDEN, 2019 | DOI:10.1163/9789004414105_004

coming out experiences, particularly in relation to families (Barringer, Sumerau, & Gay, 2017; Biblarz & Savci, 2010).

A burgeoning field of study has pointed to the fact that bi+ people navigate different issues when coming out (or assessing whether or not to come out) than lesbian and gay people (Sumerau & Cragun, 2018). For example, some scholars point to the fact that bi+ people use a process of "selective disclosure," or strategically dropping hints about their sexual identity without mentioning bisexuality specifically and/or choosing specific individuals to tell before others (McLean, 2007). Research also shows that bi+ people tend to come out later in life (Rust, 1993) and, despite generally increasing positive attitudes about lesbian and gay individuals in contemporary US society, bi+ people cannot anticipate broader acceptance of their existence in the ways that lesbian and gay people can (Mathers, Sumerau, & Cragun, 2018).

Literature that specifically focuses on bi+ people's coming out in family contexts is a small but growing body of scholarship. Thus far, such work illustrates that bi+ people navigate monosexist ideals from family members when they come out (Scherrer et al., 2015; Watson, 2014), or ideals that invalidate and violate one's experiences as a bi+ person and elevate the experiences of monosexual[3] (non-bi+) people over bi+ experiences (Eisner, 2013). Such responses from family can exacerbate the ways bi+ people already experience feelings of isolation and exclusion in contemporary U.S. society (Todd et al., 2016). While these studies incorporate bi+ experience into the literature on coming out, specifically within the family unit, they follow a similar trajectory as the research on lesbian and gay coming out experiences by focusing predominantly on parent-child or romantic partner relationships (Moss, 2012; Todd et al., 2016).

While little existing research focuses specifically on the ways bi+ people come out (or don't) to their siblings, some literature on lesbian and gay individuals points to the fact that siblings are sometimes used as a "test case" before coming out to other members of one's family of origin (Jenkins, 2008; see McLean, 2007, for some exploration of this pattern among bisexual people in Australia). Additionally, for lesbian and gay individuals, siblings may assist in helping parents understand their lesbian or gay child's identity (Haxhe et al., 2018). Importantly, some of the literature on coming out to siblings lumps bi+ people in with lesbian and gay individuals (D'Augelli et al., 2008) or lumps the process of coming out to siblings in with analyses of coming out to other family members (Scherrer et al., 2015; Watson, 2014) As such, more scholarship is needed to tease apart the complex dynamic of sibling relationships and the coming out process for bi+ people.

Considering that bi+ people comprise at least half, if not more, of the BTQLG population in the US (Gates, 2012), and sibling relationships are a unique bond that can impact the broader dynamics of family relations (Cox & Paley, 1997; Jenkins, 2008; D'Augelli et al., 2008), attending to the specific experiences of bi+ people's relationships with and coming out to siblings is an important yet overlooked area of study to date. Following calls from scholars to focus more closely to the specific experiences of bi+ people (Cragun & Sumerau, 2015; Worthen, 2013), particularly in relation to family (Biblarz & Savci, 2010; Moss, 2012) and coming out in families beyond the parent-child relationship (Barringer et al., 2017; Scherrer et al., 2015), I will use this chapter to explore the narratives from bi+ people about how they determine if and when to come out to siblings, and how their sibling relationships, within the broader context of their families of origin, factor into the decisions they make about coming out to family members.

METHODS

Data for this chapter come from 40 qualitative semi-structured interviews conducted in 2017 and 2018 with bi+ people between the ages of 20 and 30 in Chicago. Interviews are, on average, two and a half hours in length, with the shortest interview approaching one hour and the longest interview approaching five hours. I interviewed these participants specifically because I sought to talk to people for whom BTQLG politics had been a major part of popular discourse for most of their lives, particularly conversations about same-sex marriage and AIDS. I conducted recruitment through online advertisements about a study on bisexual or sexually fluid experience shared in BTQLG social media groups. In the advertisement, potential participants followed a link to a screening survey that they completed to see if they were eligible. If they were eligible, I contacted them to set up a time and location for the interview.

I asked participants a series of demographic and open-ended questions in the interview. Some of the open-ended questions focused on identity (i.e. "How would you describe your sexual identity?" "How did you arrive at that language to identify yourself?"), coming out experiences ("What was it like to come out to family?"), dating ("Tell me about your current (or past) relationship(s)"), community ("How do you feel in LGBT spaces?", "What does your bi+ (or, insert respondent's sexual identity) community look like?") and politics ("What do you think is the biggest issue facing bi+ (or, insert respondent's sexual identity) people today?"). With all of these questions, I probed and asked follow-up questions as necessary.

There are some limitations to this sample. Specifically, the respondents in this study are mostly middle-class, cisgender women, white, and have at least some college education. As such, the processes I identify in this chapter should not be assumed to apply to all bi+ individuals. As scholars have noted, gender, race, ethnicity, class, and other social structures can impact how one embodies sexual identity as well as whether or not they disclose their sexual identity to family members (Rust, 1996). That said, the data in this study still yield important information for further considering the role of siblings in bi+ people's coming out experiences.

I used a grounded theory approach (Charmaz, 2006) and open coding to identify emerging themes relating to experiences coming out in early interviews. Through this process, I began to probe more thoroughly about these experiences in later interviews. In so doing, I came to identify two overarching themes about bow bi+ people talked about coming out to siblings: (1) siblings as the first to know in the family of origin and (2) non-disclosure to siblings (and generally, non-disclosure to other members of the family of origin).

COMING OUT TO SIBLINGS: "TESTING THE WATERS" AND INVOLUNTARY DISCLOSURE

Following findings about lesbian and gay people's experiences coming out to their families (Haxhe et al., 2018), one of the main themes that emerged among bi+ people with siblings involved disclosing their sexual identity to one or more siblings before coming out to their parent(s) of origin. For some bi+ people, this was the case when they wanted to come out to their parent(s) but were not sure how they would respond. For example, a 30-year-old white, bisexual cisgender woman said:

> I called my sister first because she is like my closest in age and the one I'm closest to in my family. So, she was like kind of—she was my test case. Uhm, so I called her, and I just said, "you know, I just wanted to tell you something and let you know that I've been dating a woman (exhales) and I don't know…she's great. Yadda yadda yadda." And my sister, she just like screamed, she's like "Oh my god! Are you really??!" She's like—she's married and she's like "can I tell [my husband], is it okay??!" And I'm like, "yeah, that's fine," and she was just very happy for me.

This respondent's sister exhibited what some scholars have referred to as "complete support" (Watson, 2014) of her sister's sexual identity. While coming out to siblings is, itself, a form of selective disclosure among sexual minorities (Jenkins, 2008; McLean, 2007), the response above also illuminates the ways in which bi+ people, even when anticipating a positive response from siblings, still use rhetorical strategies of selective disclosure when coming out (disclosing a current same-gender partner instead of identifying explicitly as bisexual). In this way, bi+ selective disclosure appears to be a layered process, where one not only selects a trusted individual to whom to disclose their sexual identity, but also does so in such a way that bi+ identity labels (such as bisexual, pansexual, omnisexual) are not explicit at first.

Similarly, a 26-year-old white, bisexual, cisgender man disclosed to his sister before telling his parents, but received a slightly different response that relied on negative stereotypes about bi+ people:

I told my sister, came out to my sister over Thanksgiving 'cause I needed to tell somebody and I was also testing the waters and I wasn't ready to tell my parents…And honestly, I might not have been really ready to tell my sister but I was just sort of pushing myself forward because I felt like making up for lost time and also just when I figured it out about myself I was just like "okay yeah, I'm just gonna do this." So, I just threw myself into it. And that went not as well as I wanted because she just…didn't get it. Um, I had to do a lot of explaining. It was a lot for her to take in. She said unconsciously, or not intentionally, ran through the sort of gamut of shitty things to say to a bi person about their sexuality….But the end of the conversation she (sister) was just like, "hey, I want you to be happy and I love you" and apologizing for not quite getting it. And then with a bit of time she, you know, processed it and was like yeah okay I get it now and it just ended up being, "I just want you to be happy. You do you."

Exhibiting the "disclosure imperative" (McLean, 2007), or pressure to come out, that many bi+ people confront, as well as coming out later in life, this respondent noted feeling like he needed to "make up for lost time" in terms of coming out, reflecting the pattern of bi+ people coming out later in life than their lesbian and gay counterparts. As is the case for many bi+ individuals coming out to family members (Scherrer et al., 2015), this participant's sister responded initially with monosexist stereotypes about bi+ people but eventually warmed up to her brother's bisexuality over time. Later in the interview, the respondent quoted above notes that his sister placed pressure on him to disclose to his parents because she did not want to be the only person in the family who knew. While one may expect that increasing positive attitudes towards sexual minorities in recent years might mitigate the need for bi+ people to selectively disclose in this way, these responses show that concerns about familial response might still be prevalent among bi+ people, even if lesbian and gay people are experiencing more social acceptance (see also Mathers et al., 2018).

Sometimes for bi+ people, family members act as "gatekeepers," or those who control how and when their child or sibling's sexual identity is disclosed to other members of the family (Scherrer et al., 2015). The following example from a 24-year-old black, pansexual, cisgender woman reveals how siblings engage in gatekeeping by disregarding their bi+ kin's privacy around sexual identity, even when they are the trusted first person to find out about their sibling's bi+ identity:

> She was the first person…I was talking to my sister about [my first girlfriend] like, "you know, I really like her…." Like, she knew I liked both genders, or at that time, and she was just fascinated by it…So, she would be like "oh, okay, interesting." And I would just tell her how I feel and um, she just was like "oh, wow, you're the gay sister now," And I'm like yeah…I guess that's a thing. I guess I'll have that label. Um, and she was actually the person who outed me to my dad….We were on Face Time or Skype and I was just talking to my dad about my day and my sister is just like "tell him who you're dating!" And I'm like whyyy are you putting me on the spot? Like I didn't even want to come out in the first place and I'm like yeah…"I guess I'm dating women now, or I'm dating you know, I have a girlfriend." And he's just like *"woooow"* and then he tells the rest of our family and I'm like…(sarcastically) yay…(laughs).

This respondent's sister engaged in bi+ erasure (labeling her as the "gay" sister) and disregarded her cues that she did not yet want to be out to other members of the family. Such a response, while supportive in some ways (i.e. not explicitly disavowing her sister's partnership), also reflects the ways that people in relative positions of power may control the ways in which comparatively marginalized others narrate their lived experiences, even within the family unit. As such, while some bi+ people voluntarily came out to their siblings before their parents with the expectation of trust and support, this trust is sometimes violated.

These patterns are in line with existing research that suggests sexual minorities may use their siblings to test the coming out process within their families (Haxhe et al., 2018; McLean, 2007). While "testing the waters" by selectively disclosing to siblings sometimes works out well for bi+ people, this is clearly not always the case. Specifically, this selective disclosure strategy can sometimes backfire when siblings have a negative initial response or disclose information about their bi+ siblings to other family members. Thus, while selective disclosure to siblings may be a viable avenue for bi+ people to begin coming out to family members, it cannot be assumed that siblings will necessarily handle disclosure better than parents. In the next section, I explore how relationships between siblings, situated in the broader family context, may influence how bi+ people approach coming out to them and lead them to avoid the selective disclosure strategies noted above.

THE "GOOD CHILD/BAD CHILD" DYNAMIC AND (NOT) COMING OUT TO FAMILIES OF ORIGIN

Scholars have recently noted that in order to fully understand how sexual minority individuals approach coming out to family members, we have to understand how relationships between specific family members are situated in the broader context of the family as a whole (Scherrer et al., 2015). While a number of participants shared that their siblings were the first to know, many others shared that they were not out to their siblings. Scholarship on barriers to coming out in families has pointed out that religious and political conservatism within families of origin may prevent sexual minorities from disclosing their identity (Barringer et al., 2017). While this was the case for some respondents, this section will focus on two other important dynamics that emerged regarding why bi+ people opted not to disclose to their siblings (and families of origin more broadly): being perceived as an exceptionally good or bad child in comparison to their siblings, and thus fearing monosexist stereotypes would either challenge or confirm these familial expectations.

Family scholars highlight that understanding the family as a system, wherein no one member exists independently of others, is an important factor in understanding BTQLG people's coming out in family contexts (Scherrer et al., 2015). Within the broader family context, the sibling-to-sibling(s) relationship is important for understanding how and why bi+ people may or may not disclose their sexual identity to their siblings. Some literature suggests that the sibling order (i.e. if one is the oldest or youngest sibling), as well as the gender composition of siblings, may impact coming out within the family (D'Augelli et al., 2008). However, the findings detailed below show that perceptions of sibling relationships within the family also impact bi+ people's decisions not to come out. For example, if one sibling is perceived to occupy a position such as a "good child" or "bad child" when compared to other siblings, this can influence their feelings about revealing their sexuality to family members. Bi+ people who are held to specific expectations within the family may avoid selectively disclosing because they do not want to challenge their family's positive view of them due to common stereotypes of bi+ people as threatening, vectors of disease, irresponsible, and uniquely promiscuous (Eisner, 2013).

For example, a 28-year-old queer, cisgender woman shares how her family's perception of her as an exceptionally good child prevents her from coming out to her sister and brothers:

> My sister is like one of my best friends and I would never tell her that I am queer. I just don't think—I would never tell her I have an open marriage and I would never tell her that I'm queer because I don't think she would be supportive. I'm like known as the golden child in my family. I'm the one that got straight A's through school, did college, graduated summa cum laude, going to get my PhD. I think [my siblings] associate that with like…just a good little cis girl with her husband, which is what I am….Um, so no, I've never talked to them about it.

The perceptions of this respondent as "just a good little cis girl" prevent her from coming out, both as bi+ and in an open marriage. This is reflective of mononormative[4] social patterns, in regard to both non-monosexuality and non-monogamy, which push bi+ existence and polyamory to the margins of what is deemed acceptable in contemporary US society (Sumerau, Grollman, & Cragun, 2018). Furthermore, even though this respondent notes that she has a strong relationship with her sister (and elsewhere in the interview, she notes that such a relationship also exists with her brothers), she still opted not to share her sexual identity or relationship structure with them for fear of tarnishing their positive view of her. Quotes like this demonstrate a pattern common to working class, religious, and racial minority bisexual people wherein one's bisexuality may take a backseat to family-of-origin relationships in order to preserve said relationships (Rust, 1996). Put simply, she very consciously avoids coming out to her family in order to maintain a positive relationship with them.

Comparatively, negative expectations for bi+ individuals may also interfere with the coming out process because bi+ people may expect their coming out to confirm their family's existing negative view of them. For example, a 24-year-old white, bisexual queer cisgender man points to the fact that his parents consider him a "basket case" compared to his sister, and this intra-family dynamic drives his decision not to come out to his sister or parents:

Respondent: They already think I'm a basket case (laughs) maybe I can't do anything else to make them think I'm even more of a basket case, but it will just be uncomfortable conversations, they won't get it, they'll think there's something wrong with me, they'll probably lose respect for me.

LM: When you say that your parents already think you're kind of a basket case, what does that mean?

Respondent: I was the issue child. My sister did everything my parents wanted and still does, and I don't resent her for it. She appears to be happy. Like, she did sports in high school like my dad wanted, she went to college…and went to the same place my dad did and now works for my dad at the family practice and got married to her college boyfriend after they graduated and bought a house ten-minutes away, and that's that. Um, I was always involved in not popular causes in high school and when I was a kid…I just disagreed a lot, I fought back a lot….

This respondent expressed that the low expectations from his parents were part of the reason he wasn't out to his sister or family of origin more broadly. His response reflects a concern that coming out as bisexual and/or queer would only confirm his family's negative view of him. This may be especially so since his sister conforms to heteronormative expectations of family by being married and staying close to her family of origin.

Responses like these underscore the ways bi+ people navigate role expectations within the family, particularly role expectations between siblings, and how such expectations impact their decisions not to come out. Whether unusually high expectations or unusually low expectations when compared with their siblings, both patterns reflect that bi+ people's decisions to come out (or not) to siblings, as well as other family members, might be influenced by the ways in which they are understood *specifically* in relation to their siblings. If one is seen as exceptionally good, they may be afraid that their family will assign negative meaning to their sexual identity and thus disrupt their family's positive expectations. While if one is seen as exceptionally bad, they may be afraid to confirm these expectations, at least according to the systems of meaning that prevail within their family of origin. Attempting to avoid either tarnishing their family's positive view of them or confirming their family's negative view are both representative of the ways bi+ people navigate monosexism in the family: in both cases they avoid coming out for fear of the association family members will make between them and negative stereotypes about bi+ people. This dynamic of navigating the "good/bad child" roles, and how such roles are filtered through the lens of monosexism suggests further analysis is needed concerning bi+ coming out and sibling relations.

DISCUSSION

This chapter elaborates on some existing findings regarding bi+ coming out in the family (Barringer et al., 2017; Scherrer et al., 2015) as well new directions for future research. For example, the bi+ people in this sample, like bi+ folks in other studies, shared experiences of facing monosexist stereotypes from their families when they did choose to come out (Todd et al., 2016). Additionally, like other family members, siblings acted as "gatekeepers" about their bi+ kin's sexual identity, sometimes pressuring a bi+ person to come out to other family members or simply sharing this information without consent. This suggests that bi+ selective disclosure to siblings, which can be an affirming experience, is not necessarily guaranteed to be based on sibling-specific bonds.

These findings suggest we need more research on bi+ familial experiences. We should focus on, for example, the number and order of siblings and also the ways in which bi+ people and their siblings make sense of their role in the family. Given monosexist stereotypes about bi+ people, bi+ individuals may be especially apprehensive to come out to family members if they are seen as especially "good" or "bad" compared to their siblings since doing so could either challenge "good" beliefs or confirm "bad" beliefs. Further research is needed to better grasp the nuanced ways bi+ people assign meanings to their families, and vice versa, to fully understand how these factors play into bi+ people's coming out decisions.

This could be a new avenue of research for scholars of sexual minority experience, the family, and sibling relationships to explore in their studies. For example, it is beyond the purview of this chapter to explore how number and gender of siblings alongside their "good" or "bad" role in the family may impact bi+ people's decision to come out (or not). Future analyses should investigate these dynamics, as well as the ways race, class, and religion may specifically impact the dynamics of sibling role and coming out. Researchers could also examine potential mental health implications of navigating an especially positive or negative role, in comparison to one's siblings, while also trying to negotiate if and how to come out to one's family. How do these specific dynamics vary between bi+ people occupying different social locations?

As such, the findings here can guide scholars who seek to expand understandings of bi+ experiences and relationships within and beyond families. It is clear that sibling relationships play a vital role in how bi+ people asses the process of coming out to their families, and it is time that we, as scholars, start to more meaningfully interrogate how the sibling relationship, both independently and how it is situated within the broader family context, can tell us more about the potential gains and risks for bi+ people to come out to their families of origin. In so doing, we may develop a clearer view of not only bi+ experience, but also the dynamics within and between families and other forms of relationships in the lives of people of varied sexual identities throughout our social world.

NOTES

[1] The author elects to use the acronym "BTQLG" instead of the more common LGBTQ or GLBTQ to place emphasis on the often-ignored bi+ contingent of the BTQLG community. BTQLG stands for Bisexual, Transgender, Queer, Lesbian, and Gay.

[2] While people may use varied terms to describe their sexual identities, such as bisexual, pansexual, fluid, and queer, bi+ is an umbrella term that is used to refer to anyone who experiences sexual attraction or desire for people of multiple sexes or genders. Multiple individual identities are encapsulated under the bi+ umbrella (see, Eisner, 2013). As such, while all of the respondents interviewed for this study fall under the bi+ umbrella, I use their specifically stated sexual identities when quoting them in this chapter.

[3] Monosexuality is when a person experiences attraction exclusively to individuals of one sex and/or gender (Barringer et al., 2017).

[4] Mononormativity is a system of inequality that privileges monogamous relationship formations over non-monogamous relationship formations (Schippers, 2016).

REFERENCES

Adams, T. E. (2011). *Narrating the closet: An autoethnography of same-sex attraction.* Walnut Creek, CA: Left Coast Press.

Barringer, M. N., Sumerau, J. E., & Gay, D. A. (2017). Examining the difference in identity disclosure between monosexuals and bisexuals. *Sociological Spectrum, 37*(5), 319–333.

Biblarz, T. J., & Savci, E. (2010). Lesbian, gay, bisexual, and transgender families. *Journal of Marriage and Family, 72*, 480–497.

Charmaz, K. C. (2006). *Constructing grounded theory: A practical guide through qualitative analysis.* Thousand Oaks, CA: Sage Publications.

Cox, M. J., & Paley, B. (1997). Families as systems. *Annual Review of Psychology, 48*, 243–267.

Cragun, R. T., & Sumerau, J. E. (2015). The last bastion of sexual and gender prejudice? Sexualities, race, gender, religion, and spirituality in the examination of prejudice toward sexual and gender minorities. *Journal of Sex Research, 52*(7), 821–834.

D'Augelli, A., Grossman, A. H., & Starks, M. T. (2008). Families of gay, lesbian, and bisexual youth: What do parents and siblings know and how do they react? *Journal of GLBT Family Studies, 4*(1), 95–115.

Eisner, S. (2013). *Bi: Notes for a bisexual revolution.* Berkeley, CA: Seal Press.

Garcia, L. (2012). *Respect yourself, protect yourself: Latina girls and sexual identity.* New York, NY: New York University Press.

Gates, G. J. (2012). LGBT identity: A demographer's perspective. *Loyola of Los Angeles Law Review, 45*, 693–714.

Haxhe, S., Cerezo, A., Bergfeld, J., & Walloch, J. C. (2018). Siblings and the coming-out process: A comparative case study. *Journal of Homosexuality, 65*(4), 407–426.

Jenkins, D. A. (2008). Changing family dynamics: A sibling comes out. *Journal of GLBT Family Studies, 4*(1), 1–16.

Mathers, L. A. B., Sumerau, J. E., & Cragun, R. T. (2018). The limits of homonormativity: Constructions of bisexual and transgender people in the post-gay era. *Sociological Perspectives.* doi:10.1177/0731121417753370

McLean, K. (2007). Hiding in the closet? Bisexual, coming out and the disclosure imperative. *Journal of Sociology, 43*, 151–166.

Moss, A. R. (2012). Alternative families, alternative lives: Married women doing bisexuality. *Journal of GLBT Family Studies, 8*(5), 405–427.

Rust, P. C. (1993). "Coming out" in the age of social constructionism: Sexual identity formation among lesbian and bisexual women. *Gender & Society, 7*, 50–77.

Rust, P. C. (1996). Managing multiple identities: Diversity among bisexual women and men. In B. A. Firestein (Ed.), *Bisexuality: The psychology and politics of an invisible minority.* Thousand Oaks, CA: Sage Publications.

Scherrer, K. S., Kazyak, E., & Schmitz, R. (2015). Getting "bi" in the family: Bisexual people's disclosure experiences. *Journal of Marriage and Family, 77*, 680–696.

Schippers, M. (2016). *Beyond monogamy: Polyamory and the future of polyqueer sexualities.* New York, NY: NYU Press.

Shilo, G., & Savaya, R. (2011). Effects of family and friend support on LGB youths' mental health and sexual orientation milestones. *Family Relations, 60*(3), 318–330.

Sumerau, J. E., & Cragun, R. T. (2018). *Christianity and the limits of minority acceptance: God loves (almost) everyone.* Lanham, MD: Lexington Books.

Sumerau, J. E., Grollman, E. A., & Cragun, R. T. (2018). "Oh my God, I sound like a horrible person": Generic processes in the conditional acceptance of sexual and gender diversity. *Symbolic Interaction, 41*(1), 62–82.

Todd, M. E., Oravecs, L., & Vejar, C. (2016). Biphobia in the family context: Experiences and perceptions of bisexual individuals. *Journal of Bisexuality, 16*(2), 144–162.

Watson, J. B. (2014). Bisexuality and family: Narratives of silence, solace, and strength. *Journal of GLBT Family Studies, 10*, 101–123.

Worthen, M. G. F. (2013). An argument for separate analyses of attitudes toward lesbian, gay, bisexual men, Bisexual women, MtF and FtM transgender individuals. *Sex Roles, 68*(11–12), 703–723.

BRITTANY M. HARDER

4. AUTOETHNOGRAPHIC INSIGHTS ON MEDIA REPRESENTATIONS OF BI NARRATIVES

INTRODUCTION

Media represents an important vehicle whereby cultural ideas, values, and norms of the dominant society are reflected and become readily available to the public. Although mass media enables information to be disseminated to widespread audiences, it is often criticized for generating unnecessary moral panic among the public, framing phenomena to fit profit-seeking interests, altering public opinion through biased information and inaccurate representations, and ensuring a degree of social control in a society (Cohen, 1972; Gamson, Croteau, Hoynes, & Sasson, 1992; Garland, 2008; Giddens, 1991; Jackson, Nielsen, & Hsu, 2011; Seale, 2003; Shoemaker & Reese, 2013). It is through a general overconsumption of mass media that the public has become less critical consumers of it. Messages depicted via media channels, along with their discourses, are often able to escape public skepticism, thereby becoming embedded into the fabric of everyday social life (Hjarvard, 2013; Keller, 2003).

Heteronormativity, along with other hegemonic[1] ideals, permeate media in both explicit and implicit ways. As a primary source of information, entertainment, and communication, mass media serves as one of the most powerful and pervasive means of socialization. By deeming certain forms of families, marriages, relationships, and sexualities as culturally normal and socially appropriate, widespread audiences are taught and consistently reminded thereafter that heterosexuality is standard; any deviation from this is assumed to be a lesser status or way of life.

Indeed, increasing media representations of LGBTQI+ characters are desirable in contributing to the visibility of LGBTQI+ identities and by potentially serving as a bridge between audiences and increasing awareness (Alexander, 2007; McInroy & Craig, 2017). However, it is not just the existence of LGBTQI+ media representations that hold influence; rather, the ways in which LGBTQI+ identities are represented come to matter a great deal. The erasure and invisibility of bisexuality, in particular, has been

© KONINKLIJKE BRILL NV, LEIDEN, 2019 | DOI:10.1163/9789004414105_005

recorded by several scholars (i.e. Dyar, Lytle, London, & Levy, 2015; Eisner, 2013; Esterline & Galupo, 2013; Yoshino, 2000), including significant under- and mis-representation in the media (i.e. Alexander, 2007; Corey, 2017). In this chapter, I provide a critical discussion of media representations of bisexuality and use my own account of sexuality to discuss some of the implications of representations on lived experience. I further offer suggestions as to how media representations of bisexuality can be altered to account for lived experiences and to further promote acceptance, awareness, and inclusion of non-monosexual identities.

REPRESENTATIONS OF BISEXUALITY IN POPULAR MEDIA

Previous scholars (i.e. Alexander, 2007; Corey, 2017; McInroy & Craig, 2017; Meyer, 2009) have raised the question as to when and how bisexual media representations help to promote acceptance and inclusion of LGBTQI+ persons, and when and how these same representations are found detrimental. Through in-depth interviews with LGBTQ emerging adults, McInroy and Craig (2017) found that contemporary LGBTQ media representations allow for the validation of LGBTQ identities while providing stereotypical and one-dimensional depictions of LGBTQ people. Among several other key findings, the authors note that participants felt as if media representations continue to leave many LGBTQ subgroups invisible (McInroy & Craig, 2017). Corey (2017) concludes that the invisibility and erasure of bisexuality in contemporary culture can be largely attributed to monosexism (Corey, 2017, p. 194). Under-representation of bisexuality in media (and other sexualities that fall outside of the heterosexual or gay/lesbian dichotomy), makes the few existing representations available central to cultural understandings about bisexuality.

Yet, bisexuality is both under-represented and misrepresented in popular forms of mass media. Media representations frame bisexuality as a "deviant, inauthentic...temporary, excessive, and unstable" (Cocarla, 2016, p. 1) sexuality, and as "confused, indecisive, attention-seeking, and ultimately, closeted gays (or straights)" (Erickson-Schroth & Mitchell, 2009, p. 2466). Just like a female black widow spider, with its markedly large venom glands and life-threatening impactful bite, the provocative, hyper-sexualized, non-committed, and pleasure-seeking, bisexual character in popular culture lurks among and beyond its own classification of species as it awaits its next prey. Bisexual characters on popular drama television series and reality-dating shows including Piper Chapman of *Orange is the New Black*, Jenny Schecter and Tina Kennard of *The L Word*, and Tila Tequila of *A Shot at Love,* are a few popular examples of what bisexuality looks like in mainstream Western(ized) media (Cocarla, 2016; Del Castillo, 2015; Dove-Viebeahn, 2007; Richter, 2011).

The presence of such bisexual representations defy heterosexual assumptions and binary views of sexuality, while also reinforcing them (Alexander, 2007; Del Castillo, 2015; McInroy & Craig, 2017; Meyer, 2009). It is this *bisexual media paradox* that provides much controversy, and raises several challenges for those who identify as bisexual. For example, in a conversation between Kurt and Blaine from the hit drama series *Glee*, Kurt's reaction to Blaine coming out to him as bisexual and not gay, Kurt responds, "Bisexual is a term that gay guys in high school use when they want to hold hands with girls and feel like a normal person for a change." When asked why he is so angry, Kurt says, "I look up to you. I admire how proud you are of who you are. I know what it's like to be in the closet, and here you are about to tip toe right back in." Although such television shows are often celebrated for providing media representations of diverse casts including LGBTQI+ characters, monosexism and binegativity are embedded in the script-writing, casting, filming, editing, and other stages throughout the entire production process. By normalizing monosexism and binegativity on *Glee*, the message to audiences is that while heterosexual and gay or lesbian are valid sexualities, bisexuality is an invalid, temporary, and confused status, and one that is deemed non-credible or disingenuous (by straight and gay/lesbian people).

Similarly, in the hit-reality dating show, *A Shot at Love with Tila Tequila,* Season 1's Brandi explains, "You know we are all bicurious when we start out. We are too pushed off from being a lesbian by society and you know, that's a decision you have to make" (Season 1, *A Shot at Love with Tila Tequila*). Although this experience may be true for Brandi, she is seemingly speaking for all people who identify as bisexual. Such generalizations are encouraged to be cut from scripts or in the editing phases of TV and film production because of the serious consequences they hold for all of us. In *A Shot at Love*, Season 2, contestant Dominic says, "I feel like that's a phase. I honestly think it's a phase. I honestly don't believe there is such thing as a bisexual, you're either straight or you're not" (*A Shot at Love, Season 2*). But despite Dominic's binegativity, most of the show's heterosexual (cis men) contestants (in all Seasons of A Shot at Love) continued to talk about "girl-on-girl" action as 'hot'. Many media representations of bisexual femmes depict bisexuality as performed hypersexuality on display for the consumption, entertainment, and pleasure of heterosexual, cisgender men. Here, we see bisexuality as a disingenuous and attention-seeking sexuality, and solely for the dispense of the omnipresent male gaze. Any sort of romantic or emotional form of intimacy are automatically disregarded because bisexual femmes are often times depicted as overtly sexual beings who seek only others for immediate pleasure and attention.

Music is another popular media source whereby notions of sexuality come to influence audience understandings of sexuality. In Miller's (2016) discussion of how Lady Gaga's *Born This Way* challenges constructionist approaches of sexuality, we see just how influential musical lyrics are on shaping and reinforcing our understandings of sexuality. Through Miller's (2016) experiences teaching sexuality in the classroom, students are less able to understand how sexuality has been shaped by social and cultural forces, rather than genetic or biological ones, when popular songs such as *Born This Way* are embedded with essentialist beliefs about sexuality. This is especially difficult because some members of the LGBTQI+ community align with essentialist views of sexuality, too. In fact, *Born This Way* has become an empowering theme-song symbolizing pride and promoting acceptance among many LGBTQI+ circles. However, Miller (2016) suggests that because we are hesitant to frame sexuality "as a choice," essentialist views as embedded in *Born This Way* further reinforce essentialist beliefs that LGBTQI+ people are inherently, a different kind of people.

Specifically, music, like television, is another type of media that promotes binormativity and circulates misrepresentations of bisexuality. Although a less explored source of popular media among scholarly investigations of bisexuality (but see Johnson, 2016), pop-music similarly depicts bisexuality as an invalid, hypersexualized, temporal, and disingenuous sexuality. In many popular songs, we see a consistent framing of bisexuality as an overtly sexual, experimental, and overall disingenuous identity (Johnson, 2016). Perhaps most notably is the temporality of bisexuality as a transit stage on the way to either heterosexual or gay/lesbian, or as a risky persona that otherwise heterosexual people can try on for a night when they are feeling daring or hypersexual. What is particularly troubling in this regard is that media representations of bisexuality (or any other sexuality for that matter) frequently serve as one of few sources, if not the only source, of knowledge regarding bisexuality—who we are, what we do, how we do it, make sense of it, and feel about it.

AN APPROPRIATE BISEXUAL IDENTITY?
AUTOETHNOGRAPHIC INSIGHTS

I've considered different labels for my sexuality, tried them on, and have found myself in exasperating attempts to fit the label, rather than engaging in meaningful attempts to find a label that fits me. Bisexual has been one of these labels, and through my own experiences, including consumption of particular media, social interactions, intimate connections with others, and my interpretation of all of these, I found myself actively trying to mold myself into a replica of the ideal bisexual woman. It became evident to me that there were certain aspects of bisexuality that held social and cultural meanings of desirability (e.g., my display of physical intimacy with another cisgender, femme woman), which shaped my fitting to the label of bisexual because I understood that certain groups (i.e. heterosexual cisgender men) were likely to find it attractive, acceptable, and positive. I also found that other aspects of bisexuality held social and cultural meanings of undesirability (e.g., my experiences of emotional, romantic, committed, monogamous relationships with anyone who was not a cisgender, femme woman).

I do not identify as bisexual. In terms of my own sexuality, I understand it as fixed in the sense that it is in a constant state of fluidity. As such, my sexuality's existence in a predictable, limited, stagnant world of labels, has yet to escape hegemony or hegemonic socialization. I have long recognized the seemingly vital importance of sorting and labeling people—I've been socialized to do so. In fact, I do not embrace an identity or label to describe or summarize my sexuality. Despite this truth, throughout my daily interactions with others, their assumptions about my sexuality are made transparent. If I choose to disclose my relationship history, one that involves varying levels of intimacy with women, I prepare for the predictable question: "So, are you a lesbian or are you bisexual?" When confused with the fact that I do not embrace an identity or label to describe or best summarize my sexuality, others begin offering up suggestions that they believe to be fitting for me—like I need that and I'm seeking it, like I am unaware of the already existing choices, like I brought it up for discussion, as if I've finally succumbed to their expertise by allowing them to sort it out for me. While in monogamous relationships with others, my partners have defined our relationships as heterosexual, lesbian, or queer, based on social definitions of gender, sexuality, and relationships. Ultimately, the deciding factor is me— whatever I have been branded as—in relation to the person(s) I date, and their labeled genders and sexualities. I sometimes sit and watch while others go back and forth deciding what may be the most fitting category, *like a patient with a contested illness watching doctors try and fit experiences into their preexisting diagnostic categories.*

This tendency to label all sexualities is one I consider purposeful within socio, political, economic, legal, cultural, and historical contexts. This "tendency" is a result of historical and contemporary practices, as clear exclusive language written into law and religious scripts, as part of the order of social structures and institutions, embedded in culture and maintained through socialized ideology and circulating discourse. As a result, this obsession with labeling becomes so normalized and routine that it appears common-sense. I understand why the tendency to label sexualities exists; I do not blame people for being socialized to think about sexualities in a hegemonic way. After all, that's what makes hegemony, hegemony.

CONCLUSIONS

Akin to arguments about aligning public media representations with real-world people, situations, and experiences, I similarly follow the suggestions of scholars who argue that, because media representations serve as a vehicle for strict bodily regulation (Harder & Thuene, 2017) and circulating stereotypes that shape audience perceptions of others (Harder, Pericak, & Fleming, 2018), a viable solution to this problem is to employ those same bodies in decision-making processes of media framing (Harder & Thuene, 2017; Harder et al., 2018). Frequently, media serves as the vehicle in which such phobias circulate, and at times, serves as the vehicle necessary in addressing phobias or circulating messages of acceptance. Biphobia and bierasure are central issues in the recent #StillBisexual web-based campaign (created by bisexual author and activist, Nicole Kristal), a movement that emphasizes the problematization of stereotyping bisexuality as a temporary and invalid state (Gonzalez, Ramirez, & Galupo, 2017). A major goal of the movement is to collect a wide range of narratives from everyday people that identify as bisexual in order to change the social and cultural understandings of bisexuality (Gonzalez et al., 2017; #StillBisexual, 2018). Incorporating these narratives and voices into popular media representations of bisexuality could ultimately replace the (meta)narrative that circulates about bisexuality and that stems from popular media sources. Further, scholars who are interested in this line of research are encouraged to continuing our analyses of the ever-changing socio-historical-political landscape and what this means, at any given time, for discourses around bisexuality (e.g., see Gonzalez et al., 2017; Nutter-Pridgen, 2015).

Biphobia also appears to be the motivation for two upcoming television shows, both scheduled for release in Fall 2018: Hulu/Channel 4's *The Bisexual* seeks to address stereotypes of bisexuality within the LGBTQI+ community, and E! UK's *The Bi Life* aims to educate audiences about biphobia and the stigmatization of bi+ folks (GLADD, 2018). As an increasing amount of LGBTQI+ people are employed in media positions and media-related work sectors, a wider variety of LGBTQI+ experiences may be drawn from in decision-making processes and at every stage of production (i.e. in the planning, screen writing, casting, filming, and editing). To be clear, in order to change current bisexual representations in popular media, we must: (1) employee bisexual people in media positions and in media-related work sectors, (2) allow bisexual employees to be a part of multiple stages of production and decision-making in media, and (3) incorporate everyday bisexual narratives and voices as character stories. Scholars who study bisexuality and who are interested in future research in this area could work towards contributing a wider range of media-types and sources (analyses of a wider range of television and a variety of music genres, film, literature, advertisements/marketing, social media, etc.) into discussions of media representations of bisexuality. Likewise, continuing to incorporate bisexual authors, participants, and narratives into our work is critically important in shaping such scholarship.

Further, binormativity encourages the assimilation of those who identify as bisexual to fit within mainstream gender, sexual, and racial codes (Del Castillo, 2015, p. 10). Only few popular media representations of bisexuality are available that defy this; for example, in a character analysis of Anna Tagaro on *One Tree Hill*, Meyer (2010) suggests that Anna's overlapping Latina [*sic*] and bisexual identities provide representation of intersectional marginalized positionalities, and argues that such representations could broaden the existing frame of bisexuality in television (Meyer, 2009, 2010). Similarly, cisgender female bisexuality, compared to both cisgender male bisexuality and to non-cis bisexuality, is over-represented in popular media. Johnson (2017) argues that although more media representation may allude that bi ciswomen are privileged, the representations of bi ciswomen are pornographic and embedded with misogynistic tendencies that are exploitative (Johnson, 2016, pp. 384–385). Moving forward, we must work for a wider-range of bi-representation in media to incorporate non-cis bisexuality and cisgender male bisexuality, continue to combat the misrepresentation of bi ciswomen in media, and work towards more accurate and realistic representations of bisexuality in the media.

We cannot talk seriously about media representation of bisexuality without understanding the critical importance of how one's social positioning in the larger society, *but also among members within a given social group,* matter. As previous scholars have noted, members marginalized by one system often simultaneously face marginalization and its effects by other operating systems. Therefore, through intersecting forces of sexuality, gender, race, class, health, ability, age, etc. and their meanings within a given context, we are reminded of the potential reintroductions of power, privilege, centering, and silencing, and the inequalities that exist even within and among those who are already marginalized, underrepresented, and misrepresented in media and beyond. Historically and presently, this holds true even in moments when we show up with our best intentions at the forefront of our practices. For all of us, our everyday communications are embodied political acts where our own positionalities, choices, and language matter (we do not ever do these things from a position of "nowhere"); and we are never, and cannot ever be, divorced from the spaces in which our behavior, language, or work permeates the social worlds and lives of people whom our practices regard. Moving forward, intersectionality is recommended as the core of scholarship on and media representations of bisexuality in order to broaden the center of those who are already marginalized.

NOTE

[1] Sensoy and DiAngelo (2017) define hegemony as, "the imposition of dominant group ideology onto everyone in society, which makes it difficult to escape or to resist believing in this dominant ideology, and where social control is achieved through conditioning rather than physical force or intimidation" (p. 73).

REFERENCES

Alexander, J. (2007). Bisexuality in the media: A digital roundtable. *Journal of Bisexuality, 7*(1–2), 113–124.

Cefai, S. (2014). Feeling and the production of lesbian space in The L Word. *Gender, Place & Culture, 21*(5), 650–665.

Cocarla, S. (2016). *Straddling (In) visibility: Representations of bisexual women in twenty-first century popular culture* (Doctoral dissertation). University of Ottawa, Ottawa.

Corey, S. (2017). All Bi myself: Analyzing television's presentation of female bisexuality. *Journal of Bisexuality, 17*(2), 190–205.

Del Castillo, V. (2015). Regulating bisexuality: Binormativity and assimilation to the homonormative order in American scripted television series. *The New Birmingham Review, 2*(1), 10–22.

Dove-Viebahn, A. (2007). Fashionably femme: Lesbian visibility, style, and politics in The L Word. In *Queer popular culture* (pp. 71–83). New York, NY: Palgrave Macmillan.

Dyar, C., Lytle, A., London, B., & Levy, S. R. (2015). Application of bisexuality research to the development of a set of guidelines for intervention efforts to reduce binegativity. *Translational Issues in Psychological Science, 1*(4), 352.

Eisner, S. (2013). *Bi: Notes for a bisexual revolution.* Berkeley, CA: Seal Press.

Erickson-Schroth, L., & Mitchell, J. (2009). Queering queer theory, or why bisexuality matters. *Journal of Bisexuality, 9*(3–4), 297–315.

Esterline, K. M., & Galupo, M. P. (2013). "Drunken curiosity" and "gay chicken": Gender differences in same-sex performativity. *Journal of Bisexuality, 13*(1), 106–121.

Gamson, W. A., Croteau, D., Hoynes, W., & Sasson, T. (1992). Media images and the social construction of reality. *Annual review of sociology, 18*(1), 373–393.

Garland, D. (2008). On the concept of moral panic. *Crime, Media, Culture, 4*(1), 9–30.

Giddens, A. (1991). *Modernity and self-identity: Self and society in the late modern age.* Stanford, CA: Stanford University Press.

GLADD. (2018). *Celebrating bisexuality.* Retrieved from http://www.glaad.org/bisexual

Gonzalez, K. A., Ramirez, J. L., & Galupo, M. P. (2017). "I was and still am": Narratives of bisexual marking in the #StillBisexual campaign. *Sexuality & Culture, 21*(2), 493–515.

Harder, B. M., Pericak, K. A., & Fleming, J. K. (in press). When the game is no longer fun: Mediasport's constructions of race and gender and the enduring consequences on its audiences In *Pop culture universe: Icons, idols, ideas.* ABC-CLIO.

Harder, B. M., & Theune, F. (2017). Fat and strong to thin and frail: hyper-regulating the female athletic body. In A. Milner & J. M. Braddock II (Eds.), *Women in sports: Breaking barriers, facing obstacles* (pp. 105–121, Vol. 2). Santa Barbara, CA: ABC-CLIO Praeger.

Hjarvard, S. P. (2013). *The mediatization of culture and society.* New York, NY: Routledge.

Horncastle, J. (2008). Queer bisexuality: Perceptions of bisexual existence, distinctions, and challenges. *Journal of Bisexuality, 8*(1–2), 25–49.

Jackson, J. D., Nielsen, G. M., & Hsu, Y. (2011). *Mediated society: A critical sociology of media.* Don Mills: Oxford University Press.

Johnson, H. J. (2016). Bisexuality, mental health, and media representation. *Journal of Bisexuality, 16*(3), 378–396.

Kellner, D. (2003). *Media culture: Cultural studies, identity and politics between the modern and the post-modern.* London: Routledge.

McInroy, L. B., & Craig, S. L. (2017). Perspectives of LGBTQ emerging adults on the depiction and impact of LGBTQ media representation. *Journal of Youth Studies, 20*(1), 32–46.

Meyer, M. D. (2009). "I'm just trying to find my way like most kids": Bisexuality, adolescence and the drama of One Tree Hill. *Sexuality & Culture, 13*(4), 237–251.

Meyer, M. D. (2010). Representing bisexuality on television: The case for intersectional hybrids. *Journal of Bisexuality, 10*(4), 366–387.

Miller, A. D. (2016). The Mis-education of Lady Gaga: Confronting essentialist claims in the sex and gender classroom. In *Teaching gender and sex in contemporary America* (pp. 15–25). Cham: Springer.

Nutter-Pridgen, K. L. (2015). The old, the new, and the redefined: Identifying the discourses in contemporary bisexual activism. *Journal of Bisexuality, 15*(3), 385–413.

Richter, N. (2011). Ambiguous bisexuality: The case of a shot at love with Tila Tequila. *Journal of Bisexuality, 11*(1), 121–141.

#StillBisexual. (2018). *#StillBisexual.* Retrieved from http://stillbisexual.com/

Sensoy, O., & DiAngelo, R. (2017). *Is everyone really equal?: An introduction to key concepts in social justice education.* New York, NY: Teachers College Press.

Shoemaker, P. J., & Reese, S. D. (2013). *Mediating the message in the 21st century: A media sociology perspective*. London: Routledge.

Yoshino, K. (1999). The epistemic contract of bisexual erasure. *Stanford Law Review, 52*, 353–461.

Young, J. (2009). Moral panic: Its origins in resistance, ressentiment and the translation of fantasy into reality. *The British Journal of Criminology, 49*(1), 4–16.

PART 2

CONSENSUALLY NON-MONOGAMOUS RELATIONSHIPS

MIMI SCHIPPERS

5. POLYAMORY AND A QUEER ORIENTATION TO THE WORLD

INTRODUCTION

In this chapter I hope to demonstrate, by way of example, how being polyamorous opens up the possibility for having a queer orientation to the world. By queer orientation, I am building on the work of queer, feminist theorist Sarah Ahmed. According to Ahmed, social structure can be thought of in spatial terms. Roles, norms, and collective values set down lines for movement, and those lines compel us to take up particular ways of doing things and steer us away from alternatives (Ahmed, 2007). To the extent that normative lines reflect existing structures of inequality, they compel us to maintain the status quo and discourage us from doing things differently so that, as we "tow the line," we not only reproduce the status quo, we keep in place relations of inequality. According to Ahmed, one of the main mechanisms that keep us in line is collective ideas about what constitutes "the good life" and what paths will lead to "happiness" (Ahmed, 2010).

One of the main stories we are told in contemporary Western cultures is that a good life is only really possible through monogamous coupling and only by finding your "one and only true love" can you live happily ever after (i.e. single people are perceived as lacking something and incapable of being happy). These values are codified through norms, practices, and institutional structures that steer all of us toward monogamous couple relationship as the most desirable, beneficial, fulfilling, and moral form of adult intimacy. In other words, Western cultures are *mononormative*.

To the extent that queer is defined as a rejection of what is normative, in a mononormative world, polyamory is queer. Polyamory refers to emotionally and sometimes sexually intimate and committed relationships that include more than two adults. Generally, none of the adults are genetically related, but that isn't always the case (e.g. polygamy in which sisters marry the same man or brothers marry the same woman is common in some parts of the world). Because polyamory is queer, it is marginalized as deviant,

© KONINKLIJKE BRILL NV, LEIDEN, 2019 | DOI:10.1163/9789004414105_006

immoral, or unnatural. As is the case with most sexualities and relationship styles that are defined as deviant, those who practice polyamory experience discrimination, prejudice, and structural disadvantage (Rubin, 1984). For instance, consider all of the benefits of legal marriage in the U.S. that were denied to gay and lesbian couples and for which marriage equality was fought. None of those benefits are available to people in multi-adult relationships because polygamy is illegal. There are no laws protecting individuals on the basis of relationship status, so polyamorists can lose housing, custody of children, and our jobs and have no legal recourse because we are polyamorous.

In this way polyamory is off line from what mainstream culture would define as a "good life" (as in both happiness and morality). Living off line opens up possibilities for seeing things and doing things differently. That is, if being off line is a queer orientation to the world, then polyamory offers an opportunity to cultivate a queer orientation, not just to romantic and sexual relationships, but to the world more generally. I call this queer orientation a *poly orientation* to the world.

WHAT IS A POLY ORIENTATION?

A poly orientation to the world means living a queer life that refuses to simply follow the mononormative path we are all compelled to follow. It is as much about being able to see the operations of mononormativity and resist them as it is about being polyamorous. It also means moving through the world with openness to seeing and experiencing relationships with others in more complex, interesting, and less rigid ways. This would include being amenable to redefining what it means to be in relationship with others as well as being able to "see" poly relationships as real and possible. In other words, one does not have to be in a polyamorous relationship or identify as a polyamorist to move through the world with a poly orientation. Adopting a poly orientation is possible for anyone because anyone, if given the conceptual tools, could see how everyday interactions, the way we set up institutions, and the stories we tell encourage us to believe that monogamous coupling is the path to happiness and a "good life."

In this chapter I hope, by way of example, introduce readers to what it is like to have a poly orientation to the world. For me, being polyamorous meant that a poly orientation to the world was inevitable, desirable, and necessary. It has given me a completely new *and queer* set of criteria for what constitutes a good life and what paths might lead to happiness.

Poly Orientations toward Family

I have several people in my life that I consider family. Some of them are people I am genetically related to, and some of them are what many queer people call "chosen family." A chosen family refers to a group of people who are not necessarily biologically related, but consciously and deliberately choose one another to play significant roles in each other's lives. In my life, a poly orientation toward family has been about refusing to buy into the idea that a traditional, heterosexual, nuclear family that includes a husband/father, wife/mother, and dependent children is the key to happiness. My chosen family includes two partners, three metamours, and a chosen brother.

My "partners" are both cis gender men. One is what Elisabeth Sheff (2015) calls a "poly affective partner." According to Sheff, "Polyaffectivity is the term…for emotionally intimate poly relationships that are nonsexual. People in poly relationships who see each other as family members but are not sexually connected" (p. 20). My poly affective partner is someone I met eighteen years ago. For the first thirteen years of our relationship we were sexually involved and financially inter-dependent. We shared a household and planned our futures together, and we often traveled together and spent holidays with each other's families. In other words, we were *primary partners* for thirteen years. Five years ago, for several reasons, we decided that living together was no longer working and that, for the time being anyway, we would not be primary partners for the foreseeable future. After some bumpy times (that I'll talk more about later), we are currently chosen poly family, but not in anything remotely close to resembling a traditional heterosexual marriage. We love each other very much, share custody of our two dogs, are each others' go-to support when needed, and we are committed to each other.

My relationship with the other partner began six years ago. We experienced pretty intense new relationship energy or what polyamorists call, N.R.E., which is the euphoric, crazy, passionate feeling you sometimes have when falling in love with a new person. We live about two blocks away from each other, share custody of Chihuahua mix, and generally consider each other life partners.

My metamours are three cis gender women. By metamours, I mean that they are partners of my partners. One is my lover's poly affective partner (they were married for twenty years, but now live apart, are no longer sexual, but still very much in love and consider each other family). He is also dating another woman with whom he is sexually and increasingly emotionally involved. My third metamour has been partnered with my polyaffective partner for three years.

Last, but not least, is my chosen brother. He is a transgender man who I have known for thirty years. We didn't grow up together, but we come from very similar families and cultures, and we share a deep intellectual and political connection. Although we dabbled a time or two with being sexually involved a long time ago, being siblings makes much more sense than being lovers at this stage of our lives. I have five brothers by blood, and I love them very much, but my chosen brother is a queer, feminist intellectual-activist. As you can imagine, my relationship with him is different from what I have with my other brothers.

Most of us (me, my partners, my metamours, and my brother) spend holidays together when possible. If any one of us is in need of something, the rest of us are available and try to be of assistance if we can. Our economic dependence on each other varies a great deal, but each and every one of us would have the others' backs in a financial crisis. And just like every family, there are conflicts, but there is also incredible joy, support, and love. In other words, for us, family is not something defined by a genetic line or by legal definitions of marriage; it is something we *do*. Family ties emerge as relationships form, and because of this, we are open to reconfiguring who is family. This openness changes my relationship to others outside of my chosen family.

Poly Orienations toward Relationships

A poly orientation to the world also changes my experience of erotic desire for others. In a mononormative world, if we are partnered with another person, we are expected to shut down or ignore sexual desires for other people. It is assumed that cultivating or acting on desire for another person will severely threaten if not destroy the existing relationship. With a poly orientation, those assumptions are replaced with a kind of openness to desire and to others regardless of whether or not I am attracted to them.

This is pretty queer for a couple of reasons. In a mononormative and *heternormative* world, many people assume that men and women can't really be friends because sexual desire will always get in the way. The assumption is that people with different gender identities will automatically become erotically attracted to each other and those with the same gender identity won't. Therefore, the logical conclusion is that, when someone is in a monogamous relationship, they must avoid other-gender friends. Not only is this based on a false assumption that gender is binary (as if there are only men and women), it is also deeply heterosexist in that it assumes everyone is attracted to people of a different gender. It is also based on the sexist idea the only interest men have in women is as sexual objects, as if women aren't compelling in other ways.

My poly orientation means that I don't have to move through the world blocking out whole groups of people who could potentially become sexual partners. Although I am in committed relationships with others, those relationships are *open*, meaning we are free to develop emotionally or sexually intimate relationships with people outside of the existing relationship. With a poly orientation, I am open to having sexual desire for others without betraying my partners, and I am free to form relationships with anyone I choose regardless of gender.

A poly orientation also means resisting the automatic classification of people based on gender to decide with whom I can or cannot form relationships and what sort of relationships they can be before they have even begun. In my experience, this has led to being pleasantly surprised by erotic attraction to someone I didn't expect to be attracted to and to sometimes adding an erotic component to my friendships. It's not that I don't see gender; it's that gender doesn't determine who is in the fuckable zone and who is in the friendship zone. My erotic and friendship orientation is poly and as such, it is not defined by the gender identities of those I encounter. Instead, new relationships develop as an organic set of possibilities.

Which points to another way a poly orientation is a queer orientation toward relationships. With a poly rather than mono orientation toward the world, I don't assume that people my partners want to love, fuck, or date are a threat to me or my relationships with my partners. As I have suggested elsewhere (Schippers, 2016), being open to rather than threatened by new people in a partner's life can queer gender relations. For instance, men who are sexually involved with the same women are no longer encouraged to cultivate a violent, jealous rage toward each other or the woman. To the extent that aggression, possessiveness, and needing control are valued as hegemonic masculinity, which refers to the characteristics or practices that are seen as manly in a given culture and, when paired with a subordinate femininity, ensures men's dominance and superiority over women as a group (Connell, 1995; Connell & Messerschmidt, 2005; Schippers, 2007), then hegemonic masculinity is exposed as deeply dysfunctional when you have a poly orientation to the world. Likewise, women don't have to see each other as competitors for the attention of the same man. Instead, a poly orientation encourages women partnered with the same person to see each other as potential friends, lovers, or even political allies.

My poly orientation has led me to see metamours as people with whom I might have a relationship. I have a pretty good relationship with two of my metamours. I'm just getting to know one of them, but the other feels like a sister or good friend. Sometimes we joke about being "sister wives," which is probably a pretty un-"pc" appropriation of language used by polygamous Mormons. At the same time, my third metamour doesn't seem very interested in having a very close relationship with me. I don't doubt that we have some things in common, especially being partnered with the same person! However, perhaps due to distance (she lives in a different city from the rest of us) or something else, we aren't anything close to "besties." We do, however, contact each other when necessary, and she is always welcome to our holiday celebrations. Like all relationships, metamour relationships are not always easy. Sometimes metamours don't have much affinity and wouldn't be friends except for the relationship to the same person. Still, a poly orientation doesn't assume that metamours are competitors, poachers of property, or destructive. A poly orientation gives metamours the benefit of the doubt. Always.

A poly orientation also changes the way I think about what relationships can be and how they change over time. We live in a world characterized by what Christine Gupta (2015) calls "compulsory sexuality" and Elizabeth Brake (2012) refers to as amatonormativity. Together, these concepts refer to the way in which Western cultures define sexually romantic relationships as superior and more important than any other kinds of relationships adults can have with each other. Combined with mononormativivity, this leads to the assumption that, when people stop being sexual with each other, their relationship "failed" and is "over," and that the presence of an "ex" is a threat to current partners.

This is precisely what happened five years ago when my now polyaffective, then primary partner and I decided to live apart and eliminate sex as part of our relationship. The woman he was dating at the time—who said that she was happy with polyamory by the way, suddenly became very possessive of him and wanted him to herself. With a mono rather than poly orientation, she was deeply threatened by my presence in his life. She wanted a monogamous relationship with him and assumed that my presence was incompatible with her desires. She couldn't imagine that he and I could remain partners and not be a threat to her relationship with him. She must have bought into the heteronormative idea that men and women can only have sexual relationships with each other, and the amatonomorative assumptions that her sexual relationship with him superseded his polyaffective relationship with me in importance. She actively worked to separate us, undermined me by disparaging my character, and created all kinds of conflict with him *and* me.

Many other people made the same assumptions and defined us as having "broken up" despite our commitment to maintain our close relationship despite not sharing a household or having sex with each other. It was very difficult, and we spent many hours dealing with conflict, hurt feelings, and deciding how to be with each other, but in the end, we both were able to maintain our poly orientation toward our relationship. Five years later, and because of mononormativity and amatonormativity, it is still difficult for many people to see our relationship as "real" or committed because we are not sexually or romantically involved, we don't live together, and we have other partners. His current sexual partner (my metamour), however, also seems to have a poly orientation, and recognizes and honors our polyaffective relationship—hence the jokes about being "sister wives."

A Poly Orientation toward Kinship and Community

A poly orientation also is a queer orientation toward kinship and community. Rather than being defined as a genealogical given or a geographical *place*, kinship and community are established by what one *does*. Lauren Berlant and Michael Warner (1998) suggest that kinship and community are defined in mainstream culture according to heteronormative norms for living a "good life." They write,

> A complex cluster of sexual practices gets confused, in heterosexual culture, with the love plot of intimacy and familialism that signifies belonging to society in a deep and normal way. Community is imagined through scenes of intimacy, coupling, and kinship; a historical relation to futurity is restricted to generational narrative and reproduction. (p. 554)

Kinship and community are givens and defined by already existing norms for familial roles and by generational lines. In contrast, queer culture is something that is DIY (Do It Yourself, with the operative terms being "do") because the normative rules and roles don't fit.

> By queer culture we mean a world-making project, where 'world'… differs from community or group because it necessarily includes more people than can be identified, more spaces than can be mapped beyond a few reference points, modes of feeling that can be learned rather than experienced as a birthright. The queer world is a space of entrances,

exits, unsystematized lines of acquaintance, projected horizons, typifying examples, alternate routes, blockages, incommensurate geographies. (Berlant & Warner, 1998, p. 558)

Given Berlant and Warner's definitions, we can think of doing kinship in the context of polyamory as a world-making project that cannot fit neatly into already fixed notions of families and the different roles people are expected to play within "generational narrative and reproduction." Rather than relying on given familial and generational lines to define my family relationships, I actively do kinship with members of my chosen poly family by having their backs, supporting them, and spending meaningful and ritualized time together. For instance, my sibling relationship with my chosen brother is not defined by being related through blood as is the case with my other brothers. We can't simply take each other for granted, but instead cultivate kinship by what we do with and for each other. I cultivated kinship with him by initially supporting his decision to transition, by being there for him during that time, and by always having his back personally and professionally in the fight against cisgenderism and transphobia. He reciprocates by fighting against mononormativity. In his work he always includes polyamory in his definitions of relationships and queerness, and he always shows up for and stands up with me when I need him. Though he is not in a polyamorous relationship, he definitely has a poly orientation to the world. We also do kinship by caring for each others' dogs when needed and making sure they get to see each other regularly. Though cousins more than siblings, my dogs and my brother's dog are truly *chosen* littermates.

Community is similar to kinship in that it is not a place or a group defined by geographical proximity; it created in the doing. One way in which I *do* community is by working with others who share my feminist, queer, anti-racist political commitments and who are trying to forge a queer life. For instance, I started a polyamory "Meetup" group in New Orleans. While the group was active, we would often meet to socialize, but we would also get together to talk about navigating the ups and downs polyamory in a mononormative world. When one of the members of our community found herself fighting for custody of her daughter because she is polyamory, we not only provided emotional support, we used our networks to find legal support as well. Members of the group came from different and disparate parts of the city and surrounding area, and sometimes people visiting from out of town would join us. Despite our geographic dissimilarity, we were *doing* poly community.

A Poly Orientation toward Media

Finally, a poly orientation toward the world includes a queer orientation toward media. Because of my poly orientation, I can "see" that, with only a few and notable exceptions, every "happy ending" in television and film is a monogamous marriage between two, cisgender, heterosexual people. What does that say about what will make us happy if only monogamous marriage can be the "happily-ever-after" ending of the stories we collectively tell? As someone who has found fulfillment and support in relationships outside of monogamous marriage, I notice that I rarely see anyone like me living happily ever after in the stories told in media.

At the same time, I experience a special pleasure and joy when I see anything remotely like the way I live my life. For example, one of my favorite sources of poly content at the moment is The Netflix television show *Grace and Frankie.* The show centers on the lives of Grace, played by Jane Fonda and Lily Tomlin's character, Frankie. The premise of the show is established in the first episode when their husbands, Robert played by Martin Sheen and Sol played by Sam Waterston reveal that they, Robert and Sol, are gay, in love with each other, and want to get married. Over the course of the four seasons, Grace and Frankie develop a very close, emotionally but not sexually intimate friendship (although every once in a while Frankie flirts with Grace and suggests that it is not outside the realm of possibility that they have a more physical relationship). Grace and Frankie share a household together, care for each other, and eventually start a business in which they develop and sell vibrators specifically designed for elderly women. Sol and Robert are married, live in the same house, and dabbled in having an open relationship. Frankie and Sol are still deeply in love and say so, and although they are not consistent lovers, they have had sex with each other since the marriages broke up. Grace and Robert have a more tumultuous relationship, but there is no doubt that they, like Sol and Frankie, are polyaffective partners. For Frankie, Grace, Sol, and Robert, legal marriage or genetic lines do not define family. Instead, family is about *doing* mutual support, love, and commitment. We might say that the show offers a glimpse of what growing old with a poly orientation could be like. How many television shows or movies can you say *that* about?

CONCLUSION

A poly orientation to the world rejects the idea that "real" or "committed" or "serious" relationships are sexual and monogamous and any and all relationships that are not (1) sexual, (2) monogamous, and (3) committed are less important, serious, or fulfilling. This does not mean always rejecting monogamy as a component of some relationships. It would mean consciously choosing monogamy as a specific way you want to do a relationship with a specific person without assuming (1) monogamy is the only option, (2) that the relationships will remain monogamous forever or (3) that you would not be open to having a poly relationships in the future or with someone else. That is, rejecting mononormativity can include sometimes *consciously* choosing monogamy rather than assuming it is the default unless otherwise specified. In sum, then, a poly orientation is not about being polyamorous or identifying as a polyamorist. In fact, as I hope I have conveyed in this chapter, a poly orientation is not an identity at all. It is a way of seeing the world and choosing to doing things differently.

REFERENCES

Ahmed, S. (2007). *Queer phenomenology: Orientations, objects, others.* Durham, NC: Duke University Press.

Ahmed, S. (2010). *The promise of happiness.* Durham, NC: Duke University Press.

Berlant, L., & Warner, M. (1998). Sex in public. *Critical Inquiry, 24,* 547–566.

Brake, E. (2012). *Minimizing marriage: Marriage, morality, and the law.* Cambridge: Oxford University Press.

Connell, R. W. (2005). *Masculinities.* Berkeley, CA: University of California Press.

Connell, R. W., & Messerschmidt, J. W. (2005). Hegemonic masculinity: Rethinking the concept. *Gender & Society, 19,* 829–859.

Kristina, G. (2015). Compulsory sexuality: Evaluating an emerging concept. *Signs: Journal of Women in Culture & Society, 41*(1), 131–154.

Rubin, G. (1984). Thinking sex: Notes for a radical theory of the politics of sexuality. In C. S. Vance (Ed.), *Pleasure and danger: Exploring female sexuality* (pp. 267–319). London: Pandora.

Schippers, M. (2007). Recovering the feminine other: Femininity, masculinity, and gender hegemony. *Theory and Society, 36*(1), 85–102.

Schippers, M. (2016). *Beyond monogamy: Polyamory and the future of polyqueer sexualities.* New York, NY: New York University Press.

Sheff, E. (2013). *The polyamorist next door: Inside multiple partner relationships and families.* New York, NY: Rowman and Littlefield.

MICHELLE WOLKOMIR

6. MONOGAMY VS. POLYAMORY

Negotiating Gender Hierarchy

Romantic love is celebrated in American culture and considered a central part of living a good life. It is the framework from which we understand and build relationships and families. Yet, only one form of romantic love is culturally valued, and all other forms are stigmatized to some extent (Coontz, 2005; Ingraham, 1999; Rubin, 1993). Given the valorization of this form of romantic love, we rarely question the consequences of arranging our intimate lives in this way as opposed to another form. The following begins this examination by describing how the traditional romantic love story and monogamy emerge from and structure gender power relations. I then compare this configuration to polyamorous love and relationships to explore how varied forms of intimacy might influence cultural prescriptions for gender ideology and behavior. This comparison provides key insights into how we might begin to erode masculine dominance and gender hierarchy.

THE STORY OF ROMANTIC *LOVE* AND GENDER RELATIONS

It was October of her junior year when Makayla walked into her sociology class, looking out of the corner of her eye as she always did to see if Joel was already there. He was. He was fit and strong from all the workouts required to play collegiate soccer, and he had gorgeous eyes and a contagious smile. He said smart, and sometimes funny, things in class. As Makayla slid into her seat, she looked over at him. Just then he looked up and saw her staring at him. Their eyes met for a moment, and then Makayla turned around embarrassed, her face burning, thinking "well I'm so busted." To her surprise, Joel was waiting in the hall after class and asked if she wanted to study together for the upcoming exam. After they agreed on a time and place, Makayla walked away and almost immediately began trying to figure out what to wear to look sexy but not obvious or slutty. She decided on her best jeans and a casual cold shoulder shirt, just a little make up and expensive perfume....Makayla remembers the kiss at the end of that study date as "magical."

© KONINKLIJKE BRILL NV, LEIDEN, 2019 | DOI:10.1163/9789004414105_007

They continued dating, laughing together, making love, and telling one another their stories and secrets. They had spats, but their only big fight came when Makayla got drunk at a fraternity party and danced with one of Joel's fraternity brothers. Joel was jealous and asked if Makayla wanted to be with his fraternity brother instead of him. They had a long talk and told one another that they were in love. They agreed they would not date anyone else and then made love. Six months later, on Makayla's birthday, Joel dropped to one knee and took her hand. He said, "You are everything to me. I can't imagine my life without you or ever wanting anyone but you. Will you do me the honor of becoming my wife?" Makayla said yes immediately and joyfully. She was certain Joel was right for her. She felt closer to him than anyone else—both physically and emotionally—and she trusted him.

At the wedding, their friends made toasts to "the perfect couple" and then watched them drive off in a car decorated with interlocking hearts containing the names Makayla and Joel painted on the rear window.

This brief vignette outlines the commonly known tale of romantic love that permeates our culture. This story is the plot line for many fairy tales, books, movies, advertisements, and songs, and it exists as the guiding framework for many people's hopes, behaviors, and experiences (Galician, 2004; Kim et al., 2007; Martin & Kazyak, 2009; Ward, 2003). Though it has multiple slight variations, the basic story is that a man and woman meet and feel an inexplicable spark. He woos her, impressing her with his prowess and abilities, and fending off other suitors. She delights him with her beauty and sexual allure, as well as her caring and kind spirit. They fall in love, seem to meet one another's every need, and marry. The hegemonic romantic love ideology that undergirds this story and shapes cultural perceptions of what love should be frames the ideal intimate relationship as a unique (heterosexual) bond in which "one and only soulmates" share an intense emotional closeness, psychological compatibility, and sexual attraction that is celebrated in committed monogamy (Ingraham, 1999; Swidler, 2001). Sex and sexual fidelity play an important role in this framework. Sex serves as a symbolic enactment of couples' intertwined selves and is thus seen as "the glue that holds the special relationship together" (Jackson & Scott, 2004, p. 155). Sexual fidelity is therefore critical to marking and maintaining this "specialness" for the couple (Jamieson, 2004).

Given the importance of sex and sexual fidelity within the hegemonic romantic love ideology, monogamy as a shared cultural ideal is revered and systematically reproduced in society. In this sense, American culture is characterized by mono-normativity, or what Bauer (2010, p. 145) defines as "a complex power relation, which (re)produces hierarchically arranged patterns of intimate relationships and devalues, marginalizes, excludes, and 'others' those patterns of intimacy which do not correspond to the normative apparatus of the monogamous model." In other words, any form of intimate relationship that falls outside the boundaries of monogamy is perceived as inferior or somehow troubled, while monogamy is imbued with a sense of rightness. It is seen as *the path* to a healthy relationship and family and a good life. In sum, monogamy is romantic love done right.

This hegemonic romantic love story/ideology, however, emerges from, depends on, and recreates a system of hierarchical gender relations in which masculine superiority is systematically produced. To fully understand this statement, we must begin by examining the dominant characteristics associated with masculinity and femininity (For a fuller discussion of these characteristics see Lorber, 1994; Wade & Marx Feree, 2015). While there may be some variation, most people generally identify primary masculine and feminine traits as they are displayed in Table 1.

Table 1. Hegemonic gender traits

Masculine	Feminine
Rational, Stoic	Emotional
Provider, Protector	Nurturer, Care taker
Aggressive, Competitive	Passive, Submissive
Physically strong	Physically weak
Perpetually heterosexually horny	Sexually alluring

This table demonstrates that widely held conceptualizations of gender pose masculinity and femininity in a binary, opposing and hierarchical relationship. As you can see, the traits presented in one category are juxtaposed against the traits contained in the other. It appears one can either be masculine or feminine, and one can only be understood in opposition to the other. In other words, we understand what is masculine only in relation to what is it not—feminine—and vice versa. Further, the traits that compose masculinity are generally more culturally valued than those that comprise femininity in most situations, marking masculinity as superior. As Schippers (2007, p. 91) points out, it is this complementary and opposing relationship between hegemonic masculinity and femininity that provides the ideological framework for a "legitimating rationale for social relations ensuring the ascendancy and dominance of men."

This hegemonic gender configuration is also linked to sexuality. Consider the labels applied to people who break these gender codes. Men who act in feminine ways are often called "fags" or "queers," while women who act in masculine ways are often referred to as "butch" or "dykes." Why? Look at the last item in Table 1. People assume that if a person does not display appropriately gendered traits, then s/he will also not be properly heterosexual (e.g., there is no mixing and matching from these lists). Further, this set of gender relations establishes proper gender behaviors and codes within the context of heterosexual relationships. Men are supposed to be sexual agents—desiring, wooing and winning women—and fending off masculine competitors to claim a kind of sexual ownership (Bordo, 1999; Connell, 1995). Women, by contrast and as a complement, are supposed to be sexually passive objects of desire, more sexually alluring and pleasing than other women so a man is satisfied and will not stray (Bartky, 1990; Hesse-Biber, 2007; Wolkomir, 2004). This system of gender relations—in which men are sexual agents who act on women as passive objects—thus reproduces masculine dominance and valorizes a (hetero)sexual hierarchy. As Jeffreys (1996, p. 77) asserts, "gender is not simply the mold in which men and women learn different sexualities, but is a product of sexuality itself. The sexuality of male supremacy, heterosexual desire, requires the constant recreation of masculinity and femininity." Within this system, gendered competition is central to sexual success and love. It is by enacting gender well that men can outperform competitors and win the woman or that women can attract and keep a man. As a result, sexual partners must stay vigilant about the potential competition, and the presence of another can create jealousy and insecurity. It is thus through the proper enactment of hegemonic gendered behavior that masculine superiority and dominance are encoded into and sustained in heterosexual monogamy. Schippers (2008, p. 39) urges us to see this interconnection in monogamy, describing it as "an imagined, glorified, and compulsory relationship form [that] mirrors and supports the discursively constructed relationship between heteromasculinity and heterofemininity." Masculine superiority is thus encoded in our cultural version of monogamy. But what happens to gender hierarchy when people challenge this monogamous model of relationships?

THE STORY OF ROMANTIC *LOVES* AND GENDER RELATIONS

Fifteen years later, Makayla and Joel have 2 children, have established successful careers, and are very much in love. One night, at dinner with another couple, they discover the couple is polyamorous. Their friends explain how much joy these additional relationships have added to their lives. Makayla and Joel are surprised and intrigued and ask questions. Later that night, they talk about polyamory, and they both admit feeling attracted to and emotionally connected to another person. Makayla admits she has kissed the other man. Joel is upset, but he wonders if he should be. They agree to investigate further.

They read about polyamory and have long discussions about it both by themselves and with the two people they want to involve. When they first begin extramarital relationships, they feel anxiety, jealousy and fear. They talk through these feelings honestly, and sometimes fight. To negotiate these difficult emotions, they establish "ground rules" for their relationships and continue talking. Eventually, they feel comfortable in all their relationships. While life is often hectic, Makayla and Joel agree that their lives have never been better or more rewarding.

This brief vignette represents such an uncommonly told tale of love that it may seem unrecognizable or even impossible. Yet, many people engage in and find polyamorous relationships deeply fulfilling. Put simply, polyamory is the practice of engaging in open, honest, sexual, and loving intimate relationships with more than one person. Polyamorists believe that having more love in life enriches it and that having one love does not detract from or diminish another love (Haritaworn et al., 2006). For polyamorists, having multiple loves is analogous to having multiple friends or siblings; adding another does not erode the existing love or relationship. Polyamorous relationships can take many different forms and encompass varied behaviors. Some polyamorous couples, for example, might live together as a single family, while others may have multiple outside partners, while still others may share a single additional lover. Whatever the form of relationship, polyamorists focus on communicating openly, creating close intimate connections, and satisfying partners' needs and desires. Polyamorists, while they intensely value romantic love, largely reject the hegemonic romantic love ideology and the notion of having a "one and only" soulmate. They also therefore may not feel it necessary to engage in the same sorts of competitive gendered behavior.

Methods of Exploring Polyamorous Relationships

To examine how people who participate in multiple partner intimacies conceptualize and enact gender, I conducted 23 loosely structured, in-depth interviews with polyamorists (as part of a larger study) to explore how they negotiated these relationships and how this relationship form impacted their perceptions of gender. When possible, I interviewed both polyamorous partners/ spouses—the initial two people who decided to expand into polyamorous relationships—to capture the interactional dynamics of the relationship. These partners compose about two thirds of my sample. While not generalizable, this sample provides a lens through which to explore the intersection of non-monogamy and gender power dynamics. In what follows, I use this interview data to illustrate how negotiating successful multiple partner relationships compelled study participants to challenge traditional gender relations and to develop more egalitarian gender frameworks. As we shall see, as participants become more experienced with and immersed in polyamory, they more fully disregard the romantic love ideology and its attendant gendered prescriptions, leveling the gender hierarchy.

The Consequences of Polyamorous Love

Most study participants did not begin their romantic lives as polyamorous. Like Makayla and Joel in the first vignette, they met another person, fell in love and married. Initially, study participants largely believed in the hegemonic romantic love ideology and adhered to many aspects of traditional gender power dynamics. But then something happened in their lives to create a change. In some cases, one spouse also fell in love with another person, and, rather than divorce, the couple decided to become polyamorous. In other cases, couples simply made a joint decision that they wanted to pursue additional relationships to add to their lives. Regardless of how couples morphed into polyamory, the process and difficulties they faced were similar. They researched polyamory, had long, honest, open and often stressful discussions as a couple and with potential partners, and came to truly believe that love could be shared with multiple people without threatening their marriages.

Yet, despite this preparation and agreement, couples found practicing polyamory far more challenging than they anticipated. As polyamorists began dating and/or falling in love with others and watching their spouses do the same, many experienced surprising and difficult emotions, such as jealousy, insecurity, and fear. These feelings emerged largely because couples still retained notions of traditional gender dynamics in intimate relationships. Consider the following representative data excerpts that illustrate the feelings that emerged as spouses began extramarital love relationships:

Kyle and Cindy (married for 16 years and polyamorous for 3 years)

I felt jealous and scared she wouldn't love me as much. For me, some of it was sexual—like is he hung like a mule and better in bed? Some of it was emotional—like is she still feeling the same way about me? I was worried I wasn't going to measure up on either front. (Kyle)

I got mad at Kyle because I was jealous and uncertain. His girlfriend is so pretty, and I would see him do nice things for her. I wondered if they had better sex, and the thought drove me crazy. She made him laugh too. It was hard. What if he enjoyed her more? (Cindy)

Brad and Tawna (married for 18 years and polyamorous for 5 years)

I was surprised by how jealous I was when Tawna started having sex with her boyfriend. He's more muscular than I am—a good looking man—and I wondered if she had more orgasms with him. And he took her to nice places, and she had fun with him. I got angry because I was worried she would pick him eventually. (Brad)

I had huge initial jealousy and fear. It was hard. She is like top model gorgeous, and she is fun to be around. I was so scared I would become less important. I mean how do I beat that? (Tawna)

While these excerpts reveal that spouses felt jealous and anxious, we also see that they do so in gendered ways. Kyle and Brad reference fears about masculine competition and performance (e.g. concerns about bigger penises, more muscles, and more orgasms), worrying that, if they were outdone by another man, then they would not "measure up" and other men would win their wives. Similarly, Cindy and Tawna reference feminine concerns about girlfriends being pretty and pleasing to be around, fearing that other women may be more alluring and satisfying and thus replace them. Note that participants' initial fears are gender coded; that is, men are sexual agents who worry about being out performed, while women are more passive, fearing they will not be pleasing enough. These concerns and feelings reveal that participants maintained at least some belief in traditional gender dynamics and meanings as they entered polyamorous relationships. As a result, they had anxiety about their own gender performances, perceiving that a "poor" performance would leave them vulnerable to demotion or rejection in their relationships. At this point, success or "winning" in love was still tied to proper gender enactment.

If these couples were to establish satisfying and joyful polyamorous relationships, then they would have to develop strategies to manage and mitigate these negative emotions (Sheff, 2014, p. 119). To do so, study participants had honest ongoing conversations about how they felt about their relationships and what triggered negative feelings. They then used these conversations to develop strategies to avoid these triggers and to reassure one another of their love. In a sense, while participants certainly rejected the "only" monogamous aspect of the hegemonic romantic love ideology, they still retained remnants of this ideology, wanting to be reassured that they were "the one" most important person in their spouse's life (Wolkomir, 2015). The strategies, or what participants called "guidelines" or "foundational rules," couples developed to create these reassurances fell into two basic categories—those designed to prevent negative feelings and those constructed to repair them if they occurred.

The two most common strategies participants used to impede corrosive emotions were the establishment of "veto power" and the preservation of special spaces for the couple. Veto power generally meant that either person in the couple could say no to an additional partner, sexual behavior, or generic activity that made that person uncomfortable or created stress. For example, Joshua and Liz agreed that they could veto an additional partner if either felt that person "did not respect their marriage or time boundaries or was attempting to create fights between them." Brad and Tawna vetoed overnight trips with outside partners because they believed they should begin and end each day together. At times, couples vetoed a kind of date or a specific event because it felt dangerous or intrusive. Brett, for instance, did not want Rosie to go see their favorite band in concert with another person. To achieve similar goals, couples would also reserve special spaces just for them. Some couples promised that they would observe all holidays, birthdays, and special occasions together on their actual day, marking them as the most authentic, and that celebrations with other partners would be relegated to substitute days. Some couples agreed to reserve certain sexual practices—like oral sex or sexual role playing—only for another, again marking the couple as most special. Others reserved certain restaurants or mundane, yet meaningful, activities just for the couple. For instance, Cora and Clyde agreed that they could never take another person to the restaurant they went to on their first date. These sorts of agreements and accommodations imbued the primary relationship with a kind of authenticity and specialness and marked the spousal partner as the most important love–if not the only one.

In addition, if something happened that hurt a spouse's feeling or left him/her feeling neglected, unappreciated, or angry, then couples agreed that resolving these feelings would take precedence over anything or anyone.

Consider the following example that demonstrates how couples navigated these situations. Moira had a birthday party for Mark and invited her boyfriend. At first, all the party goers were laughing and talking together, and things seemed to be going nicely. Mark, however, became a bit morose and seemed to want to be left alone. So Moira sat with her boyfriend. Mark saw them laughing and kissing and remembers thinking, "usually I don't care, but it's MY day." He told Moira he was feeling pushed aside. She immediately found a polite way to usher everyone out, and she and Mark spent the rest of the night together. Mark explained that Moira's "instant attention to me when I said I felt left alone—the way she herded everyone else out and just sat with me—made me feel how much she values our love. It ended up a good birthday." Here, Moira's willingness to dismiss everyone else and meet Mark's needs soothed his hurt feelings and reassured him that he was the most important person to Moira.

Taken together, these sorts of strategies function to mark the couples' love as the most special and important. Veto power established a shared sense of control and centrality for partners. Reserving special spaces and events emphasized the primary relationship as the most authentic, while remediating any emotional duress a spouse experienced quickly showed unique care above others. In these ways, such strategies staved off the kinds of anxieties and fears that emerged from participants' continued adherence to an ideological framework in which gender performance was equated to worthiness and winning at love. While these couples certainly disregarded some traditionally gendered notions—such as the masculine idea of ownership of women's bodies or that women who had multiple sex partners were sluts—and now perceived men and women as comparable desiring sexual beings, they had not yet entirely transformed the connections between gender, power and relationship form. For some, men were still competing with other men to win women, and women were still competing to be the most pleasing to men to attract and keep them—an arrangement that imbues masculinity with superiority, power, and agency relative to femininity.

To alter this arrangement substantially, couples had to fully challenge and reject the last remnants of monogamy and the perceived need for gendered competition. Some study participants (12 or 6 couples) were able to fully reject monogamy as a framework for relationships. In other words, they not only dismissed the idea of a "one and only," but they also no longer felt it was important to have a ONE most important person or relationship. As a result, they could revise correspondent gender meanings through what they learned as they negotiated the difficulties of creating satisfying multiple partner relationships. Through their struggles to mitigate jealousy and insecurity and their experiences navigating the "guidelines" they established, they came to understand love differently. Through practice, they discovered—in both a felt and understood way—that love did not require any hierarchical arrangement. In fact, any hierarchical order came to be understood as antithetical to love. Instead, they began to simply perceive their love relationships as inherently valuable. Each was different and met different needs. They learned that they enjoyed and struggled with varied aspects of each relationship, and that each enriched their lives. As a result, they no longer felt they had to compete to preserve or protect their relationships, allowing them (to a large extent) to disregard traditional gender power relations and thus minimize emergent negative feelings of jealousy and insecurity. Rather, they now focused on cooperating to meet partners' needs and desires. The following two interview excerpts provide representative examples of this transformation:

> When we first had other lovers, we had all these rules because we were scared and trying to protect ourselves. You know, what if she is hotter and better in bed? What if his dick is bigger? That sort of thing. We both worried, but as we worked through those fears, we realized they were just part of the old monogamy system meant to keep us in line. Love isn't measurable as the best, and people aren't possessions. Different loves meet different needs, and they can all be wonderful. Then the rules just fell away, and we give one another the freedom to experience love and joy as we can. (Cindy)

> I used to get a sense of inadequacy as a man when Sherry (his wife) went out on dates, but now I don't. That's because of my relationship with Amy (his lover). I love Amy and we are close, but she is not competing with Sherry. They are different things, and both are important. I am a better man because I have more love. I'm not looking at myself like some macho thing anymore. I'm glad Sherry has that experience too. We know you can love more than one person, and it isn't about possession or being the best. We don't need rules; we just have to love well. (Samuel)

Here, participants explicitly link gendered power relations and competition to "the old monogamy system," noting that this system induced fear that nonconformity to gender ideals would result in threatened love relationships. Once they are able, through their lived experiences with multiple loves, to let go of the idea of love as possession that requires successful gender enactment (e.g., being "hotter" as a woman or "some macho thing" as a man), they can let go of the "rules" that were meant to ensure their number one status in a relationship. They instead focus on "loving well" in all relationships; that is, they focus on meeting partners' needs and creating mutual satisfaction and joy. Under these conditions, the relational power dynamic between masculinity and femininity is transformed and leveled.

WHAT DO WE LEARN FROM POLYAMORY?

This study of polyamory starkly reveals the inequalities that undergird and are reproduced in our existing system of gender and sexual relations. In this system, hegemonic gender ideals and hierarchy are tightly interwoven with monogamy. The hegemonic romantic love story/ideology mandates and valorizes monogamy as the only right and good form of intimate relationship. To attain this relationship, or so the romantic love story goes, couples follow a gendered prescription for behavior that continually constructs masculinity as dominant to femininity. For many people, adherence and conformity to this prescription seem critical because doing gender "right" is a way to fend off competition from others and maintain the love relationship. This configuration, and how powerfully it works in people's lives, is made visible through the examination of how polyamorous couples negotiate multiple partner intimacies. Put simply, we see that the more fully participants disregard the monogamous model as relationship form, the more fully they altered the relationship between masculinity and femininity from binary, opposing and hierarchical toward cooperative and egalitarian.

These findings do not necessarily suggest that we should do away with monogamy and adopt polyamory as a new ideal relationship form in society. Instead, an examination of polyamorous relationships provides a lens through which to glimpse alternative cultural pathways we might traverse to undo gender binaries and diminish hierarchies. Polyamorous love stories and relationships allow us to reimagine what is possible with regard to gender, power and intimacy. These stories reveal that, if love done "right" no longer requires a "one and only" held in place by vigilance about the gendered competition, then the intersection between intimacy, gender and relationship form can be more fluid. A polyamorous template for love relationships does not endorse one particular form of intimacy, or number of partners, or a set of gender relations; rather, it focuses on how well relationships function to meet all partners' needs and desires. Instead of conceptualizing love and intimacy as a zero sum game, polyamorists perceive love as additive, making notions of competition, possession, and hierarchy seem both foolish and corrosive. Put simply, polyamorist love stories show us how to think differently about how we occupy erotic and intimate spaces and how men and women exist ideologically in relation to one another. This "happily ever after" thus provides a model of how we might start to rethink gender relations, regardless of whether we choose one, two, or more partners.

REFERENCES

Bartky, S. (1999). *Femininity and domination: Studies in the phenomenology of oppression.* New York, NY: Routledge.

Bauer, R. (2010). Non-monogamy in queer BDSM communities: Putting the sex back into alternative relationship practices and discourse. In M. Barker & D. Langdridge (Eds.), *Understanding non-monogamies.* New York, NY: Routledge.

Bordo, S. (1999). *The male body: A new look at men in public and in private.* New York, NY: Farrar, Straus, and Giroux.

Connell, R. W. (1995). *Masculinities.* Berkeley, CA: University of California Press.

Coontz, S. (2005). *Marriage: A history.* New York, NY: Penguin Books.

Galician, M. L. (2004). *Sex, love & romance in the mass media: Analysis & criticism of unrealistic portrayals & their influence.* Mahwah, NJ: Lawrence Erlbaum Associates.

Haritaworn, J., Lin, C., & Klesse, C. (2006). Poly/logue: A critical introduction to polyamory. *Sexualities, 9,* 515–529.

Hesse-Biber, S. (2007). *The cult of thinness.* Oxford: Oxford University Press.

Ingraham, C. (1999). *White weddings: Romancing heterosexuality in popular culture.* New York, NY: Routledge.

Jackson, S., & Scott, S. (2004). The personal is still political: Heterosexuality, feminism and monogamy. *Feminism & Psychology, 14,* 151–157.

Jamieson, L. (2004). Intimacy, negotiated nonmonogamy, and the limits of the couple. In J. Duncombe, H. Kaeren, A. Graham, & M. Dennis (Eds.), *The state of affairs: Explorations in infidelity and commitment.* Mahwah, NJ: Lawrence Erlbaum Associates.

Jeffreys, S. (1996). Heterosexuality and the desire for gender. In D. Richardson (Ed.), *Theorizing heterosexuality: Telling it straight.* Philadelphia, PA: Open University Press.

Kim, J. L., Sursall, C. L., Collins, K., & Zylbergold, B. A. (2007). From sex to sexuality: Exposing the heterosexual script on primetime network television. *Journal of Sex Research, 44,* 1–45.

Lorber, J. (1994). *Paradoxes of gender.* New Haven, CT: Yale University Press.

Martin, K., & Kasyak, E. (2009). Heteroromantic love and heterosexiness in children's G rated films. *Gender & Society, 23,* 315–336.

Rubin, G. (1993). Thinking sex: Notes for a radical theory of the politics of sexuality. In H. Abelove, M. Barale, & D. Halperin (Eds.), *The lesbian and gay studies reader.* New York, NY: Routledge.

Schippers, M. (2007). Recovering the feminine other: Masculinity, femininity, and the gender hegemony. *Theory & Society, 36,* 85–102.

Schippers, M. (2008). *Beyond monogamy: Polyamory and the future of polyqueer sexualities.* New York, NY: New York University Press.

Sheff, E. (2014). *The polyamorists next door: Inside multiple-partner relationships and families*. New York, NY: Rowman & Littlefield.

Swidler, A. (2001). *Talk of love: How culture matters*. Chicago, IL: University of Chicago Press.

Wade, L., & Marx Ferree, M. (2015). *Gender, ideas, interactions, institutions*. New York, NY: W.W. Norton.

Ward, M. (2003). Understanding the role of entertainment media in the sexual socialization of American youth: A review of Empirical Research. *Developmental Review, 23*, 347–388.

Wolkomir, M. (2004). "Giving it up to god": Negotiating femininity in support groups for wives of ex-gay Christian men. *Gender & Society, 18*, 735–755.

Wolkomir, M. (2015). One but not the only: Reconfiguring intimacy in multiple partner relationships. *Qualitative Sociology, 38*, 417–438.

KRISTA L. BENSON

7. MARGINS OF IDENTITY

Queer Polyamorous Women's Navigation of Identity

INTRODUCTION

In the United States in the 21st century, assumptions of people's heterosexuality and monogamy abound. Unless we know otherwise, many people assume that the "average person" is heterosexual and monogamous. This assumption of the normativity of heterosexuality and monogamy—the assumption that heterosexuality and monogamy are normal, more common, and given more social value—impacts many people, but especially polyamorous queer people.

Though many people think of sexuality as being a really important part of their identities, fewer are aware that sexuality as a part of identity is actually based in a particular historical trajectory and culture. People have always engaged in sexual acts with others, but those sexual acts are not and have not always determined where a person fits in within their larger community. Sexuality as a part of identity emerged in Europe based around the Enlightenment, a preoccupation with sexual acts and how they impact people's identities which were exported to other lands alongside European colonization (e.g. Foucault, 1990; Stoler, 1995; Lacqueur, 1990). At the same time, there are other groups of people for whom the people who someone has sex with or their sense of gender have nothing to do with their place in the community. For many indigenous people of North America, for example, the important questions are not "who do you want to have sex with?" but "what work will you do?" (e.g. Driskill, 2016; Driskill, Finley, Gilley, & Morgensen, 2011; Erai, 2011; Gilley, 2011).[1]

However, within a context informed by this European history, questions about sexuality and how sexuality impacts a person's identity are common. In my interviews with polyamorous adults in the United States in 2011, I found that many of my participants explained polyamory as being a key part of their identity—a polyamorous person—and not just a set of relationship, interpersonal, or intimate practices that they engaged in. This is also often

© KONINKLIJKE BRILL NV, LEIDEN, 2019 | DOI:10.1163/9789004414105_008

true for queer people, wherein queer is as much an identity as a set of sexual or interpersonal practices (e.g. Alexander, 2008; Khayatt, 2002; Whitney, 2006).

To explore the relationship between queer identification and polyamorous identification, I examine the narratives of three polyamorous queer women who I interviewed for a larger interview and participatory ethnographic project to examine how polyamorous identity and queer identity were very important to these women. I analyze these same interviews in a related article, where I delve more deeply into queer theory and the happy object of queer identities (Benson, 2017). In this analysis, I use the theories of feminist queer theorists Lynn Huffer (2013) and Sara Ahmed (2011). Specifically, I draw on Huffer's critique of the function of stable queer identities and how they can limit queer people. This is combined with the insights from Ahmed's theoretical exploration of the role of happiness and the things that should make us happy (called "happy objects") for queer subjects. Here, by "stable identity," I am referring to the ways that people identify with and as certain things in ways that they hope will be consistent across their lifetime and understood in consistent ways by others.

In this analysis, I seek to answer the following questions: why do these queer, polyamorous women seek to establish a stable and legible identity as "polyamorous" in their interpersonal relationships? When they attempt to establish polyamorous as an identity, are they successful? Why or why not? I argue that stable identity is both something that queer polyamorous people seek as a way to find happiness and often results in queer polyamorous people who find themselves misunderstood, unsupported, and misidentified by others.[2]

THE PROMISES AND LIMITS OF IDENTITY: A CASE STUDY

Methodology

When considering the role that claims for stable identity play in the lives of polyamorous people, it immediately becomes important to consider lives that are lived queerly and the lives of people who identify as queer. Though the majority of research on polyamorous people has focused primarily on people who identify as gay or lesbian, with some exploration of heterosexual or bisexual participants, there is a significant population of polyamorous adults who identify as "queer," a term that they strongly differentiate from other sexual identity terms. From June to November 2011, I conducted

27 interviews with polyamorous-identified individuals between the ages of 24 and 42 living in or near Seattle, WA; Boston, MA; Baltimore, MD; Washington, DC; Minneapolis, MN; and New York, NY.

Interviews were conducted in locations of choice of the participants, usually their homes or coffee shops, and the names of all people who took place in this study and the names of people to whom they referred in the interviews have been changed to maintain anonymity. Participants were recruited through a variety of methods, including online polyamorous listservs, my personal connections, and referrals from other participants in the study (often referred to as a combination of "convenience sampling" and "snowball sampling"). Additionally, all initial communications identified me as an openly polyamorous person, a fact that was identified as particularly important for participants who did not know me prior to the study. Indeed, their acknowledgement of my identity was a way that identity was always at work in this study. The only criteria for participation was that the individuals must be over the age of 18 and must identify with, were currently in, or have previously been in relationships that they identified as open, polyamorous, or consensually non-monogamous.

Findings

It is important to note that my study shares a sample problem with other studies of sexuality (e.g. Kleese, 2006), in that the majority of my participants were white people with middle- or upper-middle class backgrounds with little participation from people of color or lower- or working-class individuals. Though this sample limitation is important to note, the goal of this study is not to generalize about the shared narratives of polyamorous people, but rather to explore the worlds, discourse, and meanings that inform their various understandings of the world. In the service of this exploration, this article explores three individuals selected from this larger study.

At the time of the interviews, Karen was a 31-year-old white woman from the Seattle area who had been married for four years to Corey, her primary partner, a relationship which had become polyamorous after two years of marriage. Karen was casually dating other people during that time but did not have a secondary partner or partners. Rachel was a 32-year-old white woman who lived in New York City, who was in the process of breaking up with and living in the same house as Kent, her boyfriend of five years, with whom she still described herself as being emotionally involved. Rachel was also currently dating James and had occasional sexual contact with James and his wife Lisa, while also dating at least four other people. Shira was a 31-year-old Arab and Jewish woman living in Washington D.C. who had a long-distance relationship with her primary partner, Derek, whom she had been dating for a little more than a year but had very recently established as her primary partner. A year and a half before, she had ended an 8-year abusive relationship; she had also been dating other people. This was Shira's first attempt at an open or polyamorous relationship.

Identity Foreclosed: Polyamorous Identity's Promises and Limitations

Many of my participants in the larger study and all three of the women in this case study expressed that their ideas about non-monogamy were informed by the appeal of interdependence, support, and, in Rachel's words "keeping myself open to love and loving." She explains:

> [As a polyamorous person], I feel a lot less alone…we're also social animals, right, that rely on other monkeys to help us feel better in times of stress and then also share our joy with in times of happiness….For me, it's really about support and it's about, even though loving myself has to come from myself, that support that you get, for example when [one partner] texted me on Sunday to let me know that somebody was thinking about me and concerned for my feelings, that's priceless.

Karen concurred with Rachel's assessment of the draw of being able to bring multiple people into her life in a loving or intimate way. Interestingly, she was most comfortable explaining this through connection with someone else—via telling me about a conversation that she and her husband, Corey, had about this topic. Her very articulation of the concept was a relational one.

> My husband said it best when he said "I like having the freedom to fully explore my emotions that I have with and towards other people without fearing repercussions." He's like, you know, when you first get a crush and you're all springy and in love and like "oh my god, this person is so [exciting]." You don't have to stifle that, you know? You don't have to really, like, stifle your emotions down because you're married…now we have the ability to have a full range of emotions while in the safety of knowing at the end of the day, you're going to hang out with your best friend.

For both Rachel and Karen, the explicit acknowledgement of bringing more love and connection to others into their lives were explicitly beneficial aspects of polyamorous identity. In fact, Karen's way of communicating this acknowledgement of love and community is expressed through a communal explanation: not her own words, but her words as mediated by and expanding upon her husband's ideas. Relationality is vital to how both Karen and Rachel experience their polyamorous identities.

The benefits of polyamory went beyond the practices of non-monogamy and into the communities that they built. For Shira, this benefit was actually about how polyamory allowed her to connect with her partners through being more honest. Though this was Shira's first *consensually* non-monogamous relationship, it was not her first non-monogamous one. While in previous relationships that were marked as monogamous, she explained, "I had some affairs. I've started this radical thing where I'm telling people what I'm doing." When we discussed this more in depth, she explained that it was freeing to be able to honestly express interest or attraction in people. "Maybe it wouldn't be non-monogamous if we lived in the same time zone, you know? But either way, it's nice to not have to sneak around, to be able to tell him what's really going on in my life." In many ways, these comments are way one to understand that these women were using the identity of polyamorous to convey important parts of not just their sexual and romantic practices, but about how their ethics and commitments shaped them as people.

Though all three participants expressed similar foundations of their polyamorous identity—building community, being able to be honest with partners, and being open to loving—it would be misleading to assume that those shared foundations made explaining those foundations to other people easy, both with non-monogamous people and with monogamous ones. Shira discusses a conversation that she had on a date with someone that she had recently outlined her relationship status—in a relationship with a primary long-distance partner with some casual local secondary relationships—and that the agreement with her primary partner had put some limitations on the kinds of sexual acts that she engaged in without him around. After going through a pretty detailed explanation, including her openness to intimacy and wanting to get the feedback from any potential partners on how this felt for them, she received a response that seemed to completely misunderstand all of the things that she had just set up.

He goes "So, you have a boyfriend and you just sleep with everybody and he's fine with it?" No, that is precisely not what is happening here, that is the polar motherfucking opposite of what I just said to you! And I've had that reaction of, you know, "You're just doing this to have sex with everybody." Clearly, I'm not, because I'm not having sex with anybody! I'm having different kinds of relationships and if I met somebody that I really wanted to have sex with, I would probably revisit that.

Shira had articulated foundations of the reasons for her non-monogamy, looking both for consent and understandings from any potential partners. This fundamental misunderstanding of all of that labor was, understandably, frustrating for her. Shira did not know if this date had identified with polyamory or had any experience in non-monogamous relationships. However, since polyamorous people are simply less common than monogamous people, it is likely that he had little to no consensually non-monogamous experience and didn't identify as polyamorous. Here, her identification as polyamorous and explanation of what that meant in her intimate relationships did not build the connections *or* convey accurate information to the person she was on a date with.

Misunderstandings about what it meant to be non-monogamous was not limited to potential partners, however. Rachel discussed a similar frustration with a long-term friend who was not polyamorous but who was, in Rachel's words, "a complete hippy" who she had perceived as being supportive of Rachel's polyamorous identity and all of her relationships.

I was talking with her about Kent, the person I was in a relationship with for about five years and I was, um, explaining that I was also starting to date someone new and that I was excited about it and her comment to me was "Wow, way to work on your relationship [with Kent]." You know? And I was like, "I think that shows a really deep and fundamental misunderstanding that you just don't get what this about at all and I think that that was a really shitty thing to say and that actually made me feel really shitty." You know? So then to have that conversation, she apologized to me, but I still don't think that she really gets it.

To some degree, it is understandable that the women in this case study experienced misunderstandings with people who either have an unknown relationship to non-monogamous communities and identities or who are not polyamorous. However, my participants' experiences of foreclosure or misunderstanding were not limited to monogamous people who weren't familiar with polyamory. Rachel explained her recent breakup with a partner as a result of just such a lack of understanding.

This person that just broke my heart, [he is part of] a couple who I've known for a long time who mostly [sexually] play with other people together but say that they're poly. But it turns out that the reason that he can't be involved with me [anymore], even though we both say that we're in love with one another, is because [his wife] is not comfortable with…me being sexual with him because we share such an emotional depth. And, to me, that is exactly the opposite of how I practice polyamory. Because, in my world view, that relationship is worth exploring because the depth of the love is there and, yeah, and that's really scary for people, you know, and they try to put, you know, I think boundaries are good, but I think at the same time, people try to create these false boundaries to try to keep people from "falling in love" with somebody.

It's important here to emphasize that I do not see these misunderstandings as being about misunderstanding the practice of polyamory, but rather as misunderstandings about what it means to *be* a polyamorous person. Even among other polyamorous people, Rachel's identity as a polyamorous person is intertwined with her practices of polyamory. When this couple does not share her practices, she differentiates "play [sexually] with other people" and "being poly." For her, then, engaging in polyamorous relationships or sexual play or engagement with multiple people is not the same as *being* poly.

Karen experienced a similar kind of contrast of definitions and the ways that they impact practice and identity at a polyamorous meetup in her city where she was introduced to two different identity terms by a participant in the meetup: "we-poly" and "me-poly."

So, apparently, "we-poly" is where you and your partner have other partners and they all know about each other and you do things as a group and you live as a community…and "me-poly" is where I am with my husband, [where] I go out and have a different relationship that he is not really a part of and he has other relationships that I'm not a part of.

The distinctions between "we-poly" and "me-poly" explicitly frame polyamorous practice as connected to polyamorous identity, as the terms as Karen explained them were actually identity terms.

[At the meetup], this woman was like "I'm a we-poly person and I was dating a me-poly person and I thought they were embarrassed of me or ashamed of me," blah blah blah. And I was like, I felt so attacked because I didn't come out as a me-poly person, but I was like "Yes, but don't you understand that I have two days a week with my husband? I don't want to spend them with whoever else is in my life. I don't want to spend them with my other people, I want to spend them with him."

These terms, as Karen experienced them, were not just identity terms, but felt as if they were ranked in terms of evaluation: we-poly are better, or in some way more evolved, than me-poly people. Though the other two women in this case study didn't use the terms "we-poly" or "me-poly," all three of the participants discussed the frustration or even relationships that ended when other people's understandings of what it meant to be a polyamorous person did not align with their idea of themselves, their ethics, or their experiences.

For all three of these women, the identity of queer polyamorous was one that they valued and that they wanted to convey information about who they are to others. Queer polyamorous, they hoped, would indicate certain ethical and interpersonal commitments, such as openness to loving, genuine connection with others, and honesty in their interpersonal relationships. Though this claimed identity certainly worked in some circumstances, this chapter highlights how frequently the claimed identity of queer polyamorous failed to do the work the women wanted it to do. Instead, all three of them have at various points found themselves misunderstood by both monogamous and polyamorous people at all of the points where "queer, "polyamorous," and "queer polyamorous" breakdown as a cohesive and coherent identity that is understood by other people.

CONCLUSION

In all of these examples, my participants' attempts to hold onto a stable identity of polyamorous fail, at least in part. The identity of polyamorous does not convey to other people—both polyamorous and monogamous people—what they intend it to say. The happy object of identity, of polyamorous identity in particular, to help them build connections with other people and be open to loving is frequently foreclosed. Stable identity doesn't provide the happiness that it promises, as Ahmed would predict and as Huffer explains. This chapter highlights both why these polyamorous queer women strive for a stable, coherent identity as polyamorous *and* why the work they want that identity to do is so often letting them down. Queer polyamorous women have turned away from conventional happy objects twice already—heterosexuality and monogamy. Stability of identity is one of the conventional "happy objects" that they can still have access to and yet even that happy object doesn't uniformly satisfy or work.

The attempts to imbue a stable queer polyamorous identity with their own happiness makes sense, but also often fails them. This is why Karen is so disappointed in what she perceives as judgement in how she does "me-poly" and why Shira is so frustrated when a date misunderstands her polyamory as being about sexual promiscuity. For all three of these participants, the work that they wanted the identity of polyamorous to do—to connect them authentically and accurately to other people—often fails, both with monogamous people and with other polyamorous people.

Queer polyamorous women navigating a world that normalizes and values monogamy and heterosexuality understandably strive toward stable, coherent identities—as queer, as polyamorous—to help them explain themselves to the world and build community with other people. The effectiveness of this strategy, unfortunately, is uneven. This is particularly troubling because it is this very connection to community that build the foundations of these three women's polyamorous practice and identity.

It seems that polyamorous identities provide a great deal of promise for queer polyamorous women, but there is are hidden limitations to those promises. Polyamorous identities can and sometimes do facilitate queer polyamorous women experiencing more emotional connections and closer and more honest relationships. However, it is important to recognize that these relationships and these identities are non-normative and frequently misunderstood by both monogamous and polyamorous people. The promise of identity, the happy object of stable identity, can and perhaps will always be limited for these queer polyamorous women.

NOTES

[1] Many thanks to my colleague and friend Andrea Riley-Mukavetz for helping me articulate this framing so as to not continue to normalize European settler notions of sexuality.
[2] This chapter was drafted in a meeting with my faculty writing group. Thanks to the Grand Valley State University Cook-DeWitt Center, Denise Goerisch, and Andrea Riley-Mukavetz for the inspiration. Many thanks to Wrane Soule for feedback on drafts of this chapter.

REFERENCES

Ahmed, S. (2010). *The promise of happiness*. Durham, NC: Duke University Press.
Alexander, B. K. (2006). *Performing Black masculinity: Race, culture, and queer identity*. Lanham, MD: Rowman Altamira Press.

Benson, K. (2017). Tensions of subjectsivity: The instability of queer polyamorous identity and community. *Sexualities, 20*(1–2), 24–40.

Bersani, L. (2010). *Is the rectum a grave?* Chicago, IL & London: University of Chicago Press.

Butler, J. (1999). *Gender trouble*. New York, NY: Routledge.

Butler, J. (2004). *Undoing gender*. New York, NY & London: Routledge.

Cohen, C. (1997). Punks, bulldaggers, and welfare queens: The radical potential of queer politics? In E. P. Johnson & M. Henderson (Eds.), *Black queer studies: A critical reader* (pp. 21–51). Durham, NC: Duke University Press.

Dean, T. (2000). *Beyond sexuality*. Chicago, IL: University of Chicago Press.

Deri, J. (2015). *Love's refraction: Jealousy and compersion in queer women's polyamorous relationships*. Toronto: University of Toronto Press.

Driskill, Q. L. (2016). *Asegi stories: Cherokee queer and two-spirit memory*. Tucson, AZ: University of Arizona Press.

Driskill, Q. L., Finley, C., Gilley, B. J., &Morgensen, S. L. (2011). Introduction. In Q. Driskill, C. Finley, B. J. Gilley, & S. L. Morgensen (Eds.), *Queer Indigenous studies: Critical interventions in theory, politics, and literature* (pp. 1–20). Tucson, AZ: University of Arizona Press.

Eng, D. L. (2010). *The feeling of kinship: Queer liberalism and the racialization of intimacy*. Durham, NC: Duke University Press.

Erai, M. (2011). A queer caste: Mixing race and sexuality in colonial New Zealand. In Q. Driskill, C. Finley, B. J. Gilley, & S. L. Morgensen (Eds.), *Queer Indigenous studies: Critical interventions in theory, politics, and literature* (pp. 66–80). Tucson, AZ: University of Arizona Press.

Foucault, M. (1990). *A history of sexuality* (Vol. 1, R. Huxley, Trans.). New York, NY: Vintage Books.

Foucault, M., Davidson, A. I., & Burchell, G. (2008). *The birth of biopolitics: Lectures at the Collège de France, 1978–1979*. New York, NY: Springer.

Gilley, B. J. (2011). Two-spirit men's sexual survivance against the inequality of desire. In Q. Driskill, C. Finley, B. J. Gilley, & S. L. Morgensen (Eds.), *Queer Indigenous studies: Critical interventions in theory, politics, and literature* (pp. 123–131). Tucson, AZ: University of Arizona Press.

Hames-García, M. (2011). Queer theory revisited. In M. Hames-García & E. J. Martínez (Eds.), *Gay Latino studies: A critical reader* (pp. 19–45). Durham, NC: Duke University Press.

Heckert, J. (2010). Love without borders? Intimacy, identity and the state of compulsory monogamy. In M. Barker & D. Langdridge (Eds.), *Understanding non-monogamies* (pp. 255–266). London: Routledge.

Hollinbaugh, A. L. (2001). *My dangerous desires: A queer girl dreaming her way home*. Durham, NC: Duke University Press.

Hong G. K., & Ferguson, R. A. (2011). Introduction. In G. K. Hong & R. A. Ferguson (Eds.), *Strange affinities: The gender and sexual politics of comparative racialization* (pp. 1–22). Durham, NC: Duke University Press.

Huffer, L. (2010). *Mad for Foucault*. New York, NY: Columbia University Press.

Huffer, L. (2013). *Are the lips a grave? A queer feminist on the ethics of sex*. New York, NY: Columbia University Press.

Johnson, E. P. (2005) 'Quare' studies, or (almost) everything I know about queer studies I learned from my grandmother. In E. P. Johnson & M. Henderson (Eds.), *Black queer studies: A critical anthology* (pp. 124–157). Durham, NC: Duke University Press.

Khayatt, D. (2002). Toward a queer identity. *Sexualities, 5*(4), 487–501.

Klesse, C. (2006). Polyamory and its 'others': Contesting the terms of non-monogamy. *Sexualities, 9*(5), 565–583.

Klesse, C. (2014). Polyamory: Intimate practice, identity, or sexual orientation? *Sexualities, 17*(1–2), 81–99.

Laqueur, T. W. (1990). *Making sex: Body and gender from the Greeks to Freud.* Cambridge, MA: Harvard University Press.

Muñoz, J. E. (2009). *Cruising Utopia: The then and there of queer futurity.* New York, NY: New York University Press.

Robinson, M. (2013). Polyamory and monogamy as strategic identities. *Journal of Bisexuality, 13*(1), 21–38.

Rubin, G. (2011). Blood under the bridge: Reflections on 'thinking sex.' *GLQ, 17*(1), 15–48.

Stoler, A. L. (1995). *Race and the education of desire: Foucault's history of sexuality and the colonial order of things.* Durham, NC: Duke University Press.

Whitney, C. (2006). Intersections in identity – Identity development among queer women with disabilities. *Sexuality and Disability, 24*(1), 39–52.

EMILY PAIN

8. RACE, CLASS, GENDER, AND RELATIONSHIP POWER IN QUEER POLYAMORY

Millennials are increasingly embracing nonmonogamous relationships.
(Rolling Stone)

For many millennials, polyamory is gaining popularity.
(Pride)

Polyamorous relationships may be the future of love.
(BBC)

Is the family of the future polyamorous?
(Mic)

Over the past few years, news and culture media outlets have framed polyamory as an increasingly popular relationship form among young adults. These portrayals are much improved over earlier generations of news/culture pieces that posed polyamory as 'controversial' or conflated the practice with 'open marriage,' 'infidelities,' or sexual 'fun' (see M., 2018). But do these recent portrayals gloss over the challenges of being in relationships that require ongoing communication and negotiation? Some pieces focus on managing jealousy, which is certainly a challenge for many polyamorists; however, there are other issues to consider. For instance, polyamorists value *egalitarianism*—being equals in all aspects of a partnership—but are they egalitarian in practice? How do relationship power dynamics arise in these relationships? I was interested in these questions, so I examined data relating to relationship power from my study on LGBTQ+ ('queer') polyamory. I found that race, class, and gender were sources of relationship power in queer polyamorous partnerships. In other words, social inequalities can permeate even the most egalitarian-oriented relationships.

QUEER POLYAMORY AND RELATIONSHIP POWER

Polyamory is a relationship practice that is open to involving simultaneous relationships with multiple partners. It is one form of consensual

© KONINKLIJKE BRILL NV, LEIDEN, 2019 | DOI:10.1163/9789004414105_009

nonmonogamy, where partners negotiate nonmonogamous relationship agreements or boundaries; however, polyamory is distinct for its emphasis on disclosure, honest communication, and love or emotional connections. For instance, polyamorous partners might establish agreements regarding honesty about feelings for other people, the number of partners they are comfortable with, which sexual practices are permitted with other partners, and more (Deri, 2015; Klesse, 2007; Sheff, 2014; Wosick-Correa, 2010). Polyamorous relationship negotiation processes are often ongoing, as partners (re)evaluate existing agreements and establish new boundaries (Frank & DeLamater, 2010). Whereas relationship agreements vary widely, polyamorous values are typically uniform. Many polyamorists are invested in feminist and anti-racist politics and frequently cite honesty, trust, and egalitarianism as values that guide their relationship practices (Deri, 2015; Klesse, 2007, 2010; Schippers, 2016; Sheff, 2014; Wosick-Correa, 2010). Similarly, queer partnerships are often structured around an egalitarian goal (Carrington, 1999; Weeks, Heaphy, & Donovan, 2001). Queer polyamorists are likely to be deeply invested in achieving egalitarianism in their partnerships.

However, in both queer and polyamorous relationships, partners might not be as egalitarian as they believe themselves to be (Carrington, 1999; Klesse, 2007, 2010; Weeks, Heaphy, & Donovan, 2001). For instance, polyamorists who express feminist and egalitarian ideologies can fail to realize how those ideologies do not effectively translate into practice (Klesse, 2010). Weeks, Heaphy, and Donovan (2001) found in their study on non-heterosexual intimacies that while participants strongly valued egalitarianism, nearly all "identified factors that had the potential to cause inequality" in their partnerships (p. 114). Factors that can weaken egalitarianism include differing identities or backgrounds such as race, class, gender, and other areas of 'social location.' In other words, one source of relationship power imbalances is *differential positioning*, where partners have different social locations. In a study on queer nonmonogamies, Klesse (2007) found that differential positioning "may result in unequal power between partners when they are negotiating questions around nonmonogamy," particularly "in cases of inter-partner disagreement or conflict" (pp. 124–132). Thus, a blanket characterization of queer and polyamorous partnerships as 'egalitarian' dismisses how social inequalities can impact these relationships.

Differential positioning is significant because having different social locations means that partners have diverging relations to *systems of power*: The '-isms' such as racism, classism, sexism, and cissexism[1] and their privilege counterparts such as white, middle-class, male, and cisgender privilege. Privilege and oppression are tightly intertwined within each system of power, as one cannot exist without the other (Hill Collins, 1990). Systems of power confer social and institutional privileges to dominant groups and systemically oppress people of marginalized groups. Partners with different race, class, or gender identities have diverging relations to privilege and oppression, which can impact relationship power dynamics. In queer polyamorous partnerships, having access to the privileges associated with being white, middle-class, male, and/or cisgender can enhance a partner's ability to form, negotiate, and manage partnerships in ways that align with their wishes or needs. Conversely, challenges that accompany race, class, or gender marginalization can intensify the emotions and energy necessary for relationship formation, negotiation, and management.

Furthermore, queer polyamorous partnerships exist at the intersection of heterosexism and monocentrism,[2] which privilege straight and monogamous people and systemically marginalize queer and polyamorous people. These systems of power pose challenges for people in queer polyamorous relationships. However, queer polyamorists with other marginalized identities such as people who are of color, low-income, women, or trans must *also* traverse racism, classism, sexism, and/or cissexism. Moreover, white, middle-class, male, and/or cisgender privilege can protect against queer/polyamorous sexual oppression (see Sheff & Hammers, 2011). Thus, it is important to understand the ways that systems of power can affect relationship processes, particularly in partnerships that deeply value egalitarianism and involve ongoing negotiation with multiple partners. In this chapter, I examine how race, class, and gender differential positioning produces power imbalances in queer polyamorous relationship formation, negotiation, and management processes.

THE STUDY

I conducted interviews with 44 adults who had marginalized gender and/ or sexual identities and had experience with polyamorous relationships, as part of a larger study on queer polyamory. Participants' gender identities included nonbinary, transman, transguy, transwoman,[3] ciswoman, and woman (unspecified), and several participants had multiple identities such as nonbinary/woman. Sexual identities included queer, lesbian, gay, pansexual, bisexual, and asexual, and several participants had multiple identities such as queer/lesbian. I found participants by posting electronic or physical fliers in spaces that center queer and/or polyamorous people (e.g., local pride centers, Facebook groups). I offered special energy to inclusivity by way of race, class, gender, and sexuality, as prior research primarily involved very privileged polyamorists (for instance, see Deri, 2015; Klesse, 2007; Sheff, 2014; Wosick-Correa, 2010), neglecting the voices of polyamorists with marginalized race, class, gender, and/or sexual identities. Interviews took place during the Fall of 2015 in various regions throughout the U.S., typically in-person or via Skype when necessary. I assigned pseudonyms for all participants and their partners, avoid detailed information about their relationship structures, and group some identity categories[4] to help ensure anonymity.

This study is informed by an intersectional framework, which acknowledges that people within one social group such as 'queer polyamorists' experience varying degrees of marginalization as they have multiple intersecting identities (Crenshaw, 1989; Hill Collins, 1990, 2005). I found that race, class, and gender systems of power can produce imbalanced relationship dynamics even in partnerships that prioritize egalitarianism, feminism, and anti-racism. Three overlapping themes relating to race, class, and gender arose in my participants' narratives: Communication, emotion work, and community. Each theme illustrates how systems of power can permeate queer polyamorous relationships, in interconnected and complex ways. I present these themes below and discuss how they can be viewed as mechanisms of relationship power.

COMMUNICATION

Effective communication is important for any partnership. In polyamory, however, the ability to effectively communicate feelings, needs, or intentions has implications for relationship negotiation and management processes. If communication imbalances are present, the partner(s) with stronger communication abilities might have a stronger capacity to (re)negotiate their desired relationship agreements than those with weaker communication skills. Nearly half of my participants reported that social class discrepancies produced imbalances or tensions in communication. Participants often framed communication differences in terms of class socialization, such that class-privileged people are taught stronger or more assertive communication skills than class-disadvantaged people are. Working-class/poor participants described class-privileged partners as having more "advantages" and being "entitled," more "adamant in negotiating," or more likely to "stand their ground." Sara was a white working-class/poor pansexual transwoman who had ex-partners and current partners who were raised middle-class, in contrast to her and another partner who were "lower-class." I asked Sara if she noticed differences negotiating relationship boundaries with middle-class partners and she responded:

> Yes! There's definitely a big difference because they have this expectation of having more resources. […] I find that people of a higher-class kind of stand their ground. […] They establish the terms of the relationship a lot more.

Sara felt that her partners' privileged class backgrounds benefited their communication skills and ultimately enhanced their abilities to negotiate relationship agreements.

Karl and Carrie also attributed relationship dynamics to class differentials. Karl was a white working-class/poor lesbian nonbinary/woman who was partnered with Carrie, a white lesbian transwoman raised middle-class. The two had been in a former triadic (three-person) partnership with Brian, a bisexual white middle-class cisman who lived in a different state. Brian drew on his class privilege when the partners discussed spending time together: He utilized an aggressive communication style, demanding to visit them rather than engaging in an equitable conversation about when and how the partners should visit each other. He then "used" his middle-class status as a form of manipulation when he visited them. In the following exchange, these partners illustrate Brian's manipulative behavior and Karl notes an important difference in how they responded:

> Carrie: Something that was pretty common is if he would make the trip here rather than us make the trip to him, […] he would expect us to accommodate him more because he did that.
>
> Karl: Even if we didn't want him to [make the trip].
>
> Carrie: Yeah, even if […] he was the one who was like, 'No, I really need to come down,' there was still the expectation—
>
> Karl: We still owed him. […] But you were like, 'No, I don't owe you' and I'm like, 'But he spent money and time. Those things cost money and resources, they're not cheap.' So, it would be used against me a lot and I'm more susceptible to it.
>
> Carrie: And that's something I wouldn't put up with.
>
> Karl: You're also middle-class, it's important to know.

Notably, Carrie and Karl did not indicate that their different class upbringings had any weight on their own communication, despite the fact that Karl recognized the class differential between them. Rather, Carrie's middle-class background awarded her with the ability to effectively communicate her concerns to Brian and to push back in these situations.

Similar to social class, socialization and attitudes of entitlement were central in the stories of participants who date(d) cisgender men. I heard numerous accounts of cismale partners either failing to communicate or using aggressive communication styles, which is troubling for polyamorous relationship negotiations. In fact, one-third of participants described male partners who would "just decide" on a new relationship boundary or demand boundaries that best suited them without engaging in honest communication. Additionally, cismale 'metamours' (a partner's partner) frequently intervened in women/woman partnerships. For instance, Carole was a white middle-class queer/gay woman who was partnered with a woman married to a cisman. She described an "uncomfortable" situation when he told her to give the couple more space:

> He actually caught me when, I don't know if she was like getting dressed or showering, but he basically like sat down and talked to me about how they needed—I mean it was an extensive conversation where he was like, 'You're my friend and I want to support you as my friend and blah blah blah, and also she and I need time together as a family unit.'

I asked Carole if the couple had made an agreement that he would communicate this issue rather than Carole's partner, but it appears that he planned this conversation without his wife's knowledge or consent. Carole recalled that he said, "'I don't exactly want her to hear me saying all this to you.'" Carole was already feeling "a little more down than usual" and ended up "feeling really terrible" after this experience.

My participants also referenced intersecting privileges when describing relationship communication and negotiation challenges. They listed various combinations of race, class, gender, and sexual identities to illustrate the privileges their partners had such as "straight white cismen," "straight poly men," "cisgender white males," and so on. Dee's narrative about one of her partners centered on the intersection of race, gender, and sexuality. Dee was a middle-class queer ciswoman of color who described frustrations with her partner, Dominic, a "big straight white man." Dee's ability to communicate effectively with Dominic was severely hindered by his aggressive, and at times disruptive, communication style. She said:

> I would often feel like he's interrupting me, but he was just rating my pause as a time to speak. It felt very aggressive to me, particularly in

times where we were having friction and I was like, 'You're not letting me talk.' […] He speaks more quickly and interrupts more and for me it shuts down my communication because I can't handle it.

Here we have two partners with very different relations to systems of power. The partner with enormous cultural privilege has a communication style that serves to reproduce his privilege within the relationship. In other words, Dominic's socialization as a "straight white man" can translate into greater relationship power because he takes up more space in their conversations and communicates his thoughts or needs when Dee is unable to do so.

EMOTION WORK

'Emotion work' (Hochschild, 1979) refers to emotion management processes such as working through uncomfortable or complex feelings. Polyamorists engage in substantial amounts of emotion work in relationship formation, negotiation, and management processes. For instance, emotion work is necessary to identify changing desires or needs for relationship renegotiation, to handle situations where agreements become inequitable, or to manage feelings of jealousy towards metamours. My participants' narratives revealed that race, class, and gender differential positioning is related to emotion work in several ways.

Social class discrepancies produced adverse feelings and consequent emotion work for working-class/poor participants. They experienced "stress," "frustration," "embarrassment," or "discomfort" primarily relating to housing or income disparities with their partners. Sara (white, working-class/poor, pansexual, transwoman), who recognized communication imbalances with middle-class partners, also felt insecure in her relationships due to her class status. She said:

There's more insecurity on my part because I feel like a lot of things are going to tear away from me and I'm going to lose stability or I feel like everything is temporary.

There were several points during our interview in which it was clear that Sara struggled with adverse emotions relating to class-disadvantage.

Even participants who were raised middle-class discussed having to work through adverse feelings related to income and/or housing disparities. A group of participants were 'middle-class-poor,' or "privileged poor" as one participant named it, indicating that they were currently poor at the time of our interview but had access to middle-class resources by being college-educated and/or raised middle-class. For instance, Hayden was a white lesbian nonbinary/transwoman who was raised with class-privilege but was low-income and temporarily living with a partner "on her kindness." They explained that the housing situation was "difficult" and "like a weight on me." Thus, Hayden encountered extra emotion work that their partner did not. However, Hayden was clear that her partner never exploited the situation to gain relationship power:

> That's been a large source of my stress, but that hasn't been something that she's used. But, that is an imbalance of power. Like, I don't have housing. […] She's more financially secure than I am right now. I don't have a job. I don't have a place that I'm leasing or anything. […] That's a pretty huge power imbalance in a lot of ways.

Despite this "pretty huge power imbalance," Hayden felt that their partner had never "used" class privilege to control nor manipulate the partnership. This dialogue represents how queer polyamorists understood privilege as linked to a capacity to influence relationship processes rather than as a tool of power.

Social class also intersected with gender to produce unique feelings for a few trans participants. Glen was a white working-class/poor bisexual transman who experienced gender dysphoria[5] when his partner paid for dates because it felt like they were playing into gender-stereotypical roles. He said:

> I feel a lot of frustrations being poor because I can't take him on dates or anything. I guess him paying for me feels a little dysphoric because, you know, he's supposed to pay for the girl. I don't want to deal with that.

In these situations, class disparities caused Glen to experience particularly adverse emotions because he felt like "the girl" in the relationship. Being poor was also a "source of embarrassment" for Glen and he even felt "pitied" by one or both of his partners. He said, "I think that's one of the reasons they both find me interesting is because—at least with my secondary partner, […] he had never met someone like me, who's this broke and queer and trans." I asked how Glen felt about this observation and he replied, "I feel a little weird about it, not gonna lie. I don't want to be pitied. I have a feeling of that from him." Similarly, Theo, a middle-class-poor queer transman, pointed to emotion work related to dating cisgender people. He felt that cisgender partners cannot comprehend what dysphoria is like:

There's a big difference between being with someone who is cis than trans [...] because dysphoria's a bitch, just to put it lightly. Being with cisgender people, whether they're queer or heterosexual, a lot of people just really don't understand. [...] It definitely makes relationships hard.

Theo acknowledged that dating cis people requires extra emotional labor and that dysphoria can result in an "emotional fallout" that cis people cannot understand.

Similar to the prior theme, many participants' stories that centered on emotion work were about relationships with cismen. Participants encountered "anger," "irritation," or "frustration" due to men's enactment of conventional masculinity. These participants had to "tolerate," "deal with," or "handle" these issues as part of their emotional labor. Jaz even faced extra emotion work because of misogynistic cultural assumptions rather than their male partner's behavior. Jaz was a middle-class queer nonbinary participant of color whose male partner was outwardly perceived as having two girlfriends. Jaz's emotion work in this case involved "dealing with" that perception. They explained:

I had a lot of anxieties about the fact that he was essentially living a straight white man's dream of having two girlfriends. It felt gross. It was uncomfortable. He was like, 'I don't see it that way. That's not why I'm doing this.' I'm like, 'I know, but it still feels weird. It's weird that people see it as that.' So, dealing with the outside perception of what we were doing.

Jaz's partner did not actively participate in conventional masculinity but Jaz nonetheless felt "gross" that he was perceived has living a misogynistic fantasy. Jaz's description of this cultural fantasy was also racialized: Having two girlfriends is a "straight white man's dream" rather than any straight man's dream.

Some participants' narratives on emotion work centered on the intersection of gender, race, and/or sexuality. Mae was a working-class/poor lesbian/queer nonbinary/woman of color who responded to my interview question about relationship dynamics with, "Yeaaaa, well, my partner's very privileged, being read as a cis white straight dude." Their differential positioning was a source of frustration for her, particularly regarding race and gender: Her partner would propose going out to places without considering her safety as a woman of color. She explained:

He says he'll protect me, which is a sweet sentiment, but that doesn't really address my real concerns about, 'If the police get called, what are you gonna do? You can't really protect me.'

However, Mae did not view her partner's privilege as having any impact on their relationship processes because he was a "hardcore feminist." Nevertheless, their differential positioning resulted in extra emotion work for Mae that her partner did not encounter.

COMMUNITY

People often belong to communities that align with their identities, interests, or hobbies. For instance, my participants belonged to queer, science, religious, artist, academic, and other communities. They were typically not involved in the nationally-organized or 'mainstream' polyamorous community. However, they often had experience with it such as attending local gatherings (e.g., brunches or dinners, cocktail hours, or support groups) or joining online polyamory discussion forums or dating sites. Nearly all participants who described interactions with the mainstream community had undesirable experiences with or feelings about it. They designated this community as "heteronormative," "hetero-cis," "full of straight white couples," "very white and very straight," "people with money," and so on. My participants felt that there is no equivalent queer polyamorous community, although they very much desired one. Moreover, participants' narratives suggest that issues with the mainstream community can impact relationship formation processes. Queer polyamorists with marginalized race, class, or gender identities can face difficulties finding people to form relationships with if they do not have access to a suitable community of polyamorists. Social class disadvantage can pose barriers to polyamorous community, as working-class/poor people are underrepresented there and can be excluded from events due to high costs. I asked Jordan, a white working-class/poor pansexual nonbinary/transman, if he had been to a polyamorous community event. He responded:

I went to one event only because my partners were teaching there and I came along to drive and help teach, but it was way too expensive for us. We could not afford to go otherwise.

A few participants like Jordan noted the need for community groups or events for low-income polyamorists.

Problematic gender expectations can also make people feel uncomfortable in the mainstream polyamorous community. My participants described being objectified and targeted by 'unicorn hunters'—typically white straight cisgender men or couples who were interested in sex more than committed polyamorous relationships. For instance, Brooke was a white middle-class queer transwoman who said that dating polyamorous cismen was challenging because she feels "objectified" like their "trophy." She also had to "deal with" the issue of "dudes expecting sexual interest in them," a false assumption that she "would be into their advances." Consequently, many participants explicitly stated that they are mistrusting of or no longer date polyamorous straight cismen or couples. Shari, a middle-class-poor queer/bisexual woman of color, said:

I'm always a little wary of straight poly men, because there's a lot of inherent privilege and power dynamic stuff going on there that I am not sure they've taken the time to unpack.

Another common concern with the mainstream polyamorous community was racial underrepresentation and experiences being racially stereotyped. Even white participants acknowledged these issues and called for groups or spaces that center people of color ('POC'). For instance, in describing the only organized event he had attended, Jordan (white, working-class/poor, pansexual, nonbinary/transman) said, "The only black people there were serving trays or playing music. It was like, 'Does anyone else notice this? This is really uncomfortable.'" Several participants of color drew connections between underrepresentation and struggles to find other polyamorists of color. Nikko was a working-class/poor pansexual/queer nonbinary participant of color who felt that "there are definitely queer people of color who practice polyamory who have multiple sets of identities" but that "the face of polyamory is very white and straight." Like Nikko, Shari was confident that POC do have polyamorous relationships and attributed their invisibility to the mainstream community's lack of inclusivity. Shari (POC, middle-class-poor, queer/bisexual, woman) framed this issue around finding other polyamorists of color. She explained:

I do wish there was more spaces or visibility or something for people of color who are in poly relationships. I'm on all the apps and everything and I'm like 'Where are they? Where are my people?' I don't know why that is. […] It's not like no one is doing this. It's not like we're not out there. I think the community doesn't feel very inclusive.

Shari desired a POC-centered community because she was "tired of dealing with people who don't understand" what life is like being polyamorous *and* a person of color.

Participants of color, particularly women, also described an array of adverse experiences such as being fetishized or stereotyped by straight white polyamorous couples and men. Dee's account represents the type of experiences that women of color encountered. Dee (POC, middle-class, queer, woman) explained:

> Being a queer woman, the predatory nature of some of the cis hetero couples out there. How many times on OKCupid I've gotten people that were like, 'Hey, hey!' and they're just looking—It feels very vulnerable, particularly as a black woman. They also say like, 'I've never been with a black woman.' Or their first message to me is like, 'Are you okay with white men?' Like, 'That's the first thing you say to me? No! I'm not okay with them then, okay?' […] I think that there are racialized assumptions in that as well, about black women and sexuality that folks may or may not know that they are putting on me.

Racial marginalization can exacerbate feelings of vulnerability and add to the emotion work that queer polyamorists endure, even within a community that espouses anti-racist, feminist, and egalitarian values.

CONCLUSION

Queer polyamorists' narratives revealed how systems of power can permeate their relationships. Participants described the ways that white, middle-class, and cismale people have unfair advantages in queer polyamorous relationships and conversely how having marginalized race, class, and gender identities creates unique challenges. For instance, differential positioning can produce communication imbalances that impact relationship negotiation because partners with class and/or cismale privilege are socialized into stronger or more aggressive communication skills than working-class/poor or non-cismale partners. Additionally, differential positioning can generate additional emotion work for queer polyamorists with other marginalized identities, which can weaken their ability to successfully navigate relationship formation, negotiation, and management. Further, differential positioning can result in adverse feelings or experiences with the mainstream polyamorous community, which serve to limit access to suitable partners in relationship formation processes. Thus, communication, emotion work, and community issues are mechanisms of relationship power in queer polyamory.

Race appears to be more prominent in queer polyamorists' relationship formation processes (e.g., dating within the mainstream polyamorous community), whereas class appears to be more salient for relationship negotiation and management processes (e.g., communication imbalances and extra emotion work). In contrast, gender was a central concern across all relationship processes, suggesting that gender relations are substantial even for queer partnerships. However, it is difficult to confidently identify which systems of power contribute to imbalanced relationship dynamics. For instance, Karl and Carrie discussed communication challenges with Brian as a product of class differentials but Karl also described him as "a white male cisgendered person" who felt that "he owned the world and had exclusive access to everything and everybody." Such statements highlight the complex interrelations between race, class, and gender. It is likely that Brian's white, class, and male privilege all contributed to his aggressive communication style and attitudes of entitlement. Additionally, one system of power can aggravate others, such as in Dee's case. Being a person of color intensified the feelings of vulnerability that accompanied being a queer woman in the polyamorous dating scene. Similarly, the adverse experiences that Dee encountered hinged on being a black queer woman—they existed only at the precise intersection of race, gender, and sexuality. Thus, disentangling how race, class, gender, and sexuality impact relationships might prove impossible as systems of power are 'mutually constructing' (Hill Collins, 2005). More research is needed that investigates these issues, as well as how other systems of power such as ageism or ableism impact relationship processes, how relationship power might operate through other mechanisms, or what steps partners take to minimize imbalanced relationship dynamics.

Examining race, class, and gender in queer polyamory speaks to the ways that intersecting systems of power permeate even the most ideologically-egalitarian partnerships. Queer polyamorists' narratives reveal that race, class, and gender differential positioning can impact relationship power through mechanisms of communication, emotion work, and community. These findings suggest that we must be cautious when characterizing relationships as 'egalitarian,' or when portraying them as inherently progressive as news and culture media outlets have in recent years. Social inequalities infiltrate all of our relationships.

NOTES

[1] Cissexism refers to the oppression of trans people and privileging of 'cisgender' people (anyone who is not trans).

[2] Whereas mono*centrism* is about monogamy and nonmonogamy, mono*sexism* is about 'multisexuality' (attraction to multiple genders) and 'monosexuality' (attraction to one gender).

[3] I use 'transman,' 'transguy,' and 'transwoman;' however, these terms are varied and contested. For instance, 'trans woman' and 'trans-woman' are also commonly used in the trans community.

[4] For instance, 'nonbinary' includes gender-nonconforming identities such as genderqueer, polygender, or agender.

[5] Gender dysphoria refers to feelings of distress caused by incongruency between one's gender identity/expression and their gender assigned at birth and/or their gendered body.

REFERENCES

Carrington, C. (1999). *No place like home: Relationships and family life among lesbians and gay men*. Chicago, IL: University of Chicago Press.

Crenshaw, K. (1989). Demarginalizing the intersection of race and sex: A black feminist critique of antidiscrimination doctrine, feminist theory and antiracist politics. *University of Chicago Legal Forum, 1*(8), 139–167.

Deri, J. (2015). *Love's refraction: Jealousy and compersion in queer women's polyamorous relationships*. Toronto: University of Toronto Press.

Frank, K., & DeLamater, J. (2010). Deconstructing monogamy: Boundaries, identities, and fluidities across relationships. In M. Barker & D. Langdridge (Eds.), *Understanding non-monogamies* (pp. 9–20). New York, NY: Routledge.

Hill Collins, P. (1990). *Black feminist thought: Knowledge, consciousness, and the politics of empowerment*. Boston, MA: Unwin Hyman.

Hill Collins, P. (2005). *Black sexual politics: African Americans, gender, and the new racism*. New York, NY: Routledge.

Hochschild, A. (1979). Emotion work, feeling rules, and social structure. *American Journal of Sociology, 85*(3), 551–575.

Klesse, C. (2007). *The Spectre of promiscuity: Gay male and bisexual non-monogamies and polyamories*. Burlington, VT: Ashgate.

Klesse, C. (2010). Paradoxes in gender relationships. In M. Barker & D. Langdridge (Eds.), *Understanding non-monogamies* (pp. 109–120). New York, NY: Routledge.

M., A. (2018). *Polyamory in the news!* Retrieved from https://polyinthemedia.blogspot.com

Schippers, M. (2016). *Beyond monogamy: Polyamory and the future of polyqueer sexualities*. New York, NY: New York University Press.

Sheff, E. (2014). *The polyamorists next door: Inside multiple-partner relationships and families*. Lanham, MD: Rowman and Littlefield.

Sheff, E., & Hammers, C. (2011). The privilege of perversities: Race, class and education among polyamorists and kinksters. *Psychology and Sexuality, 2*(3), 198–223.

Weeks, J., Heaphy, B., & Donovan, C. (2001). *Same-sex intimacies: Families of choice and other life experiments*. New York, NY: Routledge.

Wosick-Correa, K. (2010). Agreements, rules and agentic fidelity in polyamorous relationships. *Psychology and Sexuality, 1*(1), 44–61.

J. E. SUMERAU AND ALEXANDRA "XAN" C. H. NOWAKOWSKI

9. RELATIONAL FLUIDITY

Somewhere between Polyamory and Monogamy (*Personal Reflection*)

There are two sea shells from two different beaches on one of the night stands in our bedroom.

One of the shells came from a beach on the Gulf of Mexico during a time where we were living in separate cities. It was collected in 2014 by Xan while we walked along the beach talking about recent experiences seeing each other and other people and reminiscing about earlier periods in our relationship when we were only seeing each other. It was picked up on an evening where we were again seeing only each other while managing our own independent and shared emotional and physical chronic conditions by leaning heavily on each other for support and care. Later, Xan held it in their hands in the moonlight as they proposed marriage, both in terms of commitment and in terms of legal union, to J at the beach in question.

The other shell came from a beach on the Atlantic Ocean about an hour from where we currently share a home together and with our other two partners. It was collected by Xan and one of our other two partners in early 2018 while they shared a romantic weekend at the beach. At the same time, J was on the other coast where the first shell came from showing our other partner the beach on the Gulf of Mexico where Xan proposed in the midst of their own romantic vacation. Xan picked up the shell as both a memento of the beautiful weekend they shared with one of our partners at the beach where they first fell in love with Florida as a child, and a compliment to the other shell we hold so dear in our home. The two now live together as symbols of our love and those with whom we choose to share it.

As we began crafting this chapter, we kept going back to the sight of the shells on the night stand in our bedroom. Like the seas they came from, our relationship has evolved over time in varied ways based upon an ongoing dialogue about what we need, what we want, and what is best for each of us individually, us together, and our chosen family as a whole. This

© KONINKLIJKE BRILL NV, LEIDEN, 2019 | DOI:10.1163/9789004414105_010

seems even more salient of late as we recently co-authored and published our first collaborative novel following the release of our first collaborative edited volume after designing shared and individual career paths together predicated upon open collaboration, communication, and negotiation in all facets of our lives (see www.writewhereithurts.net for more information on such work). In fact, the books themselves focus heavily on these concepts, and much of the conceptualization in them, like the shells themselves, speaks back to an early conversation in 2011 about what we would want a relationship (at the time we were both saying "if" we tried a serious one again) to be like.

That conversation took place in a coffee shop in the city where we met. Xan was seeing someone else and J was historically uninterested in much by way of commitment to one or even multiple people. We were just starting to get to know each other at the time and talking through these other aspects of our lives when Xan wanted to know what J saw going forward. Without thinking about it much, J said, "I guess I envision relationships more like rivers that ebb and flow or shift and change in relation to what the people want over time." Laughing, Xan said, "Sounds a lot like the way we both experience our genders and sexualities." Smiling, which was rare for J back then, J said, "I guess," and Xan said, "Well, I guess you passed the first test since I'm not sure if I would be interested in anything that felt constrained or forced or too limited in the first place," and we both shared a laugh over our hot beverages.

In this chapter, we reflect on the relationship we've built—as well as the ways it has ebbed and flowed in a fluid fashion over time—from the seeds planted in that early conversation. Integrating our experiences and skills with autoethnographic, artistic, and collaborative methodologies, we reflect on a type of consensual nonmonogamy wherein we have shifted back and forth between monogamous at times and polyamorous at times based upon our individual and collective needs and desires. In so doing, we outline the ways we structure our relationship, and possibilities for consensual nonmonogamies that shift in form and practice throughout the life course. Rather than seeking to outline the contours consensual nonmonogamies more broadly or suggesting standards for other relationships (see Chapters 5–8 in this volume), here we reflect on our experiences doing consensual nonmonogamy over time as one example of the ways such practice may develop and evolve over time and in relation to the needs of a given couple, union, group, or other relationship form.

THE IMPORTANCE OF STANDPOINTS IN
RELATIONSHIP DEVELOPMENT

Researchers have long noted the importance of biographical histories, standpoints, and experiences in developing and understanding relationships. To this end, we begin by outlining our own standpoints and relevant social locations that find voice and expression in the ways we seek to craft and manage relationships—romantic and otherwise—over time. In many ways, our construction and performance of a fluid form of romantic intimacy and partnership fits well with other aspects of our biographies that have led both of us to more often need freedom and flexibility rather than more static or absolute options. In fact, we generally refer to our relationship, partnership, and marriage in varied terms as an expression of such fluidity, and most often call what we do an "open relationship" because we see it as always open to negotiation and adjustment whether monogamous, polyamorous, or anywhere in between in practice at a given time or in relation to a given context.

This interest in and pursuit of fluidity and flexibility shows up in our individual standpoints in many ways. Xan, for example, is an agender person who lives and expresses both masculine and feminine selves in varied contexts and interactions with others; a bi+ person who generally identifies as fluid, or queer as they have a preference for certain bodies (i.e., specific genital preferences) but have no preference for a certain gender (i.e., identity and/or expression along the feminine-masculine spectrum); and an agnostic person who finds interest and curiosity in relation to both believers and nonbelievers in terms of supernatural, scientific, and artistic knowledges, beliefs, assumptions, and truths. At the same time, Xan doesn't fit neatly into other binary locations in society due to their experiences as a neuroatypical person with an eidetic memory, and a multiethnic person who both benefits from the appearance of whiteness while also facing marginalization from contexts where their Polish or Tuscarora backgrounds become relevant. In fact, Xan's entire life course has required fluidity and flexibility as they live with and manage cystic fibrosis (CF), which was not diagnosed conclusively until the last couple years, and as a result, their own survival, healthcare pursuits, and understanding of their body in both positive and negative terms has been dependent upon regularly adjusting to new or different stimuli, symptomology, and both biological and social knowledges over time.

Likely very important in the development of our relationship over time, Xan and J found equally fluid and flexible people in each other when their paths crossed in 2011. Specifically, J is a non-binary transgender woman who fluctuates concerning biological intervention and transition and often lives back and forth in terms of dress, appearance, gender identity (in relation to dysphoria symptomology), and recognition of herself as J, Jason, or Erica on different days and in different contexts; a bi+ person who generally identifies as bisexual or pansexual or queer as their romantic and sexual desires are predicated upon mental attraction (i.e., internal rather than external characteristics) and connections; and an agnostic person with similar approaches to science, spirituality, and other ideological systems as Xan. J also gets lost in most statistical portraits and norms as they are a neuroatypical, orphan/adopted, and multi-racial person from the lower working class who has climbed up to the upper class thanks to much help, support, and luck over the past 20 years. J has also needed flexibility and fluidity to adopt the necessary codes and symbols of moving between class statuses over time, and to manage chronic medical conditions related to her legs, face, mental functioning, and dysphoria over time as they have only had reliable access to healthcare in the past few years.

The necessity, for both of us, for fluid and flexible options also draws from shared experience as people managing PTSD and other trauma reactions from past experience. Xan, for example, has suffered considerable trauma as a donor conceived person, a sexual and physical assault survivor, and someone who has faced the approach of death at an early age alone without support (at times) in hospitals. Similarly, J has suffered considerable trauma as an orphan/adopted person, a sexual and physical assault survivor, a hate crime survivor, and someone who has had to say goodbye to over two dozen significant connections that passed away over the years via natural and violent means. Like many trauma survivors, J and Xan both rely upon the ability to shift and change any and all aspects of their lives as a way to reclaim the loss of freedom, control, and sense of safety trauma events often take away from those who survive such events. Put simply, the combination of these background factors—as well as our roles as long term caregivers for each other and others managing such backgrounds—suggests our focus on fluidity, negotiation, and options in our relationship is not all that surprising.

NEGOTIATING THE OVERALL RELATIONSHIP AGREEMENT

As noted above, our relationship—in its committed form—begins with a series of conversations we had in the fall of 2011 after realizing very quickly that we wanted to be major parts of each other's lives. At the time, Xan and I were seeing each other, but we were also connected to other people in a romantic fashion. Xan was in a monogamous relationship with another person. J was in the process of dissolving a legal marriage with her best friend who moved to Florida with J in 2009 as they both navigated higher education. In Xan's case, the relationship in question was hitting a wall due to healing Xan and their partner needed to do from prior traumatic experiences, and Xan felt it was best to take a break from the relationship—temporary or total—for their own healing processes and needs. In J's case, the relationship in question was and remains a deeply intimate friendship that simply did not work as well while in the context of a committed, monogamous romantic relationship, and thus J and her partner were separating back into the best friends dynamic they had before coming to Florida. With these experiences taking place around our own early relationship development, we decided to be explicit about what we wanted and what rules might work for any relationship we developed over time.

This decision was also aided by previous experiences and standpoints we shared at the time. While we had both been historically polyamorous people, we had each just come out of experiences with a negative monogamous relationship (before either of us moved to Florida) followed by the positive monogamous relationships we were in when we met and noted above. At the same time, we were also both people who had historically been active in kink communities (see chapters in this volume on BDSM and kink relationships) though neither of us were very active in these endeavors at the time. As such, we both already had detailed and extensive experience in negotiating and outlining agreements that could shape a relationship, sexual activities, romantic activities, and other factors in a given connection or shared experience. We utilized these experiences to define three rules for our relationship that we continue to live by today with each other and our other two partners.

The First Rule We Agreed upon Was Egalitarianism

Put simply, we wanted to develop only equitable relationships after both having experiences with inequitable relationships that were deeply destructive. To do this, however, we had to negotiate the parameters of what would be equitable between us because we were not equal in any way socially, economically, or in our own positions in trauma recovery or health needs. If, for example, we paid for everything equally in a financial sense, we would have an inequitable or unequal relationship because Xan was (and remains) far more financially successful and from a far better financial background than J. For example, J only had a coat the first winter we spent together because Xan could afford to buy her one when J could not afford the luxury of warm clothing. We thus began, as we do now together and with our other partners, calculating and outlining equitable distributions of time, career needs, finances, housework, and other factors based on where we each stood individually in terms of resources, opportunities, and options. We further agreed to update these calculations as things changed over time, and have done so (i.e., when J got a well-paying job and better healthcare after graduate school or when Xan had more negative medical experiences in a given year and thus needed more caregiving than usual or than they could offer in return) throughout our relationship. In so doing, we agreed to pursue an egalitarian relationship, and took steps to put this into practice and monitor it as our lives changed in time.

The Second Rule We Agreed upon Was Autonomy

Especially as people managing and healing from past traumas and violence, we each sought freedom in our lives to follow our own needs, dreams, and desires. We thus conceptualized our relationship as one with at least three people active in it at all times—Xan, J, and us. This rationale has also extended the amount of people in the relationship when new partners have been added to the relationship temporarily or, on a longer term basis like at present. We see ourselves as independent beings in our relationship. For example, Xan places high priority on their career, and steps are taken by the rest of our foursome to support this priority in all ways, and at the same time, J places high priority on the ability to disappear and roam around freely, which is not only supported but also encouraged by our partners. Similarly, one of our other primary partners currently seeks to live full time in Florida again and may pursue more graduate education in the future, and thus we work towards making these goals a reality together, and our other primary partner is in pursuit of a highly competitive, high status career, and together we work with them as they continue this pursuit individually as a team of supporters and resources. Stated simply, we do not assume control, rights to, or anything else in relation to one another. Instead, we focus on how our whole, our interdependent relationships within the whole, and each of us individually can both (1) support the individual goals and needs of each partner, and (2) have the freedom to pursue our own goals and needs individually in ways that prioritize both the individual needs and desires of each of us and the overall health and affirmation of us as a whole.

126

The Third Rule We Agreed upon Was to Never Settle

Take, for example, J's class, gender, and sexual background or Xan's management of (until recently) mis or under diagnosed health conditions as case studies. In both cases, our lives have shown us how often the world and people in it can be forced to settle for less than they need, want, or even deserve. As we continue to do together, individually, and with our other partners, we decided we would commit to never settling or expecting settling from our loved ones as much as possible in our lives. We would (and do) marshal our resources, abilities, and connections to pursue any desire or need we had individually or together. We would further always remain open to adjust for any case where the other had a new potential or necessary need, desire, or adventure to express and potentially follow at some point. When J wanted to focus some of her energy and resources to regularly visit Chicago where she has a supportive and loving network who are especially capable of relaxing and recharging J's mind and body, Xan pushed J to do so, helped with the necessary budgeting (i.e., Xan is far better with math and finance planning), and encouraged the pursuit, which has become a staple of our lives and J's increasingly better mental and physical health over the last few years. Similarly, when Xan wanted to turn down a position that paid more than J ever expects to make because their real desire was elsewhere, J walked through the pros and cons with them, worked out several ways that Xan's actual desire could be achieved without any trouble for our relationship, and supported them throughout the process that led, over time, to them gaining the position they wanted most instead of the original one. In these and other cases, we commit to pushing each other to never again take less, never again be limited by others in any way that is within our power to avoid, and always look out for each other's and our collective needs and wants over time no matter how they shift and change.

As suggested throughout this section, these three rules provide the foundation of our relationship, and also reflect fluidity in the ways our relationship is or can be at any time. Further, this fluidity is built into the relationship at its core beyond whether or not we do any specific things in romantic and sexual endeavors. Rather than looking at our relationship as a thing we have, we look at it as what we do, how we do it, and how we continuously negotiate what it is and will be at given time based on our independent, shared, and disparate needs and desires over time. This, of course, means we spend much time communicating on these topics and checking in with each other about how we are feeling in relation to each of the three rules. While we could change these, like anything else, at any time, to date they have served us well as the backbone of the rest of the lives we have built together over time. In the next section, we reflect upon the ways these rules and our standpoints show up in relation to our more specifically romantic and sexual needs, desires, and endeavors over time.

NEGOTIATING POLYAMORY AND MONOGAMY OVER TIME

As suggested throughout this chapter, our approach to monogamy, polyamory, and the spaces in between derives from our overall approach to the relationship. As people focused on egalitarianism for all involved in our lives, we see the desires we share as equally valid with the desires we may not share, and we see each other's interests—romantic, sexual, or otherwise social—as important individually and collectively. Put simply, we share a commitment to each of us individually and collectively having the same opportunities to follow our desires. At the same time, as autonomous people, we do not assume or expect to have control over each other's desires or practices, but rather see whatever say we have in such things as negotiated and given in the ongoing conversation of our lives and relationships. There have been (and likely will be more) times when one or both of us was almost or completely unavailable or more available than usual in a physical, sexual or emotional sense (whether just to each other or in a broader sense) and regardless of the reasons for such fluctuations, we support each other's ability to know and inform the other in terms of what is available, necessary, and desired at a given time. Each of these factors plays into the rule for never settling.

The notion of never settling plays out in its own fluid ways. There are aspects of who we are and what we need and what we desire where we fit each other perfectly and completely. At times, this has meant all we desire is each other or simply each other and the freedom to play around or try out other people or activities. There are other aspects of who we are and what we need and what we desire that do not necessarily match at given times or ever. At times, this means we look for satisfaction of these aspects of ourselves in other places and in other ways while still sharing and communicating about them with each other. While the details in any case—as well as the complexities of our varied sides as people—may shift and change over time or in relation to specific moments, we see these fluctuations and the fluidity to embrace them within ourselves and each other as positive things and important parts of our individual and shared life satisfaction and quality.

As a result, within the rules we have for our overall relationship together and with our other partners, we also have a framework we negotiated for periods of exploration and/or developing committed relationships with others.

This framework is built on continuous conversation we call "checking in," which involves first and foremost making sure that (1) we are satisfied with each other and our life together; and (2) neither of us feel like we are missing anything or facing any problems with our own relationship. We mirror these things with our other partners now that we have shifted into a foursome alongside our own longstanding twosome in terms of committed partnerships. In the first case, we don't step outside of our commitment in any way unless we are certain that our relationship remains whole, remains a space where we each feel we're getting all we want and need from each other, and remains solid as a source of satisfaction, support, and commitment. In the second case and building on the first point, we focus on any work we need to in our committed relationship rather than stepping elsewhere if we do determine any issues in our union(s) as these are the primary focus of our lives and desires. Stated another way, we do not play with others or build other relationships in search of anything missing from our relationship, but rather, we keep our connection whole and play with others or build other relationships as experiences in and of themselves that can complement what we have and that are generally going to speak to aspects of ourselves that are not as central in what we have together.

Especially since we recognize and embrace our autonomy even in times when we have been more monogamous, we regularly talk about people who catch our interests—individually most of the time as our preferences often differ, but also collectively—in romantic, sexual, or otherwise attraction-related terms. We share these impressions, thoughts, fantasies, or interests regularly, and have a lot of fun learning and discussing the people who catch our respective attentions at varied times in our life together. At the same time, J is historically less likely to look for relationships and more likely to look for play whereas Xan is historically more likely to see play as an occasional thing and be more interested in relationships. At the same time, however, in an example of fluidity over time, at present we are both almost entirely only interested in relationships with little interest in more casual play with others. Regardless of interest or the contents of our interests or whether we were more monogamous or polyamorous in practice at a given time, we continuously utilize a system of conversations to check in, express our interests (whether passing or more serious), and reflect on our own time and relationship with each other.

When we do feel the potential for engaging others beyond simply observing and discussing them together, the process begins with a conversation about this potential. In these moments, either of us—as well as our other partners now that there are four of us in a committed whole—holds the right to veto or approve a potential new companion. This is because of the points noted above as 1 and 2. Put simply, we are only likely to veto if we (a) see something missing or off in our relationship(s); (b) see something in the potential companion that could be dangerous or troublesome for our partner or our overall lives together; and/or (c) feel some kind of insecurity or jealousy that likely owes to some problem we have yet to notice in our relationship that must be addressed before any consideration of a new companion. This process also repeats itself—as it did when we recently became a foursome of committed partnerships—when experience with a new companion becomes a possible partnership in a more committed, regular, and long term manner. This is because a more serious or long term partnership will require more engagement from the other (i.e., as a metamour[1], family member, or even as a potential companion themselves) than a casual dating scenario with a companion. In such cases, once the new partner and developing partnership is cleared by both of us, the partner who was not initially involved with the companion also begins developing a relationship—whether platonic, romantic, sexual, or all of the above—with the new partner as part of integrating them into the overall whole over time as the new committed relationship develops.

For example, the process played out (thus far) with our other current partners in the following manners. In Xan's case, their other partner is someone who they have known for some time; the development of their present relationship has involved continuous conversations and negotiations. As the present form of their partnership developed, he began getting to know and interacting with J and Xan while adjusting to the experience of a multi-faceted relationship dynamic. In so doing, he and J intend to build a metamour relationship of their own moving forward. At the same time, when J began to develop feelings for her other partner, Xan was instrumental in supporting the relationship and its development. In fact, Xan became aware of the feelings before J did, and both cleared and encouraged J to pursue these feelings before J brought them up on her own. As the relationship has developed, Xan has bonded deeply, again in a metamour fashion, with them and provided both support and encouragement as they and J develop together. In both cases, the origin of the partnerships derive from each of us supporting the other in first pursuing the relationships, and then in each of us serving as support and encouragement as the relationship became a serious, committed, partnership over time while integrating the other into our own individual lives as well. In both cases, as in any case, any potential problem or concern is talked about, and vetos could have come if any major concerns with us or with them arose, but when no such issues arise, instead we follow our desires in building relationships as we see fit.

These processes and conversations will and have played out in a similar way at the emergence of any potential companions or partners over time. In some cases, for example, things have not worked out well, and we have had to pull back together to heal, refortify our relationship, and take care of each other. In other cases, things have worked out well, but in the end, what we found were companions or we found that the best thing for us at a given time was to just focus on each other and be together without any others involved. At present, however, we have now developed very positive partnerships with the two of us at the center and connections to two others that may develop in myriad ways over time.

CONCLUDING THOUGHTS

While we are pleased to see more and more emerging academic and artistic portraits of the varieties of monogamous, fluid, and polyamorous relationships in society, here we have offered a collaborative reflection on one such relationship for readers interested in some ways consensual nonmonogamies may play out in practical cases. As one could surmise from the other chapters on nonmonogamies in this volume and elsewhere, we do not mean to suggest our path is the same as that of others, and in fact, this would be a false suggestion as consensual nonmonogamies take a wide variety of forms. Rather, our reflections here offer an in-depth, behind the scenes, or backstage view of how our own consensual nonmonogamous practice operates as well as the fluidity it represents and draws upon in practice throughout our lives. In fact, we would suggest the fluidity we utilize to make sense of our own open or fluid relationship could be useful to people who only seek monogamy or only seek polyamory in varied forms as it rests upon ongoing negotiation, conversation, and concern for those involved in a partnership no matter how many such people may number in a given time, place, or context. As we have done here, we suggest readers utilize our work here as an opportunity to reflect upon their own relationship needs, desires, and concerns in hopes of finding, building, and maintaining whatever forms would represent the healthiest and most satisfying relationships for their own lives.

With this in mind, we complete our reflection by returning to the shells that came to us from the fluidity of the sea to symbolize the fluidity in our own relationships.

NOTE

[1] As the structure of the word suggests, metamour refers to someone who is the partner of one's partner (i.e., the partner of my partner), but does not have a direct sexual relationship with said one (i.e., with me). It is a term used to capture the love and affection one feels and develops with the partner of one's partner (i.e., the emotional relationship between people who share a partner in life, love, sexuality, or all of the above).

PART 3

KINKY/BDSM RELATIONSHIPS

ROBIN BAUER

10. BDSM RELATIONSHIPS

INTRODUCTION

This chapter will provide an introduction to various kinds of BDSM-specific relationship practices, such as relationships based on a model of dominance/submission as well as relationship concepts that emerge within the BDSM context such as the model of play partnerships which defies the friend/lover dichotomy and the concept of shared intimacy, which questions the necessity of the couple and the public/private divide to generate intimate experiences.

A closer look reveals that BDSM-specific practices simultaneously question and re-instate certain elements of mono-normativity. Therefore they provide an interesting starting point for theorizing intimacy from a perspective that focuses on issues of power and consent rather than notions of equality and romantic love.

The Social Context of BDSM Relationships: Heteronormativity, Mono-Normativity and the Ideal of Harmonic Sex

The culturally hegemonic relationship model in most Anglo-European contexts is still the sexually and emotionally exclusive couple. Moreover, the ideal of a life-long commitment is still powerful and the duration of a relationship often functions as a criterion of success or failure of that relationship. Yet serial monogamy, a model of a succession of exclusive pair bonds over a lifetime, has become a standard model as well. Gay and lesbian couples have become much more culturally and in recent years also legally accepted, especially if they mimic the institution of monogamous marriage. Other types of relationships remain marginalized, such as relationships involving trans individuals, mentally disabled people, and polygamous or polyamorous constellations.

Therefore, all BDSM relationships are part of a culture that remains on the one hand structured by heteronormativity and mono-normativity, while on the other hand progress is made in some areas for some individuals (especially those who only transgress one norm or who hold significant

© KONINKLIJKE BRILL NV, LEIDEN, 2019 | DOI:10.1163/9789004414105_011

social privilege in terms of class, race or gender). The analytical concept of mono-normativity was introduced by Marianne Pieper and myself (Pieper & Bauer, 2005) to describe mechanisms that privilege monogamous relationships in both social worlds and scientific discourses alike (Barker & Langdridge, 2010). Mono-normativity tends to universalize and naturalize the exclusive, dyadic structure of the loving (usually heterosexual) couple. From the mono-normative perspective, every encounter or relationship that does not represent this pattern is assigned the status of the other, of deviation, of pathology; it is a sign of being uncivilized, racially inferior, morally inferior, in need of explanation, or it is ignored, hidden, avoided and marginalized. Sometimes monogamy is presented as natural, other times as a cultural or moral fact. Often mono-normative discourse sets the white race apart as morally superior or further developed, by crediting only white people with the ability to love in general, but to love and be faithful to only one person in particular. People of color serve as the other to this supposedly highest achievement of civilization (monogamous marriage), and are depicted as possessing a 'wild,' unconstrained sexuality that is seen at odds with modesty and fidelity, the moral high ground in terms of sexual relationships (Riggs, 2006; Carter, 2007).

One of the elements of sexual and relationship normativity, which has not yet been awarded much attention, is what I call the ideal of harmonic sex (Bauer, 2014). The ideal sexual encounter/relationship has been increasingly constructed as occurring between egalitarian partners whose intimate bodily interactions are devoid of power dynamics and anything that may be thought of as unpleasant, such as pain, humiliation, shame or discomfort. The ideal of harmonic sex is closely related to the liberal construction of the sexual as private (Leap, 1999), as a refuge, as a space remote from socio-political life. Therefore, the ideal of harmonic sex serves to obscure the fact that sexual relationships are not distinct from socio-political contexts, but infused with power dynamics (Foucault, 1978) and ongoing economic dependencies (Jamieson, 1999; Klesse, 2007). Klesse points out that much research on same-sex partnerships tends to present them as, in principle, egalitarian (2007, pp. 2, 6). Klesse sees that view as 'utterly romanticising the reality' and working with a one-dimensional concept of power (2007, p. 7); the only dimension of power that is accounted for in these narratives is the gender axis and since same-sex couples are usually of the same gender, they are considered to be equals. What this reasoning fails to consider is that people are embodying more than one social category and that social power in same-sex couples may well be distributed unevenly along lines of race, class, education, ability etc. The narrative of harmonic and synchronized sex (as in the ideal of the 'simultaneous orgasm') feeds into the illusion that, in white middle-class Euro-American contexts of monogamous, mono-racial couplehood, this ideal of the egalitarian relationship or the companionate marriage is not only achievable, but has already been established. Harmonic (and 'democratic') relationships are taken as the moral and political gold standard against which other cultures, such as Islamic and Mormon polygamy, are constructed, measured and evaluated.

BDSM relationships violate the ideal of harmonic sex with their eroticization of power imbalances, inequality, and (carefully chosen) discomforts. For instance, simultaneous orgasms are rarely the goal in BDSM interactions; they rather thrive on asynchronicity. A submissive may only be allowed to orgasm by permission of the dominant. (Queer) BDSM might, therefore, be understood as creating alternative intimacies and, more specifically, exuberant intimacies, intimacies that reject reason, moderation, mediocrity, harmony and equality as well as reproduction and usefulness. Instead, alternative intimacies celebrate difference, tension, intensity, risk, excess and so on (Bauer, 2014).

Setting the Stage: Critical Consent in BDSM Communities

The BDSM communities[1] have developed specific ethics and skills to ensure that BDSM practices and relationships are carried out in negotiated and risk-aware ways (Weiss, 2011; Bauer, 2014). Ritualized beginnings and endings of BDSM interactions, which are called 'scenes' or 'sessions' create and demarcate an alternative realty in which sexual fantasies can be enacted in a risk-reduced, semi-contained way. During the session, you can leave the ordinary world behind and enter into a negotiated role different from your everyday persona. Essentially, negotiations take place before such a BDSM encounter. They include agreeing upon the role each participant is playing, their likes and dislikes and especially their limits. As consent is considered an ongoing process rather than a one-time event, some form of communication also takes place during a session and a safeword is put into place. When used, the safeword signals that all actions must stop immediately. At the end of the session, participants are responsible for (physical, but more importantly, emotional) aftercare to make sure everyone can safely land in ordinary reality again. The extent of negotiations depends on the individuals and their familiarity with each other. If entering a BDSM relationship, consent can also be formalized in a written agreement, such as a 'Mistress-slave contract.'

To establish consent, communication and negotiation skills are crucial. These ethics and skills the BDSM sexual culture has developed are not only suitable for approaching BDSM, but can be employed to negotiate alternative ways of doing relationships such as polyamory effectively as well. People who practice non-normative sexualities for which there is no standard social script, are 'forced' to reflect on issues of establishing consent more and may then be able to transfer these skills to other areas of their life, such as relationship practices.

Liberal notions of consent are widespread within society at large but also within some BDSM and polyamory communities. They conceptualize the establishing of consent as a simple matter of entering into a contract between equals. This liberal approach to consent neglects the social context in which negotiations take place. For instance, the self-help discourses that dominate the polyamory communities (as becomes evident in polyamory manuals) tend to psychologize and individualize the processes of negotiation. They do so by a) failing to consider and reflect upon the fact that emotions and desires people may have do not necessarily represent their 'own, authentic' selves, but are also effects of social norms, pre-given forms of what and how to feel that individuals have to navigate (and are often not completely aware of). For instance, women are still generally socialized into wanting to please their partners, which may prevent them from articulating their own wishes and needs when negotiating sexual consent or relationship choices (cf. Thomas et al., 2017). Furthermore, these self-help discourses tend to b) neglect the impact power dynamics in relationships may have on the validity of consent. These may be of a social hierarchy kind, such as the level of education individuals have which may give individuals with highly developed rhetorical skills an advantage when negotiating consent, or even dependencies such as one partner relying on the other for their residence permit Or these may be power imbalances specific to the individuals in a particular relationship, such as the 'sexual market value' that may make one partner feel more dependent on their partner and make them make compromises in order to keep their partner when negotiating consent. Such power dynamics are often neglected in contexts where the ideal of harmonic sex and the myth of already achieved equality prevails. In the BDSM context on the other hand, power tends to be hyper-visual due to the popularity of playing with power. Ideally, this leads to a higher awareness and reflection of power dynamics in general. In reality, this is not automatically the case, as social power relations and their impacts permeate the BDSM communities just like any other part of society. Yet the BDSM context holds some promising potentials, which are partly realized, to learn about power in intimate contexts and put that critical knowledge to work when establishing consent. I therefore argue for the development of a notion of critical consent that takes social context into account and is power-sensitive (Bauer, 2014).

Time to Play: Renegotiating Relationship Norms

In the most visible parts of the BDSM communities,[2] negotiated, openly practiced non-monogamies of various kinds are so common that the monogamy norm seems reversed. First in terms of prevalence: the vast majority of BDSM relationship practices do not adhere to mono-normative, culturally accepted models. Rather, there is a great diversity of non-monogamous relationship styles (Rinella, 2003; Bauer, 2010; Kaldera, 2010).

Second, the monogamy norm also seems reversed in the BDSM community in terms of expected conduct. In mono-normative society at large, the expectation is that people are monogamous until proven otherwise, and people who are part of a couple are considered unavailable (at least officially). In contrast, in BDSM social contexts such as fundraising events or play parties, it is generally assumed that everybody can be approached for requesting a play date, everyone can be engaged in flirting etc. The rules of conduct of mono-normative culture are replaced by BDSM community specific standards of conduct instead. Such standards include the so-called protocol (see below) and the ethical principle of consent as explained above. In my own research on the les-bi-trans-queer BDSM communities, I proposed some explanations for this predominance of non-monogamous practices both in terms of prevalence and community standards (Bauer, 2010, 2014), four of which can be generalized across the various BDSM community subsets, such as (1) that the practice of negotiating consent for BDSM practices can include relationship choices as well.

An individual or a group can react differently to the fact that a part of their identity, behaviors or relationships violate a social norm. For instance, they can try to normalize it by emphasizing its similarities with the norm. This is the goal of some BDSM organizations like the National Coalition for Sexual Freedom (NCSF), who choose community members to represent their cause that closest resemble (white, heteronormative, mono-normative) American family values to stress that BDSM people are just like everyone else except for their special sexual tastes (Weiss, 2008). A different strategy would be to stress the difference to the norm and question the validity of the norm. Some BDSM people, especially queer ones, pursue this strategy and claim a sexual outcast identity (Califia, 2000; Landgridge, 2006). In general, if someone realizes they are different from what society expects and condones as acceptable behavior, those who fall outside the box somehow have to negotiate their relation to the norm. This leads some people interested in BDSM to question the norm around what kind of sexual behaviors are acceptable and once they have questioned this particular norm it may result in a realization that other norms can be interrogated as well. This starts what I have called (2) 'the domino effect of perversion': if you are already into BDSM, possibly also queer or trans, then you are potentially more open to experiment with non-monogamous types of relationships as well (Bauer, 2014).

(3) BDSM practices and relationships do not necessarily involve sexual activities in the normative sense. Many practices are considered sexual without involving any genital contact or nudity, for instance boot-blacking can be arousing or the flogging of a back can result in orgasm.[3] This opens up a space to experiment with different kinds of intimacies, which may be of particular interest to individuals who identify as asexual (Sloan, 2015) or for those trans people who do not wish to have sex involving certain body parts (Kaldera, 2009; Bauer, 2014). Rather than redefining non-genital BDSM acts as sexual, some practitioners distinguish 'regular' genitally focused sex from BDSM. This approach makes it possible to define relationships as monogamous that include playing with other people, if BDSM 'does not count' as sex. It may also open up a space to experiment with non-monogamy by restricting activities outside of an established relationship to non-genital BDSM. Reserving genital sex for a primary relationship while allowing for non-genital BDSM with others is sometimes considered a strategy to safeguard the primary relationship for those who prefer a model of an open relationship over polyamory. This strategy only makes sense if intimacy is associated with genital contact. Yet, the intensity of many non-genital BDSM practices holds great potential to generate deep kinds of intimacy. Therefore, pure non-genital BDSM relationships may also lead to strong emotional bonds or falling in love with someone else.

The BDSM context shows that the status of a relationship as monogamous or non-monogamous actually depends on the definitions of the people involved; what counts as sex and what are the criteria for monogamy: sexual or emotional exclusivity (or both)? Since definitions of what counts as sex or emotional intimacy may differ between individuals who play together, multiple meanings may be attributed to the same encounter. Consider a spanking session where the spankee experiences sexual arousal, while the person who delivers the spanking considers this a non-sexual BDSM activity. Both may be in relationships with other people, and to the spankee this interaction may be an expression of sex outside of that relationship, while to the spanker it may not be at odds with their monogamous commitment to another person. Likewise, an emotionally monogamous couple may partake in group play with others if they can successfully manage their personal boundaries as a couple in that situation. This may for instance be achieved by the dominant making all the decisions regarding the submissive's actions in the group play dynamic. The BDSM practitioners in both examples who define as monogamous despite erotic activities outside of their couple structure can be said to renegotiate the meaning of monogamy.

(4) A philosophy of sex-positivity pervades the BDSM communities. They have developed a sexual culture that places a high priority on exploring a multitude of sexual fantasies. The broader the range of one's specific sexual interests, the more unlikely it becomes that one partner alone can provide a 'perfect match.' A BDSM coming out thus often facilitates exploring non-monogamy as well, especially if only one partner in an existing relationship expresses an interest in BDSM.[4] Related to the concept of sex-positivity is a demythologization of the meaning of sexual intimacy, in which sex is disconnected from the discourse of romantic love and is valued as a purpose in itself outside of the context of a romantic relationship. This is a rupture with the mono-normative idea that sex and love necessarily belong together, which is sometimes even perpetuated in non-monogamous contexts such as the polyamory community with its emphasis on the value of love (Klesse, 2006).

As one consequence of both possibilities, the separation of BDSM from sex and love from sex/BDSM, playing with friends has become so common in some BDSM community contexts that the mono-normative boundary between friends and lovers is rather fluid. The term 'play partner' is used to describe a type of relationship that is situated between the normative models '(nonsexual) friendship' and 'romantic/love relationship.' A person is usually considered a play partner if they a) do not possess the status of a steady, romantic or primary relationship, but b) it is expected that you will play together again in the future. In some cases, playing together takes place on a regular basis, but in other cases it can be rather irregular and there is simply an understanding between some people that playing together remains an option. While play partners are typically not considered romantic partners, emotional attachments or certain commitments are also common (as in many nonsexual friendships as well). A spatial or symbolic separation between BDSM and ordinary life may help to share moments of sexual and/

or BDSM intimacy with friends without falling in love or entering a romantic relationship. Playing in specific BDSM venues ('dungeon') may facilitate this (in comparison with a personal space such as a private apartment). Once participants exit this particular space after a session, they seem to be able to return to a regular friendship dynamic. But the separation of spaces need not be physical. Rather, it the specific alternative reality of a session that makes it possible to be friends but share a sexual experience within that semi-contained space for a limited duration. While the intention may be to restrict the connection to a friendship dynamic, these shared BDSM experiences also add an extra value to friendships, enriching and deepening these bonds.

Bound: Dominance/Submission Relationships

BDSM-specific relationship types include Dominance/submission relation-ships (D/s), in which a consensually established hierarchy is central to the relationship. The power dynamic can take on very different shapes, depending on the particular roles. Examples are owner/property, the most common version of this would be Mistress/Master-slave; caretaker/little, also referred to as age play (Bauer, 2018), the most common versions being Daddy-boy/girl; owner/animal, the most common versions being puppy play or pony play. In an ownership relationship one (or more) dominant(s) consensually own(s) one (or more) submissive(s), sometimes explicated in a written contract. These relationships are not necessarily based on romantic love, but for instance on the submissives' need to serve. The power dynamic is in part upheld by according the dominants a high degree of control over the submissives. This often includes uneven rules in regard to non-monogamy. For instance, dominants are usually free to engage in sex and BDSM outside of the owner relationship, while the submissives often face restrictions or need permission from their owners on a case-to-case basis as an expression of the power dynamic. This kind of arrangement stands in contrast to certain polyamory philosophies such as relationship anarchy as well as the ideal of harmonic sex, which calls for equality in decision-making among partners. D/s concepts such as ownership may thus reproduce possessiveness as a normative element of romantic and mono-normative discourses. Therefore, BDSM relationships may simultaneously rupture, reproduce and re-negotiate relationship norms: Possessiveness is a tenet of mono-normativity, but it is renegotiated in an asymmetrical and explicit way, which is frowned upon in today's (pseudo-)egalitarian relationship ideals, as well as polyamory philosophy.

Another practice that is a specific form of D/s non-monogamy and based on the asymmetry between partners, is lending a submissive to someone else. This not only accentuates the power dynamic, but it can additionally foster a bonding with other dominants through the sharing of submissives. And as the submissives are regularly ordered to interact with other submissives in such a situation, it may also establish special bonds among them (e.g. as 'slave brotherhoods/sisterhoods'). This can facilitate the building of intimate friendship networks. Within such networks, the (queer) BDSM-specific tradition of leather families developed (Rinella, 2003; stein & Schachter, 2009). These are kinship-of-choice structures involving BDSM power dynamics, which may culminate in shared households with various relationships and interactions among the members, also across sexual orientations, sometimes including gay men, lesbians and trans people.

D/s relationships are often structured by what is referred to as 'protocol' in the communities. On an individual level protocol can be defined as a set of rules to live by for a submissive. This may include not being allowed to use furniture or not to speak, go to the toilet, touch oneself intimately or allow others to touch oneself without permission. It may also include rules for conduct such as how to walk (half a step behind one's dominant), how and where to stand/sit/kneel in a given situation etc. On a community level, protocol can be understood as an expression of a collective consensual hierarchy. It consists of a set of rules for conduct that resembles military protocol, for instance such as never to speak to any dominant without permission, to address every dominant with a proper title like 'Sir' etc. This tradition co-exists in the communities with a more individualistic approach, where roles and what they entail are negotiated exclusively between individuals (not on a community level) and much more flexible (allowing for 'switches,' that is, people who switch between top and bottom roles).

Both, protocol and consent, structure the interactions in BDSM spaces more than mono-normative codes of conduct. For instance, my earlier comment that everyone in a play space, regardless of their relationship status may be approached for play has to be further qualified. If the person in question is the submissive of a dominant, then protocol may require the person interested in that submissive to make a formal request to their dominant, as the dominant may be entitled to that decision. So the rules of interaction focus on the D/s dynamics, not mono-normative standards of interactions.

This kind of D/s etiquette may also provide a pre-arranged structure for non-monogamous or group situations. For instance, if a dominant has to be addressed to ask for permission for any sexual interaction with their submissive, this introduces an element of respect towards existing relationships as well as communication and negotiation about the potentials and limits of extra-dyadic activities. In this way, protocol regulates interactions in BDSM spaces in a way that is simultaneously restrictive as well as supportive of non-monogamy by providing a social structure that promotes negotiating relationship choices in a very explicit, verbal manner.

Out of Bounds: Shared Intimacy

Since many fantasies that BDSM practitioners wish to actualize involve more than two, BDSM culture provides structures to play in groups and in shared community spaces. Events that are organized by community members to provide an opportunity to meet other BDSM practitioners and play together are referred to as play parties.

There is a great variety of play beyond the couple. A larger group is crucial for role-playing scenarios like military scenes, enactments of gang rape fantasies, energy pulls (in which participants put hooks through their chests, attach chains between these hooks and then all pull on each other's hooks in a circle), simulated 'slave auctions,' Victorian tea parties etc. Other types of play can be done in pairs, but adding more people provides for more complex dynamics, such as play resembling kinship structures, puppy play (where the puppies may not only have an owner but may comprise a pack), abduction scenes, interrogation scenes etc. In both types, intimacy can be established among the whole group playing together, questioning the mono-normative idea that true intimacy is limited to the number two. The development of circles of intimate friends can be an important tool for community building in BDSM contexts. Some BDSM people consider de-privatizing sex and creating collective, non-possessive forms of intimacy in this way as radical political acts, while for others it is self-serving pleasure.

In either case, at play parties, BDSM sexuality can be taken out of the closet and celebrated in a sex-positive, semi-public environment, which inspires many to play with more than one partner. Elsewhere, I have characterized this kind of play as shared intimacy (Bauer, 2014). Four types of sessions can be broadly distinguished in such a shared play space: group play in a closed group, where it is negotiated beforehand who participates in which role; sessions that are open to a certain type of involvement from bystanders, such as humiliation play that encourages others to add to the 'shame' of the bottom(s); closed sessions that are not open to involvement of bystanders but that nonetheless feed on engaged watching by others, through adding to the bottom's experience of being exposed, on display or on stage. This may enhance the intensity of their session, increasing a sense of vulnerability, loss of control, being at the mercy of their top etc. Finally, there are closed sessions which resemble private play, and the participants may even seclude themselves to a certain agree to avoid intrusions into their play space, but still enjoy playing with others playing alongside them to create an elevated atmosphere. For all purposes, sharing a play space requires a certain etiquette and there are rules at play parties, whether they are by invitation only or open to a broader public. These may typically include the prohibition of taking pictures, disturbing a session or touching without getting permission first. Sometimes participants are also encouraged to practice safer sex or refrain from too much alcohol consumption.[5]

Under favorable conditions, playing simultaneously in the same physical space can lead to synergetic effects: collective experiences beyond the individual sessions can be created. Hearing, seeing and sensing others in close proximity can add to one's own session and produce some kind of group energy. This fragile balance can be spoiled through attitudes that focus on consumption and objectification (especially of bodies read as female or beyond the gender dichotomy) rather than a comportment of mutual respect and cooperation.

CONCLUSION

What is specific about BDSM relationships? BDSM communities developed a culture of negotiated consent, which has the potential to rupture mono-normative taken for granted assumptions about how relationships are supposed to be engaged in. Properties of BDSM such as the eroticization beyond the genitals, the demythologization of sex or the preference for power dynamics over 'the myth of equality' enables the exploration of non-romantic intimacies, including sexual friendships (play partners), D/s relationships,[6] leather families, group play and shared intimacy in play party spaces.

These practices of relating simultaneously question and re-instate certain elements of mono-normativity (such as possessiveness) in order to create intimate experiences that are characterized by intensity. BDSM relationships therefore can serve as a starting point for theorizing intimacy from a perspective that focuses on issues of power and consent rather than notions of (an illusionary) equality and romantic love.

NOTES

[1]   While there is an overarching organizational structure especially in regard to activism, for the most part, the BDSM community is divided into subsets along partner preference: the heterosexual/pansexual context, the gay male context, the les-bi-trans-queer context (in some regions, but less common the alternative is a women-only community that excludes some or all trans individuals), a queer context. Therefore I refer to the BDSM communities in plural.

[2]   What I refer to here are the more collectively organized subsets of the BDSM communities which are represented through specialized venues, play parties, gatherings etc. as opposed to an unknown number of individuals who practice BDSM in the privacy of their own homes without ever connecting to any community or attending any semi-public events. The latter are much less accessible to researchers and little is known about them. I would speculate that a significant number of BDSM practitioners practice (serial) monogamy and will not seek out the community as long as they have a partner. Therefore, the reversed norm can only be safely attributed to those who practice BDSM in some kind of community context.

[3]   This has led some researchers to discuss whether BDSM is a form of sexuality at all (cf. Newmahr, 2011 and my response in Bauer, 2014).

[4]   On the other hand, incorporating BDSM into a couple's sex life may broaden their spectrum of sexual options with one another and actually decrease the desire to play with third parties.

[5]   The degree to which there are rules differs between community subsets and locally. Gay male spaces tend to prefer a less formalistic approach, and the US-American BDSM community in general is more formal than communities in Europe.

[6]   These may well be romantic in their own perception, but not necessarily from a mono-normative perspective invested in the ideal of harmonic sex.

REFERENCES

Barker, M., & Langdridge, D. (2010). Whatever happened to non-monogamies? Critical reflections on recent research and theory. *Sexualities, 13*(6), 748–772.

Bauer, R. (2010). Non-monogamy in queer BDSM communities. Putting the sex back into alternative relationship practices and discourse. In M. Barker & D. Langdridge (Eds.), *Understanding non-monogamies* (pp. 142–153). London: Routledge.

Bauer, R. (2014). *Queer BDSM intimacies. Critical consent and pushing boundaries.* Houndmills: Palgrave.

Bauer, R. (2018). Bois and grrrls meet their daddies and mommies on gender playgrounds: Gendered age play in the les-bi-trans-queer BDSM communities. *Sexualities, 21*(1–2), 139–155.

Califia, P. (2000). *Public sex. The culture of radical sex.* San Francisco, CA: Cleis Press.

Carter, J. B. (2007). *The heart of whiteness. Normal sexuality and race in America, 1880–1940.* Durham, NC & London: Duke University Press.

Foucault, M. (1978). *The history of sexuality.* New York, NY: Panthoeon.

Jamieson, L. (1999). Intimacy transformed? A critical look at the 'pure relationship.' *Sociology, 33*(3), 477–494.

Kaldera, R. (2009). *Double edge. The intersections of transgender and BDSM.* Hubbardston, MA: Alfred Press.

Kaldera, R. (2010). *Power circuits. Polyamory in a power dynamic.* Hubbardston, MA: Alfred Press.

Klesse, C. (2006). Polyamory and its 'others': Contesting the terms of non-monogamy. *Sexualities, 9*(5), 565–583.

Klesse, C. (2007). *The spectre of promiscuity. Gay male and bisexual non-monogamies and polyamories.* London: Ashgate.

Langdridge, D. (2006). Voices from the margins. Sadomasochism and sexual citizenship. *Citizenship Studies, 10*(4), 373–389.

Leap, W. L. (1999). Introduction. In W. L. Leap (Ed.), *Public sex/gay space* (pp. 1–21). New York, NY: Columbia University Press.

Newmahr, S. (2011). *Playing on the edge. Sadomasochism, risk, and intimacy.* Bloomington, IN: Indiana University Press.

Pieper, M., & Bauer, R. (2005). Polyamory und Mono-Normativität. Ergebnisse einer empirischen Studie über nicht-monogame Lebensformen. In L. Méritt, T. Bührmann, & N. B. Schefzig (Eds.), *Mehr als eine Liebe. Polyamouröse Beziehungen* (pp. 59–69). Berlin: Orlanda.

Riggs, D. W. (2006). *Priscilla, (White) queen of the desert. Queer rights/race privilege.* New York, NY: Peter Lang.

Rinella, J. (2003). *Partners in power. Living in kinky relationships.* Oakland, CA: Greenery Press.

Sloan, L. J. (2015). Ace of (BDSM) clubs: Building asexual relationships through BDSM practice. *Sexualities, 18*(5–6), 548–536.

stein, d., & Schachter, D. (2009). *Ask the man who owns him. The real lives of gay masters and slaves.* New York, NY: Perfectbound Press.

Thomas, E. J., Stelzl, M., & Lafrance, M. N. (2017). Faking to finish: Women's accounts of feigning sexual pleasure to end unwanted sex. *Sexualities, 20*(3), 281–301.

Weiss, M. D. (2008). Gay shame and BDSM pride. Neoliberalism, privacy, and sexual politics. *Radical History Review, 100*, 86–101.

Weiss, M. D. (2011). *Techniques of pleasure. BDSM and the circuits of sexuality.* Durham, NC: Duke University Press.

ANGELA JONES

11. KINK WORK ONLINE

The Diffuse Lives of Erotic Webcam Workers and Their Clients

INTRODUCTION

Virtual space creates an environment where people feel comfortable to speak and act as they would not normally in their lives offline. In this chapter, I explore the diffuse lives of cam performers who perform kink services online. I use the term "diffuse life" to suggest that our offline and online experiences share a symbiotic relationship. Waskul and Martin (2010) studied *Second Life*[1] and sexual encounters in this interactive virtual world, and their analysis was instructive. The authors focused on the diffuse life of second lifers; they showed how a person's first life (e.g., life offline) also influenced their second life (e.g., life online). Waskul and Martin argued:

> When people write themselves into existence, one's Second Life is often remarkably like the first and vice versa. Not unlike other forms of online chat and cybersex, Second Life functions as a computer-mediated looking glass, albeit an idealized one. On the one hand, the anonymous and disembodied nature of the medium allows people to freely explore interests, desires, and curiosities with little or no constraint. On the other hand, people literally and figuratively fashion an avatar-self in both images and words—as both an ecstatic (re)presentation and in ongoing narratives. In creating these erotic avatar-selves, they draw from their own embodied self that is either credited or discredited in dramatic Second Life interactions. (pp. 309–310)

Drawing form Waskul and Martin, I posit that we must trouble the binary offline/online—the encounters people have online affect their lives offline, and our offline lives affect the interactions we have online. The pleasures we experience and the rewards we acquire in either context can stay with us, even as we move in and out of these different contexts.

The Internet creates a space where people feel uninhibited and the fear of panoptic sexual regulation ceases to exist.[2] Based on what performers

© KONINKLIJKE BRILL NV, LEIDEN, 2019 | DOI:10.1163/9789004414105_012

who I interviewed said, the online context lowers inhibitions and allows people to be a more authentic version of themselves, even if both performers and clients interact under pseudonyms. For performers and their clients, the online context allows participants to consent to enact fantasies that they would not always engage in offline, and thus the camming industry is a space in which people can experience new forms of pleasure. In addition to providing documentation of kink work in the camming industry, my goal in examining the diffuse lives of cam models and clients is to show that a symbiotic relationship between people's cam lives and offline lives exists.

THE CAMMING INDUSTRY

The camming industry is a multi-billion dollar industry and since the camming industry emerged online in 1996, the industry has employed over an estimated two million people (Jones, 2019). The camming industry is an exponentially growing field where many workers from all over the globe are finding decent wages, greater autonomy, community, and pleasure. A *New York Times* reporter, Matt Richtel wrote, "the cam business, a kind of digital era peep show, has been around for a few years, but as the technology has become better and cheaper…it has created a money-making opportunity in a pornography business eroded by the distribution of free content on the internet" (2013, p. 1). The camming industry offers sexual consumers a new and different way in which to consume pornographic content online. Camming is unique and different from traditional pornography because camming is interactive. Clients are purchasing a live and intimate encounter with an amateur—a real person—as they see it, which is substantially different than purchasing a prerecorded and scripted pornographic film.

The people who labor in this growing online sex industry are called cam models. Cam models are a cohort of sex workers who use chat rooms to sell a range of erotic fantasies to online patrons. Cam models engage in intimate conversation, exotic strip-tease, and perform explicit sex acts with clients online. Cam models are independent contractors, which means they pay the website (called a cam site) to work. The cam site pays-out a commission to the model, which is generally 35–50% of all sales made on the cam site by the performer. Many cam models also use cam sites to build-up a following of regular clients that they perform private shows for on platforms such as Skype. On some cam sites, such as Chaturbate, cam models perform in public shows and receive tips called tokens. On other cam sites, such as Streamate, cam models perform in private pay-per-minute shows. There are cam sites that offer both public shows and private shows.

For consumers, the camming industry is a safe space for the consumption of sex. The restrictions that culture places on people's sexual desires forces them to often seek out sexual gratification in secrecy, where they feel safe from surveillance, judgment, and sanctions. Therefore, people carve out alternative spaces for the exploration of sexual desires. BDSM subcultures are a clear example of one such space (Cruz, 2016; Simula, 2013; Weiss, 2011). Simula (2013) wrote about the BDSM practitioners in her study:

> First, participants frame BDSM scenes as interruptions to everyday vanilla life and describe experiencing moments of what Munoz calls "ecstatic time," which create temporal disruptions between the here and now and the then and there of past and future utopian beyond. Second, participants experience these queer moments of ecstatic time as presenting opportunities for resisting heteronormativity and gender regulation in ways they perceive as unavailable to them in other social settings. (pp. 78–79)

Engaging in BDSM in subcultures and BDSM play allow people to escape the intense sexual and gender regulation that they face in their daily lives. When people do not want to explore BDSM offline in BDSM clubs and events they can purchase these services from sex workers in private. Studies have also documented how people seek out the services of pro-dommes to explore their desires for BDSM play in privacy and secrecy (see Levey & Pinsky, 2015; Lindemann, 2010, 2012). The camming industry is an example of such a space—a space where people feel free to explore their sexual desires, in ways that for myriad reasons they might not offline.

In what follows, I specifically explore how the camming industry also provides an alternative space for the exploration of kinky sexual desires, which has numerous benefits for people's lives offline. As an additional and important note for readers, while cam models come from countries all over the globe and are diverse in their gender and racial identities, due to the scope and length of this chapter, there is a lack of diverse representation of cam models in this chapter as well as discussions that I could not explore in-depth. However, readers can find deeper conversations about the intersections of and role of gender, race, nationality, class, sexuality, ability, and age in the camming industry in my book *Camming: Money, Power, and Pleasure in the Sex Industry.*

KINK WORK ONLINE

"Kink" is an umbrella term used to describe a range of non-normative sexual practices. In the camming industry, performing kink involves enacting specific BDSM practices and role-plays, which involve exchanges of power within various forms of play, such as bondage and discipline, D/s dominance and submission, and SM sadism and masochism. BDSM scenes or interactions are characterized as play or interactions through which consenting individuals explore and transgress sociocultural boundaries. Cam performers are often asked to facilitate a wide range of BDSM scenes, many of which include role-playing scenes for which they earn top-dollar. I spoke with cam models who specialize in kink, who charge anywhere from $10–$15 USD per minute for performing kink work. For example, Rebecca, a performer whom I introduce later, makes $7,000 per month camming and has earned as much as $12,000 in one month. In what follows, I discuss the most popular role-playing requests among the cam models in my study. These BDSM role-plays were race-play, cuckholding and small penis humiliation, and incest-play and age-play.

Race-Play

Race-play is a role-playing scenario that often involves using racial slurs during sex acts and in many cases specific role-playing scripts, such as reenacting a master/slave relationship on a United States plantation. For example, a Black man wants to play as a submissive (sub) in a scene where a White woman or man to play the dominant role of a slave owner and then degrade him as a slave. In a script where the Black man is in a dominant (dom) role, the role-play could include him consensually fucking the plantation owner's White wife or role-playing a rape and raping the plantation owner's wife. In both scenarios, the fantasy is used to reconcile the historical trauma of slavery and the legacy of White supremacy that still marginalizes and oppresses Black people globally.

All role-play is about power, and Black cam models in my research generally said that race-play was empowering when they were the dom in the scene. As a sub, many felt degraded but also noted that these race-play scenes also allowed them to push and experiment with their own sexual boundaries. As one performer named Crystal explained in a post on a web form for cam models, a White man can call her an ebony goddess while she enacts pegging him (fucking him anally with a strap-on) or humiliates that same man for having a small cock, but White men may not under any circumstances call her racial epithets such as nigger. By managing these encounters in this way, she can find empowerment from the encounter by either dominating these White men or simply in having the power to deny them the power to dominate her. In a race-play scenario, where a Black woman degrades a White man the pleasurable exchange of power occurs through her exploitation and co-optation of White supremacist discourses. The power Crystal experiences in these scenes reflect specific forms of power she cannot usually exercise in her everyday life due the overlapping systems of White supremacy and patriarchy. While cam models do not actually transcend the overlapping systems of White supremacy and patriarchy, their experiences of kink work online are no doubt shaped by them and challenge them. In addition, the empowering experiences cam models often have while working affect their experiences in offline contexts. This is precisely why the cam models in my study frequently reported improved self-concept and body-image as well as feeling more sexually empowered as a result of becoming cam models (Jones, 2019).

In sum, race-play can create cathartic spaces and pleasurable spaces for Black performers, especially when they are performing a dominant role in the role-playing scene. Importantly, unlike Black BDSM practitioners in an offline club or private party, cam models are not initiating the encounter. Thus, while cam performers consent to race-play, their agency is limited because, for most models, the race-play scene is not their fantasy but rather the fantasy of their client. As Miller-Young (2014) noted, "[i]f black prostitution offered white clientele the ability to enact racial sexual fantasy and black people an economy in which to exploit these fantasies for their own economic and personal needs, illicit pornographic film production provided another arena for these conflicting desires to operate." Therefore, race-play in the camming industry is only another part of a much longer history of spaces that cater to the desires for White clientele to explore racial fantasies, which also creates economic opportunity for Black performers willing to exploit racist discourses and tropes.

Cuckholding and Small Penis Humiliation

A cuckhold is a man who encourages his wife or girlfriend to have sex with other people. Watching his partner have sex with other men brings him pleasure. There are cuckholds who want to play a role in choosing if not controlling with whom his partner has sex. Alternatively, there are also cuckholds who want the dom to select the person who will fuck his partner. Female cam models specializing in kink work told me that cuckholding is one of the most popular fetishes they are asked to facilitate. Cam models said that in private shows they get a lot of submissive cuckholds who also want to be humiliated during the scene.

In addition, small penis humiliation (SPH) is often integrated into cuckholding. SPH is a role-play involving a person(s) embarrassing a man for having a small penis. Thus, SPH is often requested as part of cuckholding shows because SPH involves humiliating the submissive for not being able to please his female partner with their small penis. Moreover, some cuckholding clients also want to add aspects of race-play to these scenarios. There are submissive White male clients, who do not only want to be humiliated by watching their wife/girlfriend get fucked by another man; they want that other man to be a Black man. In fact, the racialized component is part of the humiliation fetish.

Under White supremacy, Black men are relegated to an inferior social position. Moreover, hegemonic masculinity requires that men feel in control and dominant (Connell & Messerschmidt, 2005). In their relentless and ongoing quest for masculine validation, men often assert themselves over other men, demean women, and queer folks. Therefore, watching his wife or girlfriend get fucked by a Black man, according to these societal standards, is a great source of humiliation and assault to his manhood. The pleasure found in this particular exchange of power is derived from humiliating the submissive partner(s). However, these pleasurable experiences are also shaped by overlapping systems of oppression—namely, capitalism, patriarchy, White supremacy, heterosexism, cissexism, and ableism. In a world that places unrealistic pressures on men to be the manliest among his peers, cuckholding and SPH role-plays can feel freeing for the client, and for cam models, they told me, it is often fascinating, pleasurable, and lucrative work.

Incest and Age-Play

Incest or family play requests often involve role-playing intimate relationships between family members. Age-play involves role-playing scenes in which the cam model performs the role of a young person. However, in age-play scenes, cam models often highlighted that they will never actually say that they are under 18 years old. Age-play often overlaps with incest-play. Among performers, popular requests included daddy-daughter, and among performers who marketed themselves as mature or milf, mother-son is also popular. These fantasies and scenes allow people to push social boundaries around incest taboos, without actually breaking the incest taboo, and, thus, facing the possibility of criminal and/or social sanctions. In addition, many performers highlighted that the online context provides a space for clients to experience their fantasies in a safe, sane, and consensual[3] way. BDSM practitioners experiment and explore their own subjectivities and desires in relationship to power and, in doing so, produce pleasurable experiences. In addition, these educational and pleasurable experiences affect the lives of all participants offline as well.

CAM MODELS AND THE DIFFUSE LIFE

In my research, performers highlighted that performing kinky shows with clients also provided them with an opportunity to explore and enjoy kinky sex. Alexandra is a 28-year-old poly bisexual White cis woman from the United States, and she told me about the benefits of camming for her own sexual and romantic life. She said, "[camming] provides an avenue to experience BDSM without putting the strain on my partner who is not as into BDSM as I am. It helps me feel better about being polyamorous while being in a monogamous relationship." Alexandra explained that performing BDSM shows as part of her work is satisfying because her partner, does not want to actively engage in kinky sex and is also monogamous. Thus, for Alexandra, her cam work allows her to experience satisfaction in her relationship. It is not only that her BDSM shows are sexually pleasurable for her; her cam performances also have a lasting effect on her relationship. She identifies as polyamorous, and her cam work satisfies her desire to have sexual encounters outside of her primary relationship. The pleasure Alexandra acquires online echoes through and affects her offline life. As I argue throughout this chapter, it is important that in camming, customers can have pleasurable experiences exploring kink that they feel they cannot have offline. However, the crucial point is that, as Alexandra's comments show, these kinky encounters online have an effect on and are shaped by the individuals' lives offline as well.

As another example, I spoke with a performer named Elizabeth who specializes in kink services. Elizabeth is a 38-year-old bisexual White cis woman form the United States. Elizabeth has worked in and out of the sex industry since the late 90s. She has been an exotic dancer and dominatrix and returned to camming in 2014. Elizabeth and I talked about how her own identity and beliefs shape the pleasure she experiences in her kink shows with regular private clients. Elizabeth explained that because of her own religious identity, she also loves performing role-plays with clients that push religious social boundaries.

Elizabeth: Blasphemy is something that I always advertise. Blasphemy is a huge fetish, and I always love doing it; it must be so freeing (laughs), for some of these suppressed people. I am a nontheistic Satanist, and I enjoy the opportunity to release people from the shackles of religious convention even if it is only for a moment, because I feel that religion is a big part of what is wrong with this world. Also, I have the wardrobe and an endless imagination for the blasphemous to play this role easily and with little effort.

AJ: (Laughs) Can you tell me more about that? Like, so what would that show look like?

Elizabeth: Oh, my goodness, it depends. I do a succubus show, and I pretend and act out a lot of the stuff that I do. It's can be bizarre, like really perverse mime and spoken improvisation. (Laughs). But some more direct examples I can think of are desecrating Bibles through various means or crucifix strap-ons. Just saying really horrible things about God, describing blasphemous scenes, like bending over priests and fucking them on the altar. Speaking of really unholy descriptive scenes, insisting guys condemn God and worship Satan.

For people who have had complex and antagonistic relationships with religious institutions, especially those who have felt controlled by religion, engaging in blasphemy-play can feel freeing for the client. However, unlike other sex industries, the camming industry is built around mutual pleasure. Elizabeth also finds pleasure in her scenes as a dom and exploring her own sexuality. The pleasure Elizabeth experiences is shaped by her offline identity. In addition to the sexual pleasure she derives from dom role-play, as a nontheistic Satanist woman, it is pleasurable for Elizabeth to perform a show, which involves her fucking a man with a crucifix strap-on while he condemns god—a simultaneous fuck you to institutionalized religion and patriarchy. Cam models use their kink work to explore their own sexual desires. Again, Elizabeth's story highlighted that our offline and online lives are synergetic and inform one another, even if we are operating online under a manufactured identity.

CLIENTS AND THE DIFFUSE LIFE

Cam performers build intimate relationships with regular clients who they perform for in private shows. The kink work that performers do in the context of private shows is not merely about delivering an economic service to a stranger. Elizabeth and I were also talking about one of her regulars and the relationship they have cultivated over a period of two years:

I had this one customer; he's a hockey player, and has a really good, high-end job, [and] makes decent money. And he gets all kinky and sissy for me, and I humiliate him; and then he cums, and then he cries. And then I comfort him for like half-an-hour. It's gotten better now, but he's like, I'll never be able to have a normal life being submissive! I'm like, what? I said do you think that you need to be totally vanilla to have a wife and kids someday? I'm like you can find a girl that will kick the shit out of you and fuck you in your ass, and then have your kids. It doesn't have to be [this way], but people are so ingrained [into] *normal* [sexuality], they're made to feel guilty. You don't even understand, dude! Like, you can have it all!....But they just have this image in their head, that they're wrong, and that they'll never have a normal life because they're kinky....They never go see a therapist. I've worried about him before. I'm said maybe you should you go talk to someone. I'm not a healthcare professional, love. Yea, I've taken a ton of psych classes, but I'm not qualified. He's like, well, you are more than that [to me]; I couldn't go tell some stranger this. But he's been doing a lot better. He used to do this thing where he would throw away his lingerie and throw away his webcams. He'd throw away all of his kinky stuff, and then he'd go buy it again the next week. I'm like, ok, dude, you're gonna get a safe, and put that shit in there! (laughs). We'll have to find a way for me to open it, but stop doing it, you're spending all this money. I said, give it to me; you can buy new lingerie, and I won't throw it away (laughs)....He's doing so much better now too; I'm so happy. I've been working with him for two years, and now, he's gone on [a kink website]; he's meeting up with some dom, and he's exploring now. And he's not feeling guilt about it. And I'll pat myself on the back for helping with that, but honestly, I'm honored. If I can do that for people, then, I can't think of a more important thing to teach people than to not feel bad for their urges. As long as it's consensual and you're not hurting anyone, who the fuck cares? Like, do it up!

In this story, Elizabeth discussed the reality that kink work is about so much more than just a service worker who delivers a sexual service. She cared about this man. He cared about her. Elizabeth helped him become more comfortable with his own desires. In their sessions, they developed an intimate relationship. She assisted him to become more at peace with

157

himself. Their interactions had an effect on him outside of their sessions. Kink performers often provide clients with emotional, instrumental, and informational support. Elizabeth provided this client with emotional support by comforting him and affirming his desires. She also told me about providing him with education about BDSM and suggesting other offline sources of support. Especially in BDSM shows, the support models provide to clients can be just as important as the immediate sexual service they provide because the work the cam model and client do online can help affect their sexual lives offline—often improving clients' sex lives offline and making the client more sexually empowered offline as well.

Consider also Rebecca's story. Rebecca is a 34-year-old polyamorous White cis woman. She has been a sex worker for 16 years and has been camming for over 7 years. Rebecca, like Elizabeth also specializes in kink services in the camming industry. In our interview, we discussed the importance of the education that she provides clients:

> I'm usually pretty personable, even when I'm doing dom shows, like, my regular, slave guys will come to me and ask me questions because I'm an open book. I also know a lot about what I'm talking about. So, if we talk about lifestyle BDSM, I was in a collared relationship for two years—polyamorous collared relationship. So, I can sit there and talk about that all day long. I've been classically trained as a dom. So, I can actually talk about it, so that it that helps. I mean, yeah, and me being female and White definitely does help....Also, me doing as much fetish modeling beforehand here and there out here...and I think people automatically knew who I was or they'd come across me, oh, I watched your videos on such and such site, and that helped because I already kind of had a name before even starting to cam....I've also gotten some dom/sub couples where...it's a male dom and a female submissive, so that's been pretty interesting. I had a regular client; I haven't seen him for a few months, but, he would come and he would ask how, how like what he should do with her; and I was part of their role-play so that was kind of neat. I've watched couples and like instructed them on what to do together, so that was always interesting, 'cause that brought me back to the days when...I worked in an underground brothel out here for a little while...it was the front for a swingers club so we actually had couples in there so all us girls would be like ok, well, why don't you do this! Why don't you try this?!" Like, so, it kind of brought that back like, I'm doing the same thing I did in 2002.

Being successful as a kink performer requires skill and cultural capital. Rebecca was able to educate single clients as well as couples exploring BDSM. Rebecca's work does more than just educate; she works to validate people's desires and to support them in their sexual journeys. She continued:

> I was in a documentary a couple weeks ago; they filmed me and they were like, why do they do this? I'm like, well, they can't do it in everyday life, you know? Like, not everyone's wife is gonna be like oh, you can totally pie me in the face! (Laughs) Go ahead, hunny or like, oh, yeah, when I have to fart, I'm totally farting on you. Like, I know that turns you on. Most women would run; they'd be like, no, I can't do this. I feel that I help people a lot to realize that they're not weird; they're not strange, and the things that they are into are just things they are into and that it doesn't say anything bad about them. That's just what turns them on! And what right do I have to judge someone for what they get turned on by? Or I've had guys who were really into feet and then realized, like, after talking to me for so long, they're like it's ok if you're wanting to go, like, to a foot party and worship someone's feet. Like, I can actually, like, actualize my fantasy and not hurt anyone and the other person's into it. So that's pretty cool, too.

Rebecca performs an immediate service, but the long-term value of her work cannot be underestimated. She helps change people's everyday lives and helps them to acquire the skills they need to practice BDSM in safe, consensual, and sane ways offline. She helps them come to terms with who they are and to become comfortable practicing BDSM offline.

CONCLUSION

Performing kink online has numerous benefits for cam models. First, given that BDSM play is taboo and highly stigmatized in various societies and cultures, performers can charge a premium for these services. Therefore, performers who perform kink well can make a great deal of money by marketing and branding themselves as fetish or kink performers. Second, performers can use their interactions with clients in BDSM shows to explore their own sexual subjectivities. For performers like Crystal, Alexandra, and Elizabeth, doing kink work meant they could explore and enjoy their own sexual desires and boundaries while working. Third, the work that kink performers do with clients can have positive effects on both the lives of the client and the performer. In exploring sexual desires, and by pushing sociocultural boundaries through role-play, people can find ephemeral moments of freedom from regulatory forces in society that control human sexual behavior. In fact, it is these ephemeral moments of freedom that create the basis for their experience of pleasure. However, there are two crucial problems with this reading of kink work online.

First, BDSM play on or offline can feel like a radical experience of alterity—that is an escape from the social systems that confine our desires and restrict our bodies, which does produce pleasure. However, as Margot Weiss (2011) has argued, BDSM play can and does feel freeing to many, but BDSM play still exists within the realm of social relations and various overlapping systems of oppression. For example, race-play is a pleasurable fantasy and experience for some people. The use of racially charged epithets such as nigger during sex and role-playing involving slave narratives is a way that some Black folks, for example can move past historical and current racial trauma by taking control and ownership over how these words are used in their interactions with White people. Transgressing social boundaries and playing with race in ways that we are not supposed to can feel empowering and freeing. However, various forms of BDSM play, not just race-play, also reinforce existing systems of oppression such as White supremacy, patriarchy, and cissexism. For example, while not discussed in-depth here, despite the presence of consent, and the pleasurable outcomes for some models what are the effects of a trans woman engaging in role-play as a sub with a dom who degrades her and calls her a sissy? What are the effects of creating yet another space for White men to degrade people of color who are hired to play as a sub? The point is, as research has already shown, despite the pleasure and empowerment that many people find in these types of play scenes, these interactions still reinforce existing forms of racial, gendered, and classed-based power arrangements and entitlements.

The second issue with reading kink work online as a utopian story is that not all kinky play online will produce positive effects for clients and performers. For example, increasingly, due to market saturation, many cam performers strategically market themselves using tags such as #fetish in order to drive additional traffic to their rooms. This hashtag can have a positive effect by creating more visibility for kinky sex and, thus, potentially help to discursively push sociocultural boundaries regulating sex. However, performing kink work often involves highly specialized cultural capital. As Weiss (2011) showed in her study of BDSM, practicing BDSM requires highly specialized techniques. Performers who do not properly execute BDSM practices could not only lose clients, but could cause harm to themselves and clients. Thus, poorly performed BDSM can cause economic harm to models, and psychological harm to both model and client. Even in an online context, BDSM play should still always be safe, sane, and consensual.

When BDSM is practiced safely, sanely, and consensually by cam models and their clients the pleasures they experience are plenty. People can use the camming industry as a way to explore their sexual identities. People's offline identities will inform what services clients' seek and what services cam models will perform and how both parties experience these acts when performed online. Moreover, their experiences online can have positive effects on their lives offline. Thus, the experiences of cam models and their clients online and offline share a symbiotic relationship. Finally, these online sexual encounters also make a political contribution. As more performers tag themselves on cam sites and social media platforms, such as Twitter with tags including #fetish, #dom, #Findom #Femdom #SPH #torture #bdsm #fetishcam #kink, #humiliatrix #dominatrix, #slave, #humiliation, and so forth, they help to create further visibility for kink practices online, and even if in a small way, performing kink work online can help to challenge the rigid way societies define appropriate sexuality.

NOTES

[1] *Second Life* is an online virtual world developed by Linden Lab and launched in 2003. In 2013, SL had approximately one million active users/residents who participate in this virtual world. Residents create avatars of themselves, and interact and socialize with another. People trade virtual property and services. On the Linden Lab website, they say, "Second Life [is] the pioneering virtual world that's been enjoyed by millions of people and seen billions of dollars transacted among users in its economy .http://secondlife.com/

[2] Panoptics refers to a system of surveillance in which an authority figure can monitor and control people's behavior from one central location. For example, Jeremy Benthem famously studied the structure of prisons. If a prison is a circular tower then a guard can be stationed in the center of the cells and monitor all the prisoners from one central position. Michael Foucault, also discussed the use of panoptic surveillance in modern society. The fear of being watched and as result being caught and punished for transgressing social norms produces conformity to social norms. Contemporary society is a site of incessant surveillance and many people conform to norms regarding sexuality (however antiquated they are) out of fear of being caught and punished.

[3] Safe, Sane, and Consensual is a phrase used in BDSM communities, which empathize that all play should be performed safely by individuals who have taken care to become educated and skilled in these practices so they do not harm their partners. Second, play should be sane. This means all play should be practiced by individuals with the capacity to exercise good and responsible judgment. Finally, all play should be consensual and properly negotiated prior to the initiation of any play.

REFERENCES

Connell, R. W., & Messerschmidt, J. W. (2005). Hegemonic masculinity: Rethinking the concept. *Gender and Society, 19*(6), 829–859.

Cruz, A. (2016). *The color of kink: Black women, BDSM, and pornography.* New York, NY: NYU Press.

Jones, A. (2015). For Black models scroll down: Web-cam modelling and the racialization of erotic labor. *Sexuality and Culture, 19*(4), 776–799.

Jones, A. (2016). "I get paid to have orgasms": Adult webcam models negotiation of pleasure and danger. *Signs: Journal of Women in Culture and Society, 42*(1), 227–256.

Jones, A. (2019). *Camming: Money, power, and pleasure in the sex industry.* New York, NY: New York University Press.

Levey, T. G., & Pinsky, D. (2015). A constellation of stigmas: Intersectional stigma management and the professional dominatrix. *Deviant Behavior, 36*(5), 1–21.

Lindemann, D. J. (2010). Will the real dominatrix please stand up: Artistic purity and professionalism in the S&M dungeon. *Sociological Forum, 25*(3), 588–606.

Lindemann, D. J. (2012). *Dominatrix: Gender, eroticism, and control in the dungeon.* Chicago, IL: University of Chicago Press.

Miller-Young, M. (2014). *A taste for brown sugar: Black women in pornography.* Durham, NC: Duke University Press.

Richtel, M. (2013, September 21). Intimacy on the web, with a crowd. *New York Times*, pp. 1–9.

Sanders, T. (2005). It's just acting: Sex workers' strategies for capitalising on sexuality. *Gender, Work and Organization, 12*(4), 319–342.

Simula, B. L. (2013). Queer utopias in painful spaces: BDSM participants' interrelational resistance to heternormativity and gender regulation. In A. Jones (Ed.), *A critical inquiry into queer utopias* (p. 78). New York, NY: Palgrave.

Waskul, D. D., & Martin, J. A. (2010). Now the orgy is over. *Symbolic Interaction, 33*(2), 297–318.

Weiss, M. (2011). *Techniques of pleasure: BDSM and the circuits of sexuality.* Durham, NC: Duke University Press.

KATHERINE MARTINEZ

12. BDSM DISCLOSURES AND THE CIRCLE OF INTIMATES

A Mixed Methods Analysis of Identity and Disclosure Audience and Response

I had no problems coming out bisexual, no problems being a witch.[1] I had no problems being anything, but that one was very hard for me; it was very difficult for me and I still felt pretty isolated and alone.

(White, female, Switch)

My concept has always been that the BDSM community, we are probably 20 to 30 years behind the gay, lesbian, and transgender community in terms of our ability to be out.

(White, male, Submissive)

INTRODUCTION

Identity-based disclosures for those with invisible differences serve many different functions, such as promoting individual health and wellness, networking, and community building, all of which can be quite empowering. For instance, a White-passing person of color may disclose their racial/ethnic identity to build community around shared cultural practices and interests. Or, a heterosexual-passing cisgender queer person may disclose their sexual identity to network with other queer-identified individuals. In some of these cases, networking and building community further serve to improve one's health, safety, and wellness, as one gains a stronger sense of self and improved self-confidence (Tabaac, Perrin, & Trujillo, 2015). Further, community support ensures that those who disclose receive the resources necessary to survive and thrive post-disclosure. Yet, disclosures may also be anxiety and fear-producing; individuals may experience negative reactions from their audience, such as fear, anger, violence, and/or aggression. Disclosure, thus, is an important consideration for anybody living with an invisible difference, but perhaps especially those whose "difference" is socially stigmatized, like those who participate in bondage, discipline, dominance/submission, and sadomasochism (BDSM).[2]

© KONINKLIJKE BRILL NV, LEIDEN, 2019 | DOI:10.1163/9789004414105_013

Although many BDSM participants do not explicitly utilize BDSM and/or kink as a sexual identity, some do, and even consider their BDSM role (i.e., dominant, submissive, switch) more important to their self-conceptualization than their orientation as lesbian, gay, bisexual, pansexual, queer, or heterosexual (Better & Simula, 2015; also see Chaline, 2010; Gemberling, Cramer, & Miller, 2015). Those who do not conceptualize their BDSM practices as identity, though, often utilize the acronym as an adjective to describe their sexual practices and performances (Weiss, 2006). For instance, a heterosexual BDSM participant may identify as kinky or sadomasochistic, designating their sexual practices, fantasies, and desires as being different from those who predominantly engage in "vanilla" sex, or that which is considered conventional (i.e., missionary position, without fetishistic fantasies and desires). This difference designates BDSM participants as a group that may potentially need to disclose their sexual practices at some point in their lives, to any number of individuals (i.e., partners, parents, friends, co-workers, and even doctors or police, lawyers, and judges) and for any number of reasons (i.e., health and wellness, networking, community building, and even to allay fears of family and friends or fight criminal charges for consensual but unconventional sex practices). Although previous studies have addressed the reasons for BDSM disclosure, few studies have explored who is told and their reactions to disclosure. This is the specific goal for the current study, especially as these relate to participant gender, sexual identity, race/ethnicity, BDSM role, and participant physical location.

Reasons for BDSM Disclosure

The extant research on BDSM disclosures have revealed that these disclosures serve similar purposes to LGBTQ identity disclosures (National Sexual Violence Resource Center): they help individuals develop closer relationships with significant others and help them connect with others in their respective communities. Bezreh, Weinberg, and Edgar (2012) published one of the most comprehensive qualitative studies to describe BDSM disclosures. In their interviews with 20 adults reporting an interest in BDSM, they asked participants about their disclosure experiences and concerns surrounding behavior stigma. Most participants in this study described the challenges they faced in balancing the desire to connect with intimate others, including partners and family members, through disclosure, and the desire to avoid being viewed as strange or dangerous post-disclosure. Some participants in this study disclosed based on the desire to "be oneself," while others disclosed because a close friend requested disclosure. Most often those who chose not to disclose did so to "protect" their audience and/or because they saw sex-talk, but especially kinky-sex-talk, as taboo.

Stiles and Clark (2011) also interviewed 73 BDSM participants, asking them about their disclosure practices. They, like Bezreh, Weinberg, and Edgar, noted that participants often chose not to disclose their BDSM practices, although Stiles and Clark framed non-disclosure as an exercise in identity management.[3] In other words, non-disclosure served to "save face" for participants hoping to maintain a normative presentation of self in the workplace and home. They also chose non-disclosure to "protect" significant others from discomfort and to build a sense of in-group identity and excitement. For some, then, non-disclosure also served the purpose of building community, although they were building community as part of a subculture and perhaps even "out-group."[4] While these explanations of why BDSM participants disclose their practices and identities to significant others is important for understanding the complexities of disclosure for marginalized groups, much less is known about to whom BDSM participants disclose, or the demographic factors related to disclosure.

The audience of BDSM disclosure is particularly important for considering the work that must be done within the BDSM community to further support specific subgroups who may face additional disclosure challenges[5] because of their multiple, intersecting identities. For instance, in LGBTQ disclosure studies, researchers have found that age, gender, race/ethnicity, and location serve as important factors for determining identity disclosure (Grov, Bimbi, Nanín, & Parsons, 2006; Rosario, Schrimshaw, & Hunter, 2004; Schope, 2002; Swank, Fahs, & Frost, 2013). Specifically, Brown, Baunach, and Burgess (2015) found that those with identity-based privileges (i.e., White and male) and those who live in more populous areas are more likely to disclose their LGBTQ identities than those without these privileges and those in less populous areas, possibly because those without privilege face more challenges from their disclosure audience. Not much is known about whether these general disclosure trends exist similarly for BDSM participants, who may experience different identity-based stigmas due to their unique sexual identities, practices, and desires.

The Current Study

Several important findings from the National Coalition for Sexual Freedom (NCSF)[6] (2008) and Bezreh, Weinberg, and Edgar's (2012) studies on

BDSM disclosures highlight the various factors involved in disclosure decisions. For instance, gender and sexual identity may negatively impact disclosure, given the already high risk for violence and stigmatization. Also, age may be important to consider when analyzing disclosure behaviors, such that older generations may be less inclined to disclose due to their lack of visibility and support both within and outside the BDSM community. In addition, the circle of intimates which identifies spouses, family, friends, and acquaintances (including co-workers) in a progressive order of intimacy via concentric circles (see Figure 1), may not adequately work to determine disclosure for BDSM participants; the assumption is that one might disclose to those with whom one feels most intimate. Yet, in Bezreh, Weinberg, and Edgar's study, BDSM disclosures were often described as needs-based (i.e., who needs to know?), and spouses/partners and family were often not identified as those needing to know about specific sexual behaviors and desires. Finally, most participants in this study did not disclose at work, highlighting the reality that BDSM participants still fear discrimination in the workplace.

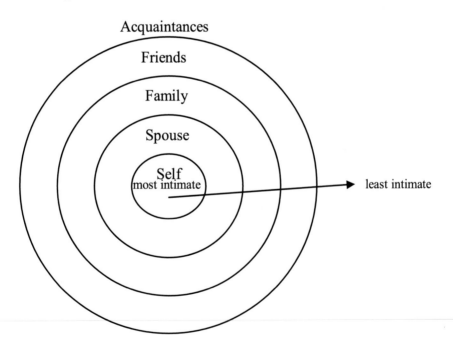

Figure 1. Circle of intimates

Given that Bezreh, Weinberg, and Edgar did not have the data to make connections between BDSM disclosure and other intersecting identities (i.e., gender, sexual identity, race/ethnicity, BDSM identity, etc.), they described one of their study limitations as relating to some subgroups within the BDSM population having specific and distinct experiences of disclosure and stigma. As was noted by the NCSF 2008 survey on violence and discrimination, women and LGBTQ individuals are subgroups that appear to experience higher disclosure violence and discrimination, although it is unclear whether they also disclose at higher rates or if they experience violence from those to whom they disclose. As a contribution to these studies, I present here a mixed-methods analysis of BDSM disclosures, with a focus on several other factors which may or may not contribute to disclosure, such as participant gender, sexual identity, age, race/ethnicity, BDSM role, and physical location; I present survey participant reports about disclosure audience and their reactions, as well as themes emerging from interviews about BDSM disclosures.

METHODS

This mixed-methods study was approved by the University of Colorado at Boulder Human Research Committee (HRC). All participants were recruited from two popular international social networking websites (Fetlife.com and TheWasteland.com) for sadomasochists and fetishists and two local BDSM clubs. The original research proposal included a 54-question survey which asked participants to report on their "experiences and perceptions of their bodies within BDSM play."[7] The survey had four sections, the first two of which were utilized for this study: (1) demographics, including gender and sexual identities, age range, race/ethnicity, and physical location and (2) experiences with BDSM play, including role identity, and BDSM identity disclosure and response. Demographic variables and BDSM role identities were treated as independent variables, while BDSM disclosures and responses were treated as dependent variables in this study.[8] Participants who completed the survey could volunteer for a face-to-face or telephone/ Skype, semi-structured interview. In interviews, participants were asked more specific questions about their BDSM disclosures, such as "Have you 'come out' to spouses, family, friends, or co-workers about your participation in the BDSM community? If so, how was this experience? If not, what are the reasons, and do you intend to do so?"[9] Surveys took an average of 35 minutes to complete, while interviews lasted 1–2 hours.

Participants

Survey. Of the 220 survey participants, 81.7% (n = 178) self-identified as United States residents, mostly from the West coast (n = 99). Most (86.8%) identified as White/Caucasian and over half (55.5%) had achieved a formal degree (e.g., Associates, Bachelor's, Master's, Professional, or Doctorate), with another 35.9% having taken up to one year of college. Participants ranged in age from 18 to 64, with 47.0% falling between the ages of 18 and 34. For gender identity, 52.3% of the participants identified as female and 45.9% as male. The other two percent identified as transgender male to female (n = 2) and transgender female to male (n = 2). Nearly half the participants (n = 103) identified as heterosexual. The rest ranged from bisexual and "open option" (n = 48), to queer (n = 28) and pansexual (n = 13). Very few identified as lesbian or gay (n = 8) and heteroflexible (n = 5). Fifteen participants did not identify a sexual identity. For BDSM identity, 42.3% identified as submissive, slave, bottom, and/or masochist, while another 30.5% identified as dominant, Master/Mistress, top, and/or sadist. Nearly a quarter (n = 52) identified as switch, and eight did not indicate their BDSM identity.[10] Overall, participants in this study were similar in these demographics to other BDSM survey participants.

Interview. Twenty-three interviewees (92.0%) identified as United States residents (7 women, 15 men, 1 genderqueer transwoman), the other two were a woman from Australia and a man from Belgium. Interviewees' racial/ethnic identities reflected that of survey participants with 88.0% (n = 22) identifying as White/Caucasian. Although I did not ask interviewees to identify their education levels because they had already done so in the survey, several did so during their interviews, reflecting 56.0% (n = 14) either with a college degree or working on one. Most women (n = 7) were between the ages of 18 and 44, the transwoman was between 18 and 24 years old, and the men (n = 13) had a broad range in age, between 18 and 64; three men did not reveal their age range. Interviewees were relatively similar in these demographics to survey participants, although differed significantly by sexual identity, with most women identifying as queer/pansexual and most men identifying as heterosexual. In addition, no heterosexual or lesbian women and no gay or queer men participated in interviews.

RESULTS

Survey Participants

BDSM disclosure audience. The relationships between the following identities and disclosure to spouses and co-workers were not statistically significant: gender, sexuality, race/ethnicity, and BDSM role identity. However, most participants who had a spouse did disclose to them (ranging from 84.2% of people of color to 97.9% of Switches), while most participants who had co-workers did not disclose to them (ranging from 73.1% of Dominants to 84.3% of people of color). In addition, most people within the various age ranges disclosed to their spouses (88.6% to 100%), but did not disclose to their co-workers (64.5% to 84.6%). Finally, most people throughout the various locations disclosed to their spouses (90.6% to 95.83%), but did not disclose to their co-workers (72.7% to 95.0%). Still, these relationships were not statistically significant.

The relationships between gender, sexual, and racial/ethnic identities and disclosure to families were also not statistically significant. Although, a good portion of participants with family members did not disclose to them (ranging from 67.4% of LGBPQs to 75.0% of people of color). Interestingly, the relationship between BDSM role identity and disclosure to families was statistically significant, such that Dominants were 2.39 and 1.17 times more likely than Submissives and Switches, respectively, to disclose to their families.[11] While there were no statistically significant differences in disclosures to families by age range, reports of disclosure to family appear to increase as one ages (ranging from 22.0% at 18–24 to 42.9% at 55–64). The relationship between location of the participant and disclosure to family was not significantly related.

Statistical significance was found for the relationship between gender and sexual identities and disclosure to friends for those who reported they had friends to tell; women were 1.20 times more likely than men,[12] and LGBPQs were 1.26 times more likely than heterosexuals[13] to disclose to their friends. Significance was also found for the relationship between BDSM role identity and disclosure to friends, such that Switches were 1.11 and 1.26 times more likely than Dominants and Submissives, respectively, to disclose to their friends.[14] Finally, a statistically significant relationship between participant location and disclosure to friends revealed that those living outside of the U.S. were between 1.71 and 1.13 times more likely than those living inside the U.S. to disclose to their friends.[15] No statistical relationship was found between racial/ethnic identity or age range and disclosure to friends.

BDSM disclosure response. Spouse and family response to disclosure did not significantly differ by gender, sexual, racial/ethnic, and BDSM role identities. However, the mean spouse response to disclosure score was significantly higher (i.e., more negative), for the oldest group of participants than for the youngest group of participants.[16] There were no statistically significant differences in mean spouse response scores by location, and there were no statistically significant differences in mean family response scores by age and location. No statistically significant differences in the means of friend and co-worker response scores existed for any of the independent variables.

There were some interesting results relating spouse, family, friend, and co-worker response to BDSM disclosures according to gender, sex, race, BDSM role identity, age, and location. First, data suggest that those in the oldest age range (55–64), versus those in youngest age range (18–24), had a lower risk for positive versus negative spouse response to BDSM disclosure.[17] Also, those in the 45–54 age range, versus those in the 18–24 age range, had a lower risk for positive versus negative friend response to BDSM disclosure.[18] These results were particularly interesting, given that age was a significant factor in differentiating comfort levels with BDSM identity; younger groups (i.e., 18–24) reported less comfort with their BDSM identities than older groups.[19] No other statistically significant risks were found for BDSM disclosure response and identity, age, or location variables.

Interview Participants

BDSM disclosure audience. Nearly all interviewees identified one or more intentional BDSM disclosure to partners, family members, friends, and/or co-workers. Only one participant identified an unintentional disclosure to his girlfriend, her parents, and his family about his cross-dressing fetish when he was younger. He explained that upon being invited to his girlfriend's house for a party, he took one of her mom's dresses, and was subsequently arrested. He noted that the entire town found out about this scenario and his fetish, including his family and friends: "All my friends alienated me; they thought I was a weirdo…that incident still haunts me to this day." Most other participants (n = 18), however, intentionally disclosed to small groups of close friends—those they often identified as being involved in BDSM themselves. Many participants cited the necessity for having significant trust within their friendships to disclose:

A very good friend of mine…I didn't have any problems coming out to her. I know all sorts about she and her family, and it didn't seem to be a problem. But in regard to other people, no, because we are [viewed as] 'sexual sadists,' and we are 'Hannibal Lecter,' and we are 'going to cut you up into little bitty parts and consume you for dinner.'

Participants with partners were either introduced to BDSM by these partners (especially female participants) or met their partners on kink websites, therefore disclosing to these significant others simply by interacting in these relationships (n = 11). Others selectively told their partners about their BDSM identities and play. Several participants (all male), for instance, only told their partners after they had found additional BDSM play partners online or were in the process of separating from their vanilla partners because they felt sexually incompatible with them. One decided not to tell his wife, because he thought she would not understand—"I basically led two lives a long time"—while another told his wife, with less than ideal consequences for their marriage:

[My wife] accepts it, but she's not enthusiastic about it, to say the least. At the same time, she loves me enough to want me to be happy, and to want to stay with me. So, it's a complex, uncomfortable relationship, but with a lot happening in it, not a dead one.

A much smaller group disclosed their BDSM identities and play to their families (n = 8) and co-workers (n = 4). None of the women explicitly disclosed their BDSM identities and play to their family members, while most of the men selectively disclosed to family members. One disclosed to a brother who was similarly interested in dominant/submissive relationships, while a couple others disclosed to their parent(s) and children, but mostly mothers and daughters, because one participant's father would "never approve" and another's son was "kind of clueless at times." Those who disclosed to co-workers (all male) were either working in the sex industry (i.e., managing online pornography websites) or were teaching sexuality-based courses at local universities and high schools. One other person disclosed to his co-worker because they had "shared secrets over a long period of time," thus trust was an important factor in this disclosure.

Importantly, participants in this study also explained to whom they would never disclose their BDSM identities and play. Of the twelve groups identified as inappropriate for disclosure, half of these related specifically to family, and most of these were reported as relating to the family's conservative values

171

and/or the fear of losing close relationships with family members who perhaps would not understand. One participant noted that he would not tell his family because "that would be a very awkward conversation to have," while another explained that her parents were weary of her having transgender friends, so "when [my parents] said, 'don't tell us,' I am not telling them." This same participant stated, "I also don't want my ex-husband to find [my online kink photos]…if he did, he might throw a hissy fit, take me to court, and try and get the kids away from me." For several of these participants, their safety and that of their families and careers was an important factor to consider prior to disclosure, especially disclosures to co-workers and neighbors. One participant debated disclosing to co-workers; his friend exclaimed, "Oh, you can't do that! They still look upon this as being sexual sadism and they will look upon you as a security risk. You just can't do that!"

BDSM disclosure response. Because most interviewees were either introduced to BDSM by partners and friends, or had friends already involved in BDSM, the responses from these people were typically supportive and encouraging (excluding the examples of the men having extramarital relationships). Non-BDSM or vanilla friends, however, were less supportive, as they struggled with understanding the reason behind their friend's BDSM participation or refused to engage in the conversation overall. One participant explained that each time she brought up her BDSM relationship to close friends they would "roll their eyes and change the subject." Another noted that her friends tried to have an intervention, telling her that her relationship choices were related to her rebellion from her former religious identity, and that she "must have a lot of shame in [her] life now." Two men who told their friends had more encouraging reactions from friends: one explained that several of his friends requested that he take them to the BDSM club so that they could "see what [it] is about," and the other clarified that because he was not pushing his interests onto his friends, they tended to show interest in learning about BDSM. However, this participant also noted, "some of them are intrigued in the way that you go to a circus [to] see something you don't see usually." Another explained, "[For my roommates], it is a source of entertainment for them. They try and give me a hard time about it, but in a joking manner."

Participants reported that family members tended to have the most extreme reactions to BDSM disclosures, although they ranged from complete acceptance, as was the case with the father who disclosed to his daughter, to financial threats. One participant said that while his family was okay with his BDSM disclosure, his wife's family would be "shocked and appalled." Another explained that he had to disclose to his mother when she thought he was sneaking out of the house to deal drugs. Upon revealing that he was going to public BDSM events, his mother exclaimed, "Oh, I just saw an episode on CSI about that the other week. It was autoerotic asphyxiation or something...." Despite this misrepresentation of BDSM, the participant explained that his mother began joking about his kinks in a non-harmful way. Others' parents were simply too uncomfortable with the disclosure to say much about it. The most severe reaction, involving financial threats, came from the mother of one participant who at first became worried, and then became angry. This participant's mother said, "What if someone in the neighborhood was raped? This is the first house the police are going to come to." When the participant tried to convince her otherwise, his mother threatened to cut off his trust fund because his BDSM participation would "damage [his] career and future."

No negative reactions from BDSM disclosures to co-workers were reported, although co-workers who were told tended to also be close, trustworthy friends.

DISCUSSION

The audience and reasoning behind BDSM disclosures, as noted in the extant research, are important to consider given the stigmas attached to BDSM practices and identities. For many people in the United States, BDSM is understood as a disordered behavior that must be feared and contained. For those who practice, however, BDSM often represents a core sense of self, even if this version of the self emerged later in adulthood, or because of an intimate relationship (Yost & Hunter, 2012). To have one's sense of self defined by the dominant culture as disordered, then, can pose real concerns for those who wish to live openly as kinky; even if "living openly" means keeping their identities and practices hidden, while living free from the violence and discrimination reported by the National Coalition for Sexual Freedom.

To disclose one's identity is an important consideration, one that the participants in this study were likely very careful in planning. As noted by the survey results, participants disclosed to spouses and friends more so than co-workers and families, with spouses and friends having more negative reactions to older than younger participants. For those who disclosed to families, Dominants (mostly men) did so more than Submissives and

Switches. Also, gender and sexual minorities and Switches disclosed to friends more so than men, heterosexuals, and Dominants and Submissives. The interviewees, on the other hand, revealed a more nuanced picture of BDSM disclosures and perhaps some reasoning behind their choice in audience for BDSM disclosure. For instance, most men told their spouses/partners about their BDSM participation after having learned about it from books or online pornography, whereas most women were introduced by spouses/partners. Also, all those who disclosed to family members and co-workers were also men, and the responses they received from family members were generally positive. The women, however, often reported having concerns about disclosing to family and friends, for fear of negative reactions; some reported negative reactions (i.e., shaming and dismissals) from vanilla friends, specifically.

Clearly, some groups must consider their disclosure audience carefully, due to the differences in consequence. If BDSM is stigmatized, especially for women who may be misrepresented in the media as being at-risk for exposure to abuse or disorder within the kink community or a kink relationship, then women would necessarily need to cautiously strategize about their disclosures. As one participant noted, she had to consider whether her children would be taken from her if her ex-partner found out about her BDSM participation. And, whereas one man's parents saw his participation as a laughing matter, it begs the question as to whether these same parents would view their daughter's participation in the same way. Women, especially LGBPQ women, in the United States are still portrayed and perceived as vulnerable to the "evils" of sexual excess (Groneman, 1995). Consequently, disclosing their BDSM practices and identities may leave them open to additional violence, harassment, and discrimination, especially if they do not have support from at least one significant person in their lives.

Limitations

One of the most significant limitations in this study is the small, non-representative survey and interview sample. Most participants identified as White and college educated, with most men identifying as heterosexual and within the Dominant BDSM spectrum and most women identifying as LGBPQ and within the Submissive BDSM spectrum. Stronger samples would have included more people of color, lesbian and gay, and transgender and gender-queer participants; there was some indication that the relationship between racial/ethnic minority identification and negative family response was approaching significance, so should be investigated further. Also, participants were mostly recruited from online kink websites, so may not be representative of those who do not participate in these forums, but do participate in public dungeons and/or private homes. For instance, some participants only engaged in BDSM online or in the privacy of their homes. It is possible that their disclosure needs are quite different from others who visit public dungeons and/or are visibly kinky (i.e., wears a collar, leather, or latex) outside the private sphere. Despite these limitations, the mixed-methods approach for this study was helpful for revealing important nuances of BDSM disclosures.

CONCLUSION

Orne (2011) explains "strategic outness" as "the contextual and continual management of identity." As such, those who choose to disclose their invisible identities must consider the context and those involved. In Orne's work, outness is never fully gained, rather it is a process that is managed on a daily basis—who one tells and how one tells is just as important as why one tells. This study revealed that similar to other sexual minority groups, BDSM participants strategically consider to whom they may disclose, given the possibility for negative reactions. Because participants in this study reported mild to severe negative reactions, it is not wonder that those with several minority identities may be more strategic about their disclosures than those who have more societal and individual privilege and power. It is still of great concern, however, that despite strategic outness, gender and sexual minorities involved in BDSM report higher levels of violence, harassment, and discrimination than those with identity-based privileges. More work must be done to destigmatize BDSM practice and identification so that participants may feel empowered to find health, wellness, and community.

NOTES

[1] Adler (2006) explained the Witch identity as related to Wicca, a pagan religious movement which is linked to visionary, artistic, and libertarian traditions, as well as ecology and feminist movements.

[2] While BDSM participation may be made visible through choice in clothing (i.e., leather and latex), style (i.e., collars), and other subcultural signifiers (i.e., kink flags), these are things that also may be hidden, and thus I consider BDSM participation an "invisible" practice and identity for this study.

[3] Sociologist Erving Goffman developed a theory in the early 1960s relating social stigma to identity management. In this theory, Goffman proposed that those with "spoiled" or socially stigmatized identities will use specific techniques to control information about

their stigmatized identities to influence the perceptions of significant and non-significant others. Some techniques include concealment, developing a "cover," and strategic disclosure.

[4] In-group and out-group designations often serve to differentiate normative (i.e., in-group) from non-normative (i.e., out-group) individuals, where the in-group is favored for achieving the norm, while the out-group is stigmatized for being different in some way.

[5] The National Coalition for Sexual Freedom (NCSF) launched their first survey on violence and discrimination faced by BDSM practitioners in SM leather-fetish communities spanning April 1998 to April 1999. They found that 36% of their sample reported experiencing some form of violence or harassment, including verbal harassment (87%) and physical (25%) and sexual violence (23%), because of their "alternative sexual practices." Thirty percent reported experiencing discrimination, including persecution (40%) and loss of job/contract (25%), due to their alternative sexual practices. Importantly, the NCSF noted that only 28% of their respondents disclosed their alternative sexual practices, but over 1/3 experienced violence and/or harassment. Nearly ten years later, and with three times as many survey respondents, the NCSF found that 38% of their sample reported experiencing some form of violence or harassment, and that a majority identified as women (53.7%) and LGBTQ (66.8%).

[6] In 1997 Susan Wright led a group in forming the National Coalition for Sexual Freedom (NCSF) with the goal of fighting for "sexual freedom and privacy rights for all adults who engage in safe, sane and consensual behavior" (ncsfreedom.org). The NCSF currently collaborates with both national and international organizations towards achieving this goal through education about and advocacy for those involved in BDSM, swing, and polyamorous relationships and communities.

[7] I use "play" in this study in to indicate participation in a BDSM "scene" or set of negotiated BDSM-related activities. While some participants prefer the term "scene" over "play," as the former denotes a serious activity that has great significance for participants' sense of self, I use "play" as an indicator of creativity in performance and to suggest that significance varies greatly between participants—some "live" D/s relationships, while others "play" as dominant, submissive, switch, or any number of other roles.

[8] I utilized chi-square and one-way analysis of variance tests to identify relationships between independent and dependent variables. In addition, I used multinomial logistic regression models to help identify the odds of positive, neutral, and negative spouse, family, friend, and co-worker responses to BDSM disclosures, given each independent variable.

[9] Interview coding occurred at two-levels. First, I coded interviews based on gender, sexual, racial/ethnic and BDSM role identities. I also looked through transcripts for references to BDSM disclosures, including audience and response, which I present as master headings within the interview results. At the second level of coding, I looked for common themes within dependent variable responses, such as methods of disclosure, reasons for disclosure and/or non-disclosure, and subsequent reactions to and/or explanations of disclosure responses; I present these as subheadings.

[10] Because most minority categories (i.e., transgender, genderqueer, lesbian, gay, African American, Latino/a, Asian American, etc.) were too small for individual analyses, I recoded: (1) transmen and transwomen within the gender category to which they transitioned (i.e., female and male), dropping the two genderqueer folks from analysis and (2) other identity groups into binaries or triads (i.e., LGBPQ and heterosexual for sexual identity; non-White and White for racial/ethnic identity; Submissive, Dominant, and Switch for BDSM role

176

identity). Age-range and location (i.e., West, Midwest, South, East, and "other") were kept as listed in the survey. Although a binary system cannot account for the unique experiences of the minority groups housed within these categories, dropping them from the study entirely would further make their experiences invisible, as was the case with the genderqueer individuals in my sample. I present the challenges of adequate representation in the limitations section of this study.

[11] Chi-square: $\chi^2(2) = 10.71, p < .01$

[12] Chi-square: $\chi^2(1) = 5.55, p < .05$

[13] Chi-square: $\chi^2(1) = 7.71, p < .01$

[14] Chi-square: $\chi^2(2) = 6.33, p < .05$

[15] Chi-square: $\chi^2(4) = 10.89, p < .05$

[16] One-way Analysis of Variance (ANOVA): $F(4, 163) = 3.98, p < .01$, oldest group ($M = 2.69$, $SD = 1.70$), youngest group ($M = 1.82, SD = 1.15$)

[17] Multinomial Logistic Regression: $\chi^2(144) = 40.36, p < .01$, CI[0.01, 0.42]; the risk for a positive versus negative spouse response decreased by a factor of 0.05 for those in the 55–64 age range, versus those in the 18-24 age range.

[18] Multinomial Logistic Regression: $\chi^2(143) = 29.05, p < .05$, CI[0.01, 0.87]; the risk for a positive versus negative friend response decreased by a factor of 0.05 for those in the 45–54 age range, versus those in the 18-24 age range.

[19] A Kruskal-Wallis test revealed that there was a statistically significant difference in comfort levels between age groups $\chi^2(4) = 26.97, p < .001$.

REFERENCES

Adler, M. (2006). *Drawing down the moon: Witches, druids, goddess-worshippers, and other pagans in America* (2nd ed.). New York, NY: Penguin Group.

Better, A., & Simula, B. L. (2015). How and for whom does gender matter? Rethinking the concept of sexual orientation. *Sexualities, 18*(5–6), 665–680. https://doi.org/10.1177/1363460714561716

Bezreh, T., Weinberg, T. S., & Edgar, T. (2012). BDSM disclosure and stigma management: Identifying opportunities for sex education. *American Journal of Sexuality Education, 7*(1), 37–61. https://doi.org/10.1080/15546128.2012.650984

Brown, M., Baunach, D. M., & Burgess, E. O. (2015). Sexual disclosure among college students in the American deep south: Toward a sexuality as structure approach. *Journal of Child and Adolescent Behavior, 3*(4). https://doi.org/10.4172/2375-4494.1000227

Chaline, E. R. (2010). The construction, maintenance, and evolution of gay SM sexualities and sexual identities: A preliminary description of gay SM sexual identity practices. *Sexualities, 13*(3), 338–356. https://doi.org/10.1177/1363460709363323

Gemberling, T. M., Cramer, R., & Miller, R. S. (2015). BDSM as sexual orientation: A comparison to lesbian, gay, and bisexual sexuality. *Journal of Positive Sexuality, 1*, 56–62.

Groneman, C. (1995). Nymphomania: The historical construction of female sexuality. In J. Terry & J. Urla (Eds.), *Deviant bodies* (pp. 219–249). Bloomington, IN: Indiana University Press.

Grov, C., Bimbi, D. S., Nanín, J. E., & Parsons, J. T. (2006). Race, ethnicity, gender, and generational factors associated with the coming-out process among gay, lesbian, and bisexual individuals. *The Journal of Sex Research, 43*(2), 115–121. https://doi.org/10.1080/00224490609552306

National Sexual Violence Resource Center, & Pennsylvania Coalition Against Rape. (2012). *The process of coming out: Sexual violence and individuals who identify as LGBTQ.* Retrieved from http://www.nsvrc.org/sites/default/files/Publications_NSVRC_Guides_Process-Coming-Out.pdf

Orne, J. (2011). 'You will always have to "out" yourself': Reconsidering coming out through strategic outness. *Sexualities, 14*(6), 681–703. https://doi.org/10.1177/1363460711420462

Rosario, M., Schrimshaw, E. W., & Hunter, J. (2004). Ethnic/racial differences in the coming-out process of lesbian, gay, and bisexual youths: A comparison of sexual identity development over time. *Cultural Diversity and Ethnic Minority Psychology, 10*(3), 215–228. http://dx.doi.org.aurarialibrary.idm.oclc.org/10.1037/1099-9809.10.3.215

Schope, R. D. (2002). The decision to tell. *Journal of Gay & Lesbian Social Services, 14*(1), 1–22. https://doi.org/10.1300/J041v14n01_01

Stiles, B. L., & Clark, R. E. (2011). BDSM: A subcultural analysis of sacrifices and delights. *Deviant Behavior, 32*(2), 158–189. https://doi.org/10.1080/01639621003748605

Swank, E., Fahs, B., & Frost, D. M. (2013). Region, social identities, and disclosure practices as predictors of heterosexist discrimination against sexual minorities in the United States. *Sociological Inquiry, 83*(2), 238–258. https://doi.org/10.1111/soin.12004

Tabaac, A. R., Perrin, P. B., & Trujillo, M. A. (2015). Multiple mediational model of outness, social support, mental health, and wellness behavior in ethnically diverse lesbian, bisexual, and queer women. *LGBT Health, 2*(3), 243–249. https://doi.org/10.1089/lgbt.2014.0110

Weiss, M. D. (2006). Working at play: BDSM sexuality in the San Francisco Bay Area. *Antrhopologica, 48*(2), 229–245.

Yost, M. R., & Hunter, L. E. (2012). BDSM practitioners' understandings of their initial attraction to BDSM sexuality: Essentialist and constructionist narratives. *Psychology & Sexuality, 3*(3), 244–259. https://doi.org/10.1080/19419899.2012.700028

13. FINDING YOURSELF IN THE DARK

On Submission, Healing, and Acceptance (Personal Reflection)

I have replayed this memory over and over again in my head. It was the night I truly found myself under Master's[1] hand and the crop. It was the night I found myself again, in a way only I could.

Our relationship as submissive and dominant did not happen by chance. It came by hours sitting across from each other and talking. It came by reading and expressing our wants and fears. We talked out exactly what we wanted. My partner and I have always been interested in the kink lifestyle. For me, I just wanted to relax and turn my brain off. I work as a crisis counselor. So much of my job is taking care of many others at one time. Submission gives me a space to just relax and focus on one person instead of many. Having someone give me tasks to do makes it simple. Instead of figuring out what someone else needs, they just tell me up front. I don't have to figure anything out. All I have to do is follow instructions. My submission is a safe space to let go of stress. For my partner, they like to feel in control. They like to plan and shape how things go and watch them play out. When my partner is in control of a scene, they feel confident. They can make anything in the scene play out how they want to. However, the power isn't one sided.

The most crucial factor in our relationship (and any relationship), kink or otherwise, is consent. Before we do a scene, we talk about it. Sometimes we'll even talk about it a few weeks before. First, we establish what we want to do. A common scene we enjoy is flogging, for example. Once a scene is agreed on, my partner and I lay out any concerns we might have. Concerns can be anything from what day of the week we have a session to how clean a tool is. We also bring up our hard limits, like where I can get hit and where my partner doesn't want to hit me. For example, I like getting hit on my chest but sometimes my partner is uncomfortable with it because it can leave a lot of marks. If either of us are uncomfortable or unsure, despite how many times we might have done something before, we don't incorporate it into a scene. Safety and security are our top priorities with each other.

© KONINKLIJKE BRILL NV, LEIDEN, 2019 | DOI:10.1163/9789004414105_014

Some people use safe words. Safe words can be anything the partners agree on in a scene. The important thing is that once that word is said, everything in the scene stops, no matter who says it. We always use the stop light system, a common check-in practice. Green means things are okay. Yellow means slow down or not has hard. Red means stop everything at once. We know it by heart. My partner knows that my life is in their hands. In turn, because they know that, they know they're not allowed to do anything I don't want to have happen to me. I give them the tools to make the scene and then they build what they want from what they're given, which is why we agreed my partner would be called Master in scenes: not because they own me but rather because they're a master of their craft, of the scene. They control the scene and I am a part of it, like an actor in a play. Or like a trainer for a pet. They help me learn new things. It was also important to have something gender neutral. In the BDSM culture, Master is often used as a gender-neutral term.

That night began like any other typical Friday night. I was getting ready to go out with a new partner and our friends. We were going to my favorite spot a local goth/fetish bar and dance club. I was completing my going out rituals with gusto. In what I could only guess looked like a flurry of flailing arms set to the music of Prince, Duran Duran, and Depeche Mode, I got ready. I put on my favorite black Stevie Nicks-esc dress, with its long flowing sleeves and lace crescent moon on the front. I laced up my Doc Martens that go to my knees, which is not as easy task, especially if you have a motor skill condition and had had a drink. I had my first drink of the night. I was allowed to have one more. I have cerebral palsy, and as a result, my muscles are tight. Having one or two drinks (never more than two on a day when we're doing a scene) or a muscle relaxer before a scene can help me position myself easier.

Next came my hair and makeup. I back combed my hair as tall as it would go, outlined my eyes with a thick dark liner, and made my lips a deep red wine color. A few dabs of lavender perfume later and I was ready for the most important part of the ritual: Master's inspection. I stepped out of the bathroom with a "ta-da!" and twirled around. They smiled, clearly pleased with my appearance. "You look beautiful! Are you ready?"

I looked at Master, then the bed, where my new valentine's present lay waiting for me: a black fur lined collar and a silver chain leash. My stomach swirled and a knee twitched. This would be the first time I'd ever been walked in public. I imagined myself paraded in front of strangers' eyes, a decoration or arm candy. A piece of art, maybe? What would they see in the red glowing rooms? A cool and confident cat, lounging with ease and pride in their chains? Or a nervous fledging?

Despite the nerves, I was quick to say I was ready. I sat down on the edge of the bed, smoothing out my dress. They picked up the collar and gently pressed my head into their chest, while they slipped it on. I closed my eyes, feeling the soft fuzz tickle then cradle my neck. I heard the clink of metal and felt the collar tighten. "Not too tight is it?"

"No, not at—"

"Tighter?"

I nodded, hearing their heart thump in their chest, taking in their scents: musk, warmth, and something faintly sweet, maybe honey or coconut. I knew it was going to be a good night as the collar was fully set in place. I could feel it breathe with me. It was just as alive as I was. My neck began to warm under the fur. I felt a kiss on my forehead. It was time to go.

With a final hair preening, I was as ready as I was ever going to be. I slipped the leash in my purse, careful to put it away quickly, despite it being just the two of us. Stepping out of the bedroom was stepping into an outside world. One that wasn't really safe. But I wasn't scared. Truth be told, as we got in the cab I forgot all about the leash and the intent that came with it. I was more concerned about what the music would be like and if my hair was still big. It was 80s night, after all. I wanted to look the part.

We met our friends outside, a line already forming. The air was a lot cooler than it should've been in Florida. Emily, my best friend, and I were glad for that, however. Going inside was a standard affair: paw at Master to get my I.D, because I don't like carrying a purse when I go dancing, get I.D (not without a kiss), present to charming door girl, say hi to door girl, get wristband, and we're in.

The downstairs bar was packed with a sea of familiar and fresh faces. Some people we recognized and smiled at. Soon we drifted into the crowd and time was lost on us. I remember all of us were sitting in the dungeon at some point. The dungeon is a special room only open on certain nights. It isn't a proper dungeon by any means. That being said, it's the only one I've been in. There were these bunk beds in the corner of the room that anyone could cuddle up with or sit with someone. Most of our friends were at the top by the time I saw them.

Master urged me to climb up to the top bunk to join the group when something clicked for both of us. I turned my head while climbing the ladder and we locked eyes. The air around me felt cool and hot at the same time. For a moment, I forgot about everyone around me, the music in the air. I felt my knees start to shake. I saw a flash of silver chain. It was time.

"We're going upstairs!" I said hand outstretched for my drink. Emily laughed and handed the glass to me, carefully. I already wasn't the steadiest climber and I'm sure the alcohol didn't help. Once I was grounded, the leash was clinked onto the O ring of my collar. All of us were laughing together. This was the first time in a long time I felt safe in public. The chain was not a way to keep me captive but rather a security blanket. I let my ability to choose go so I could relax. I no longer had to make choices of where to go or how to act. It would all be decided for me. All I had to do was follow. I could put all the thoughts and decision making behind me. All I had to do was let myself be guided. My love would guide me.

As it happened, I was being taken upstairs. I don't even remember leaving the dungeon area. One minute I was near the ladder and the next I was in the middle of the velvet-looking stairway. I felt a sudden rush of panic. I couldn't actually do this. I couldn't let my friends see me so open and vulnerable. I had always been open about being into BDSM and the kink community. But that was just talking. I'd never actually showed anyone beside partners before. And Master was the first person I've ever given a title to. We had never done anything outside the bedroom. I wanted to run but the leash prevented it. I had to face the side of me I had buried for so long.

Before my current partner, I had been in an abusive relationship. That person never hit me or left any physical scars. But he tried to change me. He hated how I wanted to be intimate, how I express my love. He hated that I didn't want to be in control for a few hours. So much of my job is taking care of other people as a counselor. In my submission, I am able to let myself be taken care of. I can turn off my brain for a little while. Submission is simple. All I have to do is make one person happy.

I've always liked getting hit. I am a masochist by nature. It's not for everyone and it's okay if it's not for you. One of the nice things about BDSM is that there's a variety of ways to have fun. It isn't always a lot of pain. Sometimes a session can be having someone brush your hair or you rub a person's back. It all comes down to what you and you partner or partners like.

For me, pain makes the softer parts of foreplay more pleasurable and more intense. It was repulsive to my former partner that someone would want to be hit. He saw it as abuse, ironically. He tried to change the way I love and take away my pleasure. I could never be affectionate with him in public. I could never pull him close to dance or kiss whenever I wanted. I was being bullied and didn't see it. If he didn't like BDSM, then why should I? According to him, everyone who did it was sick or broken somehow. I was some broken thing he tried to 'fix'. I had to grow out my hair and lose weight. I had to dress more 'like a girl,' whatever that meant. He ultimately tried to control who I was and what I would become.

I realize now that he was lazy and didn't want to put in the care and effort that comes with aftercare,[2] after sex or otherwise. There was no checking in. There was no consideration or openness, which is essential in any intimate relationship. At the worst of times, there was no consent. I was just a toy to use and discard. I didn't know it at the time, but that night I was finding myself again. I was finding the parts of me that made me really happy.

Coming to the upstairs part of the place felt like I had just climbed a mountain. My legs ached. I felt my right leg twitch. My cerebral palsy makes my right leg a lot tighter than my left. The leg went numb for a second and I had a hard time bending it. I downed the last of my drink, hoping that my muscles would relax just a little. They did not. In the corner of the room on a slightly raised platform were two big wooden beams, crossed together in the shape of an X, with metal loops at the top to hang toys like floggers or to thread rope through for people to use—a rack. People lean against it, tied up or not, and have whatever they like done to them. The platform is draped in heavy chains that people often lean on while waiting in line. Lots of people will line up to be flogged, spanked, or tied up. Without fail, the same couple whom I've never spoken to is always there. They lend out their toys and services for those who want to try, always asking what the person wants beforehand.

My body went on autopilot then. I remember wrapping my right leg around the chain and gripping tightly. I felt the feeling start to come back once the cold metal hit my skin. I stared, wide-eyed. I felt like I was eighteen again, seeing this for the first time. There were people after people getting whipped and smiling. Some were hit to the music (industrial). Some were hit with reckless abandon, no rhythm at all. Some cried happy tears. The bodies on the rack looked so relaxed, despite the pain from the various tools. The audience who watched them either looked on with calm, approving faces or they clapped and talked to people beside them. It reminded me of something out of an Anne Rice novel. Fitting. I wanted to try. Even though I was scared, I knew I was safe. The space around the rack is never quiet. It's always filled with check-ins. "Are you okay?" "Is this comfortable?" are the most common phrases.

"Does she want to try?" I heard the Master of the house (I had no other name to give him) ask my Master. I had no voice here. It is expected in these situations that the Master of the submissive knows what's best. And for that,

183

I am grateful. I don't think I could have spoken, even if I wanted to. My tongue felt like lead. It was too heavy to move. My Master rattled my chain then looked at me. Was I ready? I didn't know. But there are some things we can't ever really be ready for. The rack is one of them.

"Yeah." I squeaked out. There has to be a verbal yes for public spaces. Always. No exceptions. The Master of the House nodded, knowing it was my first time. There was a woman in the corner, watching this exchange. We made eye contact. I felt my face get really hot. It felt like she was looking right through me. She smiled looking me up and down. It didn't feel like she was sizing me up but it felt more like... I was a piece of art and I was being admired.

I remember hearing whispers about me as I went up on the platform. I couldn't exactly make out what was said. From what I heard, someone liked my dress and someone else had seen me before. I pushed those whispers away. They weren't my focus now.

Once there, I was instructed by my Master to face the crowd with my back on the beams. They would be hitting my thighs today. While it was a new experience for me, it was also new to Master. This scene was our first time together in a public space. The Master of the House had previously put ropes at the top of the beams through small metal loops on each side. Anyone could slip their wrist through and let their arms relax. I was instructed to hold onto them the best I could. Given my height, I could barely reach. But all I had to do was try.

"Are you ready?"

I nodded, making sure to make direct eye contact. Then came the sting of the crop on my thighs, just below my dress. The sound startled me and all the warmth of the alcohol rushed out of me. Air hissed out of me and I looked at Master, wide-eyed. I was terrified and curious. The people watching made it worse and better somehow. But I wasn't terrified of others but rather myself. I didn't know how I would look or sound after being silent for so long. I was scared to show my legs shaking and my hands locking in place. I didn't want my body language to stand out. I was scared people were going to know I have a different set of motor skills. I didn't want people to treat me differently.

"Spread." The world became so simple then. My life was in Master's hands. I gave it to them and they took it as they always do, with the utmost love and care. I was their pet. I was their responsibility. I was no longer the one taking care of others. At that moment, I was relieved of any sort of insecurity, if only for a moment. In their hands, all my worries about my appearance melted away. All that self-consciousness, the low self-esteem, and the doubt started to shed itself from me. Layer after layer, hit after hit, they melted away. All I had to do was what I was told. I didn't have to take care of anyone else. I didn't have to make choices. They were made for me.

"Spread!" Louder this time. I spread my legs a little and arched my back. Then the lick of the strap came. Soft at first until I shouted "Green!" Then they came harder and sharper with each blow. I felt my body start to move on its own. I felt the heat from my legs. I felt each fiber of the rope on my wrist. Every love poem I've ever read came back to me with dazzling clarity. Never had I felt so safe or vulnerable. The room was filled with kindness. As my Master, my love, continued to strike me I felt the rush of pain and warmth. I screamed loudly. I twisted in ways I didn't think possible. I let out all the pain of the past year and a half. Every hit felt like my abuser was being ripped out of me and cast out into a place where he couldn't get to me. He was beaten out of me.

The part of me that I had repressed for so long was finally freed. As the whipping went on, I yelled louder. Tears came down my face. I grinned. I didn't care what I looked like anymore. I didn't care that my body wouldn't move in the "right" way. There was so much love at this moment. I loved everyone in that room while I was on display. I heard shouts of "gorgeous!" and "look at her!" It was like I was being seen, really seen, for the first time. My intimacy and love was no longer a thing I needed to hide. I could scream and cry about being in love. I didn't care who saw me then. People called out that I was beautiful. For the first time in a long time, I believed them. I was a living art piece in a gallery. I was an exhibit to observe.

I remember my Master's face in the dim red lights. Their gaze was so intense. We were both shaking. Their hands were unsteady as they worked, with the House Master standing over them. There were always people watching. It was at this moment, this messy wonderful moment of public display, that I knew I loved them and myself, deeper than I could remember ever feeling. When I called red light, the signal to stop, all movements stilled. Before I knew it, I was scooped up in Master's arms.

After the pain came the warmth. They held me tightly, pushing my body back into the rack, leaning into me. We kissed. It was the safest I've ever felt. In a room full of mostly half-naked strangers, in a place reeking of sweat and clove cigarettes, I was whole again. I wasn't scared to show my love or show off my body anymore. My confidence was restored with the care of my love's tender hands and a leather strap.

After the embrace, I was put on the leash again. Master separated from me to take me off the platform to make room for the next couple. Our performance was met with applause. Some of the other submissives came up to me and hugged us. Some rubbed my back, patted my head, whispered praise. The woman from the corner approached me. People parted to make room for her. She dripped elegance in her black corset. Her strong arms embraced me tightly, squeezing my ribs. She gave me some orange beads like the kind you get at Mardi Gras. She draped them around my neck and scratched behind my ears.

"Good girl," she said. Her voice was deep and soft. It was soothing to hear. I nodded, unable to speak. That was the last I saw of her. I haven't seen her since then. Master guided me to the dance floor. We swayed together, not speaking or really listening. In the middle of the crowded floor, we found our peace and more importantly, the extent of our trust in each other. We didn't have to hide anymore. It was liberating.

I could still feel the welts from the strap for days after that night. In our more private moments, Master and I had fun tracing them with our fingers. They were an artist and I was a canvas. Or a garden that needed a lot of water, love, and care for those pretty purple flowers on my thighs.

From a land once thought to be dead rose a new life. Since that night I have loved deeper. I gained a strength I never thought I would have back again. Through tender hands and leather straps, I learn to be amazed by my strength, physical and mental. I learn to love my body, for all its peaks and valleys. I learn to trust and demand the same in return. In my submission, there is simplicity, there is healing, and there is always the unbreakable trust, whether it be a silver chain or a strip of leather.

NOTES

[1] It is a common practice in writing about BDSM to capitalize a Dominant's title to show their authority.

[2] Aftercare is a common term in the community for things you do after a scene to help take care of everyone involved. This can be things like cleaning up fluids, cuddling, getting water, and or asking how everyone is feeling.

PART 4

ASEXUAL RELATIONSHIPS

TIINA VARES

14. ASEXUALITIES, INTIMACIES AND RELATIONALITY

INTRODUCTION

Romantic asexual, aromatic asexual, grey-asexual and demi-sexual[1] are just some of the identity categories which sit under the umbrella of asexuality. Since the founding of the online site AVEN (Asexual Visibility and Education Network) in 2001, we have seen the development of an asexual movement in primarily western liberal democracies (Gressgard, 2013, p. 179). While AVEN defines an asexual individual as a person "who does not experience sexual attraction," the terms above highlight the diversity of ways in which asexual identified people experience and define their asexuality. This diversity includes different kinds of attraction, different ways of desiring and seeking out interpersonal relationships, and a range of intimacies, physical and otherwise (Gupta & Cerankowski, 2017). While research into asexuality has increased in the past fifteen years, there has been little academic attention to how asexual people conceive of and practice intimacy and relationships (Dawson et al., 2016, also see authors in this section).

In this chapter I add to the small body of academic scholarship that has focused on the experiences of friendship, relationships and intimacy of self-identified asexuals (Haeffner, 2011; Van Houdenhove et al., 2015; Dawson et al., 2016; Vares, 2018). Based on my research with 15 self-identified asexuals, aged 18 to 60 years, and living in New Zealand[2] (see Vares, 2018), I explore the ways in which participants are "actively and creatively renegotiating the boundaries of the platonic, the intimate and the sexual" (Carrigan, 2011, p. 476). I first consider the significance of friends in participants' lives and, in particular, the ways in which the boundary between friend/partner and friendship/relationship is being disrupted. Second, I focus on the ways in which romantic identified asexuals negotiate sexual and non-sexual intimacy in partnered relationships with non-asexuals. It is important to emphasise that, as Dawson et al. indicate, there are no distinct "asexual practices of intimacy" (2016, p. 362), as there are equivalences with non-asexual practices of intimacy. However, I suggest that the asexual narratives in this chapter, which privilege a range of primarily non-sexual intimacies and 'new' relational forms, contribute to reconfiguring and expanding the possibilities of relationality for self-identified asexuals and more broadly.

DISRUPTING THE BOUNDARY BETWEEN FRIEND/PARTNER AND FRIENDSHIP/RELATIONSHIP

As indicated in recent literature, networks of friends and friendships are increasingly cited as central sources of intimacy and support (Roseneil & Budgeon, 2004; Chambers, 2013). This was also the case for participants in this study. Madison, for example, who was open about her identification as grey-asexual with her friends and family, spoke about the importance of her friendship group as a source of physical and emotional intimacy:

> Madison (23, grey-asexual)[3]: In our group, we were all very touchy, feely, like we'd lay on each other on the couch and we'd sit next to each other and sit on each other's laps [...] and it's a source of comfort as well.

For other participants, while relationships with friends were framed in terms of intimacy this was experienced predominantly in non-physical ways:

> Philip (49, aromantic): I'm a reasonably social person. I love my friends. I love my family [...] I don't feel that I don't have intimacy in my life. I feel that I can be intimate with people. [...] I can get close to people but it's usually through speaking with them, yeah. [...] I don't have any need for physical contact. I mean physical contact can be pleasant but it's not like I desire it or want it. [...] I like to think in terms of love, you know, I do love people. I'm a caring person. I look out for them.

Philip orients himself to the construction of aromatic asexuals (who don't desire sexual or romantic relationships) as having no intimacy in their lives and thus being "isolated, disconnected and lonely"[4] (Francis, 2016, p. 28). Philip's constitution of himself as a person who: is social; loves his friends and family; thinks in terms love; and can be intimate with people, is doing the discursive work of establishing the "truth" of his account. This challenges the dominant construction of those not in romantic and/or sexual relationships (including non-asexuals) as somehow missing out on "real" love and intimacy, and therefore unhappy. This relates to a hierarchy of love and intimacy in which the presence of sex and love in a relationship puts it on a "higher plane of happiness" than a relationship without (Jamieson,

1998, p. 108). Sara Ahmed (2010), for example, discusses the way in which happiness is attributed to particular objects such as the family and the loving, sexual partnered relationship. We thus get oriented towards these objects and "happiness becomes very quickly the promotion of certain ways of living" (2010, p. 11). Philip acknowledges this orientation while simultaneously refusing to be "banished from the narrative of happiness" (Ahmed, 2010, p. 17). His explicit framing of love thus disrupts this hierarchy of love and happiness. Love, he goes on to explain, is not limited to "the one," and that, "when people do talk about 'the one' or finding my soul mate or my other half or whatever, I've really had very great difficulty getting my head around that." Rather, Philip "think[s] in terms of love" and intimacy in ways that are more expansive, collective and non-hierarchical.

Similarly, as Gabriella talked about her "vast array of friendships" she acknowledged a hierarchy which privileges sexual intimacy:

Gabriella (32, romantic): Most people—it's probably going to be a horrible generalization—[but] I understand that most people form close and intimate relationships more for the sexual relationship than they do for anything else that they get, because you can seek out close companionship and trust and really close friendship with a variety of people but you usually have a sexual relationship with one person. Whereas I have a vast array of friendships that I can draw on for that social and emotional empathic support.

Gabriella orients to what she calls a "horrible generalization" which is the dominant construction of "close and intimate relationships" being with one person and being sexual, while also challenging this through acknowledging the significance of the friendships in her life. Thus, like Philip, she emphasizes ways of connecting and belonging to many people rather than just to one person. However, For Gabriella there are some difficulties in giving meaning to her close friendships, both for herself and to others:

Tiina: So [...] you don't have a kind of a desire to be in a partnered relationship?
Gabriella (32, romantic): No. I mean I've got very close friends that *I would almost count like that,* but that conversation hasn't been had and won't be had for various reasons, whatever, you know. Moving on [laughs].

Although the boundary between friend and partner is blurred by Gabriella's comment that some very close friends "almost count" like partners, she has no intelligible way to describe such relationships to her friends (or to me in the interview). In a similar vein, Kristen Scherrer (2010) argues that we need new forms of language to describe the relationships asexual people engage in beyond simple single and coupled, and friend and relationship. It is interesting, although perhaps not surprising, that Gabriella will not discuss this with the people involved, "that conversation […] won't be had." This refusal can be understood in terms of the dominant construction of friendship as emotionally intimate but not romantically and/or sexually intimate. As Gabriella points out above, "close and intimate" relationships are constituted as those in which sexual practices occur. This is because the "presence of sex marks out romantic intimacy and love from other forms of intimacy" (Dawson et al., 2016, p. 350). Gabriella's "friendships," like Philip's, thus "trouble the larger legitimating sexual and romantic order of things" by "extending understandings of intimacy and love from couple-centric connotations to terrains of collectivity and friendship" (Francis, 2016, pp. 29, 30).

In contrast to Gabriella, James has found the AVEN forums, in which the nuances of attraction are discussed and debated, useful for naming and making sense of his "feelings" towards others. James, who identifies as aromantic and queer, employs the term "queer platonic relationship" to describe a mode of relationship he might like to have with a another man:

James: (18, aromantic)	It'd be nice if like we were in a QPR, queer platonic relationship, but I don't know if I'll want something further than that or like if I'm actually crushing on him or if I'm only squishing on him, I don't know.
Tiina:	When you say squishing?
James:	That's like platonic crushes.
Tiina:	Okay.
James:	We [AVEN online community] go very into detail in terms of attraction. There's platonic attraction, romantic attraction, sexual attraction, aesthetic attraction, there's a few others I can't remember off the top of my head but yeah.

Although James identifies as aromantic, he talked about questioning his aromantic identification and the possibility that he might be grey-romantic (where he may experience romantic attraction, although not very often, but not desire a romantic relationship). This was prompted by James experiencing an attraction to someone which he found difficult to conceptualize. He thought a

QPR (queer platonic relationship) might "be nice," that is, a relationship that is "above best friend but it's not a romantic partner, it's kind of like in the middle." He is however uncertain if he would want "something further" because he is unsure if he is "crushing" or "squishing" (James was the only participant to use the latter term). A crush is generally framed as a romantic attraction to another person.[5] However, a squish is a non-romantic or platonic crush. It is like a crush but lacking interest in forming a romantic couple. It involves an intense feeling of attraction, liking, appreciation, and/or admiration for a person you want to get to know better and become close with.[6]

The level of detail in the discussions on attraction on AVEN is debated with some arguing that terms like squish and crush are "confusing" and potentially "alienating" toasexuals,[7] while for others they are ways of reconceptualizing and understanding the attractions they experience. For James, there is confusion and uncertainty but also a sense that such terms open up possibilities which were limited with his identification as aromantic. This highlights the ways in which attraction, asexual identification and ways of relating are extremely fluid and shifting, and the possibilities for constituting 'new' subject positions and modes of affective relationality.

NEGOTIATING INTIMACY IN ROMANTIC, PARTNERED RELATIONSHIPS WITH NON-ASEXUALS

Aside from James and Philip, the other participants in this study identified as romantic asexual or grey-asexual and desired a romantic, non-sexual, partnered relationship, ideally with another asexual. However, they also acknowledged this was unlikely given most of them had not met another asexual in person. Hallie (27) was the exception, having had two online relationships with asexual men in other countries.

While only one participant was in a partnered relationship at the time of the interviews, most had been in some form sexual relationship in the past. Although Mike (22) and Aidan (23) described themselves as sex "repelled" and "repulsed," they initially felt pressured by non-asexual female partners and as a result did "try [sex] a few times." Discovering asexuality as an identity and sexual orientation (through online searches) was significant for both men and proved a turning point in their negotiation of dating and relationships.

In contrast, most of the older participants had been in long term sexual relationships or marriages (given the relatively recent emergence of asexuality as an identity). Angela (56), Sarah (47), Amelia (49) and Kathy (60) had stayed with partners or husbands because they desired the relationship but not the sex. Sarah, for example, spent many years in relationships where she "put up with" unwanted and painful sex with men or unwanted sex with women, "I thought I have to have sex because that's what you do, and it hurts and I don't like it, but I have to do it. [...] I would justify it to myself as what I had to do to get what I wanted which was a partner." Angela had married even though she was "revolted" by sex:

> Angela (56, romantic): I was revolted by sex, revolted, absolutely revolted by it, but I wanted the idealized view of what a family was, which was like children and the house [...] I wanted the whole thing, yeah, but I didn't want sex. Not at all. And so when I came to uni when I was 18, I very quickly got pregnant and married. [...] The reason why we split up was because I didn't want anything to do with my husband sexually. I loved him. I loved him but I didn't want him.

Like the younger participants, the constitution and visibility of asexuality as a sexual identity enabled these women to negotiate partnered relationships in new ways. For Sarah, identifying as asexual allowed her to say "no" to sex and to "look after herself." She is currently seeking a non-sexual, monogamous relationship (see Vares, 2018). Kathy and Angela's more recent experiences highlight different ways of negotiating partnered relationships with non-asexuals. Kathy met and married her husband after she identified as asexual and when they were both in mid-later life. Kathy's recognition of her asexuality enabled her to feel in control of her decisions, from marrying to engaging in some sexual practices. Although she didn't disclose her asexuality her husband, she was comfortable "gifting" sex to him:

> Kathy (60, romantic): So yeah, we did have relations but it wasn't full on and it wasn't one hundred percent and it wasn't scheduled. [...] I was more than happy to satisfy him or pleasure him, more from the love I felt for him than from the actual desire of doing it [...] and I mean, it makes him happy and it makes him feel like a man because he had some issues with losing mobility and stuff like that. [...] I have no problem because I figured he gave me so much [...] and you know this may sound rude but what's a blow job in the long run [...] and if it made him happy, and he was happy, then good and I got a nice cuddle. But you know we were perfectly happy sitting on the couch together watching films.

Lorca Sloan defines "gifting sex" as participating in any behavior that sexually arouses or satisfies one's partner and "not because the acts themselves are viscerally appealing or physically pleasurable" (2010, p. 557), and clearly this is not unique to those identifying as asexual. Although Kathy finds sex unappealing, she explains her actions as being for her husband out of love, reaffirming his masculinity, making him happy, and reciprocating what he gives to her in the relationship. In their study of the intimate practices of asexuals, Matt Dawson et al. (2016) refer to such sex as a practice of intimacy. They indicate that this practice occupies different positions in their participants' lives, from those offering sex as a valued part of the relationship to those who engaged in sex due to pressure. In my study, Kathy was the only romantic identified participant who gifted sex in a relationship after coming to identify as asexual.[8] Her husband's age and ill health, which resulted in infrequent sexual activity, inform Kathy's acceptance of her actions which she contextualizes as just one aspect of their intimate lives.

However, gifting sex was not considered a possibility for other participants such as Sarah and Angela (above). After separating from her husband Angela "desired a partnership." She goes on to explain, "I thought about it in terms of a male partnership, heterosexual I suppose. I desired that. I really wanted that but I don't like what comes with it [sex]." A few years ago she began a partnered relationship with a non-asexual man. Angela was clear from the start that sex wasn't a possibility for her. Her partner has been accepting of this and Angela hasn't experienced any pressure to go beyond the physical intimacy she is comfortable with:

Angela (56, romantic): We do sleep together, sometimes we hold hands in bed but we don't hug and we don't have sex. […] We always kiss each other in the morning and at night, but it's not lingering kisses or anything like that, you know, and we often hold hands. […] After work […] we make dinner together and then we usually watch something on a DVD and we just sit on the couch and yeah, it's a really nice time. It's like we're sitting close and either holding hands or he's got my feet in his lap or something like that but it's nice and it's non-threatening. […] In countless ways every day he shows me he loves me without anything physical happening.

As with Kathy, non-sexual and often non-physical intimacies featured significantly in Angela's narrative. Yet Angela's experience is one I have not yet encountered in the existing research (to date), that is, where there has never been any sexual activity in the relationship, she experiences no pressure to engage in sex, and also no guilt. When asked if she was aware of any sexual desires on the part of her partner Angela replied: "[He] just doesn't seem to be concerned about it himself […] and I suppose I just have a different view now and it's a bit more mercenary. It's kind of like, well he can sort that out himself, you know." Here Angela takes up a resistant feminine subject position in which she has no interest in, and takes no responsibility for, her male partner's sexual needs/desires.[9] As indicated above, while a non-sexual relationship of this kind is part of the lives of some non-asexuals (for example, if sexual interest, ability and/or desire decrease), what is significant here is the absence of any sexual practice from the outset of the relationship. This highlights the possibility of romantic, partnered relationships between asexual and non-asexual identified individuals where sex is not required or expected as a practice of intimacy.

CONCLUSION

Mark Carrigan argues that if "sexual intimacy ceases to be the *sine qua non* of intimacy then the boundary between friendship and relationship also become fuzzier" (2012, p. 15). In this chapter I have explored some of the ways in which some self-identified asexuals' experiences of relationality blur the boundary between friendship and relationship in various ways. For Philip and Gabriella, love and intimacy are not restricted to one person, but to many—what Mark Francis calls "collective belonging" (2016, p. 42). This disrupts the discursive privileging of consummated, (hetero) romantic love over others and opens up other ways of knowing and talking about relationality (Francis, 2016). Although language for making sense of such relationality is limited, the asexual online community is engaged in conceptualizing the diversity of attractions and creating "a new vocabulary for exploring sexuality and intimacy" (Chu, 2014, p. 191). James' reflections on his shifting attractions in a relationship which would ideally be between "best friend" and a "romantic partner" "literally *make*[s] [his] unique and often confusing relationships *make sense,* that is they render otherwise non-normative relationship intelligible" (italic in original) (Chasin, 2015, p. 177).

For the majority of romantic identified participants in this study, monogamy featured centrally as a desired or actual partnered relationship form (as it was for the asexual participants in Scherrer, 2008; Dawson et al., 2016). While mono-normativity is thus reinscribed, it is simultaneously challenged with the decentering of sexuality. Although gifting sex as a practice of intimacy is one way of negotiating a romantic relationship with a non-asexual, Angela's experience highlights the ultimate decentering of sex in a relationship with a non-asexual. It is important to acknowledge that this form of romantic and non-sexual relationality is not mentioned in the existing literature (to my knowledge), yet makes intelligible a relationship, (with a non-asexual) in which there has *never been* any sex or pressure to engage in sex. This small nature of the study on which this chapter is based, and the diversity of intimacies and relationality discussed, highlights the need for further research into asexual intimacies, for as Jacinthe Flore argues, asexuality "offers a location, both discursive and material, from which to refresh 'known' realities about intimate life" (2014, p. 74).

NOTES

[1] Romantic asexuals generally do not experience sexual attraction but do experience romantic attraction and often desire an intimate, non-sexual partnered relationship. Aromantic asexuals generally do not experience sexual or romantic attraction. For individuals who identify as grey-asexual or demi-sexual, sexual attraction is a possibility in special circumstances, for example, once a relationship has developed.

[2] Participants were recruited through a number of online sites, for example, AVEN, a queer youth support group, a student recruitment website and Asexuals New Zealand Facebook. Ten of the participants responded from the latter. Although previous studies have recruited primarily through AVEN, for this project only one participant responded to the AVEN posts. 2 participants identified as aromantic, 12 as romantic and 1 as grey-asexual. With respect to ethnicity, the majority were Pākeha (the indigenous term for non-Māori), one was Māori (the indigenous people of New Zealand), and one Iranian. Interviews were conducted either in person (10) or by phone (5). Some participants asked for a phone interview and for others, my travelling to their location was not practical at the time. The interviews lasted between 35 and 120 minutes.

[3] Following the pseudonym of the participant is their age and asexual self-identification. When presenting extracts from interviews I have generally omitted word repetitions and speech hesitations (i.e., all terms such as 'um' and 'ah').

[4] See Mark Francis' (2016) analysis of three recent films which "intentionally or unintentionally" consider asexuality (*Bill Cunningham New York*, 2010; *(A)sexual*, 2011; and *Year of the Dog*, 2007). He argues the films "overtly establish ties between asexuality and singlehood" and represent the "asexual single" as isolated, disconnected and lonely (2016, p.28). Although they "never condemn the asexual-single" they do "cast doubt on how such a person could thrive in a culture in which consummated romantic relations are the norm" (Francis, 2016, p. 31).

[5] This is distinguished from sexual attraction which is broadly referred to as a feeling that sexual people get that causes them to desire sexual contact with a specific other person.

[6] From the Urban Dictionary https://www.urbandictionary.com/define.php?term=squish

[7] see https://www.asexuality.org/en/topic/111367-squish-vs-crush/; https://asexualagenda.wordpress.com/2012/09/09/defining-crushes/

[8] In Ellen Van Houdenhove et al.'s study of the experiences of asexual women, two participants also had sex as a way of "showing love" and for their non-asexual partners and described this as a "sacrifice" they were willing to make (2015, p. 271).

[9] See Vares (2018) for a discussion of how some female participants felt responsible and/or guilty for arousing their non-asexual male partners' sexual desires and 'leading them on.'

REFERENCES

Ahmed, S. (2010). *The promise of happiness*. Durham, NC: Duke University Press.

Carrigan, M. (2011). There's more to life than sex? Difference and commonality within the asexual community. *Sexualities, 14*(4), 462–478.

Carrigan, M. (2012). 'How do you know you don't like it if you haven't tried it?' Asexual agency and the sexual assumption. In T. G. Morrison, M. A. Morrison, M. A. Carrigan, & D. T. D. McDermott (Eds.), *Sexual minority research in the New Millennium*. New York, NY: Nova Science.

Chambers, D. (2013). *Social media and personal relationships: Online intimacies and networked friendships*. Houndsmill: Palgrave MacMillan.

Chasin, C. D. (2015). Making sense in and of the asexual community: Navigating relationships and identities in a context of resistance. *Journal of Community and Applied Social Psychology, 25*, 167–180.

Chu, E. (2014) Radical identities: Asexuality and contemporary articulations of identity. In K. Cerankowski & M. Milks (Eds.), *Asexualities: Feminist and queer perspectives*. New York, NY: Routledge.

Dawson, M., McDonnell, L., & Scott, S. (2016). Negotiating the boundaries of intimacy: The personal lives of asexual people. *The Sociological Review, 64*, 349–365.

Flore, J. (2014) Mismeasures of asexual desires. In K. Cerankowski & M. Milks (Eds.), *Asexualities: Feminist and queer perspectives*. New York, NY: Routledge.

Francis, M. (2016). The asexual single and the collective: Remaking queer bonds in *(A)sexual, Bill Cunningham New York*, and *Year of the Dog. Camera Obscura, 91*, 28–63.

Gressgard, R. (2013). Sexuality: From pathology to identity and beyond. *Psychology and Sexuality, 4*(2), 179–192.

Gupta, K., & Cerankowski, K. J. (2017). Asexualities and media. In C. Smith, F. Attwood, & B. McNair (Eds.), *The Routledge companion to media, sex and sexuality*. New York, NY & London: Routledge.

Haefner, C. (2011). *Asexual scripts: A grounded theory inquiry into the intrapsychic scripts asexuals use to negotiate romantic relationships*. Ann Arbor, MI: UMI Dissertation Publishing, ProQuest.

Jamieson, L. (1998). *Intimacy: Personal relationships in modern societies*. Cambridge: Polity Press.

Roseneil, S., & Budgeon, S. (2004). Cultures of intimacy and care beyond the 'family': Personal life and social change in the early 21st century. *Current Sociology, 52*(2), 134–159.

Scherrer, K. (2008). Coming to an asexual identity: Negotiating identity, negotiating desires. *Sexualities, 11*, 621–641.

Scherrer, K. (2010). What asexuality contributes to the same-sex marriage debate. *Journal of Gay and Lesbian Social Services, 18*, 56–73.

Sloan, L. (2015). Ace of (BDSM) clubs: Building asexual relationships through BDSM practice. *Sexualities, 18*(5–6), 548–563.

Van Houdenhove, E., Gis, L., T'Sjoen, G., & Enzlin, P. (2015). Stories about asexuality: A qualitative study on asexual women. *Journal of Marital and Sex Therapy, 41*, 262–281.

Vares, T. (2018). My [asexuality] is playing hell with my dating life: Romantic identified asexuals negotiate the dating game. *Sexualities, 21*(4), 520–526.

DANIEL COPULSKY

15. AT THE INTERSECTION OF POLYAMORY AND ASEXUALITY

COMING TO TERMS: CAN SOMEONE BE ASEXUAL AND POLYAMOROUS?

When talking about minority sexualities and relationships, it is helpful to review the terms used for these identities and clarify which groups are being discussed. At the same time, it is important to acknowledge that individual use of this language varies widely. Even when a definition reflects the general consensus of a community, it can never capture the full range of personal experiences held by all those who share an identity.

Asexual means not experiencing sexual attraction to people of any gender, like homosexual means feeling sexual attraction to people of the same gender. Asexuality describes *sexual attraction*, who or what a person is sexually aroused by, rather than *sexual behavior*, with whom and how a person enacts sexuality. Just as some heterosexuals or bisexuals choose not to have sex, there are a variety of reasons some asexuals choose to engage in sexual behavior.

Sexual attraction is also distinct from *romantic attraction*, a person's romantic interests. Some aexuals enjoy romantic activities like going on dates, cuddling, or writing love letters, and may have a desire to form this kind of romantic relationship with specific people. An asexual who is interested in romantic or intimate relationships may have a *romantic orientation* towards people of one or more genders.

For example, much like homosexuals desire sexual relationships with people of the same gender, homoromantics desire romantic relationships with people of the same gender. A person's sexual and romantic orientations may align (like a bisexual who is also biromantic) or not (like a bisexual who is heteroromantic).

The degree to which people experience sexual attraction is a spectrum as well. The broader asexual (or "ace") community includes a range of desires and degrees of sexual attraction, such as gray-asexuals and demisexuals. Those who identify as *gray-asexuals* experience limited sexual attraction,

© KONINKLIJKE BRILL NV, LEIDEN, 2019 | DOI:10.1163/9789004414105_016

while *demisexuals* experience sexual attraction only after forming an emotional connection. At the other end of this spectrum are *allosexuals*, people who do experience sexual attraction.

Polyamory describes being in more than one loving relationship at the same time, or a disposition to have this kind of relationship structure. Many polyamorous relationships include sex, and this is certainly part of the appeal of polyamory for some people, but it is not a necessary component.

Polyamory is often seen as falling under the umbrella of *non-monogamy*, a broader category of being in more than one sexual, romantic, or intimate relationship. A distinction is also made between cheating and *ethical* or *consensual non-monogamy*, where multiple relationships are pursued with the knowledge and consent of all those involved.

There are a multitude of ways people structure polyamorous relationships. Polyamory might look like a triad of three partners in one relationship. It might also look like a couple who make their relationship a primary focus while each dating someone else. Or it might look like a person who has multiple partners in a web of interconnected relationships. By some definitions, a polyamorous relationship can even include a monogamous person, if they date only one partner while their partner also dates one or more other people.

There are some people who do not experience sexual attraction and are also drawn to having multiple romantic or intimate relationships. These are polyamorous asexuals, and an asexual could be in any of the kinds of polyamorous relationships described above.

BY THE NUMBERS: HOW MANY POLYAMOROUS ASEXUALS ARE THERE?

People have practiced some form of non-monogamy for as long as humans have existed, with non-monogamous relationships structured a multitude of different ways from then until now (Ryan & Jethá, 2010). Only in the past thirty years, however, was the term polyamory coined and a community formed around this particular identity (Sheff, 2013). Likewise, humans have always had a wide variety of individual experiences of sexual attraction, yet the community of self-identified asexuals came together only in the past two decades (Hinderliter, 2009). In this short time, it seems that polyamory grew particularly popular among asexuals.

Anecdotal observations of polyamorous asexuality are easy to find. One polyamorous asexual describes: "No longer a whisper, polyamory has become the main relationship model for romantic asexuals. Every panel and discussion on relationship models includes a token part on monogamy because it's assumed that everyone already knows about polyamory" (Cerberus, 2014).

It is harder to quantify the correlation between these identities. The 2015 Asexual Census surveyed people who identify as asexual, gray-a, or demisexual and found that 9.5% of respondents consider themselves polyamorous. Unfortunately, it is not clear how representative this sample is of the entire asexual community. The survey was only available online, in English, and respondents appeared to be disproportionately young and white. While the project was open to people anywhere in the world, over half of responses came from the United States.

It is even harder to get a clear picture of how many people in the population at large are polyamorous. Various studies have gotten largely different results, but also are often looking at somewhat different things (Scheff, 2014). Some studies look at people who self-identify as polyamorous while others look at specific behaviors that the study has categorized as polyamorous. There are also several studies looking specifically at sexually non-monogamous relationships, which can be particularly difficult to compare to the nonsexual relationships many asexuals have.

Best guesses tend to put the number of people in any kind of consensually non-monogamous relationship at 4 to 5% of the U.S. population (Pappas, 2013). Only some of these relationships are polyamorous. Tentatively, then, polyamory might be at least twice as popular among asexuals.

Like so much research on minority sexualities and relationships styles, the scant data available highlights the need for additional research. It would be helpful for research on polyamory and non-monogamy to be conscious of how they are defining the boundaries of these communities. It would also be particularly useful to have a large-scale representative survey that asks about both polyamory and asexuality, potentially clarifying the correlation between these understudied groups.

RELATIONSHIP ORIENTATION/RELATIONSHIP STYLE: WHAT IS POLYAMORY?

Throughout the polyamory community, there are a variety of ways different people conceive what it means to be polyamorous. Some feel that there is a part of themselves that is best suited to being in multiple loving relationships. They may think of polyamory as a *relationship orientation*, similar to the way being gay, bisexual, or asexual are sexual orientations. These individuals may consider themselves polyamorous even when they are single or in a monogamous relationship. In this view, polyamorous is something people *are*.

Others feel they are making a conscious choice to be in multiple loving relationships. They may think of polyamory as a *relationship style*, something like deciding to date casually or cohabitate. One or more relationship styles may be a good fit for a particular person, for a particular relationship, or at a particular time and place. For example, someone may decide they want a polyamorous relationship after their children have left the home or while their partner is studying abroad. These individuals may define their relationships primarily by the specific behavior that takes place presently. In this view, polyamory is something people *do*.

While it is useful to make the distinction between relationship orientation and relationship style, it is also important to acknowledge that these two frameworks are not perfectly separate. These concepts are probably better seen as two points on a continuum of how people think about polyamory. For many people, polyamorous identity builds on a combination of innate desires, behaviors, choices, experiences, and intents.

Polyamorous asexuals are found across this continuum, with the 9.5% of survey respondents who said they were polyamorous including both those who feel like polyamory is the right relationships style for them (regardless of what relationships they are currently in), and those who are currently in a polyamorous relationship (regardless of the reasons why).

UNCERTAINTY AND AMBIVALENCE: "DO YOU CONSIDER YOURSELF POLYAMOROUS?"

In the Asexual Census survey, another 26.9% of asexual, gray-a, and demisexual respondents said they were unsure whether they consider themselves polyamorous. This number is quite remarkable, at it may suggest that a very large portion of the asexual community would consider being in a polyamorous relationship. There may even be another set of people who decidedly do not consider themselves polyamorous based on their current relationship status yet would be open to the possibility in other circumstances.

There are a diversity of reasons someone might be unsure of a polyamorous identity. Someone with limited experience in relationships might not know yet what kinds of relationships work for them. Asexuals in particular may be hesitant to date while they figure out their identity and may have a harder time finding partners with compatible desires for a relationship. As mentioned, many survey respondents were also young, and simply may not yet have had much time to spend in different types of relationships.

Because the relationship orientation and relationship style models can be perceived as at odds with each other, people might be hesitant to identify as polyamorous if they only fit one of these criteria. They may feel an innate draw to polyamory but not call themself polyamorous if they are not *doing* it. Or they may be in a polyamorous relationship but not call themself polyamorous because it is not who they *are*. It can be particularly difficult for those navigating complex identities when it is not clear what the asker's intent is of a question like "do you consider yourself polyamorous?"

Asexuals may be particularly unsure or ambivalent about relationship labels since these are part of a framework culturally perceived as centering sex. For example, even academic research on non-monogamy has often focused very explicitly on sexual non-exclusivity, and asexuals are told directly that their relationships are not real if they are not having sex.

Many asexuals actively work to change these limiting conceptions of what a relationship must look like. Many have intimate, romantic relationships that they want others to acknowledge and respect. Sometimes, however, not having the clear demarcation line of sex or sexual exclusivity makes it more difficult to find a boundary between a friendship and a relationship, for researchers and individuals alike.

For some asexuals, however, making this distinction is unnecessary as long as they can find desired intimacy, partnership, or romance. Outside the framework of a relationship, asexuals may find these things from a group of people rather than one individual. In some sense, the very same things that can make polyamory a good fit for asexuals may also make it unnecessary to define as such. Thus some of the dynamics, challenges, and benefits at play when asexuals practice polyamory can be present even for asexuals who do not call what they are doing polyamory.

The Asexual Census continues as an annual project and is in a unique position to track changes in the community and to adapt what information they collect. In particular, it would be helpful for future surveys to ask about both polyamorous identity and behavior.

Results from the 2017 Asexual Census are not yet available, but should help clear up one additional reason people might have said they were unsure about considering themselves polyamorous. Where previous years offered the three answer choices "Yes," "No," and "Unsure," this past year's survey offered four: "Yes," "No," "Questioning or unsure," and "I am not familiar with this term." If there are a large number of respondents who do not know what polyamory is, it would be mistake to think they are more open to it.

MULTIPLE PATHS TO MULTIPLE PARTNERS: WHY BE IN A POLYAMOROUS RELATIONSHIP?

Across reports, there are a few common paths that lead people to polyamorous relationships, whether they are asexual or allosexual. A person might feel that polyamory fits their own desires, that their relationship needs are best met by having multiple partners.

For example, they may appreciate having people fill different roles, like one partner who is a co-parent and another that provides passionate romance. Or they may feel more secure with a sense of personal autonomy and freedom, knowing it is okay to fall in love with someone else even though they are in committed relationship.

On the other hand, a person might find that polyamory is a good fit for a specific relationship, particularly if a partner's needs are best met by having multiple partners. For example, someone might encourage their partner to seek out another relationships if their own busy schedule or desire discrepancy severely limits the time and attention they can provide in the relationship.

In cases like these, it may be possible for someone to be in a polyamorous relationship even if they are sexually or romantically monogamous to their partner. They are only involved with one person while that partner has one or more additional partners.

Sexual interests, desires, and discrepancies are a common reason people seek out additional partners, even when no one in the relationship identifies as asexual. For example, someone may have a kink or fetish that a partner does not want to explore with them. Or one partner may want to have sex frequently or regularly while their partner wants to have sex rarely or not at all.

ASEXUALITY AND SEXUAL DISCREPANCY: WHAT DOES POLYAMORY HAVE TO OFFER?

While sexual discrepancy can come up between allosexual partners who simply have different sexual desires, it is also common when an asexual person dates an allosexual person. Even if an asexual person wants to engage in some sexual activity, this may not fulfill their partner's need to feel sexually desired.

If it is possible to pursue sex outside the relationship, this can relieve some of the stress around sex within the relationship. Or course, polyamory may not resolve emotional and physical tensions around desire discrepancy entirely. While some polyamorous asexuals are happy to date allosexuals, knowing they can get sexual needs met elsewhere, some polyamorous asexuals still prefer to date other asexuals.

When asexuals do find themselves in relationships with allosexuals, struggles around sex are frequent. Mainstream couples therapists and religious advisors often pathologize or condemn both asexuality and polyamory, and offer a range of discriminatory and often wholly inadequate solutions (Decker, 2015; Weitzman, 2007). These can include ending the relationship, forced intimacy for the asexual partner, or forced celibacy for the allosexual partner.

Within the asexual community and from sex-positive allies, polyamory is frequently suggested as another option. This is likely one reason polyamory is more common in the asexual community. Asexuals who have been in this situation and tried polyamory have found a numbers of ways in which it can work well, but they have also found challenges and difficulties (Copulsky, 2016).

Along with relieving certain pressures from the allosexual partner for sex, an asexual partner may feel relief from social pressures, and from internal feelings of guilt and shame for not meeting a partner's need or from resentment if they had sex when they did not want to. Some asexuals have also found benefits from taking the focus off their partner's desires and from pursuing other partners themself. Both of these can provide avenues for deeper self-understanding of sexuality, emotions, and desire.

On the other hand, involving a new person can exacerbate existing problems in a relationship. Rather than being a relief from negative emotions, a partner's new partner can be a source of jealousy, insecurity, resentment, and feelings of neglect or abandonment, while simultaneously adding the needs and concerns of a whole additional person into the dynamic.

People may be too quick to suggest polyamory as a solution to one particular problem, centering the needs of the allosexual person and failing to consider the relationship as a whole or what other problems this arrangement could create. Calling this "band-aid polyamory," one asexual who practices polyamory cautions that "it's an unhealthy situation for one or both partners because the nonmonogamous/polyamorous status of the relationship is unwanted on at least one side, and that partner who's a monogamist at heart is going to suffer the whole time" (Crosswell, 2013).

Additionally, polyamory can be particularly challenging for asexuals. As members of two marginalized communities, they can face dual stigma and misunderstandings about what these identities mean. Since it can be difficult to navigate a polyamorous relationship or navigate a relationship as an asexual, it can be especially difficult to deal with both sets of challenges at once. This is only compounded if an individual is marginalized on additional axes, such as race, disability, or religion.

At the same time, though, polyamory can also offer some specific benefits to asexuals. Some polyamorous communities offer welcoming spaces for asexuals. As another polyamorous asexual observes, this community also "promotes healthy communication and a better handling of issues," providing a set of values and frameworks for living out those values that can be an asset to asexuals (Cerberus, 2014).

REDEFINING RELATIONSHIP: WHAT ELSE DOES POLYAMORY OFFER ASEXUALS?

Asexuals may be more likely to consider polyamory as a viable relationship option because of the way both identities challenge common assumptions about romantic or intimate relationships. Asexuality confronts the expectation that relationships must involve sexual attraction and sexual activity (even though some asexuals do engage in sexual activity). Polyamory, along with non-monogamy more broadly, similarly confronts the expectation that relationships are defined by monogamy.

In some respects, varying from relationship norms in one way may increase the pressure to conform in other ways. Media promoting acceptance for gay relationships, for example, has often highlighted couples that are otherwise normative, conventional, and "relatable." If other people may question the validity or seriousness of a relationship because it does not include sex or exclusivity, there is an incentive for people to make sure that at least that is the only thing different about their relationship.

However, many find that that defying one social expectation allows them to further question norms and makes it easier to defy another. Defying an expectation without major consequence can be reassuring, but surviving some pushback can be emboldening as well.

Our culturally traditional model for relationships is based on heterosexual marriage, lifelong monogamy, and sex for the purpose of having children. This conception of what relationships ought to look like is challenged by many different kinds of people, including those who are asexual, polyamorous, queer, kinky, sex workers, infertile, or childfree by choice.

While asexuals and polyamorous people challenge the centrality of sex and exclusivity, queer people challenge the necessity of heterosexuality, and kinky people, sex workers, and those without children challenge the focus on procreation. Once you start deconstructing any piece of these assumptions, it is easier to see how the entire model functions as a historical artifact and social construction.

All of the ways in which people relate to one another are actually up for reconsideration and recombination, and these groups are natural allies in working to change these norms. As Scherrer (2010) observed, "similar to those in polyamorous communities, asexual individuals are actively restructuring and rewriting their relationships, opening up possibilities for reimagining all of our lives."

Each of these groups is uniquely situated to reexamine what elements they want in their intimate relationships. For example, an asexual person may not want to have sex but may want to live in a household with children, while a polyamorous person may want multiple partners but not to have any kids. Sex, romance, commitment, exclusivity, independence, marriage, children, and cohabitation are just some of the options available.

Asexual, polyamorous, queer, trans, kinky, and intersex people are all expanding the rainbow of alternative sexualities and identities by creating space for each of their communities. Within these spaces, they are also making room for all the ways that these communities can overlap, including polyamorous asexuals, polyamourous kinksters, kinky queers, and queer asexuals.

Through mutual support in the face of pressure to conform to social norms, these communities collaborate to build a more expansive range of relationship options and models. This process empowers everyone to combine these possibilities in new ways and customize their relationship to work specifically for them.

REFERENCES

Ace Community Census Survey Team. (2017). *Text of the 2017 survey.* Retrieved from https://asexualcensus.files.wordpress.com/2018/02/2017rawtext.pdf

Bauer, C., Miller, T., Ginoza, M., Chiang, A., Youngblom, K., Baba, A., Pinnell, J., Penten, P., Meinhold, M., & Ramaraj, V. (2017). *The 2015 asexual census summary report.* The Ace Community Survey Team. Retrieved from https://asexualcensus.files.wordpress.com/2017/10/2015_ace_census_summary_report.pdf

Cerberus. (2014). *My ace poly manifesto.* Retrieved from transpolyasexual.wordpress.com/2014/01/30/my-ace-poly-manifesto/

Copulsky, D. (2016). Asexual polyamory: Potential challenges and benefits. *The Journal of Positive Sexuality, 2*(1), 11–15.

Crosswell, M. (2013, November 3). *The big, fat polyamorous asexual post.* Retrieved from thethinkingasexual.wordpress.com/2013/11/02/the-big-fat-polyamorous-asexual-post/

Decker, J. (2015, January 15). *Asexuality and the health professional.* Retrieved from http://www.psychologytoday.com/us/blog/the-invisible-orientation/201501/asexuality-and-the-health-professional

Hinderliter, A. C. (2009). *Asexuality: The history of a definition.* Retrieved from asexualexplorations.net/home/history_of_definition.html

Pappas, S. (2013, February 14). *New sexual revolution: Polyamory may be good for you.* Retrieved from https://www.scientificamerican.com/article/new-sexual-revolution-polyamory/

Ryan, C., & Jethá, C. (2010). *Sex at dawn: The prehistoric origins of modern sexuality* (pp. 1–2). New York, NY: Harper.

Scherrer, K. S. (2010). Asexual relationships: What does asexuality have to do with polyamory? In *Understanding non-monogamies* (pp. 154–159). London: Routledge.

Sheff, E. (2013). *The polyamorists next door: Inside multiple-partner relationships and families.* (pp. xiv–xv). Rowman & Littlefield.

Sheff, E. (2014, May 9). *How many polyamorists are there in the U.S.?* Retrieved from https://www.psychologytoday.com/blog/the-polyamorists-next-door/201405/how-many-polyamorists-are-there-in-the-us

Weitzman, G. (2007). Counseling bisexuals in polyamorous relationships. In B. A. Firestein (Ed.), *Becoming visible: Counseling bisexuals across the lifespan* (pp. 312–335). New York, NY: Columbia University Press.

C. J. CHASIN

16. ASEXUALITY AND THE RE/CONSTRUCTION OF SEXUAL ORIENTATION

INTRODUCTION

This chapter explores some conceptual complications of reconciling asexuality, with all its diversity, with ideas of sexual orientation.[1] It highlights some of the criteria that have been used to assess whether asexuality should be regarded as a sexual orientation while questioning the value of this kind of classification project. Taking a broader view of sexual orientation as a historically specific, political category, this chapter explores implications for integrating asexuality into a contemporary framework of sexual orientation, or, alternatively, for radically reconfiguring sexual orientation through an asexual lens.

WHO IS ASEXUAL/ACE?

As discussed in the introduction, there is a complex, multifaceted spectrum of experiences under the ace umbrella, including those in the vast and varied grey-zone. The ace community is extremely diverse along many dimensions. It includes high proportions of people who identify as bi+ and aromantic, and high proportions of women and people whose genders fall outside the gender binary. Ace community members engage in various kinds of significant relationships—romantic relationships (monogamous and non-monogamous; celibate and involving sexual contact, etc.); non-romantic/non-normative partnerships; conventional friendships, etc. They also include people with a wide range interest in personally participating sex, though significantly most aces are either some degree of sex-repulsed/averse, or sex-indifferent.

In short, "asexuality" as articulated by the asexual/ace community is a "hodge-podge" of different experiences that cannot be articulated by a single theoretical construct—not even the *absence of sexual attraction*—and there is no single construct or set of constructs that could function as either a necessary or sufficient condition for completely defining asexuality. The substantive multiplicity of aceness presents a problem for anyone looking to

© KONINKLIJKE BRILL NV, LEIDEN, 2019 | DOI:10.1163/9789004414105_017

define asexuality. However, regardless of the definition they ultimately adopt, if researchers define asexuality or aceness differently than ace communities do, they will produce research findings about a population that presumbably overlaps with ace community members but which is substantively different both theoretically and practically. In other words, research findings from asexuality scholarship risks only applying in limited ways to actual ace community members.

CONSIDERING ASEXUALITY AS A SEXUAL ORIENTATION

Bogaert (2015) and Van Houdenhove, Enzlin, and Gijs (2017) discussed some of the limitations of using self-identification to define sexual orientation and asexuality in particular. Relatedly, Bogaert outlined many arguments generally deemed relevant to the appropriateness of classifying asexuality as a sexual orientation—possible etiological factors, patterns of genital arousal, the theoretical overlap between asexuality and the updated DSM criterion for sexual disorders, etc. In short, Bogaert provided a thorough discussion of how conceptualising asexuality as a sexual orientation "works." Moreover, various researchers have framed their explorations of asexuality in terms of sexual orientation, and this has also seemed to "work" with little finagling, across a very disparate collection of studies. Such studies have ranged from positivist-empiricist explorations of biological markers, finding some significant differences between asexual and other sexual orientation groups (Yule, Brotto, & Gorzalka, 2014), to more *social* science scholarship, such as qualitative work with themes emerging that parallel experiences of other sexual orientation groups, such as coming to an asexual identity with respect to sexual orientation and coming out as asexual (e.g., Scherrer, 2008; Haeffer, 2011; Van Houdenhove, Gijs, T'Sjoen, & Enzlin, 2015).

Similarly, Brotto and Yule (2017a) assessed available evidence for whether asexuality should be considered a mental disorder, a sexual disorder, and/or a sexual orientation. They found insufficient evidence to justify regarding asexuality as either a mental disorder (or symptom of a mental illness) or a sexual disorder, and independently found evidence to support the tentative classification of asexuality as a sexual orientation. Others remained unconvinced (Levine, 2017), critiqued the criteria for making such determinations (Scherrer & Pfeffer, 2017; Van Houdenhove, Enzlin, & Gijs, 2017) and questioned the usefulness of attempting such judgements in the first place (Chasin, 2017; Scherrer & Pfeffer, 2017).

In their assessment, Brotto and Yule (2017a) used LeVay and Baldwin's (2012) definition of sexual orientation as "an internal mechanism that directs a person's sexual and romantic disposition toward females, males, or both, to varying degrees" (p. 623).[2] This is consistent with the definition in the American Psychological Association's Dictionary of Psychology (APA, 2015a). Similarly, they evaluated evidence of innateness from biomarker research, and also for the sexual orientation criteria outlined by Seto (2012): "age of onset, one's sexual and romantic behavior, and the stability of the attraction over time (p. 624). They found evidence lacking *only* for the criterion of temporal stability. They also acknowledged the heterogeneity of the asexual population, suggesting a complexity that bears further exploration. Meanwhile, I (Chasin, 2017) and others (e.g., Scherrer & Pfeffer, 2017) have questioned the relevance of asexuality's stability over time, given that asexual populations are predominantly women and the lifelong narrative of sexual orientation is only one of many "typical" sexual orientation narratives for women (e.g., Diamond, 2009; Golden,1987; van Anders, 2015). Furthermore, Cranney (2017) illustrated that even based on extremely limited longitudinal data, asexuality does show *some* evidence of temporal stability, noting that asexuality should not be held to a higher standard evidence than other accepted sexual orientation categories.

However, these considerations are limited to assessing whether asexuality fits with current understandings of sexual orientation. They cannot judge the value of these understandings nor can they determine whether or how they might need to be changed. Unfortunately, essentialist notions of sexual orientation (i.e., as biologically based, intrinsic and unchangeable) are so pervasive that Brotto and Yule (2017b) summarily dismissed my naming of this limitation and some of its consequences (Chasin, 2017) on the basis that the argument is not specific to asexuality. Ironically, the vastness of this issue—well beyond the scope of anything pertaining to asexuality—was precisely my point: why are people clinging to this understanding of sexual orientation and what might be gained by changing it through an asexual lens? Even the American Psychological Association is moving toward a broader definition of sexual orientation which acknowledges elements such as "social affiliations" (APA, 2015b, p. 862).

CONCEPTUAL/MORAL HISTORY OF "SEXUAL ORIENTATION"

"Sexual orientation" is an historically recent, culturally specific concept. It began emerging in freshly post-industrial Europe, in the context of turbulently shifting social mores and nostalgic backlash against them (Katz, 1996). Within this context, contemporary sexologists (e.g., Ellis, Hirschfeld, Benkert/Kertbeny, Bloch, etc.) wrote and theorised prolifically in their fight against the mounting criminalisation of same-sex sexual behaviour and those who engage in it (Robinson, 1976). Much of this work was preconfigured by a legal-moral discursive context wherein moral responsibility is predicated on free choice (i.e., grounded in post-enlightenment Liberalism and Humanism). In other words, this context provided the scaffolding for the now-familiar arguments which oppose two pairs of ideas: *non-heterosexual orientations as inborn and therefore morally neutral and worthy of protection* vs. *non-heterosexual orientations as chosen and therefore morally deficient and just targets of marginalisation.*

Between the late 19th century and mid 20th century this political struggle radically transformed the conceptual landscape, and theorists from Kertbeny to Freud in various European and American intellectual traditions produced newly-articulated "heterosexuality" as something parallel in nature to "homosexuality," to be explained in its own right. This allowed for same-sex inclinations to be conceptualized as a particular (possibly-deviant) "phenotype" or "flavour" of a characteristic that everyone has, and which drives experiences of (sexual and romantic) attraction, behaviors and relationships (Katz, 1996). In particular, sexual orientations became morally defensible *specifically* as flavours of a *universal human characteristic*. In other words, in societies of American, British and other European colonial histories, sexual orientation has become a sort of "box" that everyone is presumed to have, which can be filled with a number of different options, but that box is part of what it means to be a person. Accordingly, for people who are socially desexualised because of systemic oppression, such as ableism or racism, presuming an "emptiness" of that sexual orientation box is part of denying people their full humanity.

From that ideological perspective, arguing that asexuality is a lack of sexual orientation presupposes a limited humanity for asexual people (though others have positioned asexuality as an absence of sexual attraction while arguing that asexuality should instead be approached and understood from asexual perspectives, Van Houdenhove, Enzlin, & Gijs, 2017). Similarly, presupposing everyone has a sexual orientation, if there is no other sexual orientation box-filler that makes sense for asexual people, and if asexual people are fully real persons (as we are), then asexuality per se must be a sexual orientation. This is the framework underlying the 4-quadrant model of sexual orientation based in a two-dimensional model of erotic attraction which positions heterosexuality, homosexuality, bisexuality and asexuality all as mutually exclusive, independent sexual orientations into which all members of humanity must be classified (Storms, 1980). However, that framework is severely limited.

ASEXUALITY AND THE NEOLIBERAL MORAL ORDER OF SEXUAL ORIENTATION

Contemporary sexual orientation identity politics are framed by neoliberal ideology of decontextualised individualism and "personal responsibility" (for structural problems) (e.g., Harvey, 2005). This translates to people being responsible for their own "success" or "failure" as persons (defined in heteronormative terms) except when there is clear evidence that something is "beyond someone's control." Within this discursive context, things like homophobia and heterosexism are wrong *because* (and only to the extent that) they target innocent victims who have done nothing to deserve the marginalisation. In practice, this is accomplished by focusing on (same-gender) *attraction*/desire—constructed as passive & involuntary experiences—while generally avoiding focus on LGBTQ+ people's relationships and experiences. In contrast, emphasis is placed on the "morally respectable" choices LGBQ+ folks make toward assimilation into heteronormative society, such as the pursuit of long-term, monogamous relationships that form the basis of nuclear families (i.e., marriage).

Firstly, this framing would predict more general willingness to accept asexuality as a valid sexual orientation, worthy of protection, (a) when it is recognised to be lifelong and unchangeable, and (b) when it offers little challenge to the larger systems or structures of power. In fact, this describes the situation with regard to the recognition of asexuality within the DSM-5. Given that women comprise the vast majority of the population subject to diagnosis and treatment for "disorders of low sexual desire" (e.g., Cacchioni, 2007), psychiatric/psychological authorities hold a stronger claim over women than men with low sexual desire. Therefore, removing some of women's low sexual desire from purview of this authority should present a greater challenge than would removing some of men's low sexual desire. Indeed, women who have low sexual desire and who self-identify as asexual are now exempt from diagnosis with Female Sexual Arousal/Interest Disorder *only if their low sexual desire is lifelong* (and therefore generally regarded as "unchangeable," e.g., Montgomery, 2008); meanwhile, men with low sexual desire who self-identify as asexual have are exempt from diagnosis with Male Hypoactive Sexual Desire Disorder whether or not their low sexual desire is lifelong (APA, 2013). I have discussed elsewhere in more detail other relevant issues with these diagnostic criteria as well as the struggle between ace community and psychiatric institutions for definitional authority over asexuality (Chasin, 2013, 2015, 2017).

Secondly, this neoliberal framing of sexual orientation brings the profound disconnect between disembodied "identities" (based in "attractions" or "desires") and the lived, embodied realities of the people who "have" them. However, people's interactions and experiences with structures of oppression do not divide neatly according to identity category or classification of attraction experience(s): lived, material realities are so much more complicated than that. Homophobia is a blunt instrument, equipped to impose punitive sanctions against *perceived* violations of heteronormative masculinity (e.g. Pascoe, 2005) and heteronormative femininity (e.g. Hamilton, 2007) within an institutionally heterosexual erotic market or economy (e.g., McCall, 1992). Generally, individual internal experiences like "attraction" do not govern how people interface with systems of marginalisation & oppression in their daily lives or the resistance or violence they may encounter.

In order to understand how these regulatory forces of marginalisation act on ace people, it is first necessary to understand the diversity of aces' lived, embodied experiences, and of how aces do relationships, participate in community spaces, form group affiliations, and are perceived by others. I've argued before that *being asexual* (with all that entails) can provoke the violence of homophobia specifically targeting the asexuality—i.e., asexuality-related (or ace-related) homophobia—while also provoking homophobic and heterosexist regulatory forces in more conventional ways, i.e., by being or being perceived as gay, lesbian or to a lesser-extent bisexual (Chasin, 2015). Having said that, a more thorough understanding of the diversity of experience among people within other sexual orientation categories should be equally crucial to understanding how homophobia and heterosexism play out for everyone, and the general failure to consider such things has resulted in understandings of homophobia and heterosexism that are, among other things, often white-centric, and specific to class, ability and other factors— generally lacking in intersectional nuance.

At the same time, internal experiences of attraction indeed are often tied to state recognition and property rights, moments of homophobic violence, etc., precisely *because*, people generally build their personal lives and families around relationships that are relevant to their sexual orientations. Sexual orientations, for the most part, guide the type (i.e., gender) of person that

214

people are likely to choose to build their own nuclear families around (and some gender choices are considered "more legitimate" than others). In this way, sexual attraction is socially relevant insofar as it is connected to how people are inclined to do significant (and state-sponsored) relationships, how they interface with certain types of state-sponsored rights and prohibitions, structural and systemic heterosexism and homophobic violence, etc., and how people build their social lives and families. In other words, this framework of compulsory sexual orientation exists *because* sexual orientation (based in individual feelings of attractions and desires) and its associated outcomes (i.e., via significant relationships, criminalisation of same-sex sex, etc.) are *socially relevant*. However, asexuality troubles this relationship: (non) experiences of sexual attraction *may* or *may not* function as a shortcut to determine what is socially relevant for ace folks, and this underscores the importance of considering that possibility for others too.

ASEXUALITY RE/CONSTRUCTING SEXUAL ORIENTATION

Integrating asexuality into the framework of sexual orientation may lead in various directions. For example, given the vast diversity of romantic orientation among aces, depending on what is socially relevant in any given context, asexuality may function as a meta-category positioned in opposition to non-aceness (e.g., Chasin, 2011), as a unique sexual orientation category in opposition to other sexual orientations, as both simultaneously, and/or neither. Sexual orientation is a sociopolitical category and whether and how asexuality qualifies will depend on sociopolitical context. For example, an asexual lesbian should not be interpreted as only partly or liminally asexual and only partly or liminally lesbian: she (or xe—some lesbians are non-binary and may use non-binary pronouns) *can be* fully and legitimately both simultaneously, without contradiction. Whether one aspect of her (or xyr) identity takes precedence in terms of "sexual orientation," or alternatively whether both function together in either cooperation or combination, will likely depend on the individual and the context. Sometimes ace lesbians might have more in common with non-ace lesbians than other aces; sometimes ace lesbians might have more in common with other aces; sometimes ace lesbians might not have that much in common with either group or might relate to both. (And any/all of these things may also be true for some ace lesbians all or most of the time.)

This has serious implication for what categories might be useful or relevant when it comes to comparing "sexual orientation" groups, with respect to things like health needs/outcomes and experiences with discrimination, etc. What this means politically is still taking shape for *when/how* asexuality will function properly as a sexual orientation. Should aces as a group be compared against all non-aces collectively or against specific other sexual orientation groups? Should aces with different kinds of experiences (whether romantic orientation, approach to relationships, or something else) be compared with non-ace groups matched to those experiences? Should they be combined with non-ace folks who have those similar experiences in terms of how they do relationships or other things? (When) should various ace identities be grouped together? There will likely be times when it makes sense to consider all of those possibilities and comparisons, because which one makes the most sense in any given situation is an empirical question.

At the same time, accepting this level of nuance does not require transforming romantic orientation into a reified, compulsory orientation, nor does it require fracturing "sexual orientation" into constituent parts (e.g., of romantic, aesthetic, sensual, etc.). Granted, one possibility— the most straightforward within a neoliberal context—is the creation of a new, independent, mutually exclusive and compulsory "orientations" (like romantic orientation) corresponding to each type of attraction or desire that can be articulated, excising it from the concept of "sexual orientation." However, I caution that this set of compulsory orientations will be required to expand indefinitely to account for experiences it invariably fails to describe. Nevertheless, there are alternatives.

Asexual spectrum identities are and can be intelligible otherwise, but they may require a shift in perspective—letting go of the idea of sexual orientation as a series of obligatory, mutually exclusive categories, and reconstructing "sexual orientation" completely. Recall that sexual orientation (based in individual feelings of attractions and desires) has been reified as inherent characteristics of the neoliberal subject *because* its outcomes (i.e., via significant relationships) are—and historically had become—socially relevant. Sexual orientation situates people according to whether/how they fit within the socially normative expectations for *doing (significant) relationships*: are people inclined to do them "properly"?

Through an ace lens, the normative expectations about whether relationships are being done "properly" are revealed to govern not only the *gender* of the people involved (as is conventionally assumed), but also other factors, such as *whether* people structure their lives at all around romantic relationships, and if they do, whether these are "properly" sexual—which depends on the context and positionality of the people involved—or alternatively whether people focus on other kinds of dyadic or non-dyadic relationships altogether. For example, ace communities have produced discourses of non-romantic, non-normative relationships, such as queerplatonic/quirkyplatonic[3] relationships, which have in turn been taken up by not-specifically-ace aromantic spectrum communities, and more broadly to a limited extent as well.

Through an ace lens, the regulatory force of amatonormativity comes into focus, making it possible to recognise the normative privileging of romantic relationships that are *supposed to be* central to people's lives (i.e., as the basis of nuclear families—presupposing sexuality within marriage or civil partnership) and more intimate and valuable than other kinds of relationships. Through an ace lens, we can start to see more clearly expectations around sexual entitlement/obligation and the commodification of sex and consent, offering new perspectives for unpacking those ideas. With an ace lens, we can challenge the sexualnormative expectations that shape our desires and our sense of who/what we should be and want, and the underlying structures of compulsory sexuality (e.g., Chasin, 2013; Gupta, 2015), focusing our energy to burn these structures down.

These perspectives open up new possibilities for personal relationships—for everyone, ace and otherwise—and more broadly, radical possibilities for (re)structuring families and societies. But realising such possibilities can only happen in resistance against neoliberailism. As time passes, we will see whether/how asexuality will ultimately allow itself to assimilate into a neoliberal discursive and moral order of sexual orientation, and whether/how it will support currents of resistance against this order and toward radical change. The stakes as sexual orientation responds to asexuality's challenge are high.

NOTES

[1] This chapter addresses "sexual orientation" and not "sexual identity" for several reasons. While often used interchangeably, the words have different histories and meanings—the arguments in this chapter rely on the historical development of the social category of "sexual orientation" per se, as well as ongoing debates specifically about whether asexuality should be considered a "sexual orientation" within a discursive framing where "sexual orientation" would ascribe legitimacy. The pathologisation of asexuality has proceeded very differently than the pathologisation of lesbian, gay and bi+ identities to the point where many people accept that asexuality is a valid "identity" for an individual without accepting asexuality as a "sexual orientation" available to anyone, and therefore leaving open the possibility of "treatment" to "cure" (at least some people's) asexuality. Furthermore, framing asexuality in terms of "sexual identity" is less than straightforward: asexuality may be an identity, but it is not necessarily a *sexual* one—and individual

aces will differ on this point. Finally, much of the asexuality scholarship discussed in this chapter approaches asexuality as something other than an "identity" using various different definitions and criteria to define the "asexual" target population—since not all the "asexual" people described by this work would self-identify as asexual, it seems inaccurate and epistemologically inappropriate to label asexuality within this discussion as a "sexual identity."

[2] It is unfortunately common for definitions like this to erase intersex people—most of whom are assigned either male or female at birth—to conflate sex and gender, and to erase non-binary people of any assigned sex.

[3] Queerplatonic/quirkyplantonic relationships (QPRs) are relationships that are *not romantic relationships* but which are also *not adequately or properly described by "friendship"* (even if the people involved are indeed friends). QPRs are a meta-category "catch-all" for s diversity of non-romantic, non-normative relationships.

REFERENCES

American Psychiatric Association (APA). (2013). *Diagnostic and statistical manual of mental disorders* (5th ed.). Arlington, VA: American Psychiatric Publishing.

American Psychological Association (APA). (2015a). *APA dictionary of psychology* (2nd ed.). Washington, DC: Author.

American Psychological Association (APA). (2015b). Guidelines for psychological practice with transgender and gender nonconforming people. *American Psychologist, 70*(9), 832–864. doi:10.1037/a0039906

Bogaert, A. F. (2015). Asexuality: What it is and why it matters. *The Journal of Sex Research, 52*(4), 362–379. doi:10.1080/00224499.2015.1015713

Brotto, L. A., & Yule, M. (2017a). Asexuality: Sexual orientation, paraphilia, sexual dysfunction, or none of the above? *Archives of Sexual Behavior, 46*(3), 619–627. doi:10.1007/s10508-016-0802-7

Brotto, L. A., & Yule, M. (2017b). Response to commentaries. *Archives of Sexual Behavior, 46*(3), 653–657. doi:10.1007/s10508-017-0974-9

Chasin, C. D. (2011). Theoretical issues in the study of asexuality. *Archives of Sexual Behavior, 40*(4), 713–723. doi:10.1007/s10508-011-9757-x

Chasin, C. D. (2013). Reconsidering asexuality and its radical potential. *Feminist Studies, 39*(2), 405–426.

Chasin, C. D. (2015). Making sense in and of the asexual community: Navigating relationships and identities in a context of resistance. *Journal of Community & Applied Social Psychology, 25*(2), 167–180. doi:10.1002/casp.2203

Chasin, C. D. (2017). Considering asexuality as a sexual orientation and implications for acquired female sexual arousal/interest disorder. *Archives of Sexual Behavior, 46*(3), 631–635. doi:10.1007/s10508-016-0893-1

Cranney, S. (2017). Does asexuality meet the stability criterion for a sexual orientation? *Archives of Sexual Behavior, 46*(3), 637–638. doi:10.1007/s10508-016-0887-z

Diamond, L. M. (2009). *Sexual fluidity: Understanding women's love and desire*. Cambridge, MA: Harvard University Press.

Ginoza, M. K., Miller, T., & other members of the AVEN Survey Team. (2014). *The 2014 AVEN community census: Preliminary findings*. Retrieved September 28, 2016, from https://asexualcensus.files.wordpress.com/2014/11/2014censuspreliminaryreport.pdf

Golden, C. (1987). Diversity and variability in women's sexual identities. In Boston Lesbian Psychologies Collective (Ed.), *Lesbian psychologies* (pp. 19–54). Chicago, IL: University of Illinois Press.

Greaves, L. M., Barlow, F. K., Huang, Y., Stronge, S., Fraser, G., & Sibley, C. G. (2017). Asexual identity in a New Zealand national sample: Demographics, well-being, and health. *Archives of Sexual Behavior, 46*(8), 2417–2427. doi:10.1007/s10508-017-0977-6

Gupta, K. (2015). Compulsory sexuality: Evaluating an emerging concept. *Signs, 41*(1), 131–154. doi:10.1086/681774

Haefner, C. (2011). *Asexual scripts: A grounded theory inquiry into the intrapsychic scripts asexuals use to negotiate romantic relationships* (Unpublished doctoral dissertation). Institute of Transpersonal Psychology, Palo Alto, CA.

Hamilton, L. (2007). Trading on heterosexuality: College women's gender strategies and homophobia. *Gender & Society, 21(2), 145–172.* doi:10.1177/0891243206297604

Harvey, D. (2005). *A brief history of neoliberalism.* New York, NY: Oxford University Press. Retrieved from https://www.sok.bz/web/media/video/ABriefHistoryNeoliberalism.pdf

Katz, J. N. (1996). *The invention of heterosexuality.* New York, NY: Penguin Books.

Levine, S. B. (2017). A little deeper please. *Archives of Sexual Behavior, 46*(3), 639–642. doi:10.1007/s10508-017-0947-z

MacNeela, P., & Murphy, A. (2015). Freedom, invisibility, and community: A qualitative study of self-identification with asexuality. *Archives of Sexual Behavior, 44*(3), 799–812. doi:10.1007/s10508-014-0458-0

McCall, L. (1992). Does gender fit? Bourdieu, feminism and conceptions of social order. *Theory & Society, 21*(6), 837–867.

Pascoe, C. J. (2005). 'Dude, you're a fag': Adolescent masculinity and the fag discourse. *Sexualities, 8*(3), 329–346. doi:10.1177/1363460705053337

Robinson, P. (1976). *The modernization of sex: Havelock Ellis, Alfred Kinsey, William Masters and Virginia Johnson.* New York, NY: Harper & Row Publishers.

Scherrer, K. S. (2008). Coming to an asexual identity: Negotiating identity, negotiating desire. *Sexualities, 11*(5), 621–641. doi:10.1177/1363460708094269

Scherrer, K. S., & Pfeffer, C. A. (2017). None of the above: Toward identity and community-based understandings of (a)sexualities. *Archives of Sexual Behavior, 46*(3), 643–646. doi:10.1007/s10508-016-0900-6

Storms, M. D. (1980). Theories of sexual orientation. *Journal of Personality and Social Psychology, 38*(5), 783–792. doi:10.1037/0022-3514.38.5.783

Yule, M. A., Brotto, L. A., & Gorzalka, B. B. (2014). Biological markers of asexuality: Handedness, birth order, and finger length ratios in self-identified asexual men and women. *Archives of Sexual Behavior, 43*(2), 299–310. doi:10.1007/s10508-013-0175-0

van Anders, S. M. (2015). Beyond sexual orientation: Integrating gender/sex and diverse sexualities via sexual configurations theory. *Archives of Sexual Behavior, 44*(5), 1177–1213. doi:10.1007/s10508-015-0490-8

Van Houdenhove, E., Enzlin, P., & Gijs, L. (2017). A positive approach toward asexuality: Some first steps, but still a long way to go. *Archives of Sexual Behavior, 46*(3), 647–651. doi:10.1007/s10508-016-0921-1

Van Houdenhove, E., Gijs, L., T'Sjoen, G., & Enzlin, P. (2015). Stories about asexuality: A qualitative study on asexual women. *Journal of Sex & Marital Therapy, 41*(3), 262–281. doi:10.1080/0092623X.2014.889053

KATIE LINDER

17. QUEERING THE NUCLEAR FAMILY

Navigating Familial Living as an Asexual (Personal Reflection)

INTRODUCTION

The word "family" evokes a very specific response in people. Often, the word creates a very specific image in the minds of the people who hear it, one that we have, over the course of the past generation or so, dubbed as being the "nuclear family." When presented with this term, the image that is evoked in the minds of those who hear it is likely eerily similar among the audience.

Picture this. A father and a mother, both heterosexual and cisgender. A moderately-sized house in the suburbs. Not too big to be ostentatious, but not so small that the children don't have room to run and play and grow, as children do. Speaking of the children, there are three of them. The number I traditionally use in class, when giving examples to my students, is 2.5, but for the purposes of this analogy, I'll just round the number up to a third child. The house has a two-car garage, and one of the cars in the garage is a very sensible minivan, which the mother uses to cart the children back and forth from soccer (or basketball, baseball, dance, etc.) practice, while the father works long hours at the office as the primary breadwinner. Finally, a white picket fence surrounds the yard, giving any pets and the children ample room to play outside.

The nuclear family, one consisting of two children accompanied by their biological mother and father, has been seen as both the norm and the standard for familial living in the United States for generations (Bengston, 2001). This structure is something that people strive to attain, that is ingrained into children's minds from a time before they are even able to comprehend what the term itself means, or the implications surrounding it.

It seems that from the day that we are born, sexuality and romanticism are thrust upon us in a way that makes it feel beyond compulsory. We live in a world where, I dare to venture, homosexuality and other forms of non-heterosexuality are becoming more widely accepted, but to reject sexuality in general and as a whole is still seen as strange and unnatural.

In a world where sexuality is thrust upon us long before we are able to even begin to comprehend what the word means, what does it mean to someone who has no interest in sex or sexuality? How does that oddity, which some might claim to be contrary to human nature, fit with what we have prescribed as the "traditional" way for a family to live and function? How can one still form familial bonds, beyond those with their own parents, yet still be asexual and, sometimes, aromantic?

To examine this, and how it is possible, we must first delve into the definitions of asexuality and aromanticism. To be very blunt, asexuality has nothing to do with sex. A person can have sex, even enjoy sex, and *still* be asexual. Likewise, a person can masturbate and *still* be asexual. The presence or absence of sex does not, in and of itself, define what asexuality is, or what it is not. Simply stated, asexuality is the lack of sexual attraction. Other forms of attraction may be present, such as romantic, but the lack of sexual attraction is key to asexuality and what makes up its definition.[1]

When discussing the definition of asexuality, it is also important to establish what asexuality is *not*. Asexuality is *not* celibacy. Whereas celibacy is the choice to abstain from sexual activities, asexuality is the lack of attraction. The two could, hypothetically, exist alongside each other, but they are certainly under no obligation to. A sexual person could decide to be celibate and an asexual person could decide to be sexual, for any reason at all, and the action itself would have no affect on their sexual orientation.

Finally, to dispel two final misconceptions, possibly those that hold the most amount of annoyance for asexuals like myself, asexuals are *not* all recovering from sexual trauma, nor are we suffering from any sort of hormonal imbalance that decreases libido (Cerankowski & Milks, 2010). Like the rest of the population and people of any sexuality, asexuals are not immune to any form of sexual assault. But, that does not mean that a person's sexual assault has any bearings on their sexuality. People who have been sexually assaulted can be asexual, or they might not be. Likewise, there are people who have not been sexually assaulted who still identify as asexual. The two are not mutually exclusive. As a person who has been sexually assaulted and still identifies as asexual, hearing people attribute my assault to my asexuality is frustrating, to say the least.[2] The same logic is applicable to individuals who may have a hormone imbalance contributing to decreased libido. By no way do these factors invalidate one's asexuality.

Aromanticism falls, in some cases, in line with asexuality, but it doesn't have to. It is defined by the lack of *romantic* attraction. Those who are aromantic can be asexual at the same time, but they can also be sexual and experience sexual attraction.[3]

There's a lot of gray area when it comes to sexuality and romance, and asexuality and aromanticism are no different. Those who fall somewhere along the asexual or aromantic spectrum are often referred to as being gray asexual or gray aromantic, though the terms demisexual and demiromantic can also be applicable, depending on the situation.[4] The prefix "demi-" in these instances is used to refer to the presence of these attractions, sexual or romantic, after only a close, intimate bond is formed with an individual. Then, after this bond has developed, there is room for the attraction to grow. What is important to note, however, is that asexuality, like all other forms of sexuality, is most definitely not static. It is fluid, in constant flux for some people. As such, it is important to allow people to label themselves as they see fit, rather than assigning labels to them.

Now, with a concrete definition of asexuality in hand, as well as dispelling myths as to what asexuality is *not*, it is time to discuss navigating a sexual world as an asexual person. For myself, and the purposes of this chapter, I use the terms "asexual" and "aromantic" as larger, umbrella terms meant to include anyone who might fall under the aromantic or asexual spectrums.

Being anything other than heterosexual and heteroromantic is difficult. Anyone in the LGBBT+ community would agree. But, I would argue that being asexual is the most difficult. My entire life, everyone has tried to place me into boxes. I've tried thrusting labels on myself, hoping that they would stick, more concerned about actually being able to identify with a label than what the label itself actually was. In a world where everything is sexually charged and romance and hetero-marriage are seen as the culmination of adulthood, how does one who has no desire for any of those manage to survive? How do you survive when everyone scrutinizes all of your friendships as being "more than friends" and questions when you will, *finally*, settle down and get married?

I am asexual and gray aromantic. I want a family, and a life partner, but I want them *without* the romantic and sexual entanglements that almost always accompany them. I, along with several other asexual people that I have connected with over the years, have used various dating apps and online forums in an attempt to find people like me and, perhaps more importantly, people who would *understand* people like me. I've lost friendships and potential relationships because of my lack of romantic and sexual attraction to others. It's a concept that is lost on many people, my own family included, and often leaves me, as well as other asexuals that I know, feeling lonely and lost in the big, sexualized and romanticized world around us.

Unlike one of my best friends, who is also asexual and who I met through an asexual forum, I've always known that I don't want to spend my life alone. She is content being on her own and living her own life, independent of others, but I'm not. I've always craved having someone to spend the rest of my life with, but in a way that was vastly different from the ideas that so many others had. I've always thought of my ideal living situation as one where we have the same amount of commitment as a romantic and/or sexual couple, yet on a platonic level. A relationship that transcends the bounds of traditional friendships, yet still allows me to have a partner in life, albeit on a platonic level. Sadly, in our sexualized world, few are even willing to entertain the idea.

Something I, along with some of my asexual friends and acquaintances, have struggled with, is the lack of appropriate vocabulary to define us and the world around us. What I described in the previous paragraph is usually dismissed as being "just friends" or the slightly better "best friends" by sexual people. The former term annoys me and is mildly insulting to the type of relationship I am describing, while the second, though not untrue, still fails to convey the entire story at hand. Like many non-heterosexual people, I turned to the internet for answers, and was not disappointed.

The Asexual Visibility and Education Network, commonly referred to as "AVEN" is a virtual database of information on asexuality, and one of the premier places on the internet for asexual people to find information about themselves and others like them, and to feel less alone (Cerankowski & Milks, 2010). This site brought the term "queerplatonic partners"[5] into my life, and finally I had a word for what I had always been seeking.

Even though the social sciences have not yet conducted much in-depth research into queerplatonic relationships, some research of my own[6] directed me to a blog post from 2010,[7] which features an early usage of the term "queerplatonic relationship." In the most basic sense of the word, a queerplatonic relationship is the asexual and aromantic form of a sexual and/or romantic relationship. It is a committed relationship that is characterized by intimacy of varying degrees which are independent of the individuals involved, and centered around a platonic relationship. It is more than "just friends" or "best friends." As noted on the Aromantic wiki page for "Queerplatonic," those in a queerplatonic relationship might choose to refer to each other as "zucchinis," which originated as a joke pertaining to the lack of applicable vocabulary that partners could use to describe each other.

Queerplatonic relationships are ideal for someone like me, someone who wants to love and be loved, and have someone to share my life with, but who can't and doesn't want to do it in the way that most people do.

The words that make up the term "queerplatonic" are key to understanding it, as well as its importance to the ace and aro communities. Here, the word "queer" is not used either in a derogatory manner, or in a manner that is descriptive of both parties involved. For example, the partners in a queerplatonic relationship do not have to identify as or embrace the label of "queer." Rather, the word serves as an umbrella term, meant to identify the relationship as one that falls outside the bounds of what can be considered the societal norm.

My queerplatonic partner is my best friend, my other half, and my life partner. Our relationship is odd, to say the least. Most people assume that there is "more" to our relationship, in a sexual and/or romantic sense, and can't seem to understand the concept that two people can be as close and intimate as we are, without feeling the need to ravage each other sexually. My partner is also happily married to a heterosexual male, but our relationships have gotten to the point where they work in sync with each other, rather than competing with each other. While I am, by nature, much closer intimately and emotionally to my partner than her husband, the three of us work in tandem, as one family, to take care of household chores, entertain guests, and even raise a two-year-old dog who, even though she was adopted by my partner and her husband, is just as much my dog as she is theirs.

In the spring of 2018, around the time that I introduced my partner to various AVEN and Tumblr sources about queerplatonic partners, which she embraced with open arms, she approached me about the idea of forming our own family in the future, me, her, and her husband. The thought is one that might seem odd to many people, her husband included to an extent, but it *is* something that I have always seen myself doing. When I've thought of my future, I've always pictured myself living with a best friend, as this was long before "queerplatonic" was part of my vocabulary, and before I'd even begun to think about my asexuality.

Our life plans are simple, and we've given them quite a bit of thought. All three of us, plus the dog, living together in one large house. Three incomes would *definitely* afford us the opportunity to buy a larger house than we would be able to individually. Children are part of my partner's plan for the future, when she is done with school, and I've always seen children in my life in some capacity. If either of us is blessed enough to have children, whether they be our own or adopted, we will join forces to raise them together, treating *all of them* as our own. Her children will be mine, and my children will be hers. It takes a village to raise a child, and having three able-bodied adults to raise the children and provide for them will create a more stable, fulfilled household than the alternatives.

The purpose of this chapter, of outlining definitions of asexuality and aromanticism, of tracing the origins of the nuclear family and the development of queerplatonic relationships, and coupling them with my own, personal narrative, is to show that there is no one way to have a family, or to have a relationship. My partner and I treat our relationship with the same amount of seriousness as I have treated any of my romantic relationships, and she treats it with the same amount of commitment as she treats her own marriage. Limiting oneself to one and only one intimate[8] partner can be a fatal mistake, as I believe that there is no one person in this world who can provide me with every single thing that I need in life. I provide her with things that her husband cannot, and he likewise provides her with things that I cannot. Instead of working against each other, thus evoking jealousy and other negative emotions, we work together to create the best possible environment for all of us involved.

I may not experience sexual or romantic attraction, but I have always had and will always have a need for intimacy. Whether it's someone to come home to and talk to about my day, or someone to hug, or a partner to support me through the ups and downs that is life, I need intimacy. Being in a queerplatonic relationship, and creating our own, unique definition of a family, provides me with all of those aspects of intimacy that I need in life, while at the same time not having the "usual" sexual and romantic expectations that have long made me shy away from traditional dating.

The concept of a "family" is a social construct, one that has changed quite a bit since the definition of "nuclear family" was introduced (Bengston, 2001). Since then, we as a society have seen many fundamental changes that have shifted the way we see families as a whole, and what we see as being "normal." After the legalization across the United States of same-sex marriage in June of 2015, more and more same-sex couples have been successfully forming families of their own. My mother, who raised me as a single parent after my father left, is also an example of the changing familial dynamics that exist. In a world where we still recognize the "nuclear family," very, very few families *actually* can claim that they themselves fit that definition. If other families consisting of other people can make their own definition of a family work, then logic serves that we can do the same.

The days of thinking about a family as being a father and mother, with two children and a white picket fence are long over. It is time that we start shifting our focus to recognize other types of families that may exist. One word that I love is "queer" because, to me, its definition means anything that is not what is seen as normal. I like to think of myself as "queering the nuclear family," or changing the ideas that a family has to be one way or another. Rather, a family can be what we make of it. Regardless of sexual or romantic orientations, a family is people who love each other, in any way that they know how and are able to. No two people in the world are the same, so why should the ideal family be the same for everyone?

My ideal family is still a work in progress, but one day I'll be living with my partner, her husband, our dog, and a house full of kids, while we're all working full-time jobs doing what we love. I know that when that time comes, I won't want to have it any other way, because that will be *our* nuclear family, even if the definition fails to match that of others.

NOTES

[1] For more information about the definition of asexuality, please visit the Asexual Visibility and Education Network (AVEN) at www.asexual.org

[2] More information about common myths surrounding asexuality can be found at https://lgbt.williams.edu/homepage/10-things-you-need-to-know-about-asexuality/

[3] A more thorough breakdown of the differences between romantic and sexual attraction and orientation can be found through AVEN at http://wiki.asexuality.org/Attraction#Romantic_Attraction

[4] AVEN provides more in-depth information about both gray-asexuality and gray-aromanticism at http://wiki.asexuality.org/Gray-A/Grey-A and more in-depth information about demisexuality and demiromanticism at http://wiki.asexuality.org/Demisexual

[5] See http://wiki.asexuality.org/Queerplatonic for more information on queerplatonic relationships, as well as the more in-depth description at http://aromantic.wikia.com/wiki/Queerplatonic

[6] Tumblr has proved to be a solid source of information for me, with regards to topics about sexuality (like asexuality) that are not covered as much with more mainstream research. The post http://jasgower.tumblr.com/post/146418140149/origins-of-the-term-queerplatonic directed me to the blog post referenced later in this paragraph.

[7] See https://kaz.dreamwidth.org/238564.html for the blog post in question.

[8] The word "intimate" has many different meanings. Here, it is referring to emotional intimacy, rather than sexual intimacy.

REFERENCES

Bengston, V. L. (2001). Beyond the nuclear family: Increasing the importance of multigenerational bonds. *Journal of Marriage and Family, 63*(1), 1–16.

Cerankowski, K. J., & Milks, M. (2010). New orientations: Asexuality and its implications for theory and practice. *Sex and Surveillance, 36*(3), 650–664.

PART 5

INTERSEX RELATIONSHIPS

CARY GABRIEL COSTELLO

18. UNDERSTANDING INTERSEX RELATIONSHIP ISSUES

INTRODUCTION

This chapter will address intersex status and relationship issues. It will begin by explaining what it means to be intersex and addressing how common intersex status is. It will then address difficulties faced by intersex people with regard to finding a romantic partner and engaging in sexual relationships. Finally, it will consider the positive ways intersex status can affect relationships.

WHAT IS INTERSEX?

Contemporary Western societies espouse an ideology that sex is binary by nature. Our popular media and our biology textbooks state that humans come in two sexes: males, with XY chromosomes, a testosterone-dominant hormone profile, penis and testes; and females, with XX chromosomes, an estrogen-dominant hormone profile, vulva, uterus and ovaries. It is assumed that these factors almost always align clearly, with very rare exception. That exception is intersexuality, in which a person has sex characteristics that do not neatly align with the male and female ideal-types. Contemporary Western medicine terms intersex statuses "disorders of sex development"— that is, as "birth defects" that should be medically "corrected" via infant genital surgeries and other medical interventions aimed at erasing intersex traits (Delimata et al., 2018). The medical goal is to allow intersex people to appear to have normative endosex[1] bodies, which is framed as necessary to protect us from social stigma and poor mental health outcomes (Karkazis, 2008).

Intersex advocates oppose this framing. We understand the framing of intersex bodies as "disordered" to be akin to the way that homosexuality was considered a "disorder" by U.S. doctors until 1972, and transgender identity was classified as a "disorder" until 2013 (Stryker, 2017). We view the imposing of genital reconstructive surgeries on us as children who are given no opportunity to withhold consent as a profound violation of our human rights. In essence, such surgeries are forced surgical sex changes imposed without consent. They disregard our medical autonomy and our right to self-determination over our sex and gender. Sometimes we mature not to identify with our assigned binary sex, and doctors will have removed parts of our bodies that we do identify with, but which can never be replaced. But infant surgeries aimed at "normalizing" our appearance produce multiple harms, even when we do grow up to identify with our assigned binary sex (Viloria, 2017). The removal and/or reconstruction of phalloclitoral[2] tissue often leads to the reduction or loss of capacity for sexual sensation—especially when performed on tiny genital structures in early childhood, whose minute nerves can easily be severed. We are sent the message that our bodies are wrong and shameful. Often information about our bodies is withheld from us by doctors "for our own good;" our parents are often instructed to teach us to keep our variance a secret; frequently we are taught that our bodies are freakish curiosities by multiple interactions with medical staff (Davis, 2015).

In fact, intersexuality is commonplace. By nature, sex is not a binary, but a spectrum. Every element of physical sex—chromosomes, gonads, genitals, hormones—can vary widely and independently (Fausto-Sterling, 2000). For example, the sex chromosomes come not only in XX and XY, but Xo, XXY, XYY, XX/XY, and multiple other variations. There are XX men and XY women. Physical sex turns out to come in an amazing array of possibilities. And this is true throughout the animal kingdom, where intersex and hermaphrodite[3] statuses are myriad.

Since sex is a spectrum by nature, people have always been born intersex. But the framing of intersex bodies as "disordered" bodies that must be physically altered via surgeries, hormone treatments, etc. has been the standard practice only since the latter half of the 20th century (Reis, 2012). For the vast majority of human history, societies have had to have other, nonmedical ways to arrange their societies to account for sex variance. Most societies throughout world history have accomplished this by recognizing more than two sex categories. Rather than being "natural" and "universal," the ideology that sex is a binary is atypical in the context of world history, where recognition of three, four, five or more sexes appears to have been the norm. Thus, children born with obvious genital intermediacy had a social role or roles available to them and were not pathologized. In many societies, intersex people were seen as unusual in a positive manner, and as having special spiritual roles.

In the contemporary U.S., however, children born visibly intersex are pathologized at birth as having a "DSD" ("disorder of sex development"). Because birth certificates must be filed in 24–48 hours (depending upon the state) and are required to list a baby's sex as "M" or "F," the birth of an intersex child precipitates a crisis in which a binary sex must be quickly chosen to list on the birth certificate. The general rule of thumb applied by doctors seems to be that only in cases where the child has both testes and sufficient phalloclitoral material to construct an "adequate" penis should the child be assigned male (Greenberg, 1999).; otherwise the child should be assigned female, with the presumption that the intermediate phalloclitoris will be "surgically reduced," and a neovagina created once puberty is well-established. Note that this means doctors are choosing a binary sex for a child based upon surgical plans for maximal erasure of visible atypicality—not on gender identity or conserving sensation.

The assumption of doctors who perform "normalizing" surgeries on "children with DSDs" has been that genitals determine gender. They claim this is not magical thinking, but instead a sophisticated understanding that recognizes that parental socialization produces gendered behavior. They claim that the intersex child's genitals would presumably send confusing messages to caregivers, leading to tragic nonconformity in the child's gender. This, they claim, would put the child at risk of suicide as they matured. But by (supposedly, ideally) producing "normal" male or female genitals, the doctors will cause the parents to believe the child is "really" a boy or girl, leading them to socialize the children into normative binary genders (Karkazis, 2008).

In fact, this remains magical thinking. It glosses over the fact that children who have had infant "normalizing" surgeries continue to have atypical appearances, scarring, ongoing surgical revisions, loss of sexual sensation, recurrent urinary tract infections, and other issues that ensure parents and children will not "forget all about" the child's birth atypicality. And it ignores the fact that endosex children raised by parents with no doubts that their children have typical sex characteristics grow up to have transgender identities. Genitals do not determine gender.

Intersex people have been calling for an end to infant genital surgeries performed without consent for decades. But doctors in the U.S. continue to consider such surgeries to be the "best practice" and "standard of care" for intersex infants. So many intersex adults alive today live with the aftermath of intersex "normalizing" surgeries. And even those who have not experienced unconsented-to medical interventions must live in a society in which they understand they are framed as disordered.

HOW COMMON IS INTERSEX STATUS?

While the question of how common an experience it is to be intersex seems straightforward, it is extremely difficult to answer. This is true for several reasons. The most fundamental of these is one shared in any situation where people are trying to break up a continuous variable into discrete categories. Let's make an analogy to another famous spectrum—the rainbow.

Different societies divide the rainbow up into differing numbers of colors. All of these systems are arbitrary. For example, we learn in our science classes that the rainbow contains seven colors—red, orange, yellow, green, blue, indigo and violet. Six of these are color names English-speakers use frequently today, but one—indigo—we do not. (In fact, if you look at a pride flag today, you will see six stripes, with nothing between blue and purple.) You might think there is some "scientific" reason why the colors named in English-language science textbooks contain indigo. That's not so. It's simply the case that the colors of the rainbow were first codified by English physicist Sir Isaac Newton, and he felt that since there are seven different notes in the musical octave of Western music, there should be seven colors (Taylor, 2017). And indigo was a very socially significant color in his time because it was a color reserved for royalty, being produced using a very expensive dye extracted from certain shellfish. Because it was so culturally significant at the time in Europe, people saw the color as distinctive, as "obviously there." But in our cultural context, where there is no royalty that reserves the color as a signifier of its status, we just do not see indigo when we look at the spectrum.

Like the rainbow of colors in light, physical sex is a spectrum in nature. The physical color spectrum and sex spectrum are universal between all societies—but what we *see* when we look at them varies by culture. And whatever dividing lines we make up to break the spectrum into discrete segments are culturally subjective. So, consider a society in which intersex children are viewed as special in a positive sense, like the Bugis of Indonesia, who name five sexes, one of them, "bissu", being in the middle of the sex spectrum, and the sex from which valued shamans are drawn (Davies, 2006). In such a society, people have an incentive to be as inclusive as possible in classifying babies as intersex. In a society like ours, however, where children must be assigned a binary sex at birth, and doctors frame the birth of an intersex baby as a medical crisis, the incentives are much more complex. When a child is diagnosed with a DSD, doctors gain lucrative "cases", and an opportunity to frame themselves as heroic saviors of people with "birth defects." On the other hand, this is a traumatic experience for new parents. Parents don't want to be told their baby is defective, and doctors may wish to avoid dealing with the emotional fallout of doing so where possible. In particular, doctors today seem to defer deeply to our culture's fragile masculinity. To label a child assigned male at birth "intersex" is seen as producing a lifelong legacy of ruined masculinity, which is viewed by doctors as a horrible fate.

To get around this issue—wishing to label babies as requiring medical intervention, but also to defer to fragile masculinity—Western medicine performed some diagnostic sleight of hand. Doctors have produced dozens of diagnostic categories under which to classify differing sorts of sex variance. But the vast majority of intersex children they assign male at birth, they give one diagnostic label: hypospadias. And they are not up front about what hypospadias is—an intersex status in a child with external testes, an intermediate phalloclitoris, and a uterine structure ("prostatic utricle") that may be any size from tiny to that of a typical uterus. They classify children they diagnose with hypospadias "boys with a penile malformation," not intersex children. Thus, once doctors surgically alter the phallus, the child is deemed "cured", and no lifelong intersex classification follows them.

This is important to understand, because removing the disincentive of harming fragile masculinity makes doctors fairly free with the diagnosis of hypospadias. In the U.S., 1 in 125 children assigned male on their birth certificates are diagnosed at birth with hypospadias (Paulozzi, Erickson, & Jackson, 1997). This may be a surprisingly high number to you. After all, most popular writing on intersex issues cite a 1-in-2000 figure (see, e.g. James, 2011). But consider this: when urologists studied photographs of the penises of 500 adult men who had never been diagnosed with any genital disorder, they classified a full 45% as hypospadiac (Fichtner et al., 1995).

How can it be that medical estimates of how many people are intersex range from 0.05% to 45%—a figure 900 times larger? Well, it is because sex really is a spectrum. In order to be classified as "normal," urology textbooks say the urethra should open at the very tip of the penis. In endosex vulva, the urethra opens at the level of the pelvic floor. In intermediate genitalia, the opening may be in any position between the tip of the phalloclitoris and its base at the pelvic floor. So, when the urethra opens on a penis at some point below the tip on the penile head or shaft, a person is on the intersex spectrum. If the opening is just a few millimeters below the tip, they are just a tiny bit intersex, and nobody—doctor or penis-possessor—is likely to care, because the individual will not face any stigma. If the opening is on the shaft of the phalloclitoris, a child will definitely be diagnosed with hypospadias and surgery advised. How far the urinary opening needs to be from the exact top of a phallus before the child is diagnosed with a "DSD"...well, that's really a subjective matter. Technically speaking, 45% of all male-assigned people have hypospadias as it is medically defined. Pragmatically speaking, it's 0.8% of babies assigned male who get such a diagnosis at birth.

So, how many people are intersex? If we look at the question from the perspective of how many people receive a diagnosis of some sort of "DSD," about 1 in 150. If we look at the issue in the restrictive way many conservative scholars argue for (which excludes people with many DSD diagnoses, including those most common in children assigned male at birth), it's closer to the 1 in 2000 figure (Sax, 2002). If we look at the urologist study data, in which the assessment had no implications for the lives of the men whose photographed genitalia were studied, it's 45% of us. Of this wide range, I would argue for the 1 in 150 figure as most useful. That's because it represents about how many Americans are living their lives having been diagnosed as sex-variant and facing the consequences that follow. It is those consequences that we will turn to now.

WHAT ISSUES DO INTERSEX PEOPLE FACE IN THE CONTEXT OF RELATIONSHIPS?

Intersex people face a range of relationship issues. Many of these issues are not unique to intersex people, being shared by other marginalized groups, but the constellation of them together is. These issues include navigating sexuality after a history of childhood genital surgery, triggering sexual panics and rejection in others, and involuntary celibacy (an issue that has become fraught in an era of misogynist "incel" groups of endosex cis straight men).

Repercussions of Childhood Genital Surgeries

Intersex advocates often decry "intersex genital mutilation" or IGM, arguing that nonconsensual intersex "normalizing" surgeries are akin to female genital mutilation (FGM) (Bauer & Truffer, 2018). FGM, referred to by its practitioners as "female circumcision," is the removal of some or all of the external parts of the clitoris and labia minora, sometimes including partial closure of the vaginal outlet. It is a cultural practice in parts of Africa, the Middle East, and Asia which is traditionally understood in those areas in positive terms—as making the genitals look more feminine and culturally normative, and as protecting girls' sexual purity. Western societies decry FGM as a misogynist practice that violates women's autonomy and destroys their capacity for sexual enjoyment (Wasige & Jackson, 2017). But Western campaigns to end FGM have been resisted by mothers of girls, who have feared that not having the procedure performed upon their daughters would make them unmarriageable, ruining their lives.

Intersex genital "normalizing" surgeries are performed for similar reasons. They are intended to make our genitals adhere to Western societies' ideas of what looks "normal." They are understood as helping people to appear more feminine, or more masculine. And it is feared that unless these surgeries are performed, intersex children will face a tragic future, unable to find a mate. The fact that these surgeries impair or destroy capacity for sexual sensation is treated as irrelevant, downplayed, or dismissed, as is the case with those who perform FGM.

One obvious result is that many intersex people today have impaired or absent genital sensation. This is an experience shared by individuals around the world who were subjected to "female circumcision," and by others who have survived partial or complete genital amputation due to accidents, cancer treatments, etc. For contemporary intersex people in the U.S., the situation is complicated by two things: the very high value placed on sexual pleasure in American society today, and the secrecy that surrounds our surgeries. Many intersex people have parents who, out of a desire to ensure their children are treated as "normal," never tell them about childhood surgeries, or flatly deny that such surgeries took place when asked by their children about their genital differences. In that situation, IGM survivors experience bafflement and self-blame when their bodies do not respond as expected to stimulation.

Other intersex people were given at least some information about childhood interventions—while receiving the overt or implied message that this was a family secret that must never be disclosed. It is possible for people in a sexual relationship to work around the sensory limitations of one or both partners. But that requires communication about those limitations, which won't take place when an intersex person is keeping their history secret.

In essence, the situation intersex people face is akin to what an LGBT individual might deal with if their parents were told at birth that tests showed the child would have a marginalized sexual orientation or gender identity and would suffer unless the parents took steps to normalize their child and keep test results secret. Doctors tell parents that keeping their child's intersexuality in the closet, and raising the child to pass as endosex, is desirable. Coming out of the closet is often a difficult process. But it is especially difficult if, since infancy, one has parents who have been expecting this as a possibility that they are determined to oppose.

A relationship with parents is bound to be difficult if they have been keeping secrets from you about your body and policing the conformity of your behavior to gender stereotypes. But even when parents are open with a child about the child's intersex status, many intersex people feel betrayed by their parents' consenting to surgeries that left them feeling mutilated and numb. This experience produces intersex adults who share some characteristics with survivors of childhood abuse, having experienced trauma that their parents failed to protect them from. Consequences include lack of trust and fear that impair the ability to form healthy adult relationships.

Another consequence of childhood intersex genital reconstructive surgery relates to gender identity. Being socialized in a society that holds a binary sex ideology, the substantial majority of intersex Americans today identify as women or men and are satisfied to live in their birth-assigned binary sex. They are ipsogender.[4] But the percentage of intersex people who do not identify with their birth-assigned binary sex is much higher than it is for endosex people. We do not have good study data on exactly how much higher the likelihood of intersex people being transgender is. This is data surgeons who perform nonconsensual sex reassignments on intersex children are strongly incentivized not to collect. And that is because these surgeons have so often removed gonads and/or genital structures that the intersex trans person once had, now identifies with, but can never have restored. This is the most extreme experience of IGM, often resulting in severe emotional trauma, anger and depression. It makes having an adult sexual relationship difficult. Many trans people have written about the distress they have experienced trying to negotiate a sexual relationship when their genitals are understood as belying or undermining their gender identity (see Chapter 25 and references therein). This distress is compounded when mourning for a now-missing body part that would have been seen as affirming one's gender identity but was removed without consent.

Problems Arising from the Contemporary Sexual Orientation Paradigm

There is another thing that intersex people share with trans people—even when those intersex people are ipso gender, living in their birth-assigned sex. And that has to do with the contemporary Western ideology of sexual orientation. This sexual orientation paradigm is based on the presumption of binary sex/gender, under which people have one of two types of genitals, and those genitals determine their gender. The sexual orientation terminology of heterosexual, homosexual and bisexual has been defined based on whether a person desires those of the same, other, or both binary sex/genders.[5] By not adhering to the belief that a binary sex at birth determines a person's gender, trans and intersex people break this sexual orientation paradigm.

This rupture of the principles of the sexual orientation paradigm can cause panic, especially in cis endosex men with fragile masculinity. This form of masculinity is called "fragile" because it is so easily challenged, leading to fear of being seen as doing anything that could be deemed feminine or gay. When the man with fragile masculinity experiences such a threat to his "real man" status, he often seeks to repair this rupture by engaging in hypermasculine retaliation—for example, physical violence (Myketiak, 2016). This is what leads to the high levels of street violence aimed at trans women, and to the ongoing acceptance of the "trans panic" defense to murder in most American states. It is seen as understandable for a man who identifies himself as straight and who finds himself attracted to a woman to have suffered a blow to his masculinity if it turns out that woman has some male sex characteristic (a penis, an XY chromosome, a history of having had testes, etc.). Having been somehow "homosexualized," the man with fragile masculinity is expected to react violently to repair his reputation, and his violence deemed understandable.

The medical response to this context has been to try to "normalize" intersex bodies so that potential partners will not see any variance that would trigger violence—and to pair this with a constant emphasis on gender-conforming behavior and heterosexual activity. Doctors present being in a monogamous, monosexual-heterosexual relationship as the ultimate goal of all medical interventions (Davis, 2014). This presents intersex people assigned female at birth with a frightening double bind. Among trans people, it is transfeminine ones who are most at risk of street violence, and among intersex people, it is those legally categorized as women who most fear that a revelation of their intersex status will put them at risk of intimate partner violence from a man. Yet if they do not have a sexual relationship with a man, they know that in the eyes of the medical profession, they will have "failed."

While intersex women interested in relationships with men are particularly at risk, intersex (and trans) people of any gender and sexuality face some risks of partner rejection and social violence that cis endosex people do not. People with nonbinary gender identities, both intersex and endosex, are subjected to a great deal of social disrespect. Many are misgendered almost all the time and treated with disdain or puzzlement by potential sexual partners. And trans and intersex people with binary gender identities who are not straight often encounter a difficulty that parallels, but does not rise to the level of, trans panic[6] in straight cis endosex men. Cis endosex indviduals of any sexual orientation may reject the idea of having a partner with some sex characteristic of the "opposite" sex, deeming that characteristic repellant and the potential partner's gender as "fake." Cis endosex lesbians may frame intersex or trans lesbians as posing a risk of sexual predation. Cis endosex gay men may frame intersex or trans men as having no sexual appeal, particularly if they are not phallically-endowed. And cis endosex bi+ people may mirror these patterns as well.

The flip side of a group of marginalized people being socially viewed as sexually unattractive is often that some in the normative majority have a fetishistic interest in the stigmatized group. These fetishists pursue sexual contact with members of the group they objectify, getting a thrill from violating a social taboo via sexual relations. This is very different from a member of a privileged group being in a relationship with a marginalized individual because the privileged person is able to see past social biases about people like their partner. It is not loving a person for their unique character and qualities, and thus not caring that they are a member of stigmatized group X. It is pursuing people *because* they are a member of a particular stigmatized group, and not caring about their unique character and qualities.

There is nothing at all wrong with a consensual kinky relationship that involves a fetish object. If Person A has a fetish for ballet boots, and Person B enjoys wearing ballet boots to arouse Person A, more power to them. But in a situation in which Person A's fetish is for a kind of marginalized people, and Person A is in the privileged majority with respect to marginalized Person B, the situation rarely works out to the long-term happiness of Person B. Generally, Person A's arousal is dependent on seeing sex with Person B as taboo because people like Person B are lesser, ugly, unnatural, weird, etc. Perhaps Person A can find a Person B who shares A's belief that people like B are lesser, ugly, or unnatural or weird. But a person who embraces the idea that nobody normal could love them for themselves and that they should seek out a person who is aroused by their taboo inferiority is unlikely to be enjoying good mental health. And far more often, Person B believes Person A is pursuing them out of respectful attraction to their personality and character, not just their marginalized status. This does not meet the definition of consensual shared kink.

Today, many fetishists who seek out people who are intersex are not in fact interested in people with bodies like those we actually have. They are often fans of hentai (erotic anime and manga), specifically, in the "hermaphrodite" genre. This genre features people with idealized female body contours (substantial breasts, small waists, delicate hand and facial features), a large erecting, ejaculating phallus, a capacious vagina, uterus, and capacity for impregnation. This is a fantasy duplication of sexual characteristics, instead of the natural reality of sexually intermediate bodies. And it is not physically possible. When these fetishists discover the reality of an intersex body, they almost always withdraw in disgust. While on the whole, this withdrawal benefits intersex people in the long run, by limiting involvement with people who disrespect us, the experience confirms fears many of us have that our bodies will repel others.

Involuntary Celibacy

Because of the issues discussed above, many intersex people who would like to have a sexual partner do not have one. Some have never dated due to fear of rejection, and/or fear of violent partner reactions. Others have some limited sexual experience that went poorly. They froze up when clothing came off and a potential partner asked why their bodies looked that way, and they are afraid to repeat the experience. Or their difference went unnoticed by the partner, but they experienced no pleasure, and they didn't know how to talk about it. Or they tried to have penetrative intercourse and it was impossible or extremely painful. But the number one barrier to intersex people finding partners is shame (Davis, 2014). The whole premise of the medicalization of intersex is that sex variance is disordered, and that if other people see our bodies as intersex, they will be horrified and reject us.

The medical profession has produced a self-fulfilling prophecy for us. They say unless they erase our sex variance, we will live tragic lives of social isolation. Then they mark our bodies, our medical records, and our life histories with stigmata that can never be erased. Meanwhile, our education about science, anatomy, reproduction, and childbearing include no information intersex statuses, so parents and potential partners are unprepared to meet us. As a result, intersex people may be too traumatized, ashamed and afraid to try to enter sexual partnerships. The real tragedy here is not our bodies, it's the attempts to erase us.

It's important at this point to distinguish involuntary celibacy from two phenomena. One is asexuality. Asexual people are not interested in sexual relationships with others; demisexual people have limited sexual interest. Like endosex people, intersex people can be asexual, and that is fine. It is wrong to presume an intersex person's life is tragic merely because they do not have a sexual partner.

The other thing we must distinguish is the difference between two wrongs. One is systematic bias that frames intersex people (or any group) as living outside the boundaries of normative sexual attraction. And the other is the "incel" phenomenon. Incels are a subculture born of the internet "mansophere." They are cis straight men who believe they are entitled to "hot females" but that such women refuse to have sex with them. Incel culture is deeply misogynist. At its most extreme, it advocates a right to rape and glorifies violence against normatively attractive "Staceys," and sometimes the "Chads" they "spread their legs" for. This subculture is rightfully horrifying to people who support the dignity and autonomy of women. But most involuntarily celibate people (even those who are cis straight men) are not incels. They easily distinguish between personal suffering due to not feeling able to seek or find a partner, and some nonexistent "right" to demand sex from an individual they find attractive.

Still, the media attention paid to the incel phenomenon, especially in the wake of mass murders perfomed by incels, have made it even more difficult for intersex people to discuss the suffering caused by involuntary celibacy in our community.

WHAT POSITIVE RELATIONSHIP EFFECTS CAN INTERSEX STATUS PRODUCE?

Under the right conditions, having a sex-variant body can be, not just a neutral fact, but something with positive implications in a sexual relationship. Those conditions include that an intersex person is comfortable with their own body. They should not just be free of shame, but familiar with how their own unique body responds to sexual stimulation in ways they enjoy. It also requires a partner who is supportive, understanding, and educated about intersexuality in general, and their partner's body in particular. The partners must be able to communicate clearly and openly as they engage in sexual interactions, and willing to explore how their bodies can work together for their shared pleasure.

Under these conditions, being sex-variant can lead to a sexual relationship of high quality. Many endosex people have dissatisfying sexual relationships due to fear to deviate from sexual scripts that don't work for them. They hold beliefs about there being a "right way" to have sex, and they follow them even if they would enjoy other practices more. But when that normative sexual script is impossible to follow, or leads to pain rather than pleasure, it adds additional incentive to engage in playful, exploratory sexual interactions. And that is what makes for high quality sexual relations. Instead of adhering to a script that says, "insert tab A into slot B," partners can experiment with alternate forms of genital-genital contact; stimulating areas with mouths, hands or toys; or focusing on intense stimulation of nongenital sensitive areas of the body (neck, earlobes, nipples, toes—whatever is pleasurable to the partner). In cases where a person has lost genital sensation due to surgery, the brain has the capacity to transfer orgasmic capacity to other areas, which can be discovered through playful exploration. This leads to sexual experiences that are atypical, but pleasurable.

Finally, while it is true that life traumas can have lifelong negative consequences, it is equally true that dealing with life challenges can produce personal growth. Experiences of social marginalization can lead to insight into the difficulties faced by others, and heightened empathy. Coming to think critically about how bias has produced personal suffering can increase the sophistication of a person's social reasoning. And all of these factors are assets in personal relationships.

NOTES

[1] A person who is not intersex is endosex.

[2] The phalloclitoris is the intermediate genital form that all humans start out with in the womb. In endosex people, it differentiates into a phallus (largely external) or clitoris (largely internal). In intersex people who are genitally variant, the phalloclitoris retains an intermediate form.

[3] In scientific terminology, "intersex" is a sex status intermediate between the idealized poles of male and female, while "hermaphrodite" refers to species in which each individual has the capacity to produce both egg and sperm (such as all plants, snails, etc.). Humans can be intersex, but scientifically speaking, not hermpaphrodites. Our sex is intermediate, not "doubled," and we cannot impregnate ourselves.

[4] The term cisgender as it is used in discussing endosex people's gender identities does not apply in this context. A cis person is one who experiences privilege because the body they were born with aligns with social expectations for a person of their identified gender. A cis person may experience policing of their gender expression if they are gender-nonconforming, but their sex characteristics are not policed. Like a trans person, an intersex person's sex characteristics are policed. And intersex people's birth-assigned binary sexes do not align with our physical sex characteristics at birth. So the term "ipsogender" is used to refer to an intersex person in our society who is content to live in their birth-assigned binary gender. (In chemistry, "cis" refers to "the same side," "trans" to "the other side," and "ipso" to a substitution in the same place.)

[5] This definition of bisexuality as meaning "attracted to both binary genders" is one rejected by many bi+ people who are affirming of nonbinary people, but remains the hegemonic

definition in medical, psychological and academic contexts, and the understanding held by many people who are not themselves bi+.

[6] The phrase "trans panic" has its origin in a legal defense successfully employed in assault and murder criminal cases by cis endosex straight-identified men whose victim is a trans and/or intersex woman. The claim is made by the perpetrator that the victim did not disclose her physical sex variance while flirting or beginning sexual relations with him, and when he discovered she was not a cis endosex woman, he was so upset at being "tricked" that he lost control of himself and responded violently to her "deception."

REFERENCES

Bauer, M., & Truffer, D. (2018). *Intersex genital mutilations: Human rights violations of children with variations of sex anatomy.* NGO Report (for LOIPR) to the 2nd and 3rd Report of New Zealand on the Convention on the Rights of Persons with Disabilities. StopIGM.org

Davis, G. (2014). Bringing intersexy back? Intersexuals and sexual satisfaction. In M. Stombler et al. (Eds.), *Sex matters: The sexualities and society reader* (4th ed., pp. 11–21). New York, NY: W. W. Norton & Company.

Davis, G. (2015). *Contesting intersex: The dubious diagnosis.* New York, NY: New York University Press.

Davies, S. G. (2006). *Challenging gender norms: Five genders among Bugis in Indonesia.* Boston, MA: Cengage Learning.

Delimata, N., Simmonds, M., O'Brien, M., Davis, G., Auchus, R., & Lin-Su, K. (2018). Evaluating the term 'disorders of sex development': A multidisciplinary debate. *Social Medicine, 12*(1), 98–107.

Fausto-Sterling, A. (2000). *Sexing the body: Gender politics and the construction of sexuality.* New York, NY: Basic Books.

Fichtner, J., Filipas, D., Mottrie, A. M., Voges, G. E., & Hohenfellner, R. (1995). Analysis of Meatal location in 500 men. *The Journal of Urology, 154*(2), 833–834.

Greenberg, J. (1999). Defining male and female: Intersexuality and the collision between law and biology. *Arizona Law Review, 41*(265), 1–62.

James, S. D. (2011, March 17). *Intersex babies: Boy or girl and who decides?* Retrieved June 9, 2018, from https://abcnews.go.com/Health/intersex-children-pose-ethical-dilemma-doctors-parents-genital/story?id=13153068

Karkazis, K. (2008). *Fixing sex: Intersex, medical authority, and lived experience.* Durham, NC: Duke University Press.

Myketiak, C. (2016). Fragile masculinity: Social inequalities in the narrative frame and discursive construction of a mass shooter's autobiography/manifesto. *Contemporary Social Science, 11*(4), 289–303.

Paulozzi, L. J., Erickson, J. D., & Jackson, R. J. (1997). Hypospadias trends in two US surveillance systems. *Pediatrics, 100*(5), 831–834.

Reis, E. (2012). *Bodies in doubt: An American history of intersex.* Baltimore, MD: Johns Hopkins University Press.

Sax, L. (2002). How common is Intersex? A response to Anne Fausto-Sterling. *Journal of Sex Research, 39*(3), 174–178.

Stryker, S. (2017). *Transgender history: The roots of today's revolution* (2nd ed.). Berkeley, CA: Seal Press.

Taylor, A. P. (2017, March). Newton's color theory, ca. 1665. *The Scientist*. Retrieved June 8, 2018, from https://www.the-scientist.com/?articles.view/articleNo/48584/title/Newton-s-Color-Theory--ca--1665/

Viloria, H. (2017). *Born both: An intersex life*. New York, NY: Hachette Books.

Wasige, J., & Jackson, I. (2017). Female genital mutilation: A form of gender-based violence. In N. Lombard (Ed.), *The Routledge handbook of gender and violence* (pp. 196–207). New York, NY: Routledge.

GEORGIANN DAVIS AND JONATHAN JIMENEZ

19. NOT GOING TO THE CHAPEL?

Intersex Youth and an Exploration of Marriage Desires and Expectations

INTRODUCTION

A recent *New York Times* article reported that U.S. millennials, those born between the early 1980s and early 2000s, are in no hurry to get married (Rabin, 2018). Instead, they are focused on developing their careers, strengthening friendships, and getting their personal life "in order" before settling down. In the article, sociologist Andrew Cherlin, a families and public policy expert, is consulted to summarize this pattern which he labels "capstone marriages." "Marriage used to be the first step into adulthood. Now it is often the last.... For many couples, marriage is something you do when you have the whole rest of your personal life in order. Then you bring family and friends together to celebrate" (Rabin, 2018). While today's youth may be waiting longer to get married, that is if they want to get married at all (Luscombe, 2014), with the passage of the legalization of same-sex marriage in 2015, there is no reason to believe that anyone who desires a monogamous marriage, and the benefits it offers as a legally sanctioned institution (Calhoun, 2000), would not be able to partake in the age-old heteronormative, cisnormative, and monogamous tradition.

However, for intersex youth, those born with genitalia, chromosomes, and hormone levels that defy cisnormative expectations, marriage is likely more than a capstone that ceremoniously marks the end of youth and the beginning of adulthood. Rather, drawing on what we know from studies on intersex adults that document how marriage, notably heterosexual monogamous marriage, allow intersex adults to feel authentically gendered (see Davis, 2015a, 2015b) and the wide range of ways in which U.S. millennials navigate the gender structure (Risman, 2018), we find it reasonable, if not necessary, to explore marriage desires and expectations from the perspective of intersex youth. Do intersex youth desire marriage? Do they see marriage in their future? Drawing on data from sixteen intersex youth between the ages of eleven and twenty-five years-of-age, we ask these exploratory questions for

© KONINKLIJKE BRILL NV, LEIDEN, 2019 | DOI:10.1163/9789004414105_020

two overlapping reasons. First, outside of how intersex youth experience their diagnosis (Davis & Wakefield, 2017), we know relatively little about the lives of intersex youth. Most intersex studies, across disciplines, focus on the lived experiences of intersex adults (e.g., Davis, 2015a; Holmes, 2008; Karkazis, 2008; Preves, 2003), which we find surprising given intersex is often diagnosed at birth or during adolescence. Second, as sociocultural scholars make sense of shifts in marriage patterns and offer their theories for such changes, we wonder what we can learn by expanding the conversation to include those born with intersex traits.

Our analysis begins with an overview of the marriage desires and expectations of today's youth where we acknowledge that we are focusing specifically on monogamous marriage patterns in this chapter. We then turn to a brief description of intersex medicalization to set the stage for our discussion of how and why marriage has been relied on by intersex adults to validate their gender identity. Next we introduce our data from intersex youth that leads us to our exploratory findings that suggest the intersex youth in our study overwhelmingly desire marriage but do not feel they will get married. We begin to theorize about this pattern, but as is the case with all exploratory analyses, we conclude with a call for future research that delves deeper into how intersex youth define, make sense of, and feel about monogamous marriage.

YOUTH'S EXPECTATIONS AND DESIRES OF MARRIAGE

With the caveat that research is often heteronormative and cisnormative (Compton, Meadow, & Schilt, 2018), survey research suggests the vast majority of U.S. millennials are not rejecting monogamous marriage—a 2014 Pew Research Center report suggests 69% of unmarried millennials want to get married ("Millennials in Adulthood," 2014). Rather, they are simply waiting longer to get married (Silva, 2012; Kreider, 2005). In 1990 the median age at which men married was 26.1 and for women it was 23.9 years-of-age (Raley et al., 2010). Just over a decade later, by 2003, those numbers increased to 27.1 years-of-age for men and 25.3 years-of-age for women. And this trend is not slowing. In 2017 the U.S. Census reported that the median age for marriage was 29.5 years-of-age for men and 27.4-years-of-age for women (Geiger & Livingston, 2018).

As noted earlier, sociologist Andrew Cherlin suggests U.S. youth are postponing marriage until their lives, notably their careers, are in order for they are using their youth as a period of self-discovery (Rabin, 2018; see also, Arnett, 2000; Smock et al., 2005). Economist Robert Plotnick (2007) explains this increase in age at first marriage especially holds for those with high educational and occupational aspirations. Research by the National Center for Family and Marriage Research (NCFMR) at Bowling Green State University offers further empirical support for this claim. As reported on in a *Newsweek* article, drawing on U.S. Census Data from 1980 to 2015, NCFMR found that millennials are getting married at an older age than baby boomers, but were simultaneously more likely than baby boomers to be in college well into their twenties (Williams, 2017). Nevertheless, as age at first marriage increases for today's young adults, so does the rate of premarital cohabitation (Lundberg et al., 2016), which, for low-income couples, especially those with children, might be more economically advantageous than marriage given how household income is often a key factor in determining welfare eligibility (Lichter et al., 2006).

While young Americans are waiting longer to engage in monogamous marriage, they still value it. University of Michigan's Monitoring the Future study consistently shows that high school seniors consider having a healthy marriage and family to be "extremely important." As noted in a 2014 *Forbes* article, 78% of female high school seniors and 70% of male high school seniors reported such feelings about marriage and family, astonishing high percentages that have went virtually unchanged since the 1970s (Howe, 2014); a claim supported by The National Marriage Project at the University of Virginia. Sociologist Arland Thornton and Linda Young-Demarco's (2001) findings from five large-scale datasets yielded similar findings with 72% of all high school seniors saying that a healthy marriage and good family life were extremely important to them. Additionally, Thornton and Young-Demarco found that 78% of all high school seniors reported that they expected to marry in the future. Beyond high school seniors, Sociologist Sarah Crissey (2005) found that the majority of teens in grades 7–12 believe they had at least a 50-50 chance, or better, of being married by the age of 25, although she also noted that Black adolescents were less likely to believe in the likelihood of marriage than white adolescents. In contrast, in a 2007 study by sociologist Wendy Manning and colleagues, only 5% of teens expected not to marry at some point in the future, while 76% reported that they would "probably or definitely" get married in the future.

The research on U.S. youth's expectations and desires of monogamous marriage illustrates some changes from earlier generations as outlined above, notably that millennials are older when they marry, but nevertheless, they still see marriage in their future. As sociocultural scholars document and theorize these trends, we encourage expanding the discussion by reminding our colleagues that heterosexual and monogamous marriage has been a route for which many intersex adults validated their gender. In the section that follows, we describe intersex medicalization to set the stage for our discussion of the link between marriage and gender for many intersex people.

INTERSEX MEDICALIZATION

The experiences of intersex people have intrinsically been tied to the process of medicalization and the "medical gaze" (Davis et al., 2016), which is the practice by which medical professionals approach and diagnose bodies (Foucault, 1963). Born with a unique combination of sex characteristics— genitalia, chromosomes, and hormones—that defy cisnormative expectations about bodies, intersex people have historically been forced to undergo medically unnecessary and irreversible interventions aimed at erasing any sign of intersex status (Davis, 2015a; Holmes, 2008; Karkazis, 2008; Preves, 2003). For example, the lead author on this chapter, Georgiann Davis, has complete androgen insensitivity syndrome (CAIS)—an intersex trait where one typically is born with a vagina, but inside the body instead of ovaries, a uterus, fallopian tubes, and XX chromosomes, a person will have internal testes and XY chromosomes. As was Georgiann's case, doctors routinely lie to intersex people about their diagnosis by not telling them the truth about their bodies and instead present the diagnosis as underdeveloped reproductive structures prone to cancer (Davis, 2015a; Holmes, 2008; Karkazis, 2008; Preves, 2003). After presenting the misleading diagnosis, doctors routinely then proceed to recommend invasive and irreversible surgeries under the guise of minimizing cancer risks, when in actuality they are attempting to align sex, gender, and sexuality (Davis, 2015a). These are unfounded and dangerous lies (see Lee et al., 2006, for a discussion of the risks, and Nakhal et al., 2013, for contradictory evidence).

Intersex people have been subjected to some form of medically unnecessary and irreversible interventions since at least the 19th century (Mak, 2012; Reis, 2009; Dreger, 1998), if not earlier (Warren, 2014). However, these procedures were routinized in the 20th century in large part by the work of psychology John Money. Along with his student Anke A. Ehrhardt and with clinical data, Money argued that although the human brain is partially influenced by the hormones it is exposed to during gestation, gender socialization during childhood was the most significant factor in explaining one's gender identity (Money & Ehrhardt, 1972). Money encouraged his peers to surgically modify an intersex baby's body to match the gender the doctor chose for the intersex baby. In a complete disregard for the intersex person's bodily autonomy, Money and his colleagues claimed that an intersex person could live a happy and healthy life under this medicalization model providing that the intersex person was subjected to strict gender socialization consistent with ideologies that maintain sex, gender, and sexuality ought to all be neatly aligned (Money & Ehrardt, 1972; Money et al., 1957).

Money's work had a significant impact on the medical treatment of intersex people as well as our narrow understanding of the relationship between sex, gender, and sexuality (e.g., Rubin, 2017). Rather than accept intersex people as a challenge to the sex binary, doctors followed (e.g., Reis, 2009), and continue to follow today (e.g., Davis, 2015a), Money's logic that intersex is an abnormality that demands surgical correction. In other words, doctors assign an intersex person a gender and then surgically alter the intersex person's body to align with the gender they've assigned. They then strongly encourage the intersex person's parents to engage in strict gender socialization and policing of their intersex child's gender identity. For decades, and despite skepticism from some outspoken scholarly critics (e.g., Diamond, 1982), Money's gender theorization would shape the medicalization practices of intersex.

However, in the late 1990s, John Money was discredited on the grounds that he not only fabricated his research findings to support his theorizations about sex, gender, and sexuality, but also because he demanded his research subjects engage in unwanted dehumanizing sexual activities (see Colapinto, 2000). David Reimer—a brave former patient who publically shared his story in a *New York Times* bestseller titled *As Nature Made Him: The Boy Who Was Raised as a Girl* (Colapinto, 1997, 2000)—brought about Money's downfall. After a botched circumcision left Reimer's penis burned beyond repair, his parents went to Money for medical advice. Although Reimer was not intersex, the botched circumcision left him with "ambiguous" genitalia that Money would propose treating as he did intersex patients. Holding firm to his gender theory, Money told Reimer's parents that he and his team would remove the remainder of baby David's penis and surgically construct a vagina. Money told Reimer's parents that their son would be happy as a girl so long as they strictly socialized him as such. Following Money's medical expertise, Reimer's parents engaged in strict gender socialization and routinely brought their child to Money's office for medical follow up appointments (Colapinto, 1997, 2000). However, as an adult, Reimer shared with the world that he never felt comfortable as a girl growing up and was incredibly unhappy with his assigned gender identity (Colapinto, 1997, 2000). Reimer's experience was in complete opposition to Money's theorization, and sadly, at the age of 38, Reimer committed suicide.

Intersex activists and feminist scholars are also collectively critical of intersex medicalization practices. In the late 1980s and early 1990s, the intersex rights movement was formed as various stakeholders spoke against the ways in which medical providers treat intersex people (see Davis, 2015a; Chase, 1998). Intersex activists went to the media and organized public protests raising awareness about how doctors lied to them about their bodies while subjecting them to medically unnecessary and irreversible surgeries (Chase, 1998). Sociologist Sharon Preves drew on Judith Butler to explain: "the impetus to control intersexual 'deviance' stems from cultural tendencies towards gender binarism, homophobia, and fear of difference" (Preves, 2001, p. 524). Doctors often hold essentialist views about gender which is rooted in a white middle class understanding of femininity and masculinity and characterized by the belief that gender is biologically determined (Davis, 2015a). This has led to doctors giving medical advice and performing surgeries on children that are rooted in their essentialist views.

The navigation of intersex medicalization lasts long after childhood as intersex people age and navigate life, including romantic and sexual relationships, after being pathologized by the medical community for years. Regardless of surgical history, intersex people express sexual struggles in their life that largely stem from their anxieties about their bodily difference (Davis, 2015a; see also Davis, 2014). For example, one intersex woman reported feeling a "crippling effect of fear" when thinking about romantic relationships (Davis, 2015a, p. 93). Another stated that she worried about falling in love for fear that when she disclosed her intersex identity to her partner he would decide that he did not want to be with her anymore. While all intersex people interviewed by Davis for her earlier work experienced anxiety about their body, they employed one of three strategies to mitigate their struggles. They either avoided intimacy all together, sought out heterosexual encounters, or rejected medicalization. The first strategy of avoidance is categorized by the complete avoidance, often for decades, of any romantic engagement with another person. For those who avoided intimacy, this response allowed them to escape their fears of abnormality. The second strategy entailed engaging in heterosexual encounters in order to validate one's assigned gender. Medical professionals encouraged this strategy, as they view heterosexuality as the desired outcome of surgical intervention. Engaging in heterosexual relationships was an attempt to overcome feelings of being abnormal. The third strategy involved rejecting medicalization by using intersex as an identity characteristic. This strategy involved the embracing of intersex as an identity as well as rejecting the new language of disorder of sex development (DSD) that has come to replace intersex terminology throughout the medical profession. Those who used this strategy reported feelings of liberation.

The sexual struggles of intersex people ought to be understood as part of a broader medicalization process and not just in relation to surgical history (Davis, 2014, 2015a). The medicalization process is not just what happens in the operating room. The medicalization of intersex bodies is a complex and widespread process that often has far-reaching consequences for all intersex people, regardless of their surgical history. This is because medical professionals rely on heteronormative and cisnormative binary understandings of sex, gender, and sexuality that they then prescribe to intersex bodies. It is imperative, then, to understand the medicalization of intersex people as a process rooted in the perpetuation of heteronormativity and that intersex people are subject to a medicalization process that attempts to place them, often through surgical procedures, into a cisgender binary. In the next section, we describe how many intersex people look to heterosexual marriage to validate their gender identity.

THE SIGNIFICANCE OF MARRIAGE FOR INTERSEX PEOPLE

In the U.S., marriage has historically been a central pillar of societal organization in naturalizing and reproducing cisgendered, heteronormative, and mononormative power structures (Schippers, 2016; Wolkomir, 2009; Calhoun, 2000). Marriage employs a number of tools in the reproduction of these systems among them the "the heterosexual imaginary" which sociologist Chrys Ingraham theorizes as the normalization of heterosexuality that hides how gender is structured. As a result of the heterosexual imaginary, "heterosexuality circulates as taken for granted, naturally occurring, and unquestioned" (Ingraham, 1994). This, in turn, perpetuates not only heteronormative and cisgendered power systems but also compulsory monogamy (Mint, 2006). As a result, a singularly acceptable form of masculine and feminine cisgender performance emerges as natural and normal. These performances become intertwined with the performance of heterosexuality (Jackson, 2005; Segal, 1990), leading to a normalizing of heteronormative, cisgendered, and mononormative practices within marriage (Berlant & Warner, 1995; see also Schippers, 2016). Marriage then can be conceptualized as a mononormative societal invitation to the creation and recreation of a heteronormative and binary understanding of gender.

The complex relationship between gender, sexuality, and marriage remains even though the meaning of marriage has shifted in recent times (e.g., Bernstein & Taylor, 2013; Kimport, 2013). In 2015 the U.S. Supreme Court ruled that it was unconstitutional to deny same-sex couples the right to marry. This represents perhaps the largest shift in the meaning of marriage since Loving v. Virginia in 1967 (Carrington, 2016). Some scholars have argued that legalizing same-sex marriage will lend a sense of legitimacy for same-sex couples (Hull, 2006). Others feel the legalization of same-sex marriage will set the stage for gay and lesbian couples to gain feelings of societal normativity as they enter an institution that creates and recreates what is normal (Warner, 1999).

While same-sex monogamous couples now have federally recognized legal access to marriage, questions remain of the impact that marriage has on intersex people. Well before the U.S. Supreme Court's decision on same-sex marriage, intersex people were participating in legally recognized monogamous marriages. For example, Georgiann married a man with XY chromosomes despite the fact she had XY chromosomes. Of course, the entry into marriage has not always been a smooth process for intersex people. The heteronormative gender binary that characterizes marriage presents formidable challenges for intersex people (Uslan, 2010), which often means negotiation with institutions that privilege bodies that align with the gender binary over bodies that do not. Marriages that feature intersex people have historically been subjected to legal challenges, as intersex people do not fit neatly into the sex, and ultimately gender, binary upon which marriage was historically legally recognized (Cruz, 2010). Additionally, intersex marriages have faced additional scrutiny from politicians, religious leaders, and medical professionals (Costello, 2010), with the latter encouraging treatments or medical plans that align with a strict heteronormative cisgender binary (Davis, 2015a).

For intersex folks, monogamous and heterosexual marriage has long been an indicator of successful gender assignment (Davis, 2015b; Hass, 2004). For some surgeons, genital surgeries are performed to give intersex youth lives that are in line with their gender essentialist and heteronormative views (Davis et al., 2016). This has meant that doctors perform surgical procedures on intersex youth, in part, to put them in positions to fit the binary institution of heteronormative and mononormative marriage. These genital surgeries have long had implications on intersex people's abilities to marry (Uslan, 2010).

Doctors would assign an intersex child a gender, surgically shape the child's body to match the gender that was assigned, which in turn, limited who the intersex people would be able to marry in the future given the historically heteronormative institution of marriage (Haas, 2004).

As we enter the monogamous marriage equality era, questions remain in regards to the expectations and desires of marriage among intersex youth. In the next section, we turn to a discussion of our data that we draw on to answer two key questions: Do intersex youth desire marriage? Do they see marriage in their future? While the present study is only exploratory, our answers to these questions is a look into the lives of intersex youth that will hopefully be a springboard into future empirical studies that center the voices of young intersex people.

METHODS

Data for this study comes from intersex youth who were in attendance at the 2013 Androgen Insensitivity Syndrome-Differences of Sex Development (AIS-DSD) Support Group annual meeting. With Institutional Review Board (IRB) approval in hand, Georgiann distributed a "Recruitment Statement for Research Participants" to intersex youth who were in attendance at the meeting. The AIS-DSD Support Group's then president also voluntarily placed the recruitment statement in a registration packet that each attendee received at the conference's registration table.

Almost all of the young intersex people eligible for inclusion in this research study expressed preliminary interest, a total of 21 youth between the ages of 11 and 25 years-of-age. An unsealed manila envelope was distributed to each potential participant that contained a 40 question self-administered survey, with both closed and open-ended questions, and a pen. The goal of the survey was to further our understanding of how intersex youth navigate their lives. Background information was also collected. Participants were instructed to complete the survey at their convenience, place it in the manila envelope, seal the envelope, and return it to Georgiann sometime during the weekend long conference. All participants were verbally reminded to not put their name anywhere on the survey. They were also encouraged to answer questions however they felt comfortable. The survey also offered participants a crisis hotline they could call if they felt "sad, uncomfortable, or just need[ed] someone to talk to about [their] feelings." They were also encouraged to reach out to a well-known then board member of the AIS-DSD Support Group who is also a practicing physician and parent of two intersex adults. To our knowledge, no participant reported any discomfort from participating in the study.

Of the 21 youth who expressed interest in participating in the study, 16 completed the appropriate consent/assent forms. Participants were between 11 and 25 years old, with half of the young intersex people under the age of 18. We acknowledge there are substantial psychological, developmental, and social differences among those between eleven and twenty-five years-of-age. However, drawing on psychologist Jeffrey Arnett's (2004) theorization of "emerging adulthood" that suggests those between eighteen and twenty-five years-of-age experience delayed adulthood, we feel it is methodologically sound to explore the experiences of those between 11 and 25 years-of-age in the same analysis. The majority of participants reported living primarily with at least one parent (68.8%), whereas the rest indicated primarily living with someone other than a parent such as a grandparent.

FINDINGS

Our analysis of the marriage desires and expectations of the 16 intersex youth in our study reveals three themes: (1) gender and sexual normalcy, (2) marriage desires are consistent with the general population of U.S. youth, and (3) substantially lower expectations of marriage than consistently reported for U.S. youth. We recognize our analysis of intersex youth's marriage desires and expectations is limited, for only monogamous marriage is legally recognized in the U.S. We are also aware that our sample is not generalizable to all intersex youth. Lastly, we acknowledge that the size of our sample is small, yet we believe our exploratory analysis is valuable for spotlighting intersex youth—a group largely missing from sociocultural studies on intersex.

Theme 1: Gender and Sexual Normalcy

Given many intersex adults worry that they are not authentically gendered (Davis, 2015a; Karkazis, 2008; Preves, 2003), coupled with the fact that medical providers routinely negatively judge an intersex person if they do not identify with the gender they were assigned at birth and/or deviate from heterosexuality (Davis et al., 2016; Davis, 2015a; Karkazis, 2008), Georgiann did not want to directly ask participants to share their gender and sexuality. While this approach is far from perfect, it is favored given the cost of possibly, even if unintentionally, stigmatizing intersex youth by

256

asking them to identify their gender and sexuality. This is especially the case given research participants came from the AIS-DSD Support Group where most of those in attendance identify as woman or young girls—which is typical of the global intersex community. If an intersex youth was directly asked to report their gender and sexuality, Georgiann worried the intersex child might think their gender authenticity was being questioned and that their sexuality was being policed. Instead, as described below, Georgiann attempted to creatively gather gender and sexuality information indirectly from each participant, and while this is a crude approach, the hope is that it minimized any stigmatization.

Gender was ascertained through clothing preferences. All participants were given images, obtained from a simple Google search, of 10 young people modeling different styles of clothing ranging from stereotypically feminine, stereotypically masculine, to more androgynous clothing and asked, "Circle the teenagers below who dress most like you. Choose as many styles as you like." This question reveled that most of the participants held very diverse clothing preferences, as do most girls in the contemporary western world (Risman & Seale, 2009). However, a number of youth noted that their clothing choices were in defiance to their parents' wishes as determined by responses to a follow up question that read: "Which of the styles below do you feel your parents or guardians wished you had? You can circle more than one style."

With respect to sexuality, all participants were asked to identify a famous person (or people) they would want to go on a romantic date with. While this question is far from a perfect measure of one's sexuality, it was assumed this approach was less stigmatizing than asking youth directly about their sexual identity. Eleven of the participants indicated they would like to go on a romantic date with a famous person/s who have a masculine presentation (68.75%). One youth identified two famous people they would like to go on a romantic date with, both of whom have feminine presentations (6.25%). Two participants identified they would like to go on a romantic date with famous people of different genders, some very masculine and some very feminine (12.5%). The remaining 2 participants either did not answer the question or stated, "I don't know" (12.5%). While responses to this question offers a very crude measure of sexuality, it does suggest most of the young intersex people in this study would likely identify as straight if directly asked about their sexual identity.

Although gender and sexual normativity should not be a goal of any kind, we find it important to note that based on our crude measures of gender

257

and sexuality, we would classify most of our participants as girls and young women who are straight. While their clothing choices are quite diverse, which is not surprising given girls and young women have far more flexibility with their gender performance than boys and young men (see Risman & Seale, 2009), well over half of the young intersex people would likely identify as straight if directly asked about their sexuality. Thus, at least for the 68.75% of participants who we have classified as straight, we would expect all of the youth who desire marriage to expect that they will someday get married. Because data was collected prior to the legalization of same-sex marriage in the U.S., it is possible those who desire marriage, but are not straight (or monogamous), would be less likely to expect that they will someday get married than those who desire marriage and are straight. We return to this possibility below in our discussion of marriage expectations.

Theme 2: Marriage Desires

As described above, most U.S. millennials desire marriage ("Millennials in Adulthood," 2014). Around the same time Georgiann surveyed intersex youth for this study, the Pew Research Center conducted a generalizable study of U.S. youth that indicated 69% of unmarried millennials want to get married ("Millennials in Adulthood," 2014). Based on our exploratory study, intersex youth have similar, if not higher, desires for marriage in their future.

All of the intersex youth who participated in this study were asked, "Do you want to be married when you are older?" Response options included, "Yes," "No," and "I don't know." Almost all of the intersex youth (87.5%) reported that they would want to be married when they were older by selecting "Yes" to the marriage desire question. Only 2 of the 16 participants (12.5%) indicated "I don't know," and no respondents indicated that they did not desire marriage when they are older.

While there is only so much we can analyze from this survey question, it does allow us to see that intersex youth, at least those who participated in our study, share similar desires of marriage as the general population of U.S. youth. Furthermore, it appears that intersex youth are even more likely to desire marriage in their future than are U.S. youth at large, for 87.5% of our participants reported desiring marriage compared to only 69% of those from the general population. In the next section, we describe whether or not the intersex youth in our study expect that they will be married in their future and compare their expectations with the expectations of U.S. youth from the general population.

Theme 3: Marriage Expectations

Although we know relatively little about intersex youth, we do know that intersex youth seem to be comfortable navigating their diagnosis at the individual, interactional, and institutional levels of society, despite the occasional clash with the peers and adults in their lives (Davis & Wakefield, 2017). However, we also know that intersex adults struggle with feelings of abnormality (Davis, 2015a; Karkazis, 2008; Preves, 2003), and more specifically, a perceived lack of normalcy in romantic relationships (Davis, 2014, 2015a, 2015b). Some intersex adults avoid intimacy, others seek out heterosexual encounters to validate their gender, while the rest reject medicalization and the pathologization of the intersex body by embracing intersex as an identity (Davis, 2014).

Given these sociocultural studies, it makes sense to analyze the relationship between the marriage desires of intersex youth and whether or not they feel they will get married in the future. If intersex youth are similar to intersex adults, they will likely desire marriage but not expect it to be in their future for reasons possibly related to being differently bodied. If intersex youth are different from intersex adults who struggle with feelings of abnormality, we might expect to find intersex youth who desire marriage to expect marriage to be in their future. Of course, we caution readers from drawing any conclusions from the findings we share in this analysis, for our sample is small and not representative of all intersex youth. However, as we noted at the outset of this chapter, our hope is that this exploratory analysis will open up a dialogue about the lives of intersex youth and the importance of including youth in future sociocultural studies on intersex.

As noted in the previous section, 87.5% of the intersex youth in our study expressed a desire to get married when they are older, whereas 69% of youth from the general U.S. population expressed similar desires ("Millennials in Adulthood," 2014). However, while 87.5% of our participants desired marriage, only 50% felt marriage was in their future. This difference between marriage desires and marriage expectations is a substantial difference from the pattern we see across the U.S. youth population. Recall that U.S. youth desire marriage ("Millennials in Adulthood," 2014), and although they might be waiting longer to get married (Geiger & Livingston, 2018; Rabin, 2018; Howe, 2014; Silva, 2012; Raley et al., 2010; Kreider, 2005), they still do believe marriage will be in their future. Why is there a mismatch in our study between the percentage of intersex youth who desire marriage and the percentage of intersex youth who expect to marry?

A total of 14 of the 16 intersex youth (87.5%) who participated in our study reported that they want to be married when they are older, yet 8 of the 16 intersex youth (50%) did not feel they will be married in the future by selecting either "No" or "I don't know" to the marriage expectation question. Based on our classification of each participant's sexuality through our crude measure that asked participants to name a person or people they would like to go on a romantic date with, 5 of the 8 intersex youth in this category of desiring marriage yet not expecting it would likely identify as straight if they were directly asked about their sexuality. 2 of the 3 remaining participants who desired marriage but did not expect it also did not indicate a person or people they would like to go on a romantic date with, while the remaining participant identified people of different genders.

While our analysis is only exploratory, in this study the mismatch between marriage desires and expectations of marriage is greatest for the intersex youth who would likely identify as straight and monogamous. This finding seems to be consistent with sociocultural research on intersex adults who report sexual struggles and feelings of abnormality—experiences common among those who identify as straight (Davis, 2014, 2015a, 2015b; Karkazis, 2008; Preves, 2003). It might be that straight intersex youth who desire monogamous marriage fear a partner will not find them suitable for marriage because of their infertility—many intersex people are unable to biologically reproduce due to surgical interventions, for example the removal of their testes, that they were forced to endure (see Davis, 2015a). Or it might be that straight intersex youth who desire monogamous marriage are concerned about their ability to engage in penetrative sex. These are, of course, empirical questions that call for future research.

CONCLUSION

As we continue to learn more about the lived experiences of intersex people (Davis, 2015a; Karkazis, 2008; Preves, 2003), we encourage our sociocultural peers to actively plan future intersex studies that center the voices and experiences of intersex youth. Outside of how intersex youth navigate their diagnosis (Davis & Wakefield, 2017), we know relatively little about intersex youth, which is why we hope this chapter, with all of its limitations, will open up a larger conversation not only about intersex youth's desires and expectations of marriage (despite its mononormative boundaries), but also about intersex youth in general. This exploratory study is then meant to draw attention to some of the most invisible people in the intersex community.

U.S. youth desire marriage, and while they are waiting longer to get married, they still expect to get married (presumably they are monogamous). The intersex youth in this study, mostly straight, young women and girls, also desire marriage—even more so than their peers in the general U.S. population—however, 50% of them do not expect to get married in the future. This is quite shocking, and as described earlier, might be due to any number of reasons ranging from feelings of abnormality or fears of inadequacy in straight relationships. Of course, we know intersex people are not abnormal but rather are evidence of sex variability, and we also know that being born without a vaginal canal, with internal testes instead of ovaries, etc. does not have to predict one's sexual satisfaction (Davis, 2014). However, do most intersex youth know this? Are they aware that sex, gender, and sexuality are not neatly correlated and binary phenomenon? Do they know many people, regardless of genitalia, worry about fitting into society and/or finding romantic love if so desired? Are these even the concerns of intersex youth? Until we center intersex youth in future intersex studies, we will continue to have more questions that necessitate answers.

REFERENCES

Arnett, J. (2004). *Emerging adulthood: The winding road from late teens through early twenties*. Oxford: Oxford University Press.

Berlant, L., & Warner, M. (1998). Sex in public. *Critical Inquiry, 24*(2), 547–566.

Bernstein, M., & Taylor, V. (2013). *The marrying kind? Debating same-sex marriage within the lesbian and gay movement*. Minneapolis, MN: University of Minnesota Press.

Calhoun, C. (2000). *Feminism, the family, and the politics of the closet: Lesbian and gay displacement*. Oxford: Oxford University Press.

Carrington, A. M. (2016). Free and happy bonds: Loving v. Virginia's nineteenth-century precedent on marriage and the pursuit of happiness. *Perspectives on Political Science, 45*(2), 87–96.

Chase, C. (1998). Hermaphrodites with attitude: Mapping the emergence of intersex political activism. *GLQ: A Journal of Lesbian and Gay Studies, 4*(2), 189–211.

Colapinto, J. (2000). *As nature made him: The boy who was raised as a girl*. New York, NY: Harper Collins.

Colapinto, J. (1997). The true story of john/joan. *Rolling Stone*. Retrieved from https://www.healthyplace.com/gender/inside-intersexuality/the-true-story-of-john-joan

Compton, D., Meadow, T., & Schilt, K. (2018). *Other, please specify. Queer methods in sociology*. Berkeley, CA: UC Press.

Costello, C. G. (2010). Do I have a right to marry anyone? *Blogspot*. Retrieved from http://intersexroadshow.blogspot.com/2010/12/do-i-have-right-to-marry-anyone.html

Crissey, S. R. (2005). Race/ethnic differences in the marital expectations of adolescents: The role of romantic relationships. *Journal of Marriage and Family, 67*(3), 697–709.

Cruz, D. B. (2010). Getting sex 'right': Heteronormativity and biologism in trans and intersex marriage litigation and scholarship. *Duke Journal of Gender and Law & Policy, 18*(23), 203–222.

Davis, G. (2014). 'Brining intersexy back'? Intersexuals and sexual satisfaction. In *Sex matters: The sexualities and society reader* (4th ed., pp. 11–21). W.W. Norton & Company.

Davis, G. (2015a). *Contesting intersex: The dubious diagnosis*. New York, NY: NYU Press.

Davis, G. (2015b). What's marriage equality got to do with intersex? *Contexts*. Retrieved from https://contexts.org/blog/whats-marriage-equality-got-to-do-with-intersex/

Davis, G., Dewey, J. M., & Murphy, E. L. (2016). Giving sex: Deconstructing intersex and trans medicalization practices. *Gender & Society, 30*(3), 490–514.

Davis, G., & Wakefield, C. (2017). The intersex kids are all right? Diagnosis disclosure and the experiences of intersex youth. In P. N. Claster, S. L. Blair, & L. E. Bass (Eds.), *Sociological studies of children and youth series, "Gender, sex, and sexuality among contemporary youth"* (pp. 43–65). Emerald.

Diamond, M. (1982). Sexual identity, monozygotic twins reared in discordant sex roles and a BBC follow-up. *Archives of Sexual Behavior, 11*(2), 181–85.

Dreger, A. D. (1998). *Hermaphodites and the medical intervention of sex*. Cambridge, MA: Harvard University Press.

Foucault, M. (1963). *The birth of the clinic: An archaeology of medical perception*. New York, NY: Pantheon Books.

Geiger, A., & Livingston, G. (2018). 8 facts about love and marriage in America. *Pew Research Center*. Retrieved from http://www.pewresearch.org/fact-tank/2018/02/13/8-facts-about-love-and-marriage/

Hass, K. (2004). Who will make room for the intersexed? *American Journal of Law and Medicine, 30*(1), 301–323.

Holmes, M. (2008). *Intersex: A perilous difference*. Selinsgrove, PA: Susquehanna University Press.

Howe, N. (2014). *Don't worry America: Millennials still want to marry*. Retrieved from https://www.forbes.com/sites/realspin/2014/03/25/dont-worry-america-millennials-still-want-to-marry/#41dec0824035

Hull, K. (2006). *Same-sex marriage: The cultural politics of love and law*. Cambridge, MA: Cambridge University Press.

Ingraham, C. (1994). The heterosexual imaginary: Feminist sociology and theories of gender. *Sociological Theory, 12*(2), 203–219.

Jackson, S. (2005). Sexuality, heterosexuality, and gender hierarchy: Getting out priorities straight. In C. Ingraham (Ed.), *Thinking straight: The power, the promise, and the paradox of heterosexuality* (pp. 15–29). New York, NY: Routledge.

Karkazis, K. (2008). *Fixing sex: Intersex, medical authority, and lived experience*. Durham, NC: Duke University Press.

Kimport, K. (2013). *Queering marriage: Challenging family formation in the United States*. New Brunswick, NJ: Rutgers University Press.

Kreider, R. M. (2005). *Number, timing, and duration of marriage and divorces*. Washington, DC: U.S. Census Bureau.

Lee, P. A., Houk, C. P., Ahmed, S. F., & Hughes, I. A. (2006). Consensus statement on management of intersex disorders. *Pediatrics, 118*(2), 488–500.

Lichter, D. T., Qian, Z., & Mellott, L. M. (2006). Marriage or dissolution? Union transitions among poor cohabiting women. *Demography, 43*(2), 223–240.

Lundberg, S., Pollak, R. A., & Stearns, J. (2016). Family inequality: Diverging patterns in marriage, cohabitation, and childbearing. *The Journal of Economic Perspectives, 30*(2), 79–101.

Luscombe, B. (2014). Why 25% of millenials will never get married. *Time*. Retrieved from http://time.com/3422624/report-millennials-marriage/

Manning, W. D., Longmore, M. A., & Giordano, P. C. (2007). The changing institution of marriage: Adolescents' expectations to cohabit and to marry. *Journal of Marriage and Family, 69*(3), 559–575.

Mak, G. (2012). *Doubting sex: Inscription, bodies, and selves in nineteenth-century hermaphrodite case histories*. Manchester: Manchester University Press.

Millennials in Adulthood. (2014). Detached from institutions, networked with friends. *Pew Research Center*. Retrieved from http://www.pewsocialtrends.org/2014/03/07/millennials-in-adulthood/

Mint, P. (2006). *Compulsory monogamy and sexual minorities*. Retrieved from http://www.pepperminty.com/writing/compulsorymonogamy.pdf

Money, J., Hampson, J. G., & Hampson, J. L. (1957). Imprinting and the establishment of gender role. *Archives of Neurology and Psychiatry, 77*(3), 333–336.

Money, J., & Ehrhardt, A. A. (1972). *Man & woman, boy & girl: Differentiation and dimorphism of gender identity from conception to maturity*. Baltimore, MD: The Johns Hopkins University Press.

Nakhal, R. S., Hall-Craggs, M., Freeman, A., Kirkham, A., Conway, G. S., Arora, R., Woodhouse, C. R., Wood, D. N., & Creighton, S. M. (2013). Evaluation of retained testes in adolescent girls and women with complete androgen insensitivity syndrome. *Radiology, 268*(1), 153–160.

Plotnick, R. D. (2007). Adolescent expectations and desires about marriage and parenthood. *Journal of Adolescence, 30*(6), 943–963.

Preves, S. (2001). Sexing the intersexed: An analysis of sociocultural responses to intersexuality. *Signs: Journal of Women in Culture and Society, 27*(2), 523–556.

Rabin, R. C. (2018). Put a ring on it? Millennial couples are in no hurry. *The New York Times*. Retrieved from http://time.com/3422624/report-millennials-marriage/

Raley, R. K., Crissey, S., & Miller, C. (2010). Of sex and romance: Late adolescent relationships and young adult union formation. *Journal of Marriage and Family, 69*(5), 1210–1226.

Reis, E. (2009). *Bodies in doubt: An American history of intersex*. Baltimore, MD: The Johns Hopkins University Press.

Risman, B. (2018). *Where the millennials will take us: A new generation wrestles with the gender structure*. Oxford: Oxford University Press.

Risman, B., & Seale, E. (2009). Betwixt and between: Gender contradictions among middle schoolers. In B. J. Risman (Ed.), *Families as they really are* (pp. 340–361). New York, NY: W.W. Norton & Company.

Rubin, D. A. (2017). *Intersex matters: Biological embodiment, gender regulation, and transnational activism*. Albany, NY: State University of New York Press.

Schippers, M. (2016). *Beyond monogamy. Polyamory and the future of polyqueer sexualities*. New York: NYU Press.

Segal, L. (1990). *Slow motion: Changing masculinities, changing men*. New Brunswick, NJ: Rutgers University Press.

Silva, J. M. (2012). Constructing adulthood in the age of uncertainty. *American Sociological Review, 77*(4), 505–522.

Smock, P. J., Manning, W. D., & Porter, M. (2005). "Everything's there except money": How money shapes decisions to marry among cohabiters. *Journal of Marriage and Family, 67*(3), 680–696.

Thornton, A., & Young-DeMarco, L. (2001). Four decades of trends in attitudes toward family issues in the United States: The 1960s through the 1990s. *Journal of Marriage and Family, 63*(4), 1009–1037.

Uslan, S. S. (2010). What parents don't know: Informed consent, marriage, and genital-normalizing surgery on intersex children. *Indiana Law Journal, 85*(1), 301–323.

Warner, M. (1999). *The trouble with normal: Sex, politics, and the ethics of queer life.* New York, NY: Free Press.

Warren, C. A. B. (2014). Gender reassignment surgery in the 18th century: A case study. *Sexualities, 17*(7), 872–884.

Williams, J. (2017). The end of early marriage: Young americans would rather go to college than say 'I do.' *Newsweek.* Retrieved from http://www.newsweek.com/young-american-marriage-millennials-college-boomers-579153

Wolkomir, M. (2009). Making heteronormative reconciliations: The story of romantic love, sexuality, and gender in mixed-orientation marriages. *Gender & Society, 239*(4), 494–519.

SARAH S. TOPP

20. SHIFTING MEDICAL PARADIGMS

The Evolution of Relationships between Intersex Individuals and Doctors

INTRODUCTION

One's relationship with their doctor is among the most intimate of non-sexual relationships a person experiences. Doctors have profound access to a patient's body and medical history, and many individuals disclose information about themselves to their doctors that they do not tell others. As such, the quality of the relationship between a doctor and a care-receiver is critically important not just for achieving successful care outcomes, but also for how individuals define and value themselves. For many people with intersex variations, however, their relationships with doctors have been fraught with betrayal and abuse.

Always characterized by unease, the relationship between doctors and intersex individuals became even more troubled in the late nineteenth century, when intersex became the purview of medicine and the first intersex medical paradigm—the true sex model—was implemented. Since then, two paradigm shifts in intersex care occurred: the first in the 1950s with the introduction of the concealment-centered model of care and the second in the early 2000s with the establishment of the evidence-based model of care. Although each model remedied shortcomings from the previous paradigm, all three relied or continue to rely on the centrality of doctors, placing them in the position of authority in determining the fate of intersex bodies and stripping individuals with intersex variations of autonomy over their body. All three models also permitted, if not encouraged, the use of medically unnecessary surgeries to normalize or correct intersex bodies. In this chapter, the rationale for each of the three medical paradigms, as well as the implications for intersex individuals, is addressed.

WHAT IS INTERSEX?

Although a range of definitions exist (Aliabadi, 2004), intersex is generally understood to mean anatomical variations in sex characteristics from

© KONINKLIJKE BRILL NV, LEIDEN, 2019 | DOI:10.1163/9789004414105_021

what is typically deemed male or female (Rubin, 2017). The etiologies and manifestations of intersex variations are complex, but they relate to atypicalities in sex characteristics including chromosomes, genitals, internal reproductive organs, and hormones.

Some examples include: Klinefelter Syndrome, which can result in a chromosomal makeup of 47XXY rather than the more common 46XY; vaginal agenesis where the vagina is closed, incompletely developed or absent; Complete Androgen Insensitivity Disorder, which affects individuals who are genetically 46XY (typically male), but do not respond to androgens and thus have a vagina and no uterus or cervix; and Congenital Adrenal Hyperplasia (CAH), which affects the body's ability to produce and regulate hormones.

It has commonly been reported that, after accounting for underreporting, 1 in every 1500 births has a noticeable intersex variation (Blackless et al., 2000; ISNA, 2008b). Diamond (2007), a leading expert of intersex, says the best data suggest a greater frequency, and consensus is growing that "more than one in every hundred newborns has an intersexed condition" (p. 37).

Because of the sheer diversity of variations, the need for medical interventions differs significantly. Although some cases require immediate medical attention, such as in instances of gonadal cancer, variations that result in a metabolic disorder, or when an infant's life is in jeopardy due to the salt-wasting form of CAH, many others require no special medical care. Still, since the late nineteenth century, doctors have treated nearly all intersex individuals as medical emergencies requiring intervention and management.

THE TRUE SEX PARADIGM

Historical evidence suggests that until the 1880s, sex assignment had been a legal and social matter and physical sexual ambiguity often went undetected (ISNA, 2008c; Mak, 2005). Although visible or detectable sexual ambiguity was rejected because it challenged "public decency" and violated a strictly binary gender, it was not until advances in medicine in the late 1800s and early 1900s that doctors used surgery to "avoid the disturbing effects of visible sexual ambiguity" (Mak, p. 80). These surgical advances paved the way for the medicalization of intersex and the first paradigm of intersex care: the true sex paradigm.

Most physicians at the time agreed there were only two sexes—male and female—and one's innate true sex could be determined by their gonadal tissue. Thus, upon encountering a visibly intersex body, doctors examined gonadal tissue, looking for the existence of either ovaries or testes, to determine the true sex of their patient. Intersex individuals were labeled female pseudohermaphrodite when ovaries were present, male pseudohermaphrodite when testes were present, and true hermaphrodite when both ovarian and testicular tissue were present.

Due to the emphasis on gonadal tissue, Dreger (1999) calls this period "the age of the gonads" and argues:

> [M]edical men rallied around the idea that the...gonads...alone should determine a subject's "true sex," no matter how confusing or mixed her or his other parts. Henceforth, no matter how manly a patient looked, even if he had a full-size penis...a full beard, and a reputation for bedding down...young maidens, if he had ovaries, he would be labelled a female—in this case a "female pseudohermaphrodite." No matter how womanly a patient looked, no matter if she had a vagina...a smooth face, and a husband she loved, if she had testes, she would be labelled...a "male pseudohermaphrodite." (p. 9)

Reliance on gonads to determine true sex led to sex determinations that made no sense socially. As a result, by the 1920s, doctors developed a notion of gender as distinct from sex and began relying on surgery to bring a patient's biology in line with their gender. Although they still believed that each person could only be male or female, physicians accepted there could be multiple factors involved in defining one's true sex and it was the doctor's role to evaluate these factors to ensure a proper sex assignment. Gonadal tissue was still the primary consideration, but doctors also evaluated other physical evidence, social roles, and sexual orientation, all of which were considered through the moral assumptions of the era.

Doctors feared "social disorder" would result from ambiguous sex and believed if they allowed "an 'error of sex' to continue," they would be "engendering wrongful occupations, scandalous unions, and broken lives" (Dreger, 1998, p. 86). Seeking to correct these perceived errors of sex, doctors sought to convince patients of the perversity of their bodies (Gender and Health Collaborative Curriculum, 2012). Doctors "wanted their patients to understand their hermaphroditic conditions as deformities and not as a physical license to commit sexual immorality" (Reis, 2012, p. 68). By likening intersex bodies to "deformities such as hair-lip or club foot" (Long as cited in Carpenter, 2018, p. 2), doctors impressed upon their patients that their bodies were defects to fix, and the innovations in surgery enabled medical professionals to do just that.

The availability of surgical solutions produced "heated discussions among physicians about the patient's role" in deciding their own sex and, ultimately, "once surgical solutions to the problem of sexual ambiguity were available, the sex assignment decision was increasingly made in surgeons' consulting rooms" (Mak, 2005, p. 80).

Other doctors' reactions to the decisions made by Dr. J. Riddle Goffe demonstrates doctors' acquisition of cultural authority and subsequent denial of patient autonomy, as well as the preeminence of heterosexism in decision-making. E.C., a 20-year old "pseudohermaphodite" expressed to Dr. Goffe "annoyance" with her enlarged clitoris and requested its removal. Goffe complied with E.C.'s request, yet was attacked by other doctors for "making the wrong call" with regards to removing the enlarged clitoris, not because he removed it, but because they believed he had "misread the patient's symptoms" and had "excised a penis" rather than a clitoris (Reis, 2005, p. 437). Goffe defended his decision by pointing to E.C's love life. Goffe wrote, "She has never had any girl love affairs or been attracted passionately by any girl, but has been attracted by boys" (Goffe as cited Reis, p. 437). Goffe was unusual for the time, not because he sought to ensure heterosexuality, but because "he asked the patient what she wanted and then complied with her wishes. As a result, he had to defend himself from critics who condemned what they saw as giving undue power to the patient" (p. 438).

Codifying the centrality of doctors in determining sex and the widespread surgical response, the true sex paradigm marks the first era of the medicalization of intersex. The most common decision by doctors became the one that would eliminate visible signs of sexual ambiguity. Pressure for surgical interventions became routine and "normalizing" procedures that removed even healthy tissue became standard (Griffiths, 2018). The true sex model thus began the process of divesting autonomy from intersex individuals, depriving them of power in their relationships with doctors, and laid groundwork for the concealment-centered model.

THE CONCEALMENT-CENTERED MODEL

The concealment model was developed in the 1950s by Dr. John Money, a psychologist at Johns Hopkins University. Money argued that the true sex paradigm was flawed because it lacked focus on the psychological dispositions of a person and physical developments at puberty (Karkazis, 2008). Money hypothesized that infants are gender neutral until the age of two, and that gender identity was a consequence of one's environment and upbringing. Unlike adherents to the true sex paradigm who thought gender was a product of nature, Money and his colleagues argued that gender was a product of "nurture" and healthy gender development depended on consistent socialization in line with external genitalia. Healthy gender development, they said, could be judged by looking at sexuality: a healthy gender assignment equated to heterosexual desires and behaviors. Same sex attraction suggested that rearing had failed.

Money used a now infamous experimental case study involving twin boys, neither of whom were intersex, to support his hypothesis. In 1966, at eight months of age, twin boys Bruce and Brian Reimer underwent circumcisions. During Bruce's circumcision, the electronic cauterization equipment malfunctioned and his penis was burned beyond repair. Bruce's parents brought him to the office of Dr. Money, who had a growing reputation for his gender identity theory. After several interviews and examinations, Money concluded that a functional vagina could be surgically created, and that a surgery would help Bruce achieve functional sexual maturation as a girl. At age 22 months, Bruce underwent surgery to remove his testes and to begin the process of constructing a vagina. He was reassigned female and raised as a girl, Brenda. For years, Money published reports praising successful gender reassignment of one half of a set of identical twins (Colapinto, 2001). According to Money, Brenda was acting like a typical girl who loved dresses, hated being dirty, and eschewed the boyish ways of her twin brother (Money & Ehrhardt, 1972).

The supposed success of the case supported Money's growing influence in the medical community and solidified adoption of the concealment-centered model. Called the "optimum gender of rearing system," the model required the gender assignment of intersex children to be settled early, so they would "grow up to be good (believable and straight) girls and boys" (ISNA, 2008d, para. 1). "Settling" gender assignment required the child's anatomy to "match the 'standard' anatomy for her or his gender" (Dreger, 1998, p. 27) and surgeries to 'correct' genitals became routine. Dewhurst and Gordon (1969) claim that the number of surgeries on intersex bodies due to the concealment model became so pervasive that, by 1969, the lives and bodies of those not subjected to surgery had to be imagined.

Doctors justified surgery to parents as the avenue to provide the "right genitals to go along with socialisation" (Kessler, 1990, p. 17). The rationale was that it would be easier for parents to socialize their child as a particular sex if the genitals appeared to be 'normal' for that sex. Preves (2003) explains, "these elaborate, expensive, risky procedures are performed to maintain social order for the institutions and adults that surround that child" (p. 12). In line with this, doctors tended to limit information given to parents, both to protect the parents from feeling at fault for their child's "condition" and to encourage more seamless socialization of gender identity development (Tamar-Mattis, 2006).

Parents were instructed by doctors to withhold from their child what little information they did have. It was believed that sharing information with the child could lead to "gender confusion that all these surgeries were meant to avoid" (Dreger, n.d., para. 10). Doctors and parents used "vague language, like 'we removed your twisted ovaries' instead of 'we removed your testes'" (para. 10) when speaking to intersex children.

In an interview with Feder (2002), Mary, a mother to a 12-year old named Jessica, describes the communication she received from doctors:

> The pediatric endocrinologist asked to speak with me alone. Jessica was in a different room. The doctor…explained to me that Jessica had XY chromosomes and Jessica would not be able to bear children. She also explained…this was something I should never, ever bring up with Jessica.…We should just take care of it as quickly as possible so that Jessica could live a normal life. I agreed to this because it was what she asked me to do. I was very young. (p. 303)

Instead of telling Jessica the truth—that she had testes doctors feared could become cancerous or that a clitorectomy was being performed at the same time—Mary was instructed to tell Jessica that "her ovaries hadn't developed properly and they would have to come out" (p. 303).

Concealment model supporters argued that, left "untreated"—that is, without surgery to normalize genitals and with full information about their body—individuals with intersex variations would be depressed or suicidal and possibly end up gay or lesbian (Dreger, n.d.). As time passed, however, it became evident that the concealment model was causing the issues it sought to avoid, including shame, depression, and post-traumatic stress disorder. Commonly, the surgeries resulted in decreased sexual sensation. Human Rights Watch (2017) reports that surgical assignment of sex in young children carries the risk of assigning the wrong identity, and that, "depending on the condition, the risk can be as high as 40 percent—meaning that many children will grow up to reject the sex that has been irreversibly surgically assigned to them" (para. 16). Removal of gonads also can end fertility options and result in required lifelong hormone therapy.

Intersex people interviewed by Human Rights Watch (2017) describe that the surgeries, examinations and repeated exposures to medical practitioners caused permanent harm. The impact of these experiences with doctors extend "beyond the physical outcomes;" the feelings of "dread and horror—decades after unwanted or damaging surgeries, genital exams, insensitive disclosure of diagnosis, and other experiences" have led many to avoid healthcare as adults (para. 18).

Such negative health outcomes were evident since the inception of the concealment model. Even the acclaimed Brenda/Bruce Reimer case was a failure. Researchers Diamond and Sigmundson investigated and found that Bruce/Brenda had struggled against his reassignment as a girl from the start, and at the age of seven, rebelled against treatments. By nine, "Brenda" knew he was not girl and at fourteen, opted to live as a boy named David. He administered testosterone against the wishes of his parents and doctors. As an adult, David married a woman, adopted her kids, and had a penis reconstructed. At 38, overcome with helplessness and shame, David committed suicide (Diamond & Beh, 2006).

Despite overwhelming evidence disproving the paradigm, reliance on the concealment model remained entrenched. Money's philosophy was widely adopted, and the vast majority of published literature referenced his theories. Very few physicians contradicted him, or provided alternative management theses (Hird, 2000) until the rise of the intersex rights movement.

Concerned about dangerous effects of this model of treatment, intersex advocates pushed for reforms in care protocols. As the first and most prominent intersex advocacy organization, the Intersex Society of North America (ISNA) has been hailed as central to the struggle for intersex rights. The group was formed to fight for those harmed by their experiences with doctors and was "devoted to systemic change to end shame, secrecy, and unwanted genital surgeries for people born with an anatomy that someone decided is not standard for male or female" (ISNA, 2008a). It has since been joined by a growing group of other activists, who have pushed for alternative treatment regimens and more sympathetic perspectives. Over time, their advocacy has produced changes in medical norms. From their work, the third paradigm of intersex care, evidence-based medicine, has emerged.

EVIDENCE-BASED MEDICINE

Evidence-based medicine (EBM) seeks to integrate into clinical practice the best clinical research evidence and values (e.g., Sackett, Strauss, Richardson,

Ravenberg, & Haynes, 2000; Masic, Miokovic, & Muhamedagic, 2008). Adherents argue, "[t]he most important reason for practising EBM is to improve quality of care through the identification and promotion of practices that work, and the elimination of those that are ineffective or harmful" (Akobeng, 2005, p. 837).

Although EBM has been practiced since the 1990s, it was not generally applied to the context of intersex care until 2005, when 50 international experts on intersex-related issues attended a conference to build consensus on appropriate treatment protocols for individuals with intersex variations. The conference resulted in the 2006 publication of the "Consensus Statement on the Management of Intersex Disorders," which encouraged reliance on the best available evidence when diagnosing and managing individuals with intersex variations. Specifically, the consensus called for a shift in nomenclature and adoption of new clinical management guidelines.

Arguing that historical terms such as "intersex," and "pseudohermaphrodite" were "potentially pejorative" and "confusing to practitioners and parents" (Lee, Houk, Faisal Ahmed, & Hughes, 2006, para. 2), consensus participants proposed the adoption of "Disorders of Sex Development" (DSD). DSD, they argued, was more clinically precise and the corresponding classification system would be flexible enough to incorporate new information as clinical research developed.

In addition to the language change, consensus participants adopted several "general concepts of care," including open communication with patients and parents, and reliance on an experienced multidisciplinary team (MDT) for an immediate, thorough evaluation and long-term care management. The guidelines required all individuals to receive a gender assignment based on the best evidence available, which includes "the diagnosis, genital appearance, surgical options, need for life long replacement therapy, the potential for fertility, views of the family, and sometimes the circumstances relating to cultural practices" (Lee et al., 2006, para. 16).

The consensus differed from the previous two paradigms in its conception of gender. Rather than being essential or natural, as was believed by true sex adherents, or based on socialization, as believed by followers of Money, gender, according to consensus participants, was influenced by both. Lee et al. (2006) explains, "[p]sychosexual development is influenced by multiple factors such as exposure to androgens, sex chromosome genes, and brain structure, as well as social circumstance and family dynamics" (para. 4). Unlike previous paradigms, being gay or lesbian was not indication of incorrect gender assignment.

In concurrence, consensus participants, along with the ISNA, developed a handbook intended "to assist health care professionals in the…diagnosis, treatment…and support [of] children born with…(DSDs)" (Consortium on the Management of Disorders of Sex Development, 2006, p. 1). One chapter encourages doctors to reassure parents that clinicians are working to determine the child's gender, that the doctors will communicate with the parents once tests have been completed and that doctors should recommend being open and honest about the child's situation with friends and family to avoid a sense of shame and secrecy. The chapter acknowledges that some parents are concerned that their child may be gay and encourages doctors to tell parents that there is no any way to predict any child's sexual orientation and then affirm that the child is going to be fine:

> What we do know is that your child is always going to your child, and that this child is very lovable. The most important thing you can do is to take care of yourself and to provide this child love and honesty, and to have faith that he or she is going to do well in the world. (p. 30)

Addressing changes since the 2005 conference, consensus participants drafted an update in 2016 (Lee et al., 2016). They argued clinical evaluation standards have improved and MDTs have improved overall quality of life for many individuals with DSDs. Importantly, external sources have validated some of the consensus's successes. First, Human Rights Watch (2017) argues that specialists in intersex health have started to acknowledge there are gaps in data regarding intersex treatment. They acknowledge there has been insufficient evidence showing either harm from growing up with atypical genitals or benefits of genital surgeries. As a result, many medical practitioners have begun to concede that "parents may prefer to leave their child's body intact as a way of preserving the person's health, sexual function, fertility options, autonomy, and dignity" (p. 8). Some in the medical field, like the American Medical Association, have recommended that, except in the case of life-threatening circumstances, doctors should defer surgical intervention until the child is able to participate in decision-making (Dalke, 2017). Katharine Dalke, a practicing physician with Complete Androgen Insensitivity Syndrome, also notes that since the adoption of the consensus, "Withholding medical information…is no longer standard" (para. 15). Finally, others, like Hughes (2008), have argued that the adoption of the new nomenclature has helped doctors develop more accurate taxonomies and more aptly discuss different variations.

Despite these improvements, many are calling for further change. They note that the consensus stops short of a moratorium on non-essential genital surgeries on infants. Further, the consensus perpetuates the notion that intersex is a medical problem requiring a medical response. By selecting the term "disorder" and adopting guidelines for prompt and thorough medical evaluation, the consensus limits the potential for intersex individuals or their parents to deny treatment. This is because "the word 'disorder' implies there is something wrong...Intersex, in most cases, is not life-threatening, and is only life-limiting because society, and medicine, treat it as a disorder" (AISSG, 2011, para. 9). They argue that understanding intersex as disorder is dangerous because it legitimates invasive medical interventions.

Further, the evidence-based model maintains the supremacy of doctors making decisions for and about intersex people. Consensus participants consulted few intersex people before changing terms and only two individuals with intersex variations participated in the conference (AISSG, 2011, para. 11). As was the case in earlier models, this paradigm maintains doctors' authority.

Finally, the consensus limits individuals who identify outside of the traditional gender binary. OII argues there are more than two sexes. "There is a third, a fourth, even a fifth sex, etc. within a continuum from very female to very male" (OII, n.d., Q3). As such, some intersex individuals may identify outside of traditional categories of male and female. "Disorder of Sex Development" perpetuates reliance on the binary two-sex system by assuming that there are only two naturally occurring groups and others are disordered. Reliance on such gender essentialism erases the experiences and bodies of those who do not clearly fit into either category. Imposition of the DSD label and early gender assignment by medical professionals thus makes selection of an alternative sex category shameful and wrong.

CONCLUSION

Beginning with the true sex paradigm in the late nineteenth century, intersex has been treated primarily as a medical problem. Although each model sought to improve upon shortcomings of the previous, they share several attributes, two of which stand out.

First, all paradigms allow unneeded surgeries. Although the third paradigm discourages medically unnecessary surgeries, it stops short of a moratorium and allows doctoral discretion in determining when surgery should occur. A moratorium on procedures that could be delayed until an individual is old enough to make an informed decision is necessary to ensure the right to bodily self-determination.

Second, all paradigms rely centrally on the doctor and the belief that intersex is primarily a medical issue. Given the long history of medical mismanagement of intersex people, it is wise to consider the implications of giving disproportionate power to the medical establishment. The ability of a single group to dictate nomenclature and what is considered proper response should give pause.

These common attributes found in each paradigm have had a deleterious effect on the relationships between doctors and individuals with intersex variations. Many parents have reported that doctors made them feel unreasonable when they resisted doctors' recommendations or asked questions and many intersex individuals have reported feeling stigmatized and shamed in their interactions with doctors (HRW, 2017). The result, according to Kimberly Zieselman (2017), who learned she was intersex at age 41, is that "it is sadly common for intersex adults to avoid health care providers because of the difficult experiences we've had as children. That puts us at risk of poor health outcomes" (para. 9). It is clear that the heavy imposition of doctors and continued reliance on "corrective" procedures prevents healthy lifelong relationships with doctors. Only a shift away from the medicalization of intersex can reverse this trend.

REFERENCES

AISSG. (2011). *DSD terminology*. Retrieved from http://www.aissg.org/DEBATES/DSD.HTM#Start

Aliabadi, S. A. (2004). Gender assignment surgery for intersex infants: How the substantive due process right to privacy both supports and opposes a moratorium. *Virginia Journal of Social Policy & the Law, 12*(1), 170–196.

Akobeng, A. K. (2005). Principles of evidence based medicine. *Archives of Disease in Childhood, 90*(8), 837–840.

Blackless, M., Charuvastra, A., Derryck, A., Fausto-Sterling, A., Lauzanne, K., & Lee, E. (2000). How sexually dimorphic are we? *American Journal of Human Biology, 12*, 140–170.

Carpenter, M. (2018). The "normalization" of intersex bodies and "othering" of intersex identities in Australia. *Journal of Bioethical Inquiry, 15*(2), 1–9. https://doi.org/10.1007/s11673-018-9855-8

Colapinto, J. (2006). *As nature made him: The boy who was raised as a girl*. New York, NY: HarperCollins.

Consortium on the Management of Disorders of Sex Development. (2006). *Clinical guidelines for the management of disorders of sex development in childhood*. Rohnert Park, CA: ISNA.

Dalke, K. B. (2017, September 12). Why intersex patients need the truth and doctors need to listen. *The Nation*. Retrieved from https://www.thenation.com/article/why-intersex-patients-need-the-truth-and-doctors-need-to-listen/

Dewhurst, C. J., & Gordon, R. R. (1969). *The intersexual disorders*. London: Balliere, Tindall, and Cassell.

Diamond, M. (2007) 'Is it a boy or is it a girl?' Intersex children reshape medical practice. *Science & Spirit, 18*(4), 36–38.

Diamond, M., & Beh, H. G. (2006). The right to be wrong: Sex and gender decisions. In S. Sytsma (Ed.), *Ethics and intersex* (pp. 103–113). Dordrecht: Springer.

Dreger, A. D. (1998). *Hermaphrodites and the medical invention of sex*. London: Harvard University.

Dreger, A. D. (1999). *Intersex in the age of ethics*. Hagerstown, MD: University Publishing.

Dreger, A. D. (n.d). *Shifting the paradigm of intersex treatment*. Retrieved from http://www.isna.org/pdf/compare.pdf

Feder, E. K. (2002). Doctor's orders: Parents and intersexed children. In E. Feder Kittay & E. K. Feder (Eds.), *The subject of care: Feminist perspectives on dependency* (pp. 294–320). Lanham, MD: Rowman and Littlefield Publishers.

Gender and Health Collaborative Curriculum. (2012). *Gender and sexual diversity: Evolution of intersexuality*. Retrieved from http://www.genderandhealth.ca/en/modules/sexandsexuality/gss-historical-perspectives-02.jsp

Griffiths, D. A. (2018). Diagnosing sex: Intersex surgery and 'sex change' in Britain 1930–1955. *Sexualities, 21*(3), 476–495. https://doi.org/10.1177/1363460717740339

Hird, M. J. (2000). Gender's nature: Intersexuality, transsexualism and the 'sex'/'gender' binary. *Feminist Theory, 1*, 347–364.

Hughes, I. A. (2008). Disorders of sex development: A new definition and classification. *Best Practice & Research Clinical Endocrinology & Metabolism, 22*(1), 119–134.

Human Rights Watch. (2017, July). *"I want to be like nature made me": Medically unnecessary surgeries on intersex children in the US*. New York, NY: Human Rights Watch.

Intersex Society of North America. (2008a). *Homepage*. Retrieved from http://www.isna.org/

Intersex Society of North America. (2008b). *How common is intersex?* Retrieved from http://www.isna.org/faq/frequency

Intersex Society of North America. (2008c). *What's the history behind the intersex rights movement?* Retrieved from http://www.isna.org/faq/history

Intersex Society of North America. (2008d). *What's wrong with the way intersex has been traditionally treated?* Retrieved from http://www.isna.org/faq/concealment

Karkazis, K. (2008). *Fixing sex: Intersex, medical authority, and lived experience*. Durham, NC: Duke University Press.

Kessler, S. J. (1990). The medical construction of gender: Case management of intersexed infants. *Signs, 16*, 3–26.

Lee, P. A., Houk, C. P., Faisal Ahmed, S., & Hughes, I. A. (2006). Consensus statement on management of intersex disorders. *Pediatrics, 118*(2), e488–e500.

Lee P. A., Nordenström, A., Houk C. P., Ahmed, S. F., Auchus, R., Baratz A., ... Witchel, S. (2016). Global disorders of sex development update since 2006: Perceptions, approach and care. *Hormone Research in Paediatrics, 85*, 158–180. https://doi.org/10.1159/000442975

Mak, G. (2005). "So we must go behind even what the microscope can reveal:" The hermaphrodite's "self" in medical discourse at the start of the twentieth century. *GLQ, 11*(1), 65–94.

Masic, I., Miokovic, M., & Muhamedagic, B. (2008). Evidence based medicine: New approaches and challenges. *Acta Informatica Medica: Journal of the Society for Medical Informatics of Bosnia & Herzegovina, 16*(4), 219–225.

Money, J., & Ehrhardt, A. A. (1972). *Man & woman, boy & girl: Differentiation and dimorphism of gender identity from conception to maturity.* Baltimore, MD: Johns Hopkins University.

OII. (n.d.). *Intersex FAQ.* Retrieved from http://www.intersexualite.org/FAQ_English.html

Preves, S. E. (2003). *Intersex and identity: The contested self.* New York, NY: Rutgers.

Reis, E. (2005). Impossible hermaphrodites: Intersex in America, 1620–1960. *Journal of American History -Bloomington, 92*(2), 411–441.

Reis, E. (2012). *Bodies in doubt: An American history of intersex.* Baltimore, MD: Johns Hopkins University.

Rubin, D. A. (2017). *Intersex matters: Biomedical embodiment, gender regulation, and transnational activism.* Albany, NY: SUNY Press.

Sackett, D. L., Strauss, S. E., Richardson W. S., Ravenberg, W., & Haynes, R. B. (2000). *Evidence-based medicine: How to practice and teach EBM.* London: Churchill-Livingstone.

Tamar-Mattis, A. (2006). Exceptions to the rule: Curing the law's failure to protect intersex infants. *Berkeley Journal of Gender, Law, and Justice, 21*, 59–110.

Zieselman, K. (2017, October 26). In the intersex community, we're desperate for quality care. Doctors aren't listening. *Stat.* Retrieved from https://www.statnews.com/2017/10/26/intersex-medical-care/

PART 6

TRANSGENDER RELATIONSHIPS

CAREY JEAN SOJKA

21. TRANS RELATIONSHIPS AND THE TRANS PARTNERSHIP NARRATIVE

In college, I found myself in a relationship with someone who is transgender, and in my desire to better understand the relationship, I sought out resources and research about experiences like mine. However, at the time, there were still very few. Despite being a bit frustrating and disappointing, this lack of information propelled me to begin a deeper search of what little I could find, including online sources, books, articles, and conferences where I might learn more. Being left with more questions than answers, I then decided to pursue my own research by interviewing other partners of trans people to find out more about how people navigate relationships in which at least one person is transgender.

Since that time, we now have more information about what it can mean to partner with someone who is trans. There has been quite a bit more research; scholars have addressed issues such as how inequities are a part of many trans relationships (Brown, 2007; Pfeffer, 2010; Ward, 2010), how trans relationships often involve identity negotiations (Brown, 2009, 2010; Lenning, 2009; Pfeffer, 2017; Ward, 2009; Whittley, 2013), and how these relationships sometimes involve particular challenges (Lenning and Buist, 2013; Pfeffer, 2017). There are now also many online listservs, social media groups, vlogs, and blogs that address trans sexualities, trans intimacies, trans relationships, and the experiences of the partners of trans people. One result of this increasing information in our society, though, is that particular and limited narratives have developed about what it means to partner with someone who is trans. The creation of these narratives can lead to silencing or ignoring the actual diversity of trans relationships.

THE TRANSGENDER NARRATIVE

A similar pattern is true for trans folks themselves. The *transgender narrative* is the societally acceptable story of being trans, a narrative that varies by culture and changes over time. The transgender narrative has coalesced

© KONINKLIJKE BRILL NV, LEIDEN, 2019 | DOI:10.1163/9789004414105_022

from a variety of sources such as medicine, media, government, trans folks themselves, and trans people's families and communities. The transgender narrative suggests what it supposedly should mean to be trans, often limiting the diverse, lived experiences of people who do or would identify with this term. Particularly, this narrative is often focused on a gender binary model of 'curing' gender dysphoria through medical intervention such as hormones and surgeries and using gatekeepers, or professionals in psychiatry and medicine, to determine who is 'truly' trans.

The trans narrative has implications for trans partnerships. For instance, in the 1990s and before, many trans people were denied medical care such as hormones or gender-confirming surgeries unless it was deemed that they would be heterosexual after transitioning. The narrative determined that the correct way to be transgender was to be heterosexual, even though trans people in reality have diverse sexualities. Another aspect of the trans narrative is that dysphoria is often considered central to trans experience and thus to trans people's intimate relationships. While some trans people do experience dysphoria, others may not or do not experience it the same way.

The problem with the trans narrative is that it limits the assumptions about trans people to reflect only certain people's lives over time. Overall, the trans narrative has often been created from white normativity and ethnocentrism, classism, and heteronormativity (Valentine, 2007), and it has also historically focused on transfemininity, a focus which contributes to and is built on its articulation of trans genders as less authentic than cis genders and of femininity as less authentic than masculinity (Serano, 2007).

METHODS AND SAMPLE

My research with the partners of transgender people involved 35 in-depth, semi-structured interviews with people who were currently partnered with someone who is trans or gender variant. Participants had diverse identities and experiences, but despite their differences, they had a few similarities in common: they had all been in a relationship with someone who is trans or gender variant for at least 6 months, their partner had transitioned in some way, whether socially and/or medically, during their relationship, and they all currently lived in the United States.

I used purposive snowball sampling to find participants and then conducted interviews by phone, by video conferencing, and in person. Each interview began with the person's story of their relationship and continued with a focus on their embodiment and experiences. During the interviews, I did not specifically ask for their identity markers; instead, I asked participants to *describe* their own and their partner's experiences of gender, sexuality, and race. Therefore, these descriptions are not easily categorizable. Of the 35 participants, only four identified as heterosexual, but even of those participants, some qualified their sexuality (e.g. "heterosexual with a twist"). More had identified as heterosexual prior to their partner transitioning in some way. Participants claimed racial identities as white (n = 29), black (n = 2), multiracial (n = 1), Mexican American (n = 1), Indian (South Asian, n = 1), and Hispanic (n = 1). Twenty-four relationships were monoracial, and eleven relationships were interracial. Participants also often discussed complex gender identities, but at the risk of oversimplification, the sample included approximately four men, five genderqueer or nonbinary people, and twenty-six women. While only a few participants specifically identified as trans or a related term, many other participants complicated their gender identity beyond a simple gender conforming/gender non-conforming binary.

The transition experiences of the partners of participants that occurred during the relationship varied and overlapped. Among the trans and gender variant partners, fourteen people came out as trans during the middle of the relationship, fourteen people started to live "full-time" in their gender identity during the relationship, sixteen people started hormone therapies during the relationship (and an additional two stopped or paused hormone therapies during), and twenty people had at least one gender-confirming surgery during the relationship. Many partners of the research participants had experienced some aspects of transition prior to the start of the relationship, and nineteen partners had either tentative or concrete plans for gender transition-related changes in the future.

THE TRANS PARTNERSHIP NARRATIVE

By talking with the partners of trans folks, I found that we do not only have a problem with a limiting transgender narrative; we also have a problem with the narrative specifically about trans people's relationships, one that is not only about trans people, but also about those who partner with them. I call this the *trans partnership narrative*, which draws from aspects of the broader trans narrative but has a specific focus on and significance for relationships involving transgender people. It provides information about trans people's desire, sexuality, and relationship experiences, and occasionally addresses the experiences of people who partner with someone who is trans.

Through the interviews, a trans partnership narrative emerged that was derived not from participants' actual experiences but from their references to broader cultural and subcultural understandings of these types of relationships which they had learned through media, family, friends, work, and most often, from their connections with trans and trans partner communities through trans-related friend networks, conferences, support groups, or online forums. They often referenced this narrative in their effort to emphasize that their own experience deviated from the common story, demonstrating the narrowness of the narrative and the ways it restricts a diverse understanding of trans partnership experiences. In this way, participants both articulated common themes of the trans partnership narrative as well as their actual experiences partnering with a trans person. Participants thus found the trans partnership narrative partial and problematic, which parallels the limitations of the trans narrative. Investigating this narrative reveals how it "[forms] specific mechanisms of knowledge and power" (Foucault, 1990, p. 103). These mechanisms were highlighted by participants, who found that the trans partnership narrative is more negative than their own experiences, that it is lacking in useful information for how to navigate trans relationships, and that it often centers trans experience at the expense of understanding non-transitioning or non-trans-identified partners.

Three different participants in the study called aspects of the trans partnership narrative "horror stories," implying that this narrative suggests danger or difficulty for a non-transitioning partner. Indeed, there are not many positive aspects of the trans partnership narrative, despite the many positive experiences of participants in this research. This narrative is known well enough that deviations from it may be understood as a surprise; one participant, Janice,[1] mentioned that, upon discovering that the trans partnership narrative did not apply to her relationship, it "surprise[ed] the hell out of her." Her response indicates how much this narrative becomes entrenched in our understanding of trans lives.

CHARACTERISTICS OF THE TRANS PARTNERSHIP NARRATIVE

Some of the major characteristics of the trans partnership narrative that emerged from this research involved issues around dysphoria, sexuality and identity shifts, difficulties with embodied changes, challenges and trauma, and centering trans experience.

Dysphoria

Dysphoria was a subject that came up quite frequently in these interviews. According to participants, the trans partnership narrative they had learned suggested that dysphoria is central to the trans experience, that it negatively impacts sexual and intimate connections, that dysphoria means that particular body parts that may often be part of sexual or intimate engagement between partners are off limits, and that, if body parts do become off-limits during or because of a transition, the non-transitioning partner will mourn or grieve this loss. Some participants did experience aspects of this through their relationship, but many others noted that they had positive and fulfilling sexual relationships or that their partner did not express dysphoria at all about supposedly gendered body parts during intimate or sexual interactions. Even when particular aspects of bodies were avoided during sexual encounters, it did not necessarily impact sexual intimacy negatively.

One participant in my study, Dana, was partnered with a transfeminine person, Kendall. Dana and Kendall also had a transfeminine child who identified as a girl. Dana shared that when Kendall came out to her as transfeminine, she had expected Kendall to experience dysphoria that would negatively affect their sexual relationship. Dana remarked, "I've asked [Kendall] several times too, because…that's the only narrative I've heard." She noted that both she and Kendall intentionally tried to interrupt the dysphoria narrative for their daughter and to teach her that, for instance, "You can be a girl with a penis." However, Dana said that when it came to her relationship with her partner, she had more difficulty refuting the narrative and noted that "I was projecting this gender dysphoria narrative on Kendall" who was not experiencing it. The concept of dysphoria is central to the transgender narrative, but for Dana, at least, the particular implications of dysphoria from the trans partnership narrative were even more difficult for her to counter.

Sexuality and Identity Shifts

A second aspect of the trans partnership narrative is the idea that transition creates sexuality shifts and changing desire both for a trans person and a non-transitioning partner. One of the most common examples of this is the idea that transition changes a trans person's sexuality, particularly that trans men who dated or desired women before become gay after transition, and trans women who dated or desired women before would become straight after transition. While many trans people experience shifts in who or how they desire through a transition, many others do not, and a number of the participants were happily surprised that their partner still desired them through a transition. Erica said of her partner, Jake, "I was terrified when he starting transitioning that he was going to become gay....That was one of my biggest fears: 'What if he turns gay and leaves me?'" Erica noted that Jake expressed skepticism of this aspect of the trans partnership narrative as he was going through various aspects of his transition, and that this helped relieve Erica's fears.

There is also the idea that a transitioning partner will leave their partner after transition for someone whose sexuality identity better matches their gender identity (e.g. a trans man leaving a lesbian woman for a straight woman), which was also related to the idea that sexuality identification for a non-transitioning partner will become an issue if they do not change their social identification to match their partner's gender post-transition (e.g. a lesbian-identifying person partnering with a trans man will be a problem because her identity invalidates his). For instance, Janice's experiences, discussed below in relation to centering trans experience, aligned with this. However, many participants in this study maintained relationships where their sexuality identities did not necessarily "match," particularly straight trans men with queer/lesbian cis women and queer/lesbian trans women with straight cis women. Participants instead found new ways of defining those sexuality identities and the meanings associated with them.

Finally, the trans partnership narrative includes the idea that a non-transitioning partner will become controlling and prohibit a partner from transitioning if it threatens their identity. While this certainly can and does happen, it is by no means a given in relationships like these. Many partners of trans people, including the majority of the people in my study, are open to and accepting of a partner's transition.

Difficulties with Embodied Changes

A third aspect of the trans partnership narrative is that any embodied changes associated with gender transition are rife with difficulty. This included the ideas that bottom surgeries are dangerous because they threaten a loss of sexual sensation or that starting hormones, particularly testosterone, will make a relationship more difficult because testosterone supposedly changes personality traits such as increasing irritability or aggression. Again, while some people experience aspects of gender transition in this way, a number of participants in the study remarked that their own relationships countered this narrative. Many found that their partner having bottom surgery positively impacted their sexual relationship. Additionally, some of the partners of transmasculine people who started testosterone during the relationship noted that their partner actually became calmer, not more irritable or more aggressive, when they started hormones, which the participants attributed to their partner's hormones aligning with their gender identity. Sherri, who was partnered with T, was one such person; she noted that, "I don't see the irritability on the testosterone, as some people talk about." While she notes that this is something that "people talk about" happening, it contradicts her own experience of her partner's transition.

Challenges and Trauma

A fourth aspect of the trans partnership narrative is simply that partnering with a trans person, especially through a transition, is a challenging, traumatic, and sometimes impossible task. Participants in this study were happy to refute this aspect of the narrative. Some said that, while they heard that it was expected it would be difficult to change their use of their partner's name or pronouns, it was actually very easy for them. Others said that they had heard that partnering with someone who was transitioning would be traumatic, both through the internal workings of the relationship as well as through other difficulties such as losing family or friends. Still others noted that many people had said their relationship, particularly if they were married, would not survive a transition. Similar to the other aspects of the trans partnership narrative, while this does happen for some relationships, this is far from the norm, and presenting it as the typical narrative creates limited frameworks both for people who do not experience it as well as for people who do. Maria, who was partnered with Rain, said that, while her partner coming out as trans did affect her relationship with her mother, it was more about her mother than it was about her partner being trans. Maria said, "I hear so many horror stories [about trans relationships]. This thing with my mom is bad, but that's kind of par for the course with her. It wasn't a super great relationship to begin with. It wasn't horribly traumatic for me to have this happen." Thus, Maria says that even though something negative did come about in relation to her family and her partner, it was neither a horror story nor a traumatic experience.

Centering Trans Experience

A final aspect of the trans partnership narrative is that it centers trans people's experience. Unlike many of the other aspects of the trans partnership narrative, this was one that participants often felt reflected their experience in some way. However, it was precisely the narrative itself that typically caused the difficulties for participants. One participant called this the *classic trans partner problem*, or the expectation that the partners of trans people need to prioritize their partner's needs above their own, for a trans partner to assert their needs or identities as significantly more important, and/or for others outside of the relationship (particularly trans and trans partner communities) to prioritize trans experience over and *at the expense of* a cis or non-transitioning partner's experiences. An example of this part of the narrative is that, if a non-transitioning partner worries about their partner no longer desiring them after transition or about a potential loss of their own sexual identity or sexual community because of their partner's transition, they are being unsupportive.

This aspect of the trans partnership narrative can likely be attributed to a few factors. First, at least as compared to straight and LGBQ+ identities, the trans experience is conceptualized as highly individualistic. In part, this is because a trans experience is typically not relational in the same way as straight or other queer identities. For instance, a lesbian identity is defined not just by the self, but in reference to desiring another, in this case, typically desiring someone with a particular gender identity or expression as woman or feminine. The trans experience, in contrast, is defined by self-experiences of gender, not by desire for others. Thus, when it comes to the people who partner with trans people, their experiences do not fit within the typical trans frameworks provided.

Another reason is that, for many people, a trans experience, and particularly a gender transition, can be taxing in multiple ways. Misgendering alone is a microaggression many trans people deal with on a regular basis (Nordmarken, 2014), and embodied changes and corresponding changes in navigating others' perceptions of the self can be difficult. In many, many ways, the experience of transition is generally much more difficult than the experience of partnering with someone who is transitioning, so it would make sense that the focus should be on a transitioning partner. The classic trans partner problem occurs, however, when a non-transitioning partner puts their own needs and desires aside nearly completely during a partner's transition, and when the focus is on a trans or transitioning partner at the expense of the well-being of a cis or non-transitioning partner.

One primary way in which the classic trans partner problem asserts itself is through identity. Many participants in this study suggested that they felt pressure, either from their partner or from other people, to change how they identified their sexuality based on their partner's gender. For instance, Janice stated that many people, including friends and her partner, were pressuring her to identify herself as bisexual instead of a lesbian because her partner is a trans man. She said that while the term bisexual did not offend her because it was nothing to be ashamed of in the first place, it also was not accurate for her. From her framework, she said she is "a lesbian, but dating a boy." Her partner would even try to convince Janice that she had always desired men in addition to women, because that fit better with his understanding of her desire for him.

Another aspect of the classic trans partner problem was for partners to feel like their needs were secondary, particularly during a transition. Stella said that "I did definitely [feel] like I got lost in the process of the transition." She said she felt underappreciated during that time, and asked the question often of herself, "What about me?" Furthermore, a few participants who, during their partner's transition, asked themselves whether they would be able to stay in the relationship, said they felt guilt over even considering leaving the relationship during their partner's transition because of the potential negative consequence for their partner; their own challenges were not prioritized even by themselves. For instance, Rebecca said she had "to be brutally honest with myself like, 'Is this something you can actually do?' And it made me feel like an asshole being like, 'Am I going to be the jerk that walks out on someone who's truly becoming who they are?'" She ultimately stayed in the relationship through her partner's transition, but her self-judgment about questioning whether the relationship was right for her demonstrated her prioritizing her partner's experience over her own.

Sometimes, the classic trans partner problem showed up in more subtle ways. In closing each interview, I asked participants "What would need to change in society to make it better for *you and other people who are partnered with trans folks?*" My intention was to ask about some sense of collective experience among this diverse and non-identity-based group of people who partner with someone who is trans. Yet the answers were almost always about trans rights from an individualistic framework or a collective trans framework, about trans people and not specifically about people partnered with trans folks. In other words, their suggested solutions were about making the world better for trans people, but without connecting how that would improve their own lives as partners. Rarely did partners actually answer in ways that included their own experiences or needs. Some of the themes that arose when partners addressed their own perspectives included relationship challenges and how to handle them or the need for more education about partner experiences.

The optimistic aspect of the classic trans partner problem is that many participants who had experienced it also noted that, after significant changes associated with an active gender transition waned, they found that the relationship found or returned to a more equitable balance. Rebecca was one such participant, who said that while her partner was "struggling so much with how he identified and didn't really have the space or the time to deal with how I was struggling with my identity" during his transition, they later found better ways to mutually communicate their needs and to reciprocally support each other. This suggests that, while the trans partnership narrative focuses on trans experience at the expense of cis and non-transitioning identities, it may be more accurate to state that there is a focus on transitioning experience, which is often experienced as more temporary. As such, partners of transitioning folks may desire or require outside support for themselves during this time.

CONSEQUENCES OF THE TRANS PARTNERSHIP NARRATIVE

The trans partnership narrative is problematic not because it is untrue in some ways; indeed, it exists precisely because it is true in certain instances. For example, the story of trans men who desired women as sexual partners pre-transition and men post-transition exists because this does occur, and with enough regularity to become a part of the narrative. Yet the narrative should be examined for its potentially harmful consequences.

One such consequence is that the majority of the trans partnership narrative is negative. Presented holistically or even in partial combination, it perpetuates the message that the experience of partnering with a transitioning trans person will be filled with pitfalls and hardships with very few positive aspects. One of the reasons that participants actively refuted this narrative was that this expression of trans partnerships as negative did not fit with their own experience. While some people in this study experienced challenges in relation to their partner's transition, many others did not, and those more positive experiences are gravely lacking from the stories we tell about trans partnerships in our society. Lora, who was partnered with Tanner, said of her experience that "it was definitely positive across the board. Positive across the board. I mean from work to personal to…you couldn't have asked for a better transition. And it's nice to have a positive kind of story like that."

Second, also lacking from this narrative are useful tools for partners in handling situations that arise outside of the relationship. Maria said that, "I feel like everything I see that's meant for partners is so that they can cope with the lies and deceit and upheaval of their trans partners. I walk in [to trans partner spaces], I'm like, 'No, I'm cool with it. I need to know how to deal with everybody else.'" Many partners gravitate toward trans and trans partner community in an effort to learn how to navigate the complexities of their partnership, including how to navigate the social world beyond their relationship. However, ideas for how to handle other people's reactions to a trans relationship are more often than not secondary.

A third important aspect to note about this collective trans partnership narrative is that many of the aspects of the trans partnership narrative center the trans person as opposed to the experience of a partner of a trans person. Again, while it is critically important to address trans people's experiences of relationships, the experiences of cis or non-transitioning partners are also important to consider, both for their own sake as well as to better understand and support trans and transitioning people in relationships.

As we continue to learn more about relationships involving transgender people, we would do well to be cautious about the consequences of the types of information we share. Whose stories are heard? Whose stories are ignored or silenced or discounted? The problem with the trans partnership narrative is precisely that it functions as The Narrative. The continued emergence of new information about trans relationships gives us the opportunity to critique the limitations of the trans partnership narrative and to shift toward a more inclusive understanding of these relationships as truly diverse.

NOTE

[1] Participants chose their own pseudonyms for this research.

REFERENCES

Brown, N. (2007). Stories from outside the frame: Intimate partner abuse in sexual-minority women's relationships with transsexual men. *Feminism and Psychology, 17*(3), 373–393.

Brown, N. (2009). 'I'm in transition too': Sexual identity renegotiation in sexual-minority women's relationships with transsexual men. *International Journal of Sexual Health, 21*(1), 61–77.

Brown, N. (2010). The sexual relationships of sexual-minority women partnered with trans men: A qualitative study. *Archives of Sexual Behavior, 39*, 561–572.

Foucault, M. (1990). *The history of sexuality: An introduction* (Vol. 1, R. Hurley, Trans.). New York, NY: Vintage Books.

Lenning, E. (2009). Moving beyond the binary: Exploring the dimensions of gender presentation and orientation. *International Journal of Social Inquiry, 2*(2), 3954.

Lenning, E., & Buist, C. L. (2013). Social, psychological and economic challenges faced by transgender individuals and their significant others: Gaining insight through personal narratives. *Culture, Health & Sexuality, 15*(1), 44–57.

Nordmarken, S. (2014). Microaggressions. *Transgender Studies Quarterly, 1*(1–2), 129–134.

Pfeffer, C. (2010). 'Women's work'? Women partners of transgender men doing housework and emotion work. *Journal of Marriage and Family, 72*, 165–183.

Pfeffer, C. (2017). *Queering families: The postmodern partnerships of cisgender women and transgender men*. New York, NY: Oxford University Press.

Serano, J. (2007). *Whipping girl: A transsexual woman on sexism and the scapegoating of femininity.* Emeryville, CA: Seal Press.

Valentine, D. (2007). *Imagining transgender: An ethnography of a category*. Durham, NC: Duke University Press.

Ward, J. (2010). Gender labor: Transmen, femmes, and collective work of transgression. *Sexualities, 13*(2), 236–254.

Whittley, C. T. (2013). Trans-kin undoing and redoing gender: Negotiating relational identity among friends and family of transgender persons. *Sociological Perspectives, 56*(4), 597–621.

ALITHIA ZAMANTAKIS

22. "I TRY NOT TO PUSH IT TOO FAR"

*Trans/Nonbinary Individuals Negotiating Race and
Gender in Intimate Relationships*

INTRODUCTION

Sitting across from Fey in my apartment, we began the interview by discussing cisgender people's perceptions and understandings of trans-ness. I ask her, "Do you…feel like cis people in general have shitty perceptions of trans people?" She responds, "I don't feel like a lot of cis people understand it. I feel like if they did understand gender on a personal level, they wouldn't identify as cis." Jane Ward (2010) discusses how gender operates as a currency of exchange between bodies through sexuality. Within intimate relationships, individuals engage in strategic performances of gender identity and/or expression to give gender to significant others, intimate friends, and hook-ups (SOFHUs). Giving gender functions as a relational mechanism of diminishing or helping actualize another person's gender identity. Based on my analysis, I find that my participants engage in a form of pre-emptive gender labour to protect themselves from transphobic/racist violence that simultaneously protects cis people from realizing the socially constructed reality of their own genders. While Fey's comment on cis people's understandings of gender erases the intimate experiences and knowledge cis women of colour have of gender, her remark points out that the work cis people potentially do to express love, desire, and solidarity for trans/nonbinary people in their lives has potential to tear away at interpersonal and structural cissexism.

Ward's work on gender labour remains limited to the work that cisgender femmes do for trans men partners. Although it is critical to understand the work cis femmes perform in these relationships, it is equally critical that the experiences of trans/nonbinary individuals within intimate relationships are also analysed. Further, neither Ward nor Pfeffer explicitly engage with gender labour and gender negotiation as inherently racialized processes. Building off their work, I explore how trans/nonbinary people pre-emptively negotiate gender and race in the process of forming intimate relationships?

© KONINKLIJKE BRILL NV, LEIDEN, 2019 | DOI:10.1163/9789004414105_023

METHODS

To explore this question, I used photo elicitation and grounded theory (Charmaz, 2006) to analyse semi-structured, in-depth interviews with fifteen participants from November 2017 to January 2018. Participants were recruited through trans/nonbinary social media groups, word-of-mouth, and flyers posted across Metro Atlanta. I conducted interviews in Metro Atlanta and Salt Lake City, UT face-to-face and all others through Skype, Google Hangout, or phone. I performed line-by-line coding on transcripts and coded participant submitted photos of how they would dress on an "ideal date" according to how participants described the photo and its aesthetics. Interviews ranged from 37 minutes to two hours, with an average of one hour in length. Altogether, twenty-three photos were submitted.

Each of the fifteen participants identified as a gender other than that they were assigned at birth. Two of the participants are Black, one Black and Southeast Asian, one Asian/Indian, one Latino, and ten white. Eight participants were assigned female at birth (AFAB) and seven assigned male at birth (AMAB). Two participants were straight, two gay, three pansexual, three homoflexible/mostly gay, one Afrosensual, two lesbian, one bi, two queer, and one asexual/Panromantic, with several individuals using more than one term to identify their sexual orientation. Six were trans men, five trans women, one neutrois/femme, one trigender, one nonbinary trans femme, and one nonbinary/genderqueer. Interviews were conducted either face-to-face (at coffee shops or one of our residences), over web camera, or over the phone. Participants lived in states across the U.S. in the West, Midwest, and South.

DISCUSSION

Pre-emptive Labour

While Ward (2010) discusses gender labour as "actively suspending self-focus in the service of helping others achieve varied forms of gender recognition they long for" (p. 237), I focus here, instead, on gender labour as bodily and affective labour performed by trans/nonbinary individuals prior to and at the beginning of intimate relationships/encounters.

Pre-emptive labour does not occur to help others achieve gender; rather, it is for self-protection/-care and as a method of preventing time wasted on someone who ultimately is transphobic or feels "misled." Ten out of fifteen participants currently or previously used dating apps as a way to pre-screen people, whether by looking at the questions on OkCupid that ask whether you would date a trans person, by openly explaining their trans/nonbinary identity in their profile, or by intentionally identifying themselves as trans/nonbinary in identity markers to make sure that transphobic people do not message them in the first place. These individuals engaged in a large amount of back stage management of their presentation of self (Goffman, 1956) in an effort to ensure safety and to cultivate desired matches, messages, and SOFHUs. A 2017 YouGov survey found that 27% of individuals in the US are not open to being friends with a transgender person. Further, only 16, 17, and 18 percent of respondents were open to dating a transgender man, woman, or nonbinary person respectively. Given these findings, it is not surprising that trans/nonbinary individuals put tremendous amounts of energy into managing their presentation of self prior to engaging in intimacy with others who may or may not harbour similar sentiments. In addition to pre-emptive labour through dating apps, my participants engaged in bodily pre-emptive labour, changing how they dress, speak, and/or gesture through body language for the first few dates.

Each of my participants discussed engaging in pre-emptive gender labour. The individuals I interviewed discussed engaging in strategic actions, including changing how they dress, sound, and speak in order to gain access to intimacy with others. In doing so, they constructed a presentation of self that is desirable by cis people; however, they also internalized shame and reified cisnormative desirability politics. For example, I asked Mia, a white, trans lesbian if she perceived any differences between dating cis women and trans women. She responded,

> Well, a lot of times, what it boils down to is the fact that I like women. Like I literally prefer women. Now if she is trans, and she's gon' over and had the surgery and stuff, then we'll take and see what we do. But as far as, I prefer dating cis women, for the simple fact that…a woman doesn't stop very easily and you can never get enough [sex/orgasms].

Mia has not had bottom surgery and is a trans woman herself, yet she viewed cis women as more desirable than trans women. In seeking to make herself desirable to cis women, she internalized cissexist conflations of vaginas and womanhood and separated out cis women as more desirable than trans women for that reason.

Lewis, a queer/gay, Black, trans man who is primarily attracted to other men, instead of internalized cisnormative proscriptions regarding dating, complained about cis people's expectations regarding intimacy with trans people. Lewis sighed, "Cisgender people think someone's trans status is something that should be made clear, explicit, and explained up front, yet for them, their cisgender status is not assumed [to] operate the same way." This cisnormative expectation became discursively embedded within trans participants' discourse, as many used the phrasing of "disclosing my trans identity" or even "disclosing my trans status." Trans participants' internal sense of self shifted around the interactions and experiences they had with cisgender people. Despite several participants, Lewis included, critiquing the demand to continually out themselves and the conflation of being trans with having a sexually transmitted infection, their language continued to center trans-ness as a negative status that is ultimately "disclosed" at some point.

I asked Lewis about his own previous "disclosure," or explaining, of his gender to others prior to and/or when meeting them. He explained how his "disclosure" has shifted over time, primarily vis-à-vis dating apps:

> So I would put something in my profile that I was transgender and then noticing that would confuse people, because they thought I was a man who liked to wear dresses or something, and that's not what I meant. They would conflate being a cross-dresser or whatever. So then I would explicitly say, "I used to be a woman," because I find that was the clearest language of explaining what it meant. After awhile, I got tired of explaining to people, and so I would take it off my profile for awhile, just because I wanted to get to know people before I had that conversation, and I later put it back on again, but I think after awhile, I just got tired of explaining and would just limit my dating pool to those people who either were trans or were cisgender people who understood already…it was very angering for me that I constantly had to do this.

Lewis spoke of the seemingly perpetual questioning that he, and other trans/nonbinary participants, experienced when trying to date online. While I did not set out to primarily discuss intimacy through dating apps, the majority of my participants (including Lewis) spoke of pre-emptive gender labour and meeting people through apps or online dating sites. The barrage of questions and constant requirement to explain one's self may occur more often through online dating, as Lewis mentioned that people seem more likely to say "nasty things" online compared to face-to-face.

Additionally, Lewis elaborated how, despite pre-emptively outing himself online, he still received gendered and racialized messages that he felt like he *had* to respond to:

It was really interesting, because there were times when I put I was trans on my profile, and yet I still got white guys looking for Big Black Cock. And so they were just looking at my pictures and not really reading my profile, which I know happens all the time. But I would spend time creating, carefully crafting what I was gonna say in my profile and people weren't reading it, you know? I would just be annoyed; that was another thing that made me angry.

Here, Lewis spoke of the way in which pre-emptive gender labour and racial labour are not isolated mechanisms of intimate labour. Rather, they are interconnected. Lewis pre-emptively outed himself on dating apps like OkCupid to preserve his energy and prevent the need of explaining his trans-ness to others. However, people focused more selectively on his racial and gender markers and pictures and ignored the explanations in his profile. Lewis' body became a site of racialized gender fetishization with individuals not only wanting to have sex with a man or have sex with a Black person but particularly with a Black man. This fetishization is based on white-framed stereotypes of Black men with large penises available for white sexual consumption (Collins, 2005). Later in the interview, Lewis spoke of racist fetishization of his dark skin, and I asked him, "Do those ways of being fetishized and exotified in terms of the trans-ness and the Black-ness feel similarly exhausting to you or do they feel different in terms of the ways they affect you?" He explained that the racial fetishization is less frequent:

Given that I'm primarily interested in men of colour, so it's primarily who I'm engaging, and the apps that I use, particularly Jack'd, there's more men of colour on that app, so I would say overall, my engagement with white men on those apps is less frequent…I will say that I think the trans piece is more exhausting, because it's just more prevalent. Because it happens, it's happened, regardless of the race of the person I'm dating. Many cisgender men are just ignorant around trans stuff in general, and these apps primarily have cisgender men on them.

While trans/nonbinary individuals could choose to limit their dating/hook-up pool to other trans/nonbinary people, it remains harder to do so without apps explicitly allowing this option and the relatively smaller size of trans communities.

Lewis elaborated on how "there's less trans men available especially given I'm friends with a lot of trans friends, so the people I wanna date, either I'm already friends with or they're just really hard to find." Thus, despite one's intentions to prevent intimate encounters with cis people, the reality of having SOFHUs that are never cis is much more difficult to create. OkCupid now allows queer users to only see other queer people; however, a similar option is not available for trans people. Tinder allows users to filter by gender and sexual orientation; however, bisexual women, for example, will see queer women and heterosexual men as potential SOFHUs. Additionally, apps like OkCupid and Tinder, despite allowing individuals to identify by genders outside the binary, still require that individuals choose to be seen with "men" or with "women."

Dress, Body, and Voice

While the majority of participants spoke of a felt need to pre-emptively out themselves through dating apps, participants' responses to changing their voice, body, dress, and so forth for others were more contested. For example, Davis, a white, gay, trans man spoke of feeling like he had to change how he dresses before a date, but did not feel a need to change his voice. I asked Davis if, in the process of physically transitioning, he would "try to change [his] voice before it started to just naturally change from the hormones to deepen it around other people?" He responded, "Not really. It just, it wouldn't help. It just sounded like I was intentionally lowering my voice, right? So it didn't really help." His decision to not alter his voice was also reflected among other AFAB participants who stated a similar statement of not changing their voice, because it did not assist in "passing" as cis. However, when asked about changing his looks to feel attractive or to be seen as attractive, Davis responded,

> I think it's really hard to feel confident if, for example, none of my pants fit right now because I've lost so much weight. I've gone down two pant sizes, so I feel like on a basic level, I want to be wearing something that fits so I don't feel like I'm wearing my dad's clothes, so that I feel more confident around all these people that would have nice things. Like, I only have one pair of 34's right now, that's where I'm at a 34. So If I really wanna feel fancy, I'll wear my nice 34's and my button, my button-up. Like at least it makes me feel a little more confident in my, in my appearance, like I'm wearing clothes that I feel good in. I'm wearing clothes that fit. You know?

Whereas AMAB participants spoke more of a felt need to change how they dress for safety and/or desirability (8 out of 9 individuals), AFAB participants spoke more of a felt need to dress in a way that evoked confidence. Three of six trans men participants spoke of a need to evoke confidence specifically in regards to their dress. In five of the six trans men's submitted photos shared a similar pattern of style (comfortable and casual but dressed up), upright posture, either staring into the camera with a bright smile or staring off to the side with a look of self-assuredness and swagger.

Professional codes of dress and body language, whether explicitly acknowledged or not, were mapped onto trans men's photos in regard to portraying a masculine ethos of confidence. I coded these photos as "just one of the guys" (see Figure 1). Just one of the guys exemplifies a performative of dominant masculinities as a way of eliciting recognition as a "cisgender" man, safety through the privileges of cisgender manhood, and a reification of gender ideologies. Only white and Latino men exhibited this performative aesthetic.

In contrast, trans women's pictures were more likely to fall within the categories I termed "transdrogynous" (discussed in the next section; see Figure 2) or "just one of the girls" (see Figure 3). What contrasts just one of the guys/girls codes were participants' explanations of what they hoped to performatively elicit on a date. For example, Victoria, a white, bi, trans woman explained, "I would say that I'm a little more self-conscious on dates, because especially if I feel like the other person's on the fence, I don't wanna slip up or do something that I think might freak them out, you know...?" Just one of the girls photos portrayed trans women in stereotypically feminine dress, smiling yet demure. These photos included women posing with various objects around them or in their hands, almost as a subconscious attempt at reticent body language. While trans men experienced "social misrecognition"—a term Pfeffer (2017) uses to highlight the significance of moments when individuals are perceived as a gender/sex other than that with which they identify—trans women experienced fears of violence in addition to similar social misrecognition. For trans women, being misrecognized as a "man in a dress" carries implications of violence, death, and other threats regarding physical safety. For trans men, being misrecognized as a "woman" is emotionally harmful yet rarely physically threatening.

In addition to changing how they dress, trans women participants also spoke of changing their voice on first dates, as compared to trans men participants who said they never did. A change of dress alone did not elicit the safety and comfort trans women participants wanted in potentially dangerous spaces or interactions. Instead, a change of dress accompanied by a higher pitch in voice felt necessary to not make their SOFHUs uncomfortable and to prevent misgendering that made them feel further wary of the situation, as compared to trans men and transmasculine participants whom indicated a lack of necessity to change their voice to a more masculine pitch for safety reasons. Fey mentioned, "When I go on a first date or something like that, I usually change my voice. Um or [if] I'm in a new area, or I'm presenting really feminine, I will definitely change my voice without even thinking about it…I just make it higher pitch."

An additional code—"queer style"—was included for those that did not desire to reproduce cis-ness in how they dressed and behaved (see Figure 4). Queer style was more likely to be taken up by Black and/or nonbinary participants as an aesthetic of distancing oneself from hegemonic modes of being and eliciting new forms of intimacy.

Figure 1. Just one of the guys

This aesthetic included an exaggerated stylization of dress, including wearing a "masculine" suit and jacket with a space themed bow-tie and long hair, a tank-top that reads "Trans* Is Beautiful" with jewelry specifically chosen to add a touch of femininity for a trans man, or a dress and colourful lipstick on an individual with facial hair.

Figure 2. Transdrogynous

These participants differed from transdrogynous participants; they sought less gender-anonymity within androgyny and more to highlight their refusal to fit. Their body language was less reticent, more vulnerable (including fragmented shots of the body), and more open (with deep stares into the camera or joyful, candid shots).

Kade, a white, trigender individual, describes his picture as "very ostentatious." He elaborated, "There's a quirky femininity/asterisk about the way that I present with my hair that's supposed to invite that kind of fun question, like okay, why do you like this? This seems unusual." Rather than seeking to appear like a cisgender man or a cisgender woman, those that dressed in a "queer style" sought to appear specifically as trans, queer, and different. They wanted individuals not to ask them what gender they were

Figure 3. Just one of the girls

Figure 4. Queer style

but to ask themselves, why am I staring at this individual, what is drawing them to me, and what is this saying about me?

Isa, a Black, Afrosensual, neutrois/femme attempts to dress in ways that elicit new forms of intimacy. Isa explained, "It's the implied question of will you help me build this better world? Will you help me shift this paradigm? Will you help me? I'm asking you for help." Gender and dress become something done not according to accountable norms of manhood and womanhood but something to performatively evoke community.

Still, it is important to note that all but three participants mentioned engaging in a form of pre-emptive labour that served to reify cisnormative structures. Even those in the queer style category pre-emptively outed themselves or sought out ways of narrowing their pool of potential SOFHUs for protection from a transphobic world. As mentioned already, though this labour serves to protect trans/nonbinary individuals from a harmful social world, it also serves to protect cis people; in that, cis people know of the other individual's trans-ness prior to meeting and thus can choose whether or not to continue forth with interacting with them. Participants also highlight that theories of "doing gender" (West & Zimmerman, 1987) must be reconfigured to encompass the various ways in which trans/nonbinary individuals do gender, are held accountable for their doing of gender, and how their gender is interpreted differently in different contexts.

Pre-emptive Gender Labouring for What?

The reasons participants gave for engaging in pre-emptive labour fell into three main categories: desirability, safety, and trans-ness as complicating gender/sexuality.

Bruce, a white, straight, trans man, felt undesirable because of his trans-ness and wanted to be desired by cis women in particular. Prior to moving to Utah, he had tried to hide his trans identity until developing a relationship with a SOFHU. When he moved to Utah, he decided that this was a chance to begin being open about his trans-ness and that he needed to find a way to love his trans-ness, as well. He explained,

> When I moved here, I said I'd be open about it. So on my profiles, it says right on there: transgender. So I don't really have to be a ball buster. I had one girl ball her eyes out one time when I told her. Like we went on, 'cause I used to go on one date, and if I liked 'em, then I'd tell 'em before we kissed or anything, so they didn't feel like…I

don't know. So I liked her after the first date, so I told her in hopes for a second date, and she balled her eyes out. "How did this…how could this happen to me?!"

After several experiences like these, as well as several relationships that ultimately ended, Bruce felt like his trans-ness got in the way of intimacy with cis women. Earlier in the day before I interviewed him, he and his current partner, a cis, pansexual woman had broken up. He mentioned that the hardest part was that he had asked her if she would like him more if he had a "real dick." She told him no, but in previous relationships, cis women had told him, "Yes, it would be better, but I'll deal with what is." Constant reminders by cis women that he was not enough led him to be wary of intimacy. He said, "I get told that I'm hot a lot, and then, if they find out anything, it's like ew, what? No. No. No."

In addition to a feeling of lacking desirability by potential SOFHUs, trans/nonbinary individuals also engaged in pre-emptive gender labour out of a fear of transphobic interactions. Coke, an Indian, pansexual, trans woman, mentioned, "I've kind of…been really paranoid about going out on dates lately…not so much [because of] the dating itself, but the people around us. I'm worried about how people react if they see a trans woman with another trans woman out in public trying to get coffee. It makes me feel icky and unsure of what will happen." Coke only goes on dates in public areas where others will be around and able to help if a date becomes violent. She gives her address and the start and end time of dates to a friend as a precaution. Coke has cut out cis men as potential SOFHUs due to fears of safety, and she pre-emptively outs herself to further prevent any contact with potentially transphobic individuals.

Monroe, a Black and Southeast Asian, nonbinary trans femme, also highlighted the ways that they not only dress differently with potential SOFHUs, but, depending on the race/gender of the individual, they also behave differently. With queer/trans people of colour (QTPOC), they are "quick to be very open," but with white people, they are afraid to bring up racially relevant (even if not political) topics or jokes.

Previous experiences with white and/or cisgender individuals that raise safety flags, as well as the high murder rates for Black and Indigenous trans women and other trans women of colour, function to regulate trans/nonbinary individuals' behaviour, dress, and embodiment prior to and in the process of building intimate relationships. Several participants highlighted never experiencing violence themselves; however, the knowledge of how frequently racist/transphobic violence occurs makes them afraid to take any chances. Trans women participants that fell within the transdrogynous category of dress/embodiment often spoke of dressing in androgynous ways for safety.

The third reason highlighted by participants for engaging in pre-emptive labour comes out of a sense that trans-ness complicates gender and sexuality. Ahmed (2000) notes that, when an individual come into contact with another individual, both become mutually reconstituted by the other. My participants discussed how intimate interactions with trans/nonbinary individuals foster space for cis individuals to question their own gender/sexuality. The possibility that being with a trans/nonbinary individual says something about an individual's cis-ness and/or hetero-/homo-sexuality instills fear and a need for distance.

Kurt, a white, pansexual nonbinary participant told me, "I try not to push it too far" with partners. Kurt often wears shorts and a button-up, short-sleeved shirt tucked in with their hair in a ponytail on dates to appear less overtly masculine, but with partners, Kurt desires to wear "men's" suits, a chest binder, and a packer (a human-made phallic object) on dates. Earlier in the day before one of their first dates with their current partner, they had been out in public and wore a chest binder as they normally do. However, on their way to their partner's place, they realized that they still had the binder on. They anxiously hurried to slip out of the binder before arriving at their partner's place, because they were unsure how he would respond. As they and their partner's relationship progressed, Kurt began wearing a packer to bed with the partner, which "freaked him out." Over time, though, the partner has become more accepting. They are working together on a name to call Kurt that feels both masculine and feminine and the partner now compliments Kurt when they wear masculine clothing. What is particularly interesting, though, is that Kurt discussed their partner as becoming more "gender fluid" as he starts to accept their masculinity. Kurt's own genderqueer, transmasculinity has necessitated that their partner work to better desire them for their trans-ness. In the process, his own manhood, and how he conceives of it, has also begun to change.

Pre-emptive Gender Labour as Racial Labour

While white participants were quick to speak on the exhaustion of this pre-emptive labour, some were equally quick to demand similar forms of labour from potential SOFHUs of colour or to erase and minimize the labour done by potential SOFHUs of colour. Pre-emptive gender labour, as discussed in

305

previous sections, is also racialized in terms of the differential levels of safety and desirability white individuals have in comparison particularly to Black trans/nonbinary individuals and in terms of the ways in which sustaining cis-ness is also imbricated in sustaining whiteness. My focus, here, is not on separating and teasing out pre-emptive gender labour from pre-emptive racial labour. Rather, I touch on how whiteness is reproduced through discursive absence in discussions of forming and building intimate relationships.

Kurt mentioned that educating people is "exhausting," but they do it in relationships, because they want to build the relationships. However, as highlighted earlier, this process of education instils anxiety as they negotiate names, pronouns, binders, and packers. When I asked about the role race plays prior to and in the process of building relationships or hooking-up in regards to trans-ness, they stated that "Hispanic" [sic] people share a culture of "machismo," which "makes the gender stuff harder." At another point, they stated that, for Black people, trans-ness is not talked about, and thus, there are higher murder rates of Black trans women. Race became reductively boiled down to culture, and culture became the source of racial problems.

After the interview had ended, Kurt and I continued talking outside the café in which I interviewed them, and they told me in regard to people of colour, "You know, I expect with any marginalized group that people will educate me just like I educate them so that I can better actually advocate, and it's not that they owe it to me, but I can't advocate for them without knowing." There is an expectation BIPOC aid in constructing "good whites" implying that this education cannot occur otherwise.

Monroe also elucidated the point I make with Kurt's interview but from a Black/Southeast Asian positionality. Monroe feels desirable (physically, socially, and emotionally) among chosen family and QTPOC but feels consumable and undesirable by others for their work, scholarship, and body. Monroe told me that, although they date people of any race, they prefer QTPOC. They elaborated,

> I think that…intra-communally, there's a lot of trans anti-Blackness, so it's like I try to avoid ending up in spaces or with people who I feel like might not recognize the validity of Black trans issues.

Monroe added that they are wary to make it seem "like I only talk about race" when on a date with white people. When going on dates with QTPOC, Monroe is able to talk about racism and racially relevant topics, but when on dates with white people, they feel like they have to walk on eggshells. The discursive absence of race makes whiteness ostensibly present.

CONCLUSION

Throughout this chapter, I have shown how pre-emptive labour functioned for participants as a way of protecting white trans-ness, as racialized bodies can only be made discursively invisible. All participants engaged in pre-emptive gender labor through dress, voice, and pre-emptive outing, and BIPOC participants engaged in discursive regulation to protect themselves. However, their labor of self-protection allows cis-ness/whiteness to go unchallenged, and thus, unchanged.

The naturalization of cis-heteronormativity requires stability and a lack of ruptures within a binary way of being, loving, and fucking. Pre-emptive gender labour is the work trans/nonbinary individuals do, at least temporarily, to constrain themselves within the confines of cis-heteronormative, white notions of desirability in order to be desired and safe. It is a labour of temporarily giving cis-ness to themselves by asking others to read them as cis, and thus as desirable or to immediately know that they are not cis, allowing the cisgender person the option to choose whether or not they want to be intimately touched by trans-ness. This exhausting labour of having to explain oneself to others and contort one's body and voice so as to prevent harm and to foster intimacy weighs down on trans/nonbinary individuals, as the onus of comforting cis-ness/cis people is placed on them.

REFERENCES

Ahemd, S. (2000). *Strange encounters: Embodied others in post-coloniality*. New York, NY: Routledge.

Charmaz, K. (2006). *Constructing grounded theory: A practical guide through qualitative analysis*. Thousand Oaks, CA: Sage Publications.

Collins, P. H. (2005). *Black sexual politics: African Americans, gender, and the new racism*. New York, NY: Routledge.

Goffman, E. (1956). *The presentation of self in everyday life*. New York, NY: Anchor.

Pfeffer, C. A. (2017). *Queering families: The postmodern partnerships of cisgender women and transgender men*. London: Oxford.

Ward, J. (2010). Gender labor: Transmen, femmes, and collective work of transgression. *Sexualities, 13*, 236–254. doi:10.1177/1363460709359114

West, C., & Zimmerman, D. H. (1987). Doing gender. *Gender & Society, 1*, 125–151. doi:10.1177/0891243287001002002

YouGov. (2017). *U.S. transgender issues survey*. Retrieved from https://d25d2506sfb94s.cloudfront.net/cumulus_uploads/document/537rxhcloa/US%20 Results%20(Transgender%20Issues)%20025%2002.10.2017.pdf

STEF M. SHUSTER

23. GENERATIONAL GAPS OR OTHERING THE OTHER?

Tension between Binary and Non-Binary Trans People

INTRODUCTION

Dorothy sits poised at the head of a 15-person conference table in a meeting room at a private university centrally located in what I call Metromidwest, a large metropolitan area in the Midwest region of the United States. She looks around the room, and softly mutters under her breath, "I'm so sick of this shit. Why do we have to do this every meeting?" Some in attendance slightly turn towards her with knowing smiles, and subtly nod their heads in agreement. Andy had just introduced the topic for this evening's meeting of the trans coalition for Metromidwest to address recent concerns related to the upcoming pride festival and trans representation, which was lacking in the event programming and parade. Ze asked for everyone to introduce themselves by name and pronoun before the conversation began.[1] I look over to gauge zir reaction, and Andy looks mildly defeated but continues on with the introductions. Everyone in the room complies with the request, but noticeably, the gender normative presenting and older trans people more often than not suggest, "I think everyone knows what pronoun to use in reference to me."

Following the meeting, Andy and I go out to a bar to debrief. Ze has generously agreed to let me shadow the trans coalition meetings for the next few months while I am in Metromidwest. I ask zir about Dorothy's response to zir request for names and pronouns. Ze sighs, and says, "I can't really do anything about it. We need the older trans contingency to be a part of this conversation as it is a city-wide coalition. But, it is challenging and feels like they treat us like babies who don't really know what it means to be trans." This acknowledgment of generational differences from Andy's account sheds some light on tensions within trans communities where binary people may feel alienated from a growing cadre of people who are non-binary.[2] These identities are unintelligible to many, particularly given the pervasive and ever-present

© KONINKLIJKE BRILL NV, LEIDEN, 2019 | DOI:10.1163/9789004414105_024

structural and normative expectation of a two-gender system (Lucal, 1999). Meanwhile, non-binary people also feel alienated from the prevalent discourse from within trans, and academic, communities that more often than not understands "trans" as those who seek gender affirming medical interventions and the desire to stay within the binary categories of woman or man.

That trans people, like their cisgender counterparts, must negotiate a two-gender system is not a novel idea.[3] Drawing from broader cultural norms surrounding "gender," the scholarship on the social study of gender consistently demonstrates how gender, and the gender binary, is a taken-for-granted "fact" of life (Ridgeway and Correll, 2004). In trans-specific scholarship, earlier social scientists (e.g. Hines, 2007) focused attention on how trans people establish normative boundaries around who can claim a trans identity. Many scholars reinforced the notion that "trans" was equivocated with upholding the gender binary (e.g. Mason-Schrock, 1996). Yet these earlier studies are limited by small sample sizes and a historically contextualized moment when non-binary identities were not as prolific as they are in contemporary society. The nuances of how gender mitigates interactions between trans people have not been adequately addressed in the scholarship. Nor have the ways that trans people might police each other in these complicated negotiations around who, precisely, fits within a rapidly changing and broadly conceived category of "trans."

This chapter is guided by the question of what are the consequences of conflicting social norms regarding gender identification in trans communities, and how do these norms shape interactions between binary and non-binary trans people? As I will show, most of the trans people interviewed in Metromidwest explain away the conflict between these communities as a generational gap. Both groups are engaged in respectability politics (see Higginbotham, 1994) and policing each other. Non-binary people rely upon ageism and cast older binary trans people as being "too old" and "not in the know" to restrict them from non-binary spaces. At the same time, binarism is employed by binary trans people as a way to position non-binary people as "deviant" and othered, which helps uphold social expectations and restricts non-binary people from trans spaces. These (mis)understandings of one another exacerbate the tension that exists within communities of trans people.

HOW EXPECTATIONS SHAPE INTERACTIONS

Garfinkel's (1967) work on making visible the taken-for-granted assumptions in everyday life highlighted how our social world and interactions with others has a structure. Our shared understandings and expectations for how interactions should unfold make interactions possible. There are sanctions for those who violate norms. This interactional regulation to maintain social order operates in subtle, and often non-conscious, ways. Most individuals do not enter interactions with explicit goals to police others. But because these rules are embedded in cultural norms and structures, they come to shape expectations that govern interaction.

In the sociological scholarship on how gender shapes interactions, gender is understood as an institutionalized system of social practices that designates people as two significantly different categories—women and men (Ridgeway, 2009, 2011). Through interactions with other individuals, enacting these widely held beliefs of the binary gender system helps maintain them and perpetuate inequality. Hegemonic gender beliefs are at play, too, in these interactions. These beliefs include depictions of men and women defined by a narrow set of features, and incorporate gender stereotypes that serve as the cultural rules for enacting the social structure of difference and inequality (Ridgeway, 2009). People use cultural norms to inform behavior and evaluate others during interaction. Because the process happens automatically and sometimes outside the awareness of an individual, gender becomes a "ghost in the background," while other identities and activities are enacted in the foreground (Ridgeway & Correll, 2004, p. 522).

While scholars have documented how trans people are not immune to the broad-reaching effects of gender, and how it is enacted, sustained, and performed in everyday interactions (see, for example, Schilt, 2010), and others have focused on how the inclusion of trans people in lesbian and gay communities is fraught with conflict (see Stone, 2009), to date there is little existing research on intracommunity tension within trans communities that emanates, in part, from differing understandings of "gender" and who may claim a trans identity. This is surprising, to some degree, as a burgeoning literature has developed over the last decade documenting how "trans" is not a stable, coherent, or all-purpose category (Valentine, 2007). Yet more often than not, in academic scholarship and within trans communities, an assumption is that there is a unifying voice that emerges from within "a" trans community. Through interviews with trans people about their experiences with, and observing interactions in, trans communities, I build on the growing body of scholarship related to inequality that trans people experience, by elaborating on the relationship between binary and non-binary trans people in perpetuating trans oppression.

METHODS & DATA

I conducted in-depth interviews with 18 non-binary and 22 binary trans people in Metromidwest. Interviews were semi-structured to resemble conversations, rather than call-and-response exchanges. This interview structure enabled detailed accounts and reciprocity in the exchange (Riessman, 2008). Sharing my experiences with interviewees in trans community organizing and as a trans person helped establish greater rapport in the interview space and a mutually constituted narrative sharing.

The average interview length was 115 minutes. I met with interviewees at whatever location they selected. I asked broad questions related to interviewees' definitions of, and relationships to, LGBTQA+ communities and with others. The project began with an interest in the trans community, writ large. Over time, it evolved to centralize the tensions that exist within trans communities. That is, while in the field, I had a growing awareness that there was not a coherent singular trans community, but rather multiple iterations of "trans" across different communities (see Valentine, 2007, for a similar observation). These differences were often distinguished by binary and non-binary trans people inhabiting separate spaces.

I used a thematic narrative analysis to analyze the interviews. I began by coding the interviews, then observational field notes to identify underlying assumptions in each person's account regarding how gender matters in trans spaces, and to what effect. Particular cases were selected to illustrate general patterns and "mapping the contours of the interpretive process and sense-making" (Riessman, 2008, p. 57). In so doing, I focus here on two themes that emerged in analyzing the data on interactions between binary and non-binary people: (1) explaining away tension between binary and non-binary people as a generational divide; and (2) constructing some trans people as "others" in attempting to draw boundaries around trans communities and who may lay claim to a trans identity.

RESULTS

Historically, "trans" was defined as those individuals who desired to transition from one binary gender to the other. More recently in U.S. society, a proliferation of gender categories has expanded "trans" to hundreds of possibilities. Yet, not all in the trans community embrace these additional ways of understanding one's self as trans, nor recognize those who identify as trans but not within the gender binary. In what follows, I first focus on the narrative that the tension between binary and non-binary people is due to a generational divide. While a persuasive idea, the data does not reflect such simplicity. Instead, I suggest the different norms that shape binary and non-binary identification are a plausible explanation for intracommunity tension. Following this section, I then examine how binary and non-binary trans people are engaged in a process of othering each other. In so doing, I demonstrate how these efforts to restrict each other, by boundary policing, shore up uncertainty about who may claim a trans identity.

Generational Divides?

An oft-cited explanation for the conflict present in trans communities in Metromidwest was rooted in generational divides. Non-binary people expressed in a number of ways that older trans people simply did not understand or respect their desire to identify with a gender that was outside of the gender binary. As exemplified in the opening quote to this chapter, Andy, a white 24 year-old genderqueer person had suggested that Dorothy (a 77 year-old white trans woman) and other older trans people treated non-binary people like "babies" in processing through Dorothy's reaction to being asked to share gender pronouns at the start of a trans coalition meeting. Picking up on this idea of generational differences, Billy, a 29 year-old white femme genderqueer person shared,

> In Metromidwest we had a few groups who are supposedly welcoming of everyone on the gender spectrum, but those groups didn't work very well with each other. You know whenever that happens it can be a huge problem. A group or two actually imploded. Basically there was a fairly high profile trans group that had pretty broad membership, and/or personal conflicts within the group. It seemed that a lot of the tension was between older trans people, often women—because in Metromidwest trans women are more active in activism than older trans men—and younger people of all different kinds of gender identities.

While Metromidwest has had some success in organizing broad-based coalitions, as Billy and Andy both suggested, tension arose within these groups when some refused to consider non-binary people as being a part of "the" trans community.

The explanation of generational divides holds sway among non-binary people, as they frequently recounted trying to engage in city-wide coalition building among trans people, and these efforts were challenging because, from their perspective, older trans people consistently denigrated younger non-binary people. D., a black 28 year-old femme-presenting genderfluid person shared that many times, the older people have this attitude of, "Like you crazy kids, you will figure it out one day." This notion that non-binary identification represents a youthful narrative of trans, and one that will eventually give way to a binary identity, was perceived as offensive. D. continued to share that there have been efforts for reconciling these differences, to some degree. But non-binary interviewees consistently suggested that it was challenging at best, and a source of estrangement from the broader trans community, at worst. As D. commented, "There have been pretty explicit conversations where some older trans people that I have talked to, are like 'I don't get it. I don't get genderqueer. I don't know what that is. I don't get non-binary trans, I just…don't get it."

Many non-binary people used as their reference point one organization in Metromidwest that was explicitly for non-binary people, to make comparisons with how it felt in the city-wide trans organizations. Interviewees who were a part of this non-binary group recalled that it is a space where, "People can just be themselves. We don't talk over one another. We don't engage in respectability politics. And we have a lot of rules to help protect people. No one is ever expected to speak for one's group, and only from lived experience." In a current cultural landscape of safe space and widespread lists of rules for do's and don'ts, non-binary people felt safer in community spaces that had these norms in place for organizations meetings.

But, while non-binary people were quick to point to older binary trans people as the source of the problem, a different accounting of the tensions within trans communities emerged from the perspective of binary trans people. Maria, a 72 year-old Latina trans woman, acknowledged the conflict between binary and non-binary people as a generational gap, but also suggested that the norms governing these groups are fundamentally different. She shared,

> We have had social mixers with older people and younger people, but it never quite stuck. We have had a couple of younger trans people come into the meeting space, and there seems to be that wall divide of experience. We try to have a good time and let the young ones into our space because we feel an obligation to mentor them. Being trans is hard. But I have noticed that there are a lot of rules in those [non-binary] spaces. You have to speak from your own experience. Not generalize. Not make connections between people's experiences. That kind of stuff. And if you do, you get "ouched." In our groups, we just want to have conversations about life and not have to follow all of these rules.

314

Here, Maria referenced the generational gaps, but explicitly identified how the tension was not because older people were intolerant, but rather the norms in these communities were different. Norms established around speaking from one's experience and ways of communicating were cited by many of the older trans participants as difficult to bear because they were not used to following such explicit rules for interaction. These explanations pointed to structures of the rules shaping each space, rather than any given individual's fault. In some ways, then, while often invisible to many quick to point the finger at older trans people, these older interviewees consistently recognized broader structures and norms that shaped interactions.

As Shelly, a white 78 year-old trans woman also said,

> I've made it a point since coming out to be active. I've been involved in the community for over forty years now. And there are a lot of old traditions that some may find it difficult to let go of. We had a brochure that people would use for outreach programs. It was a really basic brochure. There was a faction of people in trans communities that I didn't even know, but when they saw the new version of our materials, they went ballistic. And they should have. It was a terrible document and reinforced negative stereotypes about trans people. But rather than using that as an opportunity to have conversations across generations and teach each other about our communities, a lot of the younger people just left the group and have refuted us since then.

In leaving the group because of outdated materials, Shelly suggested that there are many people in the older trans community who were open to conversations and wanted to learn about new ideas and perspectives surrounding gender. Other older people also indicated that some of the new norms, or rituals, in younger spaces were rarely explained, but the expectation was that if one did not understand them, they were not "with it," and subsequently shunned. Mel, a white 63 year-old trans person shared that, "I went to this one meeting and people kept snapping. I didn't know what that meant. I leaned over and asked a younger person why everyone was snapping. And they just rolled their eyes and pretended like I hadn't said anything." This instance by Mel was followed with, "I just worry sometimes that the young ones assume we are all just old tired fuddy duddies."

Creating the "Other" Trans Person

In the previous section I showed how the misunderstandings that existed between binary and non-binary people was explained away by generational gaps. But, looking beneath the surface of their accounts revealed how norms governing these different ways of understanding "trans" and specific rituals have been established within these communities. Policing and calling each other out, both groups engaged in respectability politics. However, there remains the problem of who is acknowledged as being a part of the trans community. In spite of the different norms that govern binary and non-binary spaces that led to vast misunderstandings about the intentions of people, one way that binary trans people grappled with such difference was to construct non-binary people as "othered" and, thus, not legitimate in claiming a trans identity. And, as I suggested in the opening pages of this chapter, "gender" is a systemic mechanism for organizing people and creating inequality across gender categories. While many scholars assume a coherency in "trans" identities, few have examined intracommunity tensions within trans communities.

Non-binary people were frequently understood as being so different and "out there" that they did not belong in trans community spaces. As River, a 21 year-old mixed race genderqueer person shared, after attending a trans group populated by mostly binary trans people,

> Just teaching them about what genderqueer was. Their minds were baffled. They could not understand. They were like, "This is really complicated and confusing. How could you not know your gender? I understand how you might not know your identity or your sexuality, but how could you not know your gender?"

As River explained, in trying to teach binary trans people about what it meant for them to identify as genderqueer, the assumption was that River did not know their gender, delegitimizing their claim to not only a trans identity, but any gender identity. It is within these moments as non-binary people move through trans spaces, that they frequently recounted being met with bafflement, mistrust, and sometimes amusement. Another 27 year-old genderqueer person shared,

> I was at this meeting for trans people in the suburbs, mostly older trans people. I think I might have been the only genderqueer person there. Which is fine. But I shared that I was genderqueer identified and it was like everyone's heads snapped in my direction and their eyes got really wide. It just felt like, "look at this curious oddity."

Within trans spaces, sometimes non-binary people were treated as objects of fascination, as binary people may not have the tools to grapple with one who identifies as non-binary and being in a trans space.

This way of handling difference was not relegated to older binary trans people. But it helps explain some of the friction in the generational gap. The locus of othering, however, is often misunderstood as coming exclusively from the *older* trans community. In reflecting upon their experiences at an open-mic event for trans people, D. was told by the MC (a 22 year-old binary trans woman) that the event was only for trans people. D. was, "Absolutely pissed. Especially because this is supposed to be a trans space. These people are all a part of the trans community, I almost felt betrayed, I guess. Like how can you say that to me? I'm a part of your community." D. went on to share that they felt that the MC misread them as a cisgender gay man. In policing the boundaries of who could participate in the event, D.'s voice was literally erased from the space because of assumptions about who they are, and how they identified.

Pronouns of reference also sometimes emerged as a way of being inclusive and in the spirit of recognizing that people may inhabit a vast array of gender identities. But, in other moments—as Jay a white 35 year-old genderqueer person, and other non-binary participants shared—pronouns became a staging ground for crafting notions of difference and the "other" onto the experiences of non-binary people. Ze said,

> Pronouns are meant to be a gesture of goodwill and we were going around the circle and a lot of the binary people in the group were saying, "oh, I don't care." And it's like yes you do. Maybe some of them really really really don't care, maybe. I have to cut that a little slack. But I also can't believe that every single person in that group doesn't care. So it turned into a really ridiculous exercise with no benefit, except for the people who said use 'ze' or gender-neutral pronouns. The problem was no one was actually using those pronouns for those people. So it failed on multiple levels.

From Jay's account, using non-binary pronouns became a way to demarcate difference, rather than serving as a way to recognize everyone in the trans space in the ways that they desired to be referenced. And, in the process, when binary trans people refuted the notion that they must declare their pronouns, non-binary people become "othered."

Beyond pronouns of reference as an othering device, and binary trans people marking boundaries around who was identified as fitting in the trans community, some non-binary people expressed frustration with how medical interventions were equivocated with being a "real" trans person. Ari, a 32 year-old mixed race trans* person reflected,

> I've been on hormones for a few months now and I can already tell a difference in how people treat me. Like, before, I was singled out and made to feel like I didn't belong in trans spaces because I was weird and ambiguous. But now, I'm accepted by binary trans people as one of them. This is not really true. Like, I might look like them, but I've now been deemed an acceptable trans person because I am on hormones.

Before starting hormones, Ari had been told that they were not really trans and in one instance, was told by a binary trans person that they were, "giving trans people a bad name and needed to pick one." This level of regulation in trans spaces was not often as transparent as Ari's experience, but the point remains that non-binary people felt excluded from trans spaces as their claim to a trans identity was met with suspicion by binary trans people. Sam, a 37 year-old binary trans man, in reflecting on boundary policing in trans spaces illuminated this logic, "I just don't really understand what we have in common. I am a man. I want to be understood as a man. And I want people to call me a man. For those who are non-binary, I don't think they fit in our spaces because their goal is not to transition all the way." Here, Sam is invoking a double-barreled logic in that while he wants to be understood in social life as a man, he still holds to the belief that "trans" should be defined as those who desire to transition from one binary gender to the other.

Addressing these gaps in understanding between non-binary and binary people, and the conflict that ensues as a result, Summer, a 47 year old trans woman said,

> A lot of people in my community don't understand non-binary people. And as a result of their confusion, have pushed them out. They [binary trans people] want broader society, or even the LGB community, to take us seriously and perceive that non-binary people are undermining that work. Like, I might not understand it, but some of my friends have been pretty mean to the non-binary groups because they think that our credibility is destroyed, and plays up on the idea that we are just men who wear dresses.

This poignant quote by Summer directly addressed the tensions between binary and non-binary people. Yet even in her own generous and critical description of the boundary policing that exists in trans spaces, as she gave voice to how non-binary people were a widely misunderstood group in Metromidwest, she went on to reflect that perhaps it is better for "them to find their own spaces because they likely will never feel made to belong by many in my community." In spite of her ability to acknowledge how binary people police non-binary people in trans spaces, she conceded that non-binary people do not belong. In these instances, and across the interviews of binary and non-binary people, non-binary people were made to feel like "others" and how they understand themselves as being a part of the trans community was not aligned with how some binary trans people attempt to assimilate into mainstream society. In efforts to maintain a respectable image to the broader Metromidwest community, the majority of binary people felt that non-binary people ought to develop their own groups and not identify as a part of the trans community.

CONCLUSION

In Metromidwest, the norms governing binary and non-binary communities are built upon fundamentally different assumptions and ideological perspectives. Beholden to their roles as mentors who have a wealth of lived experience, older trans people sought opportunities to work with younger trans people, many of whom in Metromidwest were non-binary identified. In spite of the oft-cited narrative from non-binary people that they are "more" oppressed, they fail to realize the ways that they set up space in restrictive ways that keep binary people feeling left out and not in the know on new traditions and rituals. Yet in establishing these norms that not all are privy to, they created boundaries around who is enabled and emboldened to inhabit non-binary space.

For younger non-binary people however, they too face boundaries and borders around who may lay claim to a trans identity, and often invoked in binarist ways from older trans people. In so doing, binary trans people are unknowingly crafting boundaries around the identities of non-binary people. In holding younger non-binary people to expectations of the gender binary, binary trans people police who is admitted into trans spaces, and regulate those who offer counter-narratives to the binary gender system by shunning non-binary people, and labeling them as "others" who ought not participate in trans communities. These expectations that are placed onto non-binary people are unobtainable to meet, and also norms that non-binary people often intentionally choose not to meet.

Both binary and non-binary people give voice to assumed generational gaps in the interviews. Met with hostility, non-binary people left city-wide coalitions to form their own organizations out of frustration for being sidelined by older trans people. Yet, from the perspective of older trans people, the young ones were operating from different rules—rules that they were not privy to, and left them feeling frustrated as well. Taken together, the perpetuation of inequality between binary and non-binary people is a two-way street. In examining the narratives of both binary and non-binary trans people, the explanation of a generational gap does not hold much theoretical weight as each of these communities ultimately ended up otherizing each other—one from a place of ageism, and the other from binarism.

Resoundingly, however, both seem to believe that all trans people ought to establish a coherent community. But to what effect might this be accomplished, and to fulfill what function? The answers to this question points back to the tension between binary and non-binary people and in the current system, is unlikely to be reached through a middle ground. Each of these groups of trans people seeks to establish a singular trans community, but they are built from different norms and understandings of gender. Beyond the confines of this one locale, a provocative question is raised in what might a coherent trans community look like, and how might these fissures between binary and non-binary people be resolved? In naming the perpetuation of oppression that is slung both ways across binary and non-binary people, this chapter has a broader-based goal of illuminating the resiliency of assumptions that comes from within trans community spaces. In so doing, this work demonstrates how trans people are not immune to re-creating and perpetuating inequality within their communities.

This work provokes larger questions for trans studies scholars and those who work within cultural and social explanations for inequality. In what ways might we look beneath the surface of what people say, to hone in on the disjunctures between what is stated and what is communicated in other ways that ultimately upholds social order—order that hinges on community expectations and norms that might be placed under the broad category of "trans" but on the ground level of interaction, holds little use value as these communities are clearly not singular, but are insulated and insulating themselves from each other.

NOTES

[1] In this chapter, I use the pronouns of reference that interviewees self-identified. While not an exhaustive list, the pronouns typically used by interviewees include: she/her/hers, they/them/theirs, ze/zir/zir, he/him/his.

[2] While difficult to pinpoint exact definitions because of quickly changing terminology, in general "binary gender" refers to people whose gender identities are within the binary categories of woman or man, while "non-binary" refers to people whose gender identities

are not so easily contained by these distinctions. Thus, readers will be introduced to non-binary people who use identity categories such as "genderqueer," "genderfucked," and "non-binary." All, in some way, denote people whose identities are above, beyond, and/or outside of woman or man.

[3] "Cisgender" means people whose gender identities align with the gender assignment at birth. In contrast, "trans" means people whose gender identities are not aligned with the gender assignment at birth.

REFERENCES

Garfinkel, H. (1967). *Studies in ethnomethodology*. Englewood Cliffs, NJ: Prentice-Hall.

Higginbotham, E. B. (1994). *Righteous discontent: The women's movement in the Black baptist church, 1880–1920*. Cambridge, MA: Harvard University Press.

Hines, S. (2007). *Transforming gender: Transgender practices of identity, intimacy and care*. Bristol: Policy Press.

Lucal, B. (1999). What it means to be gendered me: Life on the boundaries of a dichotomous gender system. *Gender & Society, 13*(6), 781–797.

Mason-Schrock, D. (1996). Transsexuals' narrative construction of the "true Self." *Social Psychology Quarterly, 59*, 176–192.

Ridgeway, C. L. (2009). Framed before we know it: How gender shapes social relations. *Gender & Society, 23*(2), 145–160.

Ridgeway, C. L. (2011). *Framed by gender: How gender inequality persists in the modern world*. New York, NY: Oxford University Press.

Ridgeway, C. L., & Correll, S. J. (2004). Unpacking the gender system: A theoretical perspective on gender beliefs and social relations. *Gender & Society, 18*(4), 510–531.

Riessman, C. K. (2008). *Narrative methods for the human sciences*. Thousand Oaks, CA: Sage Publications.

Schilt, K. (2010). *Just one of the guys? Transgender men and the persistence of gender inequality*. Chicago, IL: University of Chicago Press.

Stone, A. (2009). More than adding a t: American lesbian and gay activists' attitudes towards transgender inclusion. *Sexualities, 12*(3), 334–354.

Valentine, D. (2007). *Imagining transgender: An ethnography of a category*. Durham, NC: Duke University Press.

GRIFFIN LACY

24. RESEARCH ON GENDER IDENTITY & YOUTH

Incorporating Intersectionality

Popular discourse surrounding gender identity and youth is highly contentious. Indeed, in the professional realm, there is often resistance to research on transgender children—including within the discipline of sociology. Incorporating race, class, and gender into the conversation ensures even greater controversy. In particular, the experiences of trans girls and trans youth of color are fraught with cultural opposition. In the social realm, gender-nonconformity is often met with rejection, violence, or attempts to dissuade gender nonconforming behavior. Class location also contributes to difficulties and social resistance faced by low income and working-class children. How trans and gender nonconforming children and youth are particularly situated at the intersection of race and gender identity is a pressing research question for sociologists to explore.

Cisnormativity and binary gender norms are deeply embedded in American society. For trans and cisgender children alike, gender nonconforming traits are discouraged. Youth are socialized as either *girls* or *boys* to become *women* or *men* respectively, in the rigid and binary sense those terms are popularly understood. Children are pressured to fit neatly within the gendered expectations culturally assigned to them at birth or sooner. Some children resist these expectations, while others do not. Videos of "gender-reveal parties" are growing in popularity and are sweeping the internet. Digital clips display strong emotional reactions of elated or disappointed "big brothers" and "big sisters" hoping for a particular outcome of the sex of their unborn sibling. As the dramatic responses to their prenatal siblings' gender go viral, their reactions are telling. In the cultural scripts we provide children—even before they are born—*gender matters*.

This chapter explores the state of the field of sociological research on trans youth and puts forth a call to scholars to center on the unique and important experiences of trans youth of color. I review the scholarship on transgender and gender nonconforming youth, with attention to intersections of various structural identities. Finally, I discuss points of possible intervention and research methodologies that will likely prove to be useful in exploring this area of research.

Transgender *adults* have existed in the popular US imagination for decades, fuelled by mainstream media attention in the 1990s. Additionally, there are more support groups and different types of resources available to the transgender community than ever before—yet public awareness of transgender *youth* is much more recent. "The nature of sex/ualities, gender and schooling has changed considerably over the last 20 years, with global political, social and cultural shifts bringing the lives of queer youth to the fore" (McGlashan & Fitzpatrick, 2018, p. 239). Societal awareness of transgender children has led to a cultural push toward acceptance and acknowledgment of diverse gender identities, unfortunately corresponding with backlash in the form of active political threats to the rights of transgender students. These threats will hopefully inspire a growing academic realization of the importance of research on this topic. The timeliness of this research is emphasized by the scholarly consensus that reveals the high degree of trauma experienced by transgender youth, especially trans youth of color and trans girls. This disproportionate suffering contributes to economic and social inequalities later in life. Despite this shift in research on gender identity youth over the past decade, critical information is still lacking, particularly regarding youth of color.

Patricia Hill Collins (2000) explores Kimberlé Crenshaw's (1993) concept of intersectionality. This framework adds an important element of embedded racial domination, which must be considered when discussing trans youth of color. Within Hill Collins' framework, race is uniquely understood as an invisible subjugated system within white supremacy. We can examine the concept of racialized systems from the perspective of trans youth of color through an intersectional lens. Hill Collins' insight on the dual identities of black women in the United States, and the competing roles of feminism and black unity in *Black Feminist Thought*, is useful when explaining social phenomena that prevent a universal experience of trans youth identity. These dual identities inform the debate regarding strategies for inclusion of racial minorities in gender minority advocacy, with the goal of reducing gender inequality. Hill Collins highlights access to forms of language and power, which privileges dominant voices in the production of knowledge. Intersectionality forces us to challenge the current discourse surrounding trans youth.

Most sociological literature, prior to the turn of the century, neglected the intersecting topic of gender identity and youth entirely, let alone the intersections of gender identity, youth, *and* race. Twelve years ago, Grossman and D'Augelli (2006) called for more research on transgender youth generally. They described many harms experienced by trans youth and relayed an urgent call for help from many of their youth who served as focus group participants in one of the very first studies: "There is nothing for transgender youth. Please help us" (p. 125). They describe a toolkit moving forward to help build "strategies to enhance emotional, social and physical development...to assist transgender youth in building the resiliency they need to live in a culture that tenaciously maintains a binary concept of gender" (p. 126). Fortunately, we are now seeing more interdisciplinary literature on the topic of transgender youth published with greater frequency, particularly within the last few years.

Two essential sociological texts specifically about transgender children and their families were just released in the summer of 2018: *The Trans Generation: How Trans Kids (and Their Parents) are Creating a Gender Revolution* by Ann Travers (2018); and *Trans Kids: Being Gendered in the Twenty-First Century* by Tey Meadow (2018). These texts are welcome additions to the lack of conversation surrounding these crucial topics. The multiracial populations observed in these recent publications included trans youth of color.[1] However, more research is needed, especially when it comes to the unique experiences of trans youth of color. Prior to their work, according to Singh (2013), transgender youth of color have effectively been missing from the conversation around best practices and family strategies.

Among scholars and activists, there are divergent viewpoints regarding potential strategies for gender identity recognition and increased equality for transgender and gender nonconforming youth. However, Simons et al. (2013), Travers (2018), and Meadow (2018), all find that family support can be one measure of protection for LGBT youth. Simons et al. (2013) describe how family rejection places trans youth at higher risk for mental health issues, including depression. They plea with professionals to practice interventions by conveying the importance of family support to their clients. Pearson et al. (2007) discuss the stigmatization of nonheterosexuality in school environments and the negative consequences that result from those stigmas, impacting young people's ability to participate in academic environments and threatening their ability to succeed in the future. This has particular implications for trans and gender nonconforming youth, even more so for trans youth of color.

Contemporary sociological and psychological findings clearly indicate that a lack of gender identity support in childhood and adolescence can lead to a decrease in well-being and negative health outcomes, including depression, drug-use, self-harm, and the single most catastrophic: suicide. Suicide rates of transgender youth are particularly striking when compared to gender-conforming peers and other marginalized subgroups (Pritchard, 2013). Bullying, harassment, and forced-homelessness are just a few of the many forms of victimization trans and gender nonconforming youth face disproportionately. Grollman (2012, 2014) suggests that cisgender adults and youth who have more than one disadvantaged status experience a "double disadvantage" due to their "disproportionate exposure to discrimination" (2014, p. 3). This theory can be applied to trans youth of color as well. Findings also suggest that *families*, along with their transgender children, suffer due to a lack of societal and institutional support related to their children's stigmatized gender identities (Prichard, 2013; Singh, 2013).

Though the sociological field has progressed since King and Ekins' (1999)—now outdated[2]—study on "body femaling" and "transgendering," in which they describe "the new interdisciplinary field of transgender studies" to be in an "infant state" (599), there is still work to be done. Sociologists have not collected enough data to know how society can best support gender identity expressions in youth, nor are we able to identify the appropriate support mechanisms required of caregivers and professionals as proposed by Simons et al. (2013). "The literature is virtually devoid of transgender and transsexual families" (Pfeffer, 2010, p. 165).[3]

As mentioned, transgender youth identities have only recently come to the forefront of public discourse, and only in the last few years have sociologists begun incorporating trans youth into their research. It is long past due that we include more trans youth voices of color together with systematic study of transgender youth—more broadly—along the intersectional axes of age, race, class, and gender.

In an attempt to understand gender identity and youth with little prior research, we can extrapolate theoretical frameworks from literature on youth, gender, and sexuality. For instance, McGuffey and Rich (1999) provide a provocative analysis of hegemonic masculinity within middle childhood play. Because the article was written almost two decades ago, childhood transgender identities were not on the forefront of sociological investigation. Nevertheless, McGuffey and Rich's theory involving "the gender transgression zone" is useful for future studies and can be extended to incorporate a similar study of childhood gender play and boundary maintenance. Using a child-centered approach, it is relevant for future research on gender identity and youth to explore the play obstacles faced by young transgender children as they begin to push against gendered boundaries (McGuffey & Rich, 1999). In the case of trans youth, these gendered boundaries uniquely conflict with their internalized sense of gender. Furthermore "gender transgression zones" will likely be experienced in particular ways for trans youth of color, warranting further intersectional ethnographic exploration to uncover some of these unique distinctions.

Averett's (2016) intersectional study, "The Gender Buffet," investigates how social location permeates parental approaches to hegemonic sexuality, particularly for parents who identity as LGBTQ. Averett's investigation unveils an interesting and unique "queering" of childrearing that allows children greater freedom of gender expression. This approach is useful in the study of parents of transgender children, as both an example of an exemplar methodology, as well as a philosophical approach.

Another model for the type of data that will be useful is the work of Barrie Thorne (1987), who challenges the adult-centered nature of feminist research and traditional knowledge structures. She situates child representations as most often described as either "threats" or as "victims" and challenges the ways that we think about children (p. 89). Thorne argues that how we think about children are reflective of adult interest which are limiting to sociological understanding and calls for "conceptual autonomy" from their shaping by dominant groups to be granted in order to bring their experiences to the forefront" (p. 104).

Additionally, Thorne and Luria (1986) investigate the heteronormative social scripts that are enacted in elementary schools that prepare youth for early adolescence. They find that girls and boys are often separated by gender and thereby learn different patterns of interaction. They claim that "entry into adolescence entails the assumption of sexuality as a core of identity" (188). Their studies of childhood interaction and reinforcement of societal cultural norms regarding sexuality and gender expression are important when considering the experiences of transgender youth in early and middle childhood, as well as in adolescence. Moving forward, it is important for educators and caregivers to create and provide new non-cisnormative cultural scripts. A plurality of these scripts will be required for trans youth to flourish as they develop and grow into their own sense of sexuality. Removing systematic gendered separation is recommended to reduce harmful isolation of trans and gender nonconforming youth. Creative and inclusive ways of building new cultural norms around gendered behaviors in classrooms will

327

likely benefit an internalized sense of self for gender-expansive youth. The sexual polarization contributing to the different patterns of interaction that exist between groups of boys and girls in schools is arguably detrimental for cis and trans students alike, particularly non-heterosexual students. Furthermore, the specifications of these suggested strategies must to take race and class into account in a meaningful way to improve their effectiveness.

Literature on gender identity and youth, specifically in relation to transgender children, has been published primarily within the field of psychology. Eve Sedgwick (1998) references the now-outdated[4] gender identity diagnosis in the DSM III: "Gender Identity Disorder of Childhood (GIDC)" (p. 20). She claims GIDC attracted little attention at the time and reveals a historical precedent to disproportionately diagnose natal males compared to natal females. Her findings show that any expression of gender nonconformity in natal males is more likely to result in a GIDC diagnosis than in natal females, who she claims require an "actual biological development" of a future penis to even be considered for a GIDC diagnosis. Conversely, natal males who simply *express a dissatisfaction* with their own penis were likely to be diagnosed. This gendered look at the ways gender identity was pathologized and disproportionately applied to trans girls may be an important consideration for any research on trans youth moving forward.

In 2008, Karl Bryant published a piece titled "In Defense of Gay Children," through which he explored the pathologization of "Gender Identity Disorder of Childhood" (or GIDC) and its direct link to homosexuality, homophobia and homonormativity. Bryant argued that "GIDC is a site where an idealized gender conforming gay subject is produced...where gayness is valued over and above other forms of queerness, especially transsexual and transgender forms" (p. 456). He goes on to state that both defenders and critics of GIDC diagnoses produce some form of homonormativity. He describes an era of increasing tolerance toward gay identities which, he claims, has deep connections to transphobic expression as the new form of antigay sentiment. He argues that the defense of homosexuality comes at the expense of queer outcomes. Bryant's nuanced argument challenges us to examine "the ways that homophobia and antihomophobia sometimes work together" (p. 470). Though the types of diagnoses have changed, and the DSM-V now utilizes more progressive language, issues pertaining to gender identity and youth are inextricably linked to a pathologization within the medical field (Johnson, 2015). Current debates have not reached consensus regarding the value of medical diagnoses associated with trans youth, and future research on this topic is required.

Grossman and D'Augelli (2006) focus on the invisibility and vulnerability of transgender youth in their late teens. Their findings display the negative implications of this invisibility on the mental health of trans youth. They categorize the reports from the focus groups into four problem areas, including "the lack of safe environments, poor access to physical health services, inadequate resources to address their mental health concerns, and a lack of continuity of caregiving by their families and communities" (p. 112). Part of their invisibility, Grossman and D'Augelli claim, is due to the western gender binary and our society's failure to recognize the existence of anything outside that structure. Adequate healthcare and other services cannot be provided without specific information on the needs of this population. The authors also call for research to be drawn from a greater cross-section of different populations within the community using—what mainstream sociologists now would refer to as—an *intersectional*[5] approach (p. 125).

Given the increased visibility of trans youth, it may be relevant to gain a sense of public attitudes that accompany this increased awareness. Elischberger et al. (2018) describe the attitudes of adults toward transgender gender identities in youth. Generally, adults reported favorable attitudes toward transgender youth, with some hesitation regarding bathroom use. This finding is in contrast with previous research, which has concluded that people have predominantly negative views toward transgender individuals (Cragun & Sumerau, 2014). It is possible that the shifting cultural climate in the last few years and the increasing visibly of transgender people in the popular media, along with both the growing political acceptance of lesbian and gay adults and anti-bullying movements in schools, has led to an increased acceptance of transgender children. According to Elishberger et al. (2018), more negative attitudes toward transgender minors were reported in adults who had an association with religion, political conservatism, and strong gender conformity, particularly in men. Those who felt that transgender identities were more environmental than biological also reported more negative attitudes (Elishberger et al., 2018). These findings are relevant when examining the usefulness of the currently popular "born this way" discourses surrounding LGBTQ activism.

Elischberger et al. (2018) suggest a need for increased education around the topic of gender identity and youth. This may have policy implications moving forward, especially related to school environments and parenting. Because many people conflate gender identity and sexual orientation, there is a need for awareness regarding the distinctions between the two. Furthermore, current sociological literature is primarily derived from data on transgender adults and parents of transgender children. While the adults who interact with the children are essential when considering the levels of support children are given as a result of the attitudes and beliefs of their parents, teachers, and other caregivers, there is a need to expand the literature to include the lived experiences of transgender children themselves. Views from the standpoint of the marginalized position are not adequately represented in the literature on trans youth (Elishberger et al., 2018).

Bullying has become a popular discussion in scholarly discourse on gender and sexual minorities (Pritchard, 2013). However, previous work has "not had a critical and sustained analysis of the ways that race, ethnicity, class, and other identities complicate discussions of how bullying and bias-motivated violence affect a diversity of queer youth" (p. 320). This is also true for people with differing sexual minority identities. Pearson et al.'s (2007) finding that age and race place an important role in determining different outcomes for sexual minority youth is relevant to future research on gender identity and youth. There is a gap in the sociological literature regarding the intersecting forms of oppression experienced by trans and gender nonconforming youth, particularly youth of color (Singh, 2013). If we extrapolate from adult literature, which has shown trans women of color to have the highest rates of victimization, then we might expect transfeminine youth of color to also experience the highest rates of marginalization. Yet only additional research can show if that's the case.

Ridgeway and Kricheli-Katz (2013) have "considered gender, race, and class as culturally distinct systems of inequality not because they really are separate but because people routinely treat them as such, and this has consequences" (p. 313). In conducting an intersectional analysis, "multiple characteristics of individuals are simultaneously present—some more essentialized that others—and therefore intersect to create challenges and possibilities for actors" (p. 313). Mental and emotional impacts of gender and racial oppression on individuals lead to very high rates of depression, anxiety and suicide attempts for queer youth of color (Pritchard, 2013).

Race also plays an enormous role in high school social dynamics relating to gender expression and sexuality (Pascoe, 2007; Jones, 2009). Morris and Perry (2017) show how African American girls experience unique attempts to restrict their assertive behaviors in an effort to force them to become more hegemonically "feminine," thereby restricting their ability for growth and academic achievement. Pascoe found that black boys were disproportionately punished for behaviors that their white counterparts could get away with, such as being singled out for "over-sexualized" dancing and, according to

Pascoe, "it was the relationship between race, gender, and sexuality that rendered black boys so potentially dangerous to the delicate balance of the (hetero)sexual order established by the school" (Pascoe, 2007, p. 49). These findings on the intersections of race and gender are relevant to future studies on gender identity and youth moving forward.

The stress theory employed by Lu and Wong (2013) can also be applied to transgender children and youth of color. Racism, sexism and transphobia affect people on a personal level. There are net effects of racism on a person's health. "Devalued identities" are connected to "negative experiences and specifying conditions" that "lead to poor mental health" (p. 365). Similar to the Asian American men that Lu and Wong studied, transgender children, particularly those of color, "might initially possess positive identity standards, but others project stereotyped appraisals, resulting in distress" (p. 365). Trans children also suffer from not being able to "successfully perform role-identities in certain domains" (p. 365).

There is a dearth of literature on trans youth of color prior to the onset of adolescence. Additionally, existing literature is primarily focused on the vulnerability and victimization of later-stage youth. One of the first studies to include a positive framework regarding aspects of the lives of transgender adolescents of color was conducted recently by Singh (2016), who distinctively explores the resilience of these youth. This unique study—along with Robinson's (2018a, 2018b) research on gender expansive homeless youth—are some of the very few articles that exists relating to youth of color with transgender identities that does not present trans youth of color through a framework of victimization. Singh (2013) conducted a small qualitative analysis of only thirteen transgender youth of color using a feminist, intersectional, intercategorical approach. Singh explores the question, "what are the daily lived experiences of resilience transgender youth of color describe as they negotiate intersections of transprejudice and racism?" The study found that the youths' racial and gender identities evolved contemporaneously. Specifically, the participants recognized that as children their experiences were less validated, but they self-advocate and find a place within the LGBTQ youth community and social media as a way to find affirmation for their intersecting identities. Similar studies ought to be conducted with the goal of empowering trans youth of color.

In terms of parenting trans youth of color, there are distinct fears and responses that mothers of color have in response to their children. Hurtado (1989) argues that all marginalized groups, which includes gender variant, gender nonconforming, and trans youth, are situated relationally, specifically in their distinct and particular position to the dominant group. While gender oppressions occur, they alone do not determine a specific individual's subordinate position. Race and ethnicity play a major role in determining these subjugated positions. Hurtado argues that white women worry that their children will grow up and join the patriarchy, while black women worry that their children will be shot in the street. "These differences in childhood experiences with racism and classism, in the necessity of developing survival skills" (Hurtado, 1989, p. 854) will, theoretically, have impacts on the ways in which mothers of color raise their children with regard to gender identity relative to white mothers.

Clashes in feminist discourse concerning race and families might provide a useful frame to understand similar differences in forms of mothering relating to transgender children. Many black women have had to teach their children forms of survival that are different from white women, due to systemic racism. One survival technique black mothers may convey to their transgender children might involve a deeper suppression of a nonconforming gender identity. Parents may justifiably fear that the intersection of transphobia and white supremacy could lead to increased exposure to systematic violence and further risk in society.

Despite increased visibility and social recognition in recent years, transgender and gender non-conforming children and youth face renewed threats in the current political climate. Trans and gender nonconforming youth of color are responding to the rising oppressive forces with vigor and resilience but would benefit from additional empirical data that documents their lived realities, and the outcomes of their strategies of resistance. Researchers should continue to explore the experiences of trans and gender nonconforming children and youth, who suffer from intersecting forms of gendered oppression and racialized victimization in varying economic social locations.

NOTES

[1] Participant samples: 13 youth of color, including 4 children with some portion of their ethnicity labelled "black" (Travers, 2018, pp. 217–218) and 17 youth of color, including only 4 black children (Meadow, 2018, pp. 242–245) respectively. The numbers were calculated by adding any participant who was not listed by the authors as only "white," or of European descent.

[2] While some people in the trans community (typically older and some newer members) continue to use some of the terminologies cited above, in general, sociologists no longer refer to transgender identities and experiences as "transgendering" or "transgendered."

[3] Moore's (2011) work on black lesbian mothers with gender non-conforming presentations—whom she calls "transgressives"—highlights the importance of looking at racial differences to qualitatively understand specific gender minority experiences, and differing gender and sexual minority categorization of women of color.

[4] This is likely in part due the official categorization of transgender children as having a mental disorder, in tandem with the lack of social recognition outside of that field. The evolving language of diagnoses for transgender identities changed most recently in 2013 to "Gender Dysphoria" with the release of the DSM-V. Some advocates prefer "Gender Incongruence" in lieu of such stigmatized language. It's possible that—like homosexuality—transgender identities will not always be categorized as a mental disorder.

[5] Scholars of color at the time were already using the term.

REFERENCES

Averett, K. H. (2016). The gender buffet LGBTQ parents resisting heteronormativity. *Gender & Society, 30*(2), 189–212.

Bryant, K. (2008). In defense of gay children? 'Pro-Gay' homophobia and the production of homonormativity. *Sexualities, 11*, 455–475.

Cragun, R. T., & Sumerau, J. E. (2014). The last bastion of sexual and gender prejudice? Sexualities, race, gender, religiosity, and spirituality in the examination of prejudice toward sexual and gender minorities. *The Journal of Sex Research, 52*(7), 821–834.

Crenshaw, K. (1993). Demarginalizing the intersection of race and sex: A Black feminist critique of antidiscrimination doctrine, feminist theory and antiracist politics. *University of Chicago Legal Forum, 140*, 139–167.

Elischberger, H. B., Glazier, J. J., Hill, E. D., & Verduzco-Baker, L. (2018). Attitudes toward and beliefs about transgender youth: A cross-cultural comparison between the United States and India. *Sex Roles, 78*(1–2), 142–160.

Grollman, E. A. (2012). Multiple forms of perceived discrimination and health among adolescents and young adults. *Journal of Health and Social Behavior, 53*(2), 199–214.

Grollman, E. A. (2014). Multiple disadvantaged statuses and health: The role of multiple dimensions of discrimination. *Journal of Health and Social Behavior, 55*, 3–19.

Grossman, A. H., & D'Augelli, A. R. (2006). Transgender youth: Invisible and vulnerable. *Journal of Homosexuality, 51*(1), 111–128.

Hill Collins, P. (2000). *Black feminist thought: Knowledge, consciousness, and the politics of empowerment* (2nd ed.). New York, NY: Routledge.

Hurtado, A. (1989). Relating to privilege: Seduction and rejection in the subordination of white women and women of color. *Signs, 14*, 833–855.

Johnson, A. H. (2015). Normative accountability: How the medical model influences transgender identities and experiences. *Sociology Compass, 9*(9), 803–813.

Jones, N. (2009). *Between good and ghetto: African American girls and inner-city violence.* New Brunswick: Rutgers University Press.

Lu, A., & Wong, Y. J. (2013). Stressful experiences of masculinity among U.S.-Born and immigrant Asian American men. *Gender & Society, 27*, 345–371.

McGlashan, H., & Fitzpatrick, K. (2018). 'I use any pronouns, and I'm questioning everything else': Transgender youth and the issue of gender pronouns. *Sex Education, 0*, 0.

McGuffey, C. S., & Rich, B. L. (1999). Playing in the gender transgression zone: Race, class, and hegemonic masculinity in middle childhood. *Gender & Society, 13*(5), 608–627.

Meadow, T. (2018). *Trans kids: Being gendered in the twenty-first century.* Berkeley, CA: The University of California Press.

Mohanty, C. T. (1991). Under western eyes: Feminist scholarship and colonial discourses. In C. Mohanty, A. Russo, & L. Torres (Eds.), *Third world women and the politics of feminism.* Bloomington, IN: Indiana University Press.

Moore, M. (2011). *Invisible families: Gay identities, relationships, and motherhood among Black women.* Berkeley, CA: University of California Press.

Morris, E. W., & Perry, B. L. (2017). Girls behaving badly? Race, gender, and subjective evaluation in the discipline of African American girls. *Sociology of Education, 90*(2), 127–148.

Pascoe, C. J. (2007). *Dude you're a fag: Masculinity and sexuality in high school.* Berkeley, CA: University of California Press.

Pearson, J., Muller, C., & Wilkinson, L. (2007). Adolescent same-sex attraction and academic outcomes: The role of school attachment and engagement. *Social Problems, 54*, 523–542.

Pfeffer, C. (2010). 'Women's Work?' Women partners of transgender men doing housework and emotion work. *Journal of Marriage and Family, 72*, 165–183.

Pritchard, E. D. (2013). For colored kids who committed suicide, our outrage isn't enough: Queer youth of color, bullying, and the discursive limits of identity and safety. *Harvard Educational Review, 83*(2), 320–345.

Ridgeway, C. L., & Kricheli-Katz, T. (2013). Intersecting cultural beliefs in social relations: Gender, race, and class binds and freedoms. *Gender & Society, 27*, 294–318.

Robinson, B. A. (2018a). Child welfare systems and LGBTQ youth homelessness: Gender segregation, instability, and intersectionality. *Child Welfare, 96*(2), 29–45.

Robinson, B. A. (2018b). Conditional families and lesbian, gay, bisexual, transgender, and queer youth homelessness: Gender, sexuality, family instability, and rejection. *Journal of Marriage and Family, 80*(2), 383–397.

Rubin, G. (1993). Thinking sex: Notes for a radical theory of the politics of sexuality. In *The lesbian and gay studies reader.* New York, NY: Routledge.

Sedgwick, E. K. (1998). How to bring your kids up gay. In H. Jenkins (Ed.), *The children's culture reader* (pp. 231–240). New York, NY: New York University Press.

Simons, L., Schrager, S. M., Clark, L. F., Belzer, M., & Olson, J. (2013). Parental support and mental health among transgender adolescents. *Journal of Adolescent Health, 53*(6), 791–793.

Singh, A. A. (2013). Transgender youth of color and resilience: Negotiating oppression and finding support. *Sex Roles, 68*(11–12), 690–702.

Thorne, B. (1987). Re-visioning women and social change: Where are the children. *Gender & Society, 1*, 85–109.

Thorne, B., & Luria, Z. (1986). Sexuality and gender in children's daily worlds. *Social Problems, 33*(3), 176–190.

Travers, A. (2018). *The trans generation: How trans kids (and their parents) are creating a gender revolution.* New York, NY: New York University Press.

SHALEN LOWELL

25. SYMBIOTIC LOVE

*On Dating, Sex, and Interpersonal Relationships between Transgender
People (Personal Reflection)*

INTRODUCTION

I love being in love with another transgender[1] person. My fiancé, Shea, is the
nicest, most genuine person I know, and he's all I've ever wanted in a life
partner. As is, he's amazing; but Shea also being trans allows us to connect,
understand, and love one another on a deeper level. Let's face it, dating and
navigating relationships as a trans person is hard. I'm a bisexual, genderfluid,
nonbinary trans person. I don't identify as a "man" or "woman," or as any
sort of binary gendered identity; nor do I identify as a transman or as being
transgender in any binary sense or presentation. Therefore, I prefer the term
"nonbinary transgender." To boot, my gender often fluctuates as part of my
genderfluidity, changing between feeling like I am just gender nonbinary in
the most general sense to more agender to genderqueer, and others, each term
particular unto my personal definitions of those genders. For years I felt that
finding anyone worth my time (where romantic and sexual relationships are
concerned) was impossible—especially as a nonbinary trans person. I was
uncertain about myself, my genders, and my body. If I was this insecure with
myself, how could I expect anyone else to love and to accept me without
being uncertain about me, too?

Nonetheless, I've seen myself only being with other nonbinary and trans
people for years. To me, cisgender people didn't quite understand me, my
gender dysphoria, my nonbinary gender, and my nonbinary body enough for
me to enter into a romantic and sexual relationship with them. To this end, too
often in "dating preferences" dialogues, there's a particular focus on cismen
who date transwomen and ciswomen who date transmen. The focus here
is essentially still on cis people, and their experience dating a trans person.
In a strikingly metanarrative moment that jolted me back to my undergrad
critical theory days, when in research preparation to pen this chapter to
further illustrate my points made here and deepen my own understanding of

© KONINKLIJKE BRILL NV, LEIDEN, 2019 | DOI:10.1163/9789004414105_026

trans relationships, I noticed a resounding lack of just that: resources. Here's where I'm bridging that divide: it's time to talk about romantic, sexual, and interpersonal relationships between and among trans people.

ON STRUGGLING TO ATTAIN SYMBIOTIC RELATIONSHIPS

Let's start with sexuality. I'm bisexual. Bisexuality was, in a more archaic fashion, traditionally defined as an individual's attraction to both men and women. But ever since the word "bisexual" was established, the term's meaning has expanded to indicate attraction to two or more genders. The definition expanded the more people identified as bi, evolving the boundaries of what it means to be bi. The definition of bisexuality can vary based on each bisexual person; but for me, bisexuality means I'm attracted, both romantically and sexually, to almost every gender except for cisgender, heterosexual men. When it comes to my attraction to men and women, transmen and transwomen are included in that attraction. Transmen are men; transwomen are women—simple as that. Furthermore, on a personal level, I'm much more attracted to nonbinary people, gender nonconforming people, and trans people more so than anyone who is cisgender. Although transgender people are just one category of people to whom I'm attracted, with those that are trans, I find deeper romantic and sexual connections than with cis people—for countless reasons that will be addressed.

As a trans person, I faced constant discrimination by potential partners— some of which I was aware, and some of which I was not. Dating as an adult can be difficult—and sometimes seem nigh on impossible as is—never mind factoring into the equation the possibility that your gender, especially as a nonbinary trans person, could dissuade potential partners from seeking a relationship with you. Wherein cis people are concerned, the few cis individuals with which I went on dates drew out more doubt—on my part as well as theirs—than I was willing to handle. I would question their attraction to me, and ask myself, "How do they really see me or my gender? Am I "trans enough" for them to recognize me as trans? Am I nonbinary enough for them to validate me as such? Do I dress in a way that suggests I'm nonbinary? Do they like that? Do they see me as I want to be seen? Do they accept me as trans and nonbinary? Will they assume the genitals I have?" The list of questions that reverberated in my head was relentless, a nonstop internal dialogue. I'm sure the same could be said for my other trans siblings in the dating scene. Riley J. Dennis calls attention to this struggle in her article, "Your Dating 'Preferences' Might Be Discriminatory," touching on discriminating against potential date mates, particularly in relation to genitalia. When discussing the challenges trans people may encounter when dating cis people, Dennis (2016) says, "The main concern that people have in regards to dating a trans person is that they won't have the genitals that they expect. Because we associate penises with men and vaginas with women, some people think they could never date a trans man with a vagina or a trans woman with a penis." This sentiment was always at the forefront of my thoughts when I encountered someone I might like to date (or who I thought might like to date me). Based on countless conversations with my fellow trans siblings, I'm far from the only transgender person who's concerned with how potential date mates will react to my set of genitalia—and even before the inception of any kind of relationship, what kind of genitalia they I assume I have based on how I present my gender. Strangers see me, and I can feel their eyes roam my body as they check off in their head: breasts? Yes. Wider hips? Yes. Does it look like they (meaning, me) have a penis? No. And then quickly come to the gendered conclusion that "that is a female, woman, lady; therefore, they have a vagina." But what if I had the genitalia you didn't expect? What if I don't have a vagina? Does it matter? And, if so, why does it matter? Oftentimes, people want immediate affirmation and gratification of "yes, this person has the genitals I expect them to have based on their appearance." The same is true when dating as trans. We face this constant genital interrogation.

To complicate matters, what if you yourself are unsure of, or are exploring, your gender identity? What if you don't know if you want to medically, or in any form or fashion, transition or change or alter your gender expression? What if you want to transition sometime in the future? If that's a possibility, would a potential partner accept that? I've transitioned clothing- and appearance-wise, but not medically (I'm not currently undergoing Hormone Replacement Therapy (HRT), though I am taking the first steps in considering HRT; I am not pursuing any surgeries.), so I wasn't sure how that uncertainty would be perceived by potential date mates, whether those people were transgender themselves or not. All the above concerns could be applied to potential partners of any and all genders, but I found them particularly prevalent when I thought about/went on dates with cis people.

Though this uncertainty occurs in cases where trans and cis people date, that issue is not our main topic of focus. However, the point is important to note as it pertains to the struggles us trans people face when dating cis people. The notion of judging someone based on the genitals you assume they have doesn't just come into play as a concern trans people have when dating, having sex with, and such with cisgender people. These concerns extend to trans people dating other trans people, as well. Herein lies the complex and chaotic whirlwind of factors that could complicate potential relationships. What I've found is that if a potential partner or partners doesn't accept you, your gender, and your gender expression, ditch them. Surround yourself with friends and partners who wholeheartedly respect you for who you are.

Even if we don't mean to, or are actively training ourselves against doing so, we judge people, we assume things about the person they are and their body. This can happen in relationships among trans people, too, much as we might not want to admit it. When dating, for example, one might assume that because someone is a transguy, he or they wear(s) or want(s) to wear a packer or enjoys penetration as part of sex.[2] This may be the case for some individuals, transguys or not; but more than anything, these above notions are gender-informed assumptions. To the contrary, I know tons of transguys who don't like packing at all, and are fine with their lower bodies. Unfortunately for us trans people, we face judgement along gender lines at every turn.

Onto my relationship with Shea—my fiancé. Shea and I are monogamous, and we are both trans; he's a pansexual transguy. There's no relationship like that of a romantic and sexual relationship as a trans person with another trans person, bar none. My relationship with him, as a fellow trans person, directly contradicts all of the challenges and uncertainty that arise at the thought of pursuing an intimate romantic and sexual relationship with any cisgender person. There exists between Shea and I an unmatched understanding of what it's like to be trans (though how we identify as trans, and our individual struggles and history, may differ slightly), one of the many connections tying us together. Our relationship is symbiotic: Shea acknowledges, accepts, and loves me for who I really am and the genders with which I identify, without question or inhibition, and the same is true for me about him. He relates to my chest dysphoria (though mine is minor comparatively) and offers any help and support he can; he respects both my emotions and my body (and is careful of the areas of which I am most self-conscious). We're cognizant of each other's previous struggles in dating and transitioning. To cap off all these wonderful things, I absolutely love that he is trans, and he's communicated similar sentiments about being with me. We love that we've found lifelong love with each other, as trans people, with trans people.

To that end, Shea and I embrace our mutual queerness. He emphatically told me one day, "No matter how much I may pass as a cisguy, I never want to lose my queerness. I want people to know and recognize that I'm queer, and that we're queer. I'm proud of it, and of us." Shea and I see our relationship as an extension of the LGBTQ community—and in particular, the trans community. As such, we have not only our other trans friends, but ourselves as a couple, to lean on in times of joy, tragedy, sadness, and dysphoria. We rely on one another much as any trans people rely on their community, for acceptance, love, honest conversation, understanding, and support. Together, we navigate our lives as trans people in tandem, trying to live happily and freely in the face of this country's widespread and rampant transphobia. As much as anyone (myself including) has a litany of great cis friends who are also trans allies that support me and love me for who I am, they can't quite relate to my life in the same way another trans person can.

On the day-to-day, the commitment, comfort, and compassion I feel from being with a fellow trans person in a romantic and sexual relationship is unmatched. Shea and I can so casually, and without judgment, prejudice, or second-thought discuss topics like, "Should I pack today? I'm feeling incredibly uncertain about it and every time I pack I feel that it's too obvious. How does this look?" This very conversation could transition to, "Why don't we pack together?" By Shea suggesting we pack in unison, that offer immediately bridges the gap of discomfort and loneliness, in which I no longer feel as if I'm in this alone. I do not experience these instances in isolation; there will always be other trans people that share your thoughts, feelings, and uncertainties.

On a more vulnerable note, earlier this year, I had a complete mental breakdown with regards to my physical appearance, and the disconnect that only seemed to be strengthening between how I saw my body, how I felt others see my body, and how my body actually is. Specifically, I was—and still remain—concerned with my wide hips, my fat distribution (as someone who is "female" bodied, or assigned female at birth), and my thick thighs. On my part, the breakdown was unexpected and shattered my assumption that I could "just deal" with my body as is. My body as is, is trans enough. However, I'm no longer completely satisfied with my physical appearance. The outcome of talking through all of this with Shea was deciding to improve my mental health with therapy, and my physique with HRT by going on testosterone. This conclusion is one years in the making. And without Shea's emotional and personal guidance (he's been on T for three years now), on which I leaned throughout the working-through process, I wouldn't have felt comfortable enough coming to the conclusion that I did.

Relying on this mutual support for comfort is critical to our survival, not just in the day-to-day, but in the wider scope of our lives, and especially when tragedies occur within our community. No one of us in the queer community will forget the attack on Pulse nightclub in Orlando, Florida on

339

June 12, 2016, which was later ranked as one of the deadliest mass shootings in the history of the United States. At the club, 49 people were killed and over 60 injured. (Kreps, 2017) The attack was a terrible and sobering reminder of just how much hatred and we face and prejudice we endure as queer people, despite the insistence that we live in a "progressive society." The LGBTQ community is still shaken and grieving from this attack, which occurred during Pride Month. I was at a Pride party of my own that very night, fresh from a day out at the Boston Pride Parade, when the news broke. We remember the immediate and omnipresent terror and fear that our own LGBTQ spaces could and would be targeted in a similar fashion. I still feel this fright to the core. I'm afraid of going out to queer-friendly clubs, of attending Pride events. I still go, but the fear has almost stopped me before—and understandably so. In a recent report released by the Human Rights Campaign (Crary, 2017), the organization "calculated that 102 transgender people have been killed in the U.S. over the past five years—including 25 this year," most of them attributed to hate crimes. David Crary (2017) of the Associated Press continues, in his appropriately titled article, "Killings of Transgender People Hit a Record High in 2017, Advocacy Groups Say," that "another monitoring group, the National Coalition of Anti-Violence Programs, has tallied 26 homicides of transgender and gender-nonconforming people in the U.S. so far this year." Considering these staggering stats, we have a right to be afraid as trans people. We face violent discrimination even as we try to live our lives and navigate our worlds living as authentically as we can. It's no hyperbole to say that sometimes I fear going out in public as a trans person, afraid of being targeted. However, any fear that I personally have about being assaulted or targeted because of my transgender identity, I fully recognize my inherent privilege as a white, fairly female-passing queer individual. Transwomen (especially Black and Hispanic transwomen) face more violence and prejudice than I do in these circumstances.

From fearing for your life as a trans person, to fearing rejection, our mutual trans friends and lovers better understand the issues we face, the shunning of our identities and violence towards us exacted by wider societal forces. I would be remiss if I didn't talk about the physical aspect of relationships among trans individuals, as well. Sex between two consenting transgender individuals is wonderful, beautiful, revolutionary sex, and the same goes for romantic intimacy. To love and respect your body and another partner's body (or multiple partners' bodies), and to receive that love and respect in turn—it's an amazing experience, making love to one another as we are with our bodies as they are. On the flip side, though, sex is also scary; it involves being intimate in one of the most vulnerable ways. And for trans people like myself, it can be terrifying.

When I finally was ready for sex, shedding my carefully constructed gender identity by way of my (ironically) genderless clothing, what is there left? Just my body and my person, nothing else. When considering sex in the theoretical, for years I wondered, "Will my body be respected? Will my genderfluid and trans body be respected and accepted as such, even though in anatomy, I retain all that I was assigned at birth (AFAB)? I haven't gotten top surgery and am not on hormones. Am I still trans enough, then?" I'm sure I'm not alone in these ruminations. Even with sex between trans people, sometimes we still enter into the situation with certain expectations of what another's body could be like. Sam Dylan Finch (2014) succinctly reflects on this in his post, "8 Tips on Respectfully Talking Pleasure, Sex, and Bodies With Your Trans Lover": "[One] common assumption is that all trans folks have similar bodies and goals in transition. However, this is completely untrue. All trans bodies are different, just like cisgender (non-trans) bodies are. Don't go into the conversation [about sex] with the expectation that your partner has had certain surgeries or will ever choose to undergo surgery." Each trans person's body is as individual and special as they are. Not all transmen want top (or bottom) surgery, bind their chests, have copious amounts of body hair from testosterone from HRT, or emulate the stereotypical picture of "masculinity" that social expectations place upon them.[3] Whether any trans person desires to undergo HRT, pursue surgeries, or alter their appearance in anyway, is completely their call. Each and every trans person has their own transition goals. Their bodies are as individual as they are. And because not only sex, but emotional intimacy, creates an atmosphere of vulnerability, each trans person's body must be equally respected and assumptions not placed upon them—especially if gender dysphoria plays a part in how they feel about their bodies.

Discomfort with your body can unhinge and unsettle even the most confident individual. As in many relationships among transgender individuals, whether they are sexual in nature or no, one or more people in the relationship may experience gender dysphoria. Dysphoria can be broadly defined as an individual's discontent or discomfort with their assigned gender. Examples of dysphoria include, but are not limited to, extreme discomfort with one's genitals and/or assigned gender, anxiety triggered by forced reinforcement or reminder of one's assigned gender (with which one might not identify), and/or discomfort with or dislike of any of one's body parts. Gender dysphoria can range from minor physical or emotional discomfort to

341

deep-seated anxiety and depression. On more than one occasion, my dysphoria has exacerbated, and even played a part in, my depression. Dysphoria differs for everyone, and can even can be related to how others perceive you and your identity. As an example: Based on my appearance, strangers still seem to think I am a woman, and I hate this because I'm a nonbinary trans person who is not a woman, and who has gone to great lengths to present in a way that suggests otherwise. I've spent years coming to terms with my trans identity and am finally happy (for the most part) with my appearance; when someone misgenders me or sees me and still thinks "woman," "female," "lady," or any of the alike, I'm extremely annoyed. I'm not as distraught as I used to be on these occasions, but I'm unsettled and slightly dysphoric nonetheless.

As I've previously mentioned, my gender fluctuates. Just as gender can fluctuate, so too can gender dysphoria change in intensity, and the areas that cause dysphoria can alter. I almost never experience chest dysphoria, but do have bottom dysphoria on the occasion (most often, before and after menstruation). But as with each trans person, gender dysphoria is completely individual. To circle back to our discussion of physical intimacy, dysphoria can be exacerbated by sex. Sam Dylan Finch (2014) suitably address how dysphoria relates to sex, writing, "[…] But what one partner liked or found triggering may be completely different from what a new partner might experience. Some trans people have significant body dysphoria (which is the distress or discomfort that occurs when the gender someone is assigned does not align with their actual gender) where certain parts of their bodies can cause them incredible amounts of distress. Interacting with these parts of the body may be traumatic. Others do not have any dysphoria at all, or only at specific points in their lives." Initiating a dialogue about sex is crucial, discussing your partner's likes, dislikes, and needs during sex. But this is especially the case in relationships between trans people and between people who experience gender dysphoria or any amount of discomfort with their bodies. Gender dysphoria may inform each of those preferences—likes and dislikes with regards to touching certain areas of the body, comfort in initiating that contact, or off-limits areas of the body (whether those off-limits areas are linked to genitalia or not). Dysphoria doesn't always affect sex, but it can. For example, if one experiences bottom dysphoria, another individual touching that person's genitals could trigger the dysphoria related to that area. The same goes for other body areas, such as a person's chest. Another instance is this: if you're intimate with someone who binds their chest and who experiences dysphoria in that area of their body (however, the two are not always mutually exclusive), they may not want to be touched

Table 1. Gender terminology reference chart[4]

Agender	Individual who feels they have no gender identity, or who identifies not as male or female but 'neutral'
Bigender	Individual who sees themselves as having two gender identities. The separate genders could be male, or female, mixed or other—and may exist at the same time or entirely distinctly and separate from the other gender
Cisgender	Individual who identifies with the gender they were assigned at birth
Genderfluid	Individual for whom gender is unfixed; they fluctuate between different gender identities, one of which may or may not include their assigned gender at birth. These gender identities may be binary, nonbinary, both, neither, or fluctuate—and may all exist at the same time or separately
Genderqueer	Individual who does not subscribe to conventional gender distinctions but identifies with neither, both, or a combination of male and female genders. Genderqueer is often used as an umbrella term referring to gender identities that do not fit into the socially constructed binary gender norms
Hormone Replacement Therapy (HRT)	A procedure in which the body's natural hormones are replaced or boosted by medical means, such as with pills or injections. As an example, for someone assigned female at birth, this might mean taking testosterone to replace the estrogen in their body, and vice versa for someone assigned male at birth
LGBTQIA	Acronym that stands for: Lesbian, Gay, Bisexual, Transgender, Queer, Intersex, Asexual
MOGAI	Acronym that stands for: Marginalized Orientations, Gender Identities, and Intersex. This acronym is often used to be more inclusive than LGBTQIA
Nonbinary	Individual does not identify as male, female, or any concrete binary gender identity. Examples of binary genders include "man" and "woman"
Transgender	Individual whose gender identity is different from the gender they were assigned at birth.
	Nonbinary transgender: Individual whose gender identity is different from the gender they were assigned at birth, and whose identity is not that of a binary gender (see: *Nonbinary*)

or fondled there. These are just a few examples, but there are many more instances in which gender or body dysphoria influences how a trans person wants to experience sex. As long as there's an open dialogue between all members of the relationship, and each person in the relationship respects the gender(s), boundaries, and safety of the other(s), sex can be empowering, and incredibly validating.

CONCLUSION

On the symbiosis implicit in healthy relationships among trans people, my concluding message is this: you are loved. Take it from a fellow trans person, dating is difficult. Baring yourself before others, physically and emotionally, is equally as difficult. Compound those factors with the abounding uncertainties and internal struggles inherent in in discovering, and accepting, your own identity or identities, whether that be as a trans person, a nonbinary person, both, or any LGBTQ identity.

At the onset of this chapter, I sought out to shed light on the challenges trans people experience in dating, in sex, and in interpersonal relationships of all kinds—but particularly trans people's relationships with other trans people. While I've certainly done that, the exercise also prompted me to take a look back at my life and assess how far I've come in my personal journey and transition. On that note, everyone's journey deserves a voice. Trans and nonbinary narratives are as unique as each trans and nonbinary person; this is mine. My life is by no means representative of all trans lives, but I do hope to inspire others to share their stories in an effort to expand, extend, and diversify our narratives. To all the trans folks in our worldwide community, I hope you, too, find meaningful, symbiotic relationships.

NOTES

[1] For definitions of the gender and sexuality terms discussed here, please see Table 1.
[2] As a note, a packer is a prosthetic penis. They vary in size, shape, shade, and function. Some can be used during sex, some function as stand-to-pee (STP) devices, and more.
[3] I use transmen as an example here because I can relate to their experiences, as a transmasculine genderfluid person (that sometimes identifies as a transman), more so than those experiences of transwomen and transfeminine folks.
[4] Not meant to be comprehensive; these gender terms are subject to change based on the individual.

REFERENCES

Crary, D. (2017). Killings of transgender people hit a record high in 2017, advocacy groups say. *TIME*. Retrieved December 9, 2017, from http://time.com/5029561/transgender-murders-2017/; https://www.yahoo.com/news/killings-transgender-people-hit-record-170607964.html

Dennis, R. J. (2016, December 9). Your dating 'preferences' might be discriminatory. *Everyday Feminism*. Retrieved November 22, 2017, from https://everydayfeminism.com/2016/12/dating-preferences-discriminatory/?utm_content=buffere117e&utm_medium=social&utm_source=facebook.com&utm_campaign=buffer

Finch, S. D. (2014, December 16). 8 tips on respectfully talking pleasure, sex, and bodies with your trans lover. *Everyday Feminism*. Retrieved November 22, 2017, from https://everydayfeminism.com/2014/12/8-tips-on-respectfully-talking-pleasure-sex-and-bodies-with-your-trans-lover/

Kreps, D. (2017, April 21). Orlando to remember pulse victims on anniversary of nightclub shooting. *Rolling Stone*. Retrieved December 9, 2017, from http://www.rollingstone.com/culture/news/orlando-to-remember-pulse-victims-on-anniversary-of-shooting-w478103

ANDREA MILLER

FOR USE IN THE CLASSROOM

Notes on Teaching Outside the Rainbow

The three co-editors are fully aware that we teach in our classrooms, interact with our colleagues, engage with several levels of administrators, and produce research that is contested in what sociologists Kristin Schilt, Tey Meadow and D'Lane Compton have called doing "queer work in a straight discipline" (2018). This is also why we decided to create this volume—what is the existing work that not only expands the rainbow but also questions the current rainbow? Is there a place for kink, ace, BDSM, etc. in the rainbow or has the rainbow itself become sanitized and heterosexualized in its presumed queer space? These are the questions that we believe that this volume has addressed.

With that being said, there is always more work to do in our "straight discipline," but we hope you agree that this is a satisfying place for readers to begin, refresh, or expand their knowledge and that of their students. Like this book, this final chapter is not a traditional "resources for additional research" but a look at how instructors and alternative academics might approach the idea of what "Expanding the Rainbow" looks like in the classroom itself. First, we consider how those of us who teach outside of the rainbow often invite (purposeful or not) discomfort for our students. Second, we review some of the strategies that instructors use to teach about the relationship between sexuality, gender and other power-driven work. Third, we consider how we (or should we) normalize discussions of alternative sexualities and genders with our students by asking if creating a "safe space" in classrooms is warranted or even possible. Lastly, we provide a discussion of teaching strategies and activities to incorporate into the classroom.

Discomfort is something that most all sociology instructors are aware of. Anyone teaching critical pedagogy, whether it centers on race, class gender, sexuality or some combination undoubtedly invites discomfort into our lives—it is part and parcel of our "profession." While making students purposefully uncomfortable has been the subject of many teaching essays

© KONINKLIJKE BRILL NV, LEIDEN, 2019 | DOI:10.1163/9789004414105_027

(see Ludlow, 2004; Valerio, 2001) the editors and authors in this volume add multiple layers of uncomfortability as our entire curriculum or semester may center around alternative sexualities and genders that we have situated as outside of the rainbow.

In their essay "From Safe Space to Contested Space," Ludlow (2004) asserts that LGBTQIA faculty are always teaching in "contested spaces," spaces marked by a privileging location (as instructor) and simultaneously in an oppressed one where students carry and live out their heteronormative expectations (p. 52). Many students have become impervious to acronyms like LGBTQIA because many of these acronyms find their way onto syllabi (if even for a week). However, we contend that discussions that appear in this volume are non-normalized and thus create a sense of unease for many students and instructors.

This embodied unease is echoed in Tre Wentling's essay "Critical Pedagogy: Disrupting Classroom Hegemony" (2016). Here Wentling describes how they invite unease or disruption because to engage in critical pedagogy means to re-situate taken-for-granted norms and "invite disruption" (p. 231). By "destabilizing all that is familiar" Wentling (2016, p. 231) reminds us that this can cause outrage not only by those students who hold more normalized worldviews, but it may throw their entire identity structures into question. As instructors, we no-doubt take some pleasure in undermining students' heteronormative belief systems but we are also always aware of the social and psychic cost to not only our presentations of self as we stand before the classrooms engaging in (and oftentimes with) our own alternative genders and sexualities. Meadow too is also highly attuned to the costs Wentling discusses. In their aptly titled essay "The Mess," Meadow (2018) specifically speaks to the discomfort of queer bodies doing fieldwork. They also acknowledge the "corrosive forces" that lead researchers and professors to "undertake tremendous emotional and intellectual labor" (p. 153), corrosive because we are often cajoled to present and embody our own genders and sexualities in "palatable ways" (p. 153).

To be clear, some students will be angry, irritated, or even indifferent when learning and critically engaging in classrooms centered around alternative genders and sexualities. All of the contributors in this volume are expert at doing what is the first task in any alternative genders and sexualities classroom—deconstructing popular understandings of gender, sex, and sexuality as well as re-socializing students, so to speak, away from the inherited hegemonic discourses around genders and sexualities in U.S. society. Doing this is necessary if authentic (if there is such a thing) or at least critical discussions that challenge traditional worldviews are to be met. Some of us tell our own stories so that students and colleagues can feel free to tell their own. Drawing on hooks (1994), Kunkel (2016) reminds us that storytelling has unexpected benefits as it provides an outlet for the assumed "expert" professor to decenter authority (p. 168).

Another strategy can be found in Hidalgo's (2016) essay "Teaching Spaces of Possibility" where they outline a strategy called "making the sensational mundane"—otherwise, normalizing classroom discussions of sexualities. Hidalgo details how they treat every topic as "worthy of discussion" by refusing to sensationalize or "other" a topic, as well as tending to each topic equally by "requiring just as much extensive reading (on say, erotica) as any other topic" (p. 200). This equalizing discourse allows Hidalgo to "make the material accessible by making it mundane." Earlier work by Valerio (2001) also discusses using a "non-defensive demeanor" whereby Valerio discusses not making herself out to be an authority and finds it important to disclose her personal identity to ease possible vulnerabilities. Echoing Hidalgo and Valerio, in her remarks on her essay "Porn is good pedagogy," Penley (2013) advises the reader/teacher that uses sexually explicit material in the classroom (in Penley's case, teaching porn) to "never make an exception for pornography "in terms of issuing disclaimers or warnings." Penley goes as far as to note that these warnings may be seen as "disrespectful and patronizing to students…" (p. 197).

Contrasting Hidalgo's quest for "hope" through "normalizing" techniques, we are also met with the pedagogical query of "who" and "what" can be normalized in the first place. Here we are referring to the question(able) technique of building a "safe space" in alternative sexualities and genders classrooms. In thinking about pedagogical spaces, Allen (2015) is forthright in claiming that even musing that a lecture might provide a safe space for students and faculty is an outright "fantasy" (p. 767). Before we might be able to "normalize" or make alternative genders and sexualities "mundane," Ludlow challenges the "safe space" framework by asking us to define the space in question and who is in the space—in other words, what bodies are in the classroom and where bodies are in the classroom. Who is in the seats and who is front—what sort of space do they embody and how are their bodies are rendered (as powerful or powerless)? Teachers like Ludlow present the reader early on with her conclusion—"a 'safe space classroom' that serves both feminist inquiry and any question of diverse individuals is neither possible or desirable." Drawing on Harris (1998), Ludlow reiterates that a "safe space" is not feasible in a space where inequalities exist among students.

We are aware these "normalizing" practices may be more practical at some universities than others, for example private universities may have different codes of speech than public ones. In this case, we point you to scholars like Baber and Murray (2001); Davis (2005); Galbreath (2012); and Wagner (2017) who make an equally persuasive argument in favor of the possibility and productiveness of working toward "safe space" classroom settings, especially for sexual assault survivors who welcome content warnings and appreciate boundary settings. For example, Penley's (2013) practice of admonishing those who make "exceptions for pornography" may not be possible at universities that are governed by local and State laws with regard to course content.

Ludlow (2004) examines her own privilege by stating, "I have learned that I cannot offer my less-privileged students, students of color, LGBT students… safety, nor should I try" (p. 45). Ludlow understands that it is from privileged lenses that "safe" environments are even possible. Hierarchies are fields of power and many students (and professors) may never feel safe. Attempting to make classrooms "neutral" places is a fiction that many of us may have attempted and prioritized. Following Ludlow, however, we think considering a "contested" space might be more fruitful as we attempt to "expand the rainbow." If we start with the premise that alternative sexualities and genders are not neutral but fraught with inequalities, then perhaps we could better serve ourselves and our students. And let's be clear, by "contested" we do not mean rage-full or ill-serving, but following Ludlow, we mean critical with room for (respectful) conflict. To "contest" something is to call into question its stability as a concept, norm, identity, etc.—the work that sociologists are always doing regardless of whether they are teaching alternative sexualities and genders.

For Ludlow, in the "contested classroom" instructors recognize and teach that knowledges are always marked by power and privilege. To mark the difference between "safe" and "contested" spaces, Ludlow concludes that in a "safe space" classroom the goal is an "environment free from domination and authority;" while in a "contested space" classroom everyone knows that "no space is free from domination" (2004, p. 48). And because no space is "free from domination," we question the fields of power and the hierarchies of privilege to seek better understandings. Like Ludlow, Henry (1993–1994) knows that "there are no safe spaces" and points out that as a Black feminist woman her "pedagogy is not only a political act, but an act of courage" (p. 2).

Kimberly Kay Hong (2018) begins her essay "Gendering Carnal Ethnography with a discussion of Loïc Wacquant's (2005) concept "carnal sociology." Indeed, we each put ourselves and body in front (and center) every-time we teach our students, communicate with colleagues or even enter the field. In this final section, we provide some active resources that may help alleviate some of the anxieties and friction that are bound to arise when we expand the rainbow. At the recent 2018 American Sociological Association pre-conference meeting "Sexualities: Race, Empire: Resistance in an Uncertain Time," I (Andrea) had the privilege of organizing a panel on how to incorporate trans and intersex concepts and activities into the classroom. Claire Forstie (2018) discusses her use of a pronoun activity during the first day of class. She states, "sharing pronouns is a radical act, but for whom?" In other words, Forstie invites us to interrogate our own teaching practices when we call on students' identities and bodies to educate others." To alleviate "who we are using to educate," Forstie never requires her students to state their pronouns out loud in class but instead asks them to think about ways they have been misgendered in the classroom.

Coston (2018), too asks their students to think about places or social situations where they can imagine being uncomfortable expressing their gender. Using primers like Serano's *Whipping Girl* (2016), and her more recent essay "On Transgender People and 'Biological Sex Myths" (2017) as well as Nik Moreno's "Queer and Trans: A Primer (2016)" to explain the idea that identities are fluid and that problems will undoubtedly arise when social actors assume that one's gender identity is based on the sex assigned at birth. Coston also uses the popular teaching graphic "The Gender Unicorn" developed by Trans Student Educational Resources (TSER) (http://www. transstudent.org/gender/) to encourage students to ask what their unicorn would look like if they viewed their gender identity as fluid? How would students gender identities look if their gender was based on the multiple axes that the "unicorn" activity provides versus a binary, either/or system of understanding gender? (Conston, 2018).

Costello (2018) (also see Chapter 18 this volume) and Becker (2018) both talk about how they use their own bodies to talk about transgender, intersex, sex, gender, and sexuality but often look to other bodies as well to use as exemplars. Becker questions whether we have enough "diverse bodies" in the room and asks, "who is allowed in the room in the first place?" Costello follows up some of Becker's concern with providing various vignettes on intersex persons and bodies so students are aware that intersex bodies and persons exist as well as using their blog "The Intersex Roadshow" as an invitation to students to explore transgender and intersex identities in more detail (https://intersexroadshow.blogspot.com).

Finally, Sarah Hemphill and Dan Copulsky (see Chapter 16 for activity) re-situate students' understandings about intimacy and relationship structures through their activity "Relationship Yes/No/Maybe List." Instead of focusing on type of sexual activity, relationship options are instead highlighted. Asking students to define what "being romantic would look like," and giving students the option to choose "no preference" to types of sexual activities expands their understanding that sexual activity is not always central to one's relationships and that asexual folks may prefer various types of relationships that may include (or not) any physical touching or physical intimacy. Probing students to contemplate that they may not want any types of sexual activity is key to this activity and furthers socio-cultural understandings of the varying aspects of what it might mean to be asexual.

Expanding the Rainbow compels us to stretch our teaching, decide how we comport ourselves in a "straight discipline," and investigate how our bodies and the bodies of our students are situated alongside ours. This chapter is offered as inspiration to the ways we can (and already do) engage our teaching praxis with our students and colleagues. The activities and classroom etiquette issued here will no doubt be contested as our discipline tries to keep hold to its boundaries and boxes; all the while, we, the teacher-agitators unapologetically shake it up, stretch it out, and contort it into different configurations. We invite you to join us!

REFERENCES

Allen, L. (2015). Queer pedagogy and the limits of thought: Teaching sexualities at university. *Higher Education Research & Development, 34*(4), 763–775.

Baber, K., & Murray, C. (2001). A postmodern feminist approach to teaching human sexuality. *Family Relations, 50*(1), 23–33.

Becker, J. (2018, August). *Using trans and intersex scholarship in a non gender/sexuality course*. Paper presented at the sexualities pre-conference meeting of the American Sociological Society. Philadelphia, PA.

Coston, L. (2018, August). *Using trans and intersex scholarship and activities in the intro to sociology classroom*. Paper presented at the sexualities pre-conference meeting of the American Sociological Society, Philadelphia, PA.

Costello, C. G. (2018, August). *Introducing intersex issues and advocacy in the sociology classroom*. Paper presented at the sexualities pre-conference meeting of the American Sociological Society, Philadelphia, PA.

Davis, N. J. (2004). Taking sex seriously: Challenges in teaching about sexuality. *Teaching Sociology, 33*, 16–31.

Forstie, C. (2018, August). *What do you mean, my pronouns? First-day activities in the classroom*. Paper presented at the sexualities pre-conference meeting of the American Sociological Society. Philadelphia, PA.

Galbreath, B. J. (2012). An argument for teaching a human sexuality course within the context of a women and gender studies program. *American Journal of Sexuality Education, 7*(1), 62–77.

Harris, J. (1998). 'Rock the boat, don't tip the boat over': A classroom activist's perspective on women's studies. *Conflict, and Community Building, Atlantis, 22*, 2.

Hemphill, S., & Copulsky, D. (2019). Relationship yes/no/maybe list.

Henry, A. (1993–1994). There are no safe spaces: Pedagogy as powerful and dangerous terrain. *Action in Teacher Education, 15*, 4.

Hidalgo, D. A. (2016). Teaching spaces of possibility: Cultivating safe, relaxed, and challenging classrooms. In K. Haltinner & R. Pilegram (Eds.), *Teaching gender and sex in contemporary America.* Springer.

Hoang, K. K. (2018). Gendering carnal ethnography: A queer reception. In D. Compton, T. Meadow, & K. Schilt (Eds.), *Other, please specify: Queer method in sociology*. Berkeley, CA: University of California Press.

hooks, b. (1994). *Teaching to transgress: Education as the practice of freedom.* New York, NY: Routledge.

Kunkel, C. A. (2016). From protest to praxis or being real in the classroom. In In K. Haltinner & R. Pilegram (Eds.), *Teaching gender and sex in contemporary America.* Springer.

Ludlow, J. (2004). From safe space to contested space in the feminist classroom. *Transfromations: The New Jersey Project Journal, 15*, 1.

Meadow, T. (2018). The mess: Vulnerability as ethnographic practice. In D. Compton, T. Meadow, & K. Schilt (Eds.), *Other, please specify: Queer method in sociology*. Berkeley, CA: University of California Press.

Miller, A., & Lucal, B. (2009). The pedagogy of (in)visibility: Two accounts of teaching about sex, gender, and sexuality. *Teaching Sociology, 37*(3), 257–268.

Penley, C. (2013). A feminist teaching pornography? That's like Scope's teaching evolution. In T. Taormino et al. (Eds.), *The feminist porn book: The politics of producing pleasure.* New York, NY: CUNY Press.

Schilt, K. (2018). The 'not sociology' problem: Identifying the strategies that keep queer work at the disciplinary margins. In D. Compton, T. Meadow, & K. Schilt (Eds.), *Other, please specify: Queer method in sociology*. Berkeley, CA: University of California Press.

Schilt, K., Meadow, T., & Compton, D. (2018). Introduction: Queer work in a straight discipline. In D. Compton, T. Meadow, & K. Schilt (Eds.), *Other, please specify: Queer method in sociology*. Berkeley, CA: University of California Press.

Serano, J. (2016). *Whipping girl: A transsexual woman on sexism and the scapegoating of femininity.* New York, NY: Seal Press.

Valerio, N. L. (2001). Creating safety to address controversial issues: Strategies for the classroom. *Multicultural Education*, Spring.

Wacquant, L. (2005). Carnal connections: On embodiment, apprenticeship, and membership. *Qualitative Sociology, 38*(4), 445–474.

Wagner, L. M., et al. (2017). Teaching philosophies guiding sexuality instruction in U.S. colleges and universities. *Teaching in Higher Education, 22*(1), 44–61.

Wentling, T. (2016). Critical pedagogy: Disciplining classroom hegemony. In K. Haltinner & R. Pilegram (Eds.), *Teaching gender and sex in contemporary America.* Springer.

NOTES ON CONTRIBUTORS

EDITORS

Andrea Miller (she/her/hers) is a full adjunct faculty member in the Department of Anthropology and Sociology at Webster University in St. Louis where she is also a fellow for the Institute for Human Rights and Humanitarian Studies. She received her Ph.D. (Sociology, 2006) from American University. Her dissertation research and subsequent publications focus on the research areas of gender and sexuality, with a specific focus on bisexuality. Her work has been published in *Teaching Sociology*, *Teaching and Learning Inquiry*, and in the edited volume *Sociology Through Film* (Sage). Her most recent publication, "The Mis-education of Lady Gaga: Confronting Essentialist Claims in the Sex and Gender Classroom" was published in *Teaching Gender and Sex in Contemporary America*. Miller is a founding and current area editor of TRAILS (Teaching Resources and Innovations Library for Sociology) for the American Sociological Association and is a recipient of the William T. Kemper Award for Excellence in Teaching. For more information about her work please contact me at andreamiller31@webster.edu

Brandy L. Simula (she/her/hers) is a post-doctoral faculty fellow on The Nature of Evidence initiative at Emory University, where she is also affiliated with the department of sociology. Her research examines how individuals navigate cultural beliefs about gender, power, and sexuality in everyday interactions. Using feminist and queer theory and methods, her scholarship centers the experiences of people who hold marginalized social identities. Her research has been published in *Sexualities*, *Journal of Homosexuality*, *Journal of Bisexuality*, and *Sociology Compass*, and in anthologies including *Somewhere over the Rainbow: A Critical Inquiry into Queer Utopias* and *Selves, Symbols, and Sexualities: An Interactionist Anthology*. For more information about her work, visit: www.brandysimula.com

J. E. Sumerau (they/them/she/her) is an assistant professor and the director of applied sociology at the University of Tampa. She is the author of 10 books and over 60 articles and chapters focused on the intersections of sexualities, gender, health, religion, and violence in society. Dr. Sumerau is

355

also a two time finalist for the Lambda Literary Award in Bisexual Fiction, and an award winning sociological social psychologist recognized for their scholarly writing and teaching by regional and national sociological associations. They are also the co-creator and co-editor of the academic blog site www.writewhereithurts.net, a regular contributor to Conditionally Accepted at Inside Higher Ed, and the editor for the Society for the Study of Symbolic Interaction Music Blog. For more information, please visit www.jsumerau.com

AUTHORS

Robin Bauer is a professor for Epistemology and Theories of Difference at the Faculty of Social Work, Baden-Wuerttemberg Cooperative State University Stuttgart, Germany, where he teaches sexuality, gender and social work, disability studies, critical whiteness, intersectionality, social theory and epistemology. He studied chemistry, philosophy and educational sciences and attained his PhD in sociology with a qualitative study on les-bi-trans-queer BDSM at the University of Hamburg (published as "Queer BDSM Intimacies" in 2014). He has published widely in the fields of transgender studies, BDSM, sexuality, non-monogamies, queer theory, and queer-feminist science studies, seeking to connect his research with his activism.

Krista L. Benson is an Assistant Professor of Liberal Studies at Grand Valley State University. Krista's current project, *The Kids Who Aren't There: Indigenous Youth, Child Removal, and Juvenile Detention*, examines the ways in which heteropatriarchal gender norms are imposed on Native children through the system of "in state care," including children educated in compulsory state education, those fostered outside of tribal families, and those with contact with the juvenile justice system. This past, current, and future research has considered the interrelationships of sexuality, colonization, racialization, and legal systems and their impacts on people in the United States.

C. J. Chasin, M.Sc., is a queer aroace, long-time ace community member, and PhD Candidate in Community Psychology. CJ has published several papers on asexuality (in the *Archives of Sexual Behavior, Feminist Studies* and elsewhere), in addition to work on other topics including friendship. Grounded in feminist psychology, CJ's current academic work focuses on consent, voluntary unwanted sex and gender-based violence. As a community educator, CJ also develops and facilitates workshops exploring asexuality, aromanticism and non-normative relationships—primarily alongside other neurodivergent and chronically ill aces.

Daniel Copulsky is a sex educator and researcher with the Center for Positive Sexuality. His research interests include non-monogamy, sexual orientation, and queer identities. Dan presents regularly at conferences and colleges, and creates comics about sex and relationships as SexEdPlus.com.

Cary Gabriel Costello is Director of LGBT+ Studies and an Associate Professor of Sociology at the University of Wisconsin-Milwaukee. Intersex by birth, ze has a lifelong interest in studying the sex spectrum and advocating for sex-variant people. Dr. Costello's areas of specialty include human sexuality, sociology of the body, medical sociology and intersectional identity. Ze blogs about intersex issues at http://intersexroadshow.blogspot.com/. Dr. Costello is a gestational father, and is married to an intersex woman who, like Dr. Costello, transitioned from her inappropriate birth sex assignment.

Georgiann Davis is an associate professor of sociology at the University of Nevada, Las Vegas. She is also the current board president of inter ACT: Advocates for Intersex Youth (2017–present) and the former president of the AIS-DSD Support Group (2014–2015). She has written numerous articles on intersex in various outlets ranging from *Ms. Magazine* to the *American Journal of Bioethics*. In her book, *Contesting Intersex: The Dubious Diagnosis* (2015, NYU Press), Davis explores how intersex is defined, experienced, and contested in contemporary U.S. society.

Ashley Green is a PhD student in Sociology at the University of South Florida. She received her MA in Women's Studies from San Diego State University in 2015 with a primary research focus on pansexuality. Her current research is centers around fluid sexualities, non-binary gender identities, language, meaning making, and narratives of identity. Additionally, she is interested in exploring queer femininities and LGBTQ space and place, particularly as they intersects with experiences of community.

Brittany M. Harder, Ph.D., is an Assistant Professor of Sociology at the University of Tampa. Her research employs a wide array of quantitative and qualitative methods to address issues including those of minority health/

well-being, intersectional inequality and discrimination, racial and gender media representation, and the sociology of health and illness. She is actively involved in the community through several activities including employment with the Human Rights Campaign, and volunteer work with local, state, and national political campaigns and community organizations. Brittany frequently runs food, hygiene, and school supply drives, and engages in other efforts to improve issues of hunger and homelessness in Miami Dade County and Hillsborough County. Her community participation and activist efforts aim to raise awareness of people, processes, and barriers that foster inequality.

Jonathan Jimenez is a doctoral student in the department of sociology at the University of Nevada, Las Vegas. Jonathan's research focuses on the coming of age experiences of trans youth. Specific areas of study include examining the intersections of age and gender identity and the role that gender identity plays in shaping the life course.

Angela Jones is Associate Professor of Sociology at Farmingdale State College, State University of New York. Jones's research interests include: African American political thought and protest, gender, and sexuality. Jones's is the author of *Selling Sex Online: Work, Community, and Pleasure in the Erotic Webcam Industry* (NYU Press, 2019) and *African American Civil Rights: Early Activism and the Niagara Movement* (Praeger, 2011). She is a co-editor of the three volume *After Marriage Equality* book series (Routledge, 2018). Jones has also edited two other anthologies: *The Modern African American Political Thought Reader: From David Walker to Barack Obama* (Routledge, 2012), and *A Critical Inquiry into Queer Utopias* (Palgrave, 2013). She is also the author of numerous scholarly articles, which have been published in peer-reviewed journals.

Griffin Lacy is a doctoral student and instructor in the Department of Sociology at University of Albany, State University of New York. Griffin's research interests include gender & sexuality, feminist theory, qualitative research methods, and childhood. Their current ethnographic project focuses on the intersectional experiences of trans and gender nonconforming children and youth and their families in Upstate NY.

Nik Lampe is pursuing a Master's degree in applied sociology at the University of Central Florida. Their research focuses on health, gender, and sexualities in the experiences of transgender and gender non-conforming populations.

Katie Linder is a second-year graduate student in the Sociology Department at the University of Iowa, where she is hard at work on her master's degree. Her primary research interests are in criminology and race studies, and gender and sexuality studies. She graduated from Illinois College in Jacksonville, IL, in May 2017, with a degree in sociology and minors in psychology and Spanish, and as a member of the Phi Beta Kappa honor society. Currently, she lives in Iowa City, IA, with her best friend/partner, her partner's husband, and their two-year-old pitbull.

Shalen Lowell is a transgender and genderfluid author, blogger, and poet from Boston, MA, now living in southern Maine. They specialize in fiction which represents the intersection of fantasy and postmodern genres and queer literature, with particular emphasis in calling attention to the lives, struggles, and experiences of nonbinary LGBTQ+ folx. Shalen's work has been featured in *Æther & Ichor*, *The Writing Disorder*, *Privilege Through the Looking Glass*, and they were most recently named one of Massachusetts' Best Emerging Poets. Shalen can be contacted at shalenlowell@gmail.com.

Katherine Martinez (they/them/their pronouns), Associate Professor of Gender, Women, and Sexualities Studies at Metropolitan State University of Denver, writes and teaches on a range of topics relating to bodies/embodiment, gender, race, class and sexuality. In 2011, they received their PhD in Sociology from the University of Colorado at Boulder, with additional certification in Women's Studies and Ethnic Studies. Katherine teaches courses related to queer theories and identities and serves as a sexualities studies minor advisor at the Gender Institute for Teaching and Advocacy (GITA). Their research interests are in queer theories, practices, and activism.

Lain A. B. Mathers is a doctoral candidate in sociology at the University of Illinois at Chicago. Zir research focuses on the intersections of gender, sexualities, religion, and health as well as the experiences of bi+ and transgender populations. Zir work has been published in numerous academic journals and edited volumes.

Mar Middlebrooks is currently a student in the Masters of Social Work Program at the University of South Florida. She received her bachelors in

Sociology with a minor in Women's Studies from the University of Tampa. She continues working within the LGBTQIA+, kink, and differently abled communities as a writer and a counselor.

Alexandra "Xan" C. H. Nowakowski is an Assistant Professor in the Departments of Geriatrics and Behavioral Sciences and Social Medicine at the Florida State University College of Medicine. They are a medical sociologist and public health program evaluator focused on health equity in aging with chronic disease. Lived experience of queer sexuality, agender identity, polyamorous relationships, partner abuse, and cystic fibrosis inform all of their work. Dr. Nowakowski's interest in centering scholarship and outreach informed by lived experience led them to found the Write Where It Hurts advocacy project and blog (www.writewhereithurts.net) along with their spouse, Dr. J Sumerau.

Emily Pain is an instructor of sociology at the University at Albany, SUNY. Her research interests are in sexualities, families, queer studies, intimacies, and qualitative methods. More specifically, she is interested in LGBTQ+ ('queer') polyamory, families of choice, creative kinship, (anti) assimilationism, and sexual citizenship. She focuses on questions such as: 'How do queer people participate in a "queering" of intimacy and family in an era of assimilationism?,' 'How do those with radical queer political ideologies navigate assimilationist cultural expectations?,' and 'How do heteronormative forces continue to constrain queer lives?' Her current book project explores queer polyamorous relationships, families, and community. She details how queer polyamorists form, manage, navigate relationships and families at the cultural intersection of heterosexism and monocentrism. She also illustrates how queer polyamorists participate in a 'queering of intimacy' in America but are simultaneously constrained by monocentric forces that weaken this transformative potential. Please see empain.blog for more details.

R. F. Plante has had the great privilege to work with and mentor under-graduates for over 25 years, studying, teaching about, and writing about genders and sexualities. She also advocates for faculty governance, diversity, and inclusion. This has been her life's work, dating back to 1987, in the form of peer sexuality education, sexuality advocacy, and social justice work. She is grateful to be able to continue doing this as a professor of sociology.

Mimi Schippers received her PhD in Sociology from the University of Wisconsin-Madison and is Professor of Sociology and Gender and Sexuality

Studies at Tulane University. Her research focuses on masculinities, femininities, and the intersections of gender, race, and sexuality in everyday interactions, relationships, and subcultures. Her current research agenda focuses on compulsory monogamy, polyamory, and the queer, feminist, and anti-racist potential of sex and relationships that include more than two people. She is author of *Beyond Monogamy: Polyamory and the Future of Polyqueer Sexualities* and *Rockin' out of the Box: Gender Maneuvering in Alternative Hard Rock.*

stef m. shuster is an assistant professor in Lyman Briggs College and the Department of Sociology at Michigan State University. Their research examines the social construction of "evidence" in three domains including medicine, social movements, and the construction of knowledge. Their research has recently appeared in the *Journal of Health and Social Behavior, Gender & Society,* and *Social Psychology Quarterly.*

Carey Jean Sojka is an Assistant Professor of Gender, Sexuality, and Women's Studies at Southern Oregon University. Dr. Sojka's research and teaching focus on embodiment, intersectionality, transgender studies, and feminist and queer theory. As an extension of her academic work, she also conducts community education workshops on transgender, lesbian, gay, bisexual, and queer issues.

Sarah S. Topp is a consultant at JurySync Litigation Consulting in Olathe, KS. She received her PhD in Communication Studies from the University of Kansas, where she studied rhetorical theory, gender, and social movements. Her dissertation was on the rhetoric of intersex rights advocates.

Tiina Vares is Senior Lecturer in Sociology at the University of Canterbury, New Zealand. Her research interests include sexualities and identities, sexualization, and sexuopharmaceuticals. Here current project explores the experiences of self-identified asexuals in New Zealand, particularly in relation to intimacy and relationality.

Michelle Wolkomir is the Tracie Whitehurst Woods Board of Regents Endowed Professor of Sociology and the Director of Gender Studies at Centenary College. Her book, *Be Not Deceived: The Sacred and Sexual Struggles of Gay and Ex-Gay Christian Men*, received the 2006 American Sociological Association's book award in sexualities. Other publications focus on mixed orientation marriage, non monogamy, gender power dynamics among various groups, and interviewing techniques for sensitive populations. She was appointed to the Shreveport Human Relations Commission by the mayor of Shreveport.

alithia zamantakis (they/she) is a nonbinary trans femme graduate student in the Department of Sociology at Georgia State. Their research focuses on the ways in which whiteness and transphobia are constructed and/or challenged within intimate relationships, the co-constructions of white supremacy and transphobia through discourse, and reproductive justice. They are a member of the Sociologists for Trans & Intersex Justice and a poet/fiction author when not consumed by academic writing.

Printed in the United States
By Bookmasters